THE REGULATION OF INTERNATIONAL COMMERCIAL ARBITRATION

This book addresses how the regulation of international commercial arbitrators takes place. International commercial arbitrators are a unique category of service providers because they are not organised as other professionals such as accountants, lawyers and doctors. The book provides an overview of how and why the regulation of international commercial arbitrators diverged from that of other professions. It also argues that, despite these differences, there is an effective regulatory environment overseeing the behaviour of international commercial arbitrators.

The book unpicks the different elements that contribute to the creation and enforcement of professional norms in this field. It explains how the specific characteristics of the arbitral market create strong incentives for ethical norms to be created, even in the absence of the institutions that usually address these issues in other fields. It also describes how market and social forces drive arbitrators to comply with these norms in most circumstances. Finally, the book addresses the ways in which this regulatory system also explains some of the perceived weaknesses of arbitration, namely the rising costs of proceedings and the perceived unfairness of appointments.

Volume 15 in the series Civil Justice Systems

Civil Justice Systems

Series General Editor: Christopher Hodges OBE,
Centre for Socio-Legal Studies, University of Oxford

This series covers new theoretical and empirical research on the mechanisms for resolution of civil disputes, including courts, tribunals, arbitration, compensation schemes, ombudsmen, codes of practice, complaint mechanisms, mediation and various forms of Alternative Dispute Resolution. It examines frameworks for dispute resolution that comprise combinations of the above mechanisms, and the parameters and conditions for selecting certain types of techniques and procedures rather than others. It also evaluates individual techniques, against parameters such as cost, duration, accessibility, and delivery of desired outcomes, and illuminates how legal rights and obligations are operated in practice.

Volume 1: *The Costs and Funding of Civil Litigation: A Comparative Perspective*
Edited by Christopher Hodges, Stefan Vogenauer and Magdalena Tulibacka

Volume 2: *Consumer ADR in Europe*
Christopher Hodges, Iris Benöhr and Naomi Creutzfeldt-Banda

Volume 3: *Law and Corporate Behaviour: Integrating Theories of Regulation, Enforcement, Compliance and Ethics*
Christopher Hodges

Volume 4: *A Comparative Examination of Multi-Party Actions*
Joanne Blennerhassett

Volume 5: *Redress Schemes for Personal Injuries*
Sonia Macleod and Christopher Hodges

Volume 6: *Ethical Business Practice and Regulation: A Behavioural and Values-Based Approach to Compliance and Enforcement*
Christopher Hodges and Ruth Steinholtz

Volume 7: *Delivering Collective Redress: New Technologies*
Christopher Hodges and Stefaan Voet

Volume 8: *Pharmaceutical and Medical Device Safety: A Study in Public and Private Regulation*
Sonia Macleod and Sweta Chakraborty

Volume 9: *Delivering Dispute Resolution: A Holistic Review of Models in England and Wales*
Christopher Hodges

Volume 10: *Regulatory Delivery*
Graham Russell and Christopher Hodges

Volume 11: *Access to Justice for the Chinese Consumer: Handling Consumer Disputes in Contemporary China*
Ling Zhou

Volume 12: *Public and Private Enforcement of Securities Laws: The Regulator and the Class Action in Australia's Continuous Disclosure Regime*
Michael Legg

Volume 13: *Outcome-Based Cooperation: In Communities, Business, Regulation, and Dispute Resolution*
Christopher Hodges

Volume 14: *No-Fault Approaches in the NHS: Raising Concerns and Raising Standards*
Sonia Macleod and Christopher Hodges

Volume 15: *The Regulation of International Commercial Arbitration: Arbitrators' Duties and the Emerging Arbitral Market*
João Ilhão Moreira

The Regulation of International Commercial Arbitration

Arbitrators' Duties and the Emerging Arbitral Market

João Ilhão Moreira

•HART•
OXFORD • LONDON • NEW YORK • NEW DELHI • SYDNEY

HART PUBLISHING

Bloomsbury Publishing Plc

Kemp House, Chawley Park, Cumnor Hill, Oxford, OX2 9PH, UK

1385 Broadway, New York, NY 10018, USA

29 Earlsfort Terrace, Dublin 2, Ireland

First published in Great Britain 2024

A catalogue record for this book is available from the British Library.

A catalogue record for this book is available from the Library of Congress.

Library of Congress Control Number: 2024934249

ISBN: HB: 978-1-50996-269-3
ePDF: 978-1-50996-271-6
ePub: 978-1-50996-270-9

Typeset by Compuscript Ltd, Shannon

ACKNOWLEDGEMENTS

This book is the result of several years of research, first as part of my DPhil in Law at the Centre for Socio-Legal Studies at the University of Oxford and later during my time as an Assistant Professor at the Faculty of Law of the University of Macau. Many people have, therefore, contributed with ideas, comments and support. In particular, I owe a deep debt of gratitude to Prof. Bettina Lange, my supervisor during my DPhil, and Prof. Christopher Hodges, whose guidance, teachings and comments greatly enriched my academic knowledge and without whom this book would not exist. I also owe an immense thank you to the many friends and colleagues who aided me with their friendship and thoughts during my time at the University of Oxford and at the University of Macau, both academically and personally. Your support is truly appreciated and will not be forgotten.

This book would also not have been possible without the support of several institutions. Beyond my time at the Centre for Socio-Legal Studies, research stays at the Lauterpacht Centre for International Law at the University of Cambridge, the Max Planck Institute Luxembourg for Procedural Law, and the University of Hong Kong greatly contributed to this book. I extend my heartfelt thanks to these institutions' academic and fantastic support staff as well as to the many friends I have made during those stays. Fundação de Ciência e Tecnologia and the Institute of Advanced Studies in Humanities and Social Sciences of the University of Macau further supported this endeavour, and I am deeply grateful for their support. Beyond these institutions, this book also owes its existence to the extensive support of the Faculty of Law of the University of Macau and Prof. Tong Io Cheng, Dean of the Law Faculty, to whom I am deeply grateful. My colleagues' unwavering backing, trust and patience at the Faculty of Law was inspiring. To all of you, I extend my gratitude.

Finally, I owe a deep debt of gratitude to the many members of the arbitral community with whom I had the opportunity to learn and discuss the ideas that eventually shaped this book. These discussions were truly inspiring, and the experience of writing this book would have been significantly less pleasant and the final work considerably weaker without the patience of many of you to discuss these topics with me. Still, as usual, any errors or misconceptions in this book remain my own.

CONTENTS

1

Introduction

I. Introducing the Debate Regarding the 'Regulation' of International Commercial Arbitrators

When entering a hospital, the average patient rarely questions the commitment of its doctors to their well-being.[1] Likewise, when visiting a lawyer, most have confidence that the professional they visit has their best interests at heart. Professionals perform their roles due to the existence of a complex web of incentives and deterrents that are not always easy to identify. Doctors care for the life and health of their patients and lawyers for the fate of their clients due to a wide range of factors, from simple monetary and professional incentives, such as the desire to gain more customers[2] or avoid disciplinary action, to complex and deeply ingrained cultural values and moral judgements.

Society expects many professions to act ethically and fulfil a role that goes beyond simply complying with strictly defined contractual obligations. Communities trust many professionals to perform key tasks with profound public interest implications, from providing life-saving procedures to guaranteeing legal rights. A society, however, rarely trusts solely in market incentives, social pressures, and moral judgements to lead professionals to behave per their professional and ethical obligations. Many jurisdictions establish complex institutional and legal arrangements to ensure that professionals uphold public interest goals. Such arrangements range from establishing or endorsing the power of professional associations to dictate and enforce behavioural norms, to the state directly establishing detailed limits on who can perform such professional services and how they must be delivered.

However, one significant exception relates to international commercial arbitration. International commercial arbitrators, deciding cases often valued at millions of dollars and with profound implications for the fate of companies, workers and communities, certainly qualify as agents of central importance in many legal jurisdictions.[3] Despite their crucial importance, arbitrators and arbitral institutions can, in theory, enter the market in

[1] It should be noted that trust in physicians is, however, quite distinct in different countries. For an overview, see Robert J Blendon, John M Benson and Joachim O Hero, 'Public Trust in Physicians – U.S. Medicine in International Perspective' (2014) 371 *New England Journal of Medicine* 1570.

[2] As noted by a commentator, '[M]ost contracts, both formal and informal, are "enforced" simply by the latent threat of withdrawing future business from the violator'. William M Landes and Richard A Posner, 'The Private Enforcement of Law' (1975) 4 *The Journal of Legal Studies* 1, 1.

[3] See Susan D Franck, 'The Role of International Arbitrators' (2005) 12 *ILSA Journal of International and Comparative Law* 499.

international arbitration services without being previously licensed and, in practice, are subject to little or no disciplinary oversight from state-backed institutions.[4] This makes international commercial arbitrators a particularly unique 'profession' from a legal, sociological and economic perspective.[5]

It should be noted that, despite lacking institutional and legal arrangements that regulate behaviour in many other markets in professional services, international commercial arbitration is today seen by many as able to guarantee an efficient and trusted system of solving international disputes.[6] It works as the main dispute resolution system for international commercial disputes and is increasingly supported by courts and legislators in most jurisdictions.[7] Reflecting this success, arbitral institutions report an increasing number of new cases,[8] surveys of users of the system indicate general satisfaction with international arbitration,[9] and several pieces of national legislation have been amended to further support the use of arbitration.[10]

Against this background, the governance of international commercial arbitration has been very much left to the inner discussions of the arbitral community, with the field being, for the most part, far from the media spotlight. Indeed, while arbitration has grown exponentially, it has often remained opaque, with those outside it largely uninterested in its inner workings. This has allowed the arbitral community to have, by and large, a monopoly in shaping the norms that regulate the field, spearheading many of the most relevant changes arbitration has gone through in the last century.

[4] See Gary Born, *International Commercial Arbitration*, 2nd edn (Alphen aan den Rijn, Wolters Kluwer Law & Business, 2014) 2047. For an overview of the lack of certification and licensure practice in the US in regard to arbitrators, see Stephen K Huber, 'State Regulation of Arbitration Proceedings: Judicial Review of Arbitration Awards by State Courts' (2009) 10 *Cardozo Journal of Dispute Resolution* 509, 544.

[5] The definition of what constitutes a 'profession' is contentious, with its precise definition being context-dependent. For an overview of the different approaches to the concept, see Mike Saks, 'Defining a Profession: The Role of Knowledge and Expertise' (2012) 2 *Professions and Professionalism* 1, 1-2. Within arbitration circles, the majority view tends to qualify arbitrators as not being a profession. See, for example, Emilia Onyema, *International Commercial Arbitration and the Arbitrator's Contract* (London, Routledge, 2010) 65. Despite this, and while arbitrators do not indeed fit neatly into most definitions of what constitutes a 'profession', the term will be sometimes used as a short-hand throughout this book.

[6] In the words of Lord Neuberger, referring in particular to the 1996 Arbitration Act, '[a]s unlike in the banking sector, such modern light touch regulation is not merely what the market wanted, but nearly twenty years on, it is generally seen to be working well.' See Lord Neuberger, Key Note Speech, Chartered Institute of Arbitrators Centenary Conference, 2 July 2015, available at www.ciarb.org/docs/default-source/centenarydocs/london/lord-neuberger.pdf?sfvrsn=0.

[7] In the words of Lew: 'International arbitration, before neutral arbitrators, in a third country, with non-national or international procedures being followed, has become the essential mechanism for the settlement of all kinds of international business disputes.' Julian DM Lew, 'Achieving the Dream: Autonomous Arbitration' (2006) 22 *Arbitration International* 179, 185. See also, Thomas E Carbonneau, *Law and Practice of Arbitration*, 5th edn (New York, Juris Publishing, Inc, 2014) xiii; Karl-Heinz Böckstiegel, 'Past, Present, and Future Perspectives of Arbitration' (2009) 25 *Arbitration International* 293, 295.

[8] Gary Born, *International Arbitration: Law and Practice* (Alphen aan den Rijn, Kluwer Law International, 2012) 16.

[9] QMUL's 2015 International Arbitration Survey, for example, shows that '90% of respondents indicate that international arbitration is their preferred dispute resolution mechanism, either as a stand-alone method (56%) or together with other forms of ADR (34%).' '2015 International Arbitration Survey: Improvements and Innovations in International Arbitration' 2 www.arbitration.qmul.ac.uk/docs/164761.pdf accessed 16 October 2015.

[10] Amongst many others, Nigeria (2023), Tanzania (2021), Russia (2016), Brazil (2015), Slovakia (2015), Colombia (2012), France (2011) have recently amended their legislation to further support arbitration.

II. Too Closed, Too Slow, Too Expensive: The Growing Pains of Commercial Arbitration

While international commercial arbitration is living, by all measures, an era of unprecedented popularity, its legitimacy has, however, been increasingly questioned. It is true that most criticism has been directed not to commercial arbitration but rather to investment arbitration, which has been derided in some political quarters as an untrustworthy system of protecting multinational companies.[11] These criticisms, nevertheless, have spilt over to affect the perception of the traditionally less controversial commercial arbitration, with some of the attacks simply casting negative aspersions over arbitration in general, pointing to its opacity and lack of diversity.[12]

However, it should be noted that criticisms of arbitration have not only been raised by politically motivated outsiders. Some elite members of the commercial arbitration community have increasingly expressed concerns about commercial arbitration's level of transparency, cost, and fairness.[13] While these are in the larger picture, minor quibbles in what is usually the self-congratulatory tone of most self-analysis that the arbitration community provides,[14] they show a level of discomfort with the evolution of the field, serving as a catalyst for more comprehensive discussions of how arbitration should be regulated and, in particular, how arbitrators are selected.

It is worth noting, at this point, that inner criticisms of arbitration have not coalesced into an organised critique of arbitration but rather spotlight different issues that are perceived as problematic or inherently unfair. In this regard, while speed and cost have been traditionally presented as one of the major advantages of arbitration, many within the community have expressed concerns with a so-called 'judicialisation' of proceedings, noting that arbitral proceedings have increasingly become similar to court proceedings. Indeed, concerns with mounting costs and decreasing efficiency date back at least two decades, with a practitioner noting in the late 1990s that:

> Over the years we have often talked of arbitration as being less formal, more flexible, speedier and less costly than litigation, but do we really fight hard to keep it that way? Both lawyers

[11] For an extensive analysis, see Michael Waibel and others (eds), *The Backlash Against Investment Arbitration: Perceptions and Reality* (Alphen aan den Rijn, Kluwer Law International, 2010).

[12] Stavros L Brekoulakis, 'Introduction: The Evolution and Future of International Arbitration' in Stavros L Brekoulakis, Julian DM Lew and Loukas A Mistelis (eds), *The Evolution and Future of International Arbitration* (Alphen aan den Rijn, Kluwer Law International, 2016) 12.

[13] David W Rivkin, for example, in a well-known speech in the 2015 ADR Asia Conference, chastised arbitrators for often not meeting parties' expectations. David W Rivkin, 'Keynote Address: A New Contract Between Arbitrators and Parties' (2016) 18 *Asian Dispute Review* 4. See also Park, who notes that 'recent literature laments that a golden age of cheap and cheerful arbitration has yielded to backlash against a system marked by too many rules, excessive rules and undue delay'. William Park, 'Procedural Tension in International Arbitration: Arbitration in Autumn' in John Norton Moore (ed), *International Arbitration: Contemporary Issues and Innovations* (Leiden, Martinus Nijhoff Publishers, 2013) 3.

[14] In the words of Born: 'There have been periods of lesser, and periods of greater, judicial and legislative support for the arbitral process. […] Judicial skepticism or hostility has typically been cyclical, not infrequently coinciding with outbreaks of extreme nationalism or totalitarianism, while in most instances the enduring needs of the business community, the respect of enlightened governments for the parties' freedom to order their commercial affairs and the relative advantages of the arbitral process have eventually overcome limitations or prohibitions on the arbitral process.' Born (n 4) 69.

and arbitrators have commented on how often arbitrations today are converted into court-like battles.[15]

Beyond these more practical concerns with the potentially diminishing appeal of arbitration, discussions have also focused on more macro issues related to perceived unfairness in the appointments of arbitrators. Traditionally, this has mostly revolved around contesting assertions that arbitration works as an old boy's club or, using more colourful language, a 'mafia'.[16] These debates evolved, however, in the last two decades to an increasing acknowledgement that there are systemic issues in arbitration leading to continuous under-representation of many groups, with the still unresolved gender imbalances being a particular point of concern.

At the same time that there is an increased appeal to open the field, a few have expressed apprehension regarding the increased number of arbitrators. Indeed, as the community became more heterogeneous, the idea that arbitration was entering a period where commitment to professional values was waning seemed to have taken hold around some circles.[17] The core concern in this aspect centres around the idea that new entrants might be less committed to the norms of the field, given that a larger community may be less capable of policing itself.[18] These views raise challenging questions, particularly the possibility that an increased number of arbitrators and arbitral practitioners could render the current unique self-regulation governing arbitration unworkable.

III. The Emerging Distrust in the Ability of Arbitration to Self-regulate

Parallel to these community-driven concerns, academic analysis of arbitration has increasingly considered the ability of arbitration to provide a fair and efficient system of resolving disputes. A particular point of interest relates to the lack of monitoring of unethical behaviour in the field, a concern compounded by a perceived lack of transparency. As with the more practitioner-driven discussions,[19] academic analysis of the governance of arbitration and the role of arbitrators has been spurred by the growing importance of the field, also showing a level of scepticism regarding the ability of the arbitrators and the arbitration market to self-regulate.

[15] Gray Whitmore, 'Is There a Growing International Arbitration Culture?' in Albert Jan van den Berg (ed), *International Dispute Resolution: Towards an International Arbitration Culture: Towards an International Arbitration Culture* (Alphen aan den Rijn, Wolters Kluwer Law & Business, 1998) 28. See also Rémy Gerbay, *The Functions of Arbitral Institutions* (Alphen aan den Rijn, Kluwer Law International 2016) 53. Noting, even earlier, the same concerns in regards to French arbitration, see Philippe Fouchard, 'Conclusion' [1990] *Revue de l'Arbitrage* 483, 483.

[16] See, eg, Yves Derains, 'Le Professionnalisme Des Arbitres Internationaux' [2019] *Revue de l'Arbitrage* 659, 682.

[17] See Sundaresh Menon, 'Some Cautionary Notes for an Age of Opportunity' (Chartered Institute of Arbitrators International Arbitration Conference, Penang, 22 August 2013), available at www.singaporelaw.sg/. See also Catherine A Rogers, 'Regulating International Arbitrators: A Functional Approach to Developing Standards of Conduct' (2005) 41 *Stanford Journal of International Law* 53, 62.

[18] Still, in some arbitral circles, it has become common to mention that a 'golden-age' of arbitration has passed. See, eg, Rivkin (n 13); William Park, 'Arbitration in Autumn' (2011) 2 *Journal of International Dispute Settlement* 287, 288.

[19] It should be noted that in arbitration the line between academic and practitioner is often blurry, with many involved in the academic research of the field, also practising in this area.

At this point, it should be noted that, for a long time, little academic literature could be found regarding the regulation of arbitrators or, more broadly, the socio-economic position of arbitrators.[20] Undoubtedly, it is true that the current 'golden age' of international arbitration was built on top of a large body of legal analysis, providing a thorough and increasingly intricate discussion of the many legal issues surrounding this field.[21] By comparison, analysis of international commercial arbitration as a socio-legal and economic phenomenon – ie, a legal institution with social and economic consequences for service providers, disputing parties and the community at large – was for a long time comparatively much scarcer.[22]

Several factors contributed to the limited study of international commercial arbitration from a socio-legal perspective. First, for a long time, international arbitration was a reasonably marginal legal phenomenon which attracted little attention outside arbitration circles and the limited number of experts in the field. Second, the reasonably closed nature of international arbitration,[23] the lack of readily available public information regarding how arbitral tribunals truly deliberate,[24] and the complex legal arrangements underlying this

[20] Key exceptions include the following monographies: Catherine A Rogers, *Ethics in International Arbitration* (Oxford, Oxford University Press, 2014); Joshua DH Karton, *The Culture of International Arbitration and The Evolution of Contract Law* (Oxford, Oxford University Press, 2013); Yves Dezalay and Bryant G Garth, *Dealing in Virtue: International Commercial Arbitration and the Construction of a Transnational Legal Order* (Chicago, University of Chicago Press, 1996).

[21] Some of the most well-known works in the legal analysis of international arbitration, include: Gary Born, *International Arbitration: Law and Practice* (Alphen aan den Rijn, Kluwer Law International 2012); Philippe Fouchard and others, *Fouchard Gaillard Goldman on International Commercial Arbitration* (Alphen aan den Rijn, Kluwer Law International, 1999); Julian DM Lew, Loukas A Mistelis and Stefan Kröll, *Comparative International Commercial Arbitration* (Alphen aan den Rijn, Kluwer Law International, 2003); Alan Redfern, *Law and Practice of International Commercial Arbitration* (London, Sweet & Maxwell, 2004); Mauro Rubino-Sammartano, *International Arbitration Law* (Alphen aan den Rijn, Kluwer Law International 2001). Many other authors – who often are also leading practitioners – working in this academic side of international commercial arbitration, have also provided detailed legal analysis regarding national arbitration statuses and arbitration in particular regional settings or jurisdictions.: Jean-Louis Delvolvé, Jean Rouche and Gerald H Pointon, *French Arbitration Law and Practice: A Dynamic Civil Law Approach to International Arbitration* (Alphen aan den Rijn, Kluwer Law International, 2009); Jalal El-Ahdab, *Arbitration with the Arab Countries* (Alphen aan den Rijn, Kluwer Law International, 2011); Gabrielle Kaufmann-Kohler and Blaise Stucki, *International Arbitration in Switzerland: A Handbook for Practitioners* (Alphen aan den Rijn, Kluwer Law International, 2004); Michael J Moser, *Arbitration in Asia – 2nd Edition* (New York, Juris Publishing, Inc, 2008); Essam Al Tamimi, *Practitioner's Guide to Arbitration in the Middle East and North Africa* (New York, Juris Publishing, Inc, 2009); Jingzhou Tao, *Arbitration Law and Practice in China* (Alphen aan den Rijn, Kluwer Law International, 2008).

[22] See Emmanuel Gaillard, 'Sociology of International Arbitration' (2015) 31 *Arbitration International* 1, 2. Despite the shortage of socio-legal analysis when compared to more traditional doctrinally oriented legal literature, a significant number of studies have shed light on the nature, functioning and evolution of arbitration as a social and economic institution. For example, they have provided guidance on the role played by competing generations of arbitrators in creating a transnational dispute system; argued that economic incentives have helped to create 'a culture of arbitration'; and evaluated the market for international arbitrator services, in light of the obligations that arbitrators assume as custodians of the international arbitration system. See, Yves Dezalay and Bryant G Garth, *Dealing in Virtue: International Commercial Arbitration and the Construction of a Transnational Legal Order* (Chicago, University of Chicago Press, 1996); Tom Ginsburg, 'The Culture of Arbitration' (2003) 36 *The Vanderbilt Journal of Transnational Law* 1335–1345. Catherine A Rogers, 'The Vocation of the International Arbitrator' (2004) 20 *American University International Law Review* 957.

[23] Jean-Babtiste Racine, 'Éléments D'une Sociologie de L'arbitrage: Actes de La Journée D'étude Du Groupe Sociologie de L'arbitrage Du Comité Français de L'arbitrage' [2012] *Revue de l'Arbitrage* 709.

[24] Christopher R Drahozal, 'Arbitration by the Numbers: The State of Empirical Research on International Commercial Arbitration' (2006) 22 *Arbitration International* 291, 293.

field discouraged general discussions of the grid of incentives that international arbitrators face in relation to compliance with professional standards.

Over the last two decades, against the background of a growing influence of interdisciplinary methodologies, the academic literature has, however, started to consider the governance of the field. This research has often been built on the notion that arbitrators operate as economic agents competing in a market and deploying complex economic strategies.[25] At the same time, research has increasingly acknowledged that arbitrators' actions are influenced by a broad range of psychological, social, cognitive, and emotional factors.[26] Finally, increased attention has been paid to the networks formed by arbitrators,[27] with some arguing that an exclusive 'culture' amongst the arbitral community has developed.[28]

Importantly, some have manifested distrust regarding the ability of the arbitration market to regulate behaviour. The most well-known of these voices is undoubtedly Rogers, who has repeatedly warned about the imperfections of the arbitration market and how these imperfections impede the arbitration market from distinguishing ethical from unethical arbitrators:

> In addition to an absence of formal sanctions, international arbitrators are largely insulated from market-based regulation. International arbitration is an ostensibly private process. As a result, international arbitrator conduct is largely insulated from public scrutiny and broad-based reputational sanctions.[29]

Still, while concerns have been raised, commercial arbitration has been moving forward without a true impetus for fundamental reform taking hold. In this sense, voices wanting to significantly change commercial arbitration have been limited. While some, most notably Paulsson, have proposed significant modifications to the process through which arbitrators are selected,[30] such proposals have not found traction.[31] Rather, both the commercial arbitration community and those studying the field – groups which have significant overlap – appear mostly uninterested in entertaining significant regulatory modifications.[32]

[25] Thomas Clay, 'El Mercado Del Arbitraje' (2014) 7 *Arbitraje: revista de arbitraje comercial y de inversiones* 15.

[26] Susan D Franck and others, 'Inside the Arbitrator's Mind' (2017) 66 *Emory Law Journal* 1115.

[27] Sergio Puig, 'Social Capital in the Arbitration Market' (2014) 25 *European Journal of International Law* 387.

[28] See, in particular, Karton (n 20), focusing on how values such as party autonomy, the service of business, neutrality, and internationalism dominate arbitration.

[29] Rogers (n 20) 58.

[30] Paulsson's – a worldwide leading arbitral practitioner – criticism of the system of party appointed arbitrators has been specially noted. Jan Paulsson, 'Moral Hazard in International Dispute Resolution' (2010) 25 *ICSID Review* 339. Also criticising the prevalent system of party appointed arbitrators, see Albert Jan van den Berg, 'Dissenting Opinions by Party-Appointed Arbitrators in Investment Arbitration' in Mahnoush H Arsanjani, Jacob Katz Cogan, Robert D Sloane and Siegfried Wiessner (eds), *Looking to the future: essays on international law in honor of W. Michael Reisman* (Leiden, Martinus Nijhoff Publishers, 2011).

[31] Others have proposed changes to institutions' behaviour with the aim of augmenting the level of transparency, reducing costs, and increasing the speed of arbitral proceedings. For an overview of the debate, see Albert Jan van den Berg (ed), 'Survey: Arbitral Institutions Can Do More to Foster Legitimacy. True or False?' in *Legitimacy: Myths, Realities, Challenges* (Alphen aan den Rijn, Wolters Kluwer Law & Business, 2015).

[32] Even Rogers's proposals to increase transparency and correct perceived market imperfections through the project 'Arbitration Intelligence', while having found more grassroots support within the community, do not represent an attempt to overhaul the essential features of how arbitrators are selected. Rather, these efforts are often framed as attempts to maintain arbitration legitimacy and protect it from unwanted external interventions.

IV. The Need to Re-evaluate the Ability of Commercial Arbitration to Self-regulate

The current moment in which arbitration is living invites, therefore, further reflection. Indeed, despite its sui generis regulatory system and the above-mentioned concerns, the general perception seems to be that serious deviations from professional norms by international commercial arbitrators are rare and that, overall, arbitration operates well.[33] Against this background, there has been a dearth of discussion regarding the underlying forces that are leading members of the arbitral community to comply with applicable professional standards and norms.

Presenting an answer to these questions is the key objective of this book. Understanding the set of incentives and motivations that lead the different agents working within commercial arbitration to regulate behaviour is an essential step: i) to understand if the commercial arbitration community can be 'trusted' to create and enforce their own rules of behaviour;[34] and ii), in the case of a negative answer, to ascertain if reform is possible and what steps should be undertaken to develop different regulatory approaches in this field.

This book ultimately concludes that, in most respects, the arbitration market works well in steering arbitrators' behaviour to comply with their professional duties. The core of the argument relies on the notion that the arbitration market, albeit unique in many respects, fosters a tight-knit community where its members are strongly incentivised to network and participate in community-wide initiatives. This, in turn, creates the conditions for the community, despite lacking the institutional trappings of most organised professions, to create norms and monitor behaviour within the field.

Before advancing to an analysis of this argument, it is important to clarify some of the concepts and options underlying this book. First, despite acknowledging the lack of traditional professional regulation mechanisms, this book describes arbitrators as regulated. Second, this book deals specifically with commercial arbitration rather than with arbitration as a whole. Third, it focuses particularly on arbitrators rather than the whole set of agents offering services related to arbitration. Finally, this book will refer to arbitrators' professional norms and arbitrators' duties rather than relying on the more restrictive concept of ethics. The way that these concepts are addressed in the book will be discussed next.

A. 'Regulation': An Enlarged Notion to Include All Forms of Social and Economic Control

The word 'regulation' is often used to refer to a reasonably straightforward concept, ie, the actions undertaken by a public authority to oversee activities that are valued

[33] In an interview, Born summarised what seems to be the view dominant amongst the community: 'arbitration is more efficient, more expeditious, more expert, more even-handed and more enforceable'. *Modern Arbitration: Live – An Interview With Gary Born* (19 March 2019), available at: www.wilmerhale.com (last accessed 25 February 2020).

[34] In the words of Paulsson, '[c]onfidence in the ethical standards of arbitrators and arbitral institutions is the Alpha and Omega of the legitimacy of the process.' Jan Paulsson, *The Idea of Arbitration* (Oxford, Oxford University Press, 2013) 147.

by a community.[35] In this narrow definition, regulation is used to refer to an authoritative set of rules accompanied by some mechanism, typically a public agency, responsible for monitoring and promoting compliance with rules.[36] When it comes to professional regulation, a body controlled by professionals is usually responsible for determining the rules that shape who can offer services and create legal constraints on how these services can be provided. Typically, this body also has the power to apply legal sanctions for those who infringe on these norms.

Regulation is, however, sometimes also used to refer to a much broader idea: all forms of social or economic incentive that influence an agent.[37] In this sense, regulation is used to refer to incentives beyond state-based interventions. It also encompasses the effects of the interventions of a host of other bodies, including corporations, self-regulators, trade bodies and other organisations, and even social or economic forces (such as markets, cultural understandings, or even language).[38] In this sense, regulation includes not only intentional interventions but also the effects of all other factors that influence behaviour.

Arbitration could be described as unregulated, given the aforementioned differences from most organised professions. However, relying on the second, broader concept of regulation allows uncovering a clear regulation system. This is to say that arbitrators are 'regulated' in the sense that their behaviour is shaped by a wide spectrum of forces, including state and non-state actors and social, economic, and cultural forces. This book will use the term regulation in this broader sense. This conceptual preference derives mainly from the fact that, in the context of arbitration, it is often very difficult to separate the effects of 'intentional' regulation from other forces shaping behaviour, inviting the usage of regulation in that wider sense.[39]

Some within the arbitration community tend to resist the idea of a 'regulation of arbitrators', as they may perceive this as equating arbitration to other professions, a notion deeply opposed by many. Nevertheless, it is uncontroversial that arbitrators are constrained by a complex set of norms and expectations of legal and non-legal origin, which are, in turn, enforced by deeply intertwined legal and market reputation mechanisms. Therefore, discussing a regulation of arbitrators should not be understood as necessarily advocating further intervention in this market. Instead, it intends to encapsulate the idea that arbitration is bound to a complex set of norms and equilibriums rather than an anarchic field.

B. Why Analyse Commercial Arbitration Separately from Investment Arbitration?

The second important conceptual caveat to the scope of this book is that it will mostly deal with commercial arbitration. As is well known, this is only a subset of a larger legal

[35] Robert Baldwin, Martin Cave and Martin Lodge, *Understanding Regulation: Theory, Strategy, and Practice*, 2nd edn (Oxford, Oxford University Press 2012) 2–3.

[36] Robert Baldwin, Colin D Scott and Christopher Hood, *A Reader on Regulation* (Oxford, Oxford University Press 1998) 3.

[37] For a discussion see ibid.

[38] See also Rogers (n 20) 222.

[39] Also opting for the usage of this broader concept of regulation when referring to arbitration, see Rogers (n 20).

institution known collectively as arbitration or, when talking in a transnational context, as 'international arbitration'. While the rising popularity of arbitration has meant that these distinctions are widely known even for those outside the world of arbitration, it is still useful to clarify the meaning of these different concepts. This will allow an understanding of the scope of this book and the choice to deal separately with commercial arbitration.

While definitions vary, in general terms, arbitration can be defined as a consensual means to resolve disputes via a non-governmental decision-maker, selected by or for the parties involved, which produces a binding decision through the use of impartial adjudicative procedures which afford each party the opportunity to present their case.[40] It is then possible to subdivide arbitration between international arbitration and domestic arbitration, where the first refers to arbitrations with a transnational element and the second to arbitrations which deal uniquely with matters internal to a specific national jurisdiction.[41]

Taken in its broader sense, international arbitration itself encompasses different subsets of arbitration, most notably international commercial arbitration, which in general refers to arbitration proceedings resulting from contractual disputes, and investor-state arbitration, which refers to arbitration between private investors and states regarding possible violations of investment protection agreements; and state-to-state arbitrations, which refers to arbitration proceedings between two or more states regarding international law disputes.[42]

In the context of a socio-legal or economic analysis of this field, the option of many authors has often been to offer an analysis of international arbitration and international arbitrators as a whole.[43] As it is well known, there are many similarities between the legal rules and main values that provide a framework for these different kinds of arbitration. Furthermore, many of the people and institutions who operate in these different fields are often the same.[44] Therefore, a degree of overlap exists between the professional communities linked to each of these types of arbitration.[45] For these reasons, many of the regulatory mechanisms leading commercial arbitrators to comply with their professional and ethical obligations are similar to those that lead investment arbitrators to comply with their professional and ethical obligations.

[40] Gary Born, *International Arbitration: Law and Practice* (Alphen aan den Rijn, Kluwer Law International, 2012) 3.

[41] See UNCITRAL Model Law Article 1(3).

[42] Besides these types of consensual arbitration, some jurisdictions also establish some forms of mandatory arbitration. Whether this kind of arbitration should be considered 'truly' a form of arbitration is subject to controversy. For a discussion, see Charles Jarrosson, 'Les Frontières de l'arbitrage' [2001] *Revue de l'arbitrage* 5, 5–42. These kinds of arbitration, despite also serving as a basis for markets, often have structures, supply and demand formation mechanisms considerably different from commercial arbitration.

[43] This was, eg, the option of Gaillard in Emmanuel Gaillard, 'Sociology of International Arbitration' (2015) 31 *Arbitration International* 1 and Rogers in Rogers (n 20).

[44] For example, many of the most well-known arbitrators of international commercial arbitration cases also act as arbitrators in international investment cases. Also, often the same law firms and counsel work in both fields.

[45] See Alec Stone Sweet and Florian Grisel, *The Evolution of International Arbitration: Judicialization, Governance, Legitimacy* (Oxford, Oxford University Press, 2017) 72. This proximity has practical implications. For example, an arbitrator who can build a career within the field of international investment arbitration may be able to leverage their reputation to obtain more appointments within the international commercial arbitration market and vice-versa. Therefore, there are reputational effects across these markets.

Consequently, this book could have analysed the regulation of international arbitration and international arbitrators as a whole instead of focusing specifically on international commercial arbitration. It should be noted, however, that commercial arbitration and these other types of arbitration also differ in considerable ways. They possess distinct legal frameworks and institutional arrangements and rely on different narratives and sources of legitimacy.[46] Further, these different markets, despite appearing somewhat similar from a distance, upon closer inspection, have considerable differences regarding the demand and supply structures, potentially favouring different attitudes and leading market actors to adapt differently.

For example, in investment arbitration, an arbitrator will have to take into consideration that the parties have unique contrasting characteristics (investment arbitration typically pits an investor who acts as a claimant against a state who acts as a respondent). In contrast, in commercial arbitration, claimants and respondents are often both commercial enterprises. Further, in investment arbitration, a single institution, the International Centre for Settlement of Investment Disputes (ICSID), has a key position in the market. In the commercial arbitration market, the arbitrator will take into consideration that a multitude of arbitral institutions operate in the market. Also, while most awards are public in investment arbitration, in commercial arbitration, awards are most often confidential.[47] Finally, investment arbitration often raises fundamental issues of public interest, which are usually absent from international commercial arbitration.[48]

Arbitrators' optimal market strategies in those two markets – ie, how they operate within certain institutional constraints to achieve their market goals – will hence not fully coincide. Consequently, while several of the underlying methods that regulate behaviour are present across these markets, considerable differences in the characteristics of the disputing parties that use the system, the levels of information available, the size of the community, and governing institutions mean that players are likely to adapt and behave differently within these markets. Hence, the regulatory superstructure and incentives overviewing behaviour are distinct.

Overall, an in-depth analysis of the regulatory mechanisms taking place within the arbitral market is, therefore, better conducted through a separate analysis of the different types of arbitration. On this basis, due to its importance, international commercial arbitrators will be the focus of the analysis of this book.[49] Commercial arbitration, when considering the absolute number of cases and their aggregated value, is certainly the most relevant subset of international arbitration, especially in its international strand, with an

[46] Investment arbitration in particular has been subject to heavy criticism. For an overview, see Waibel and others (n 11).

[47] For an overview, see Bernardo M Cremades and Rodrigo Cortes, 'The Principle of Confidentiality in Arbitration: A Necessary Crisis' (2013) 23 *Journal of Arbitration Studies* 25.

[48] See Nigel Blackaby, 'Public Interest and Investment Treaty Arbitration' in Albert Jan van den Berg (ed), *International Commercial Arbitration: Important Contemporary Questions* (Alphen aan den Rijn, Kluwer Law International, 2003).

[49] While there are great similarities in proceedings, institutional arrangements and social practices between both international and domestic commercial arbitration, the communities of practitioners and applicable legal rules do not fully overlap. Still, and while the text will mostly focus on the international commercial arbitration market, many of the conclusions in this text will be applicable to domestic commercial arbitration.

increasing number of practitioners in a variety of jurisdictions dedicating themselves full-time or close to full-time to this area.[50]

Accordingly, and for the purpose of this book, 'international commercial arbitration' will be used throughout to refer to a method of settling disputes, usually of a private-law nature, based on an agreement between two parties, usually located in different jurisdictions, in front of an arbitral tribunal constituted in accordance with the parties' agreement and the applicable law. 'International arbitration' will be used in a broader sense to mean both international commercial and investor-state arbitration. 'Arbitration' will be used even more broadly to incorporate both cross-border and domestic disputes referred to as arbitration.

C. Why Focus Specifically on the Regulation of Arbitrators?

As mentioned in the sections above, instead of focusing on the ethical quandaries and regulatory issues of arbitration as a whole, this book focuses on arbitrators. In particular, this book focuses on how the market strategies deployed by arbitrators affect the creation and enforcement of ethical and professional norms in this field. Often, this discussion is complemented with reference to how the market shapes the behaviour of other agents, such as arbitral institutions and counsels, but most often with the aim of understanding how these agents, in turn, influence the behaviour of arbitrators.

The option to focus on commercial arbitrators is taken as this analysis explains many of the perceived successes and drawbacks – such as the perception that costs of arbitrating are rising and the proceedings are often not efficient – of modern international arbitration. Indeed, different levels of compliance with different kinds of obligations may be a result of how strong the incentives are for an arbitrator to comply or deviate from a particular obligation. As it will be argued, there are peculiarities in arbitration as a service that, in turn, lead to arbitrators generally being incentivised to comply with their ethical obligations while, at the same time, creating little pressure for arbitrators to compete on prices or solve perceived structural issues regarding appointments.

Further, focusing on international commercial arbitrators allows for uncovering interesting questions that are often overlooked when arbitration is discussed as a whole. In particular, it allows for exploring the regulation of 'arbitrators' as a professional group – a topic rarely touched upon in the literature. Arbitrators are an interesting sociological category as they do not fit squarely into the definition of a 'profession' from a sociological perspective. A 'profession' is a concept, at least in the Anglo-American context, usually defined as a paid occupation associated with advanced knowledge,[51] usually acquired in institutions of advanced learning. Professional status is linked to special power and prestige, and most often, members of a profession are organised around professional associations and shaped by a specific culture and professional ethical norms.[52]

[50] However, due to the larger amount of publicly available information, most empirical research on arbitration has so far dealt with investor-state arbitration.

[51] See Keith M Macdonald, *The Sociology of the Professions* (London, SAGE Publications, 2013) 2.

[52] See, for all, Harold L Wilensky, 'The Professionalization of Everyone?' (1964) 70 *American Journal of Sociology* 137. The exact definition of what constitutes a profession in sociological terms, however, continues to be debated. For an overview, see Saks (n 5).

The question of how arbitrators are regulated is in itself an interesting question that facilitates revealing how an elite 'profession' is regulated outside the more typical methods of a national-based, legal-centric regulation system. As this book will argue, traditional regulatory mechanisms of professional oversight take a backseat to reputation amongst peers and market mechanisms in the case of arbitrators. Further, analysing the arbitration market reveals how the mechanics of selecting service providers and price formation deeply affect the regulatory structure, providing an interesting contrast to other professions, such as auditors and lawyers.

V. Structure of the Book

This book is composed of nine chapters. After this first introductory chapter, chapter two will introduce the reader to how, in the twentieth century, modern international commercial arbitration was formed and how it acquired its main features, such as its autonomy from courts and the finality of its awards. Particular attention will be paid to the idea that a consensus developed around the notion that private arbitrators can be trusted to uphold the integrity and fairness of the arbitration process,[53] and therefore, minimal court oversight is necessary. From there, this chapter will argue that this legal framework created a potentially profitable 'market' where both arbitrators and law firms could obtain significant proceeds. It will be shown that such actors quickly took advantage of this opportunity. This is important as it explains the importance given to economic incentives in the subsequent chapters of this book.

Chapter three will detail the main features of the market in international commercial arbitration services. More specifically, this chapter will detail how arbitrators and arbitral institutions are selected, how prices are formed, and which strategies these actors undertake to prosper in the market. This chapter will clarify how this market's specificities have led to an environment where arbitrators and arbitral institutions mostly compete by trying to increase their reputation and visibility. Based on an analysis of the market structure, how arbitrators are selected, and how fees are determined, it will be shown that price is often not a relevant driver of competition in this context. Instead, the dominant strategy for arbitrators involves networking and improving one's standing and reputation within the arbitral community.

Chapter four will then start linking the particularities of the market described in the previous chapter to the regulation of arbitrators. After briefly contextualising the regulation of arbitrators against the background of the evolution of the regulation of professional services, this chapter will pay particular attention to how the characteristics of arbitration and the arbitral market have led the regulation of arbitrators to be distinct from that of other professions, such as doctors or lawyers. The key focus will be on why states and state-backed institutions have a less detailed regulation of arbitrators compared to these other professions. This will help explain why, in the context of regulating arbitrators, understanding markets, the community and other forces outside traditional legal interventions are particularly relevant.

[53] For a more detailed analysis, see Dario Alessi, 'Enforcing Arbitrator's Obligations: Rethinking International Commercial Arbitrators' Liability' (2014) 31 *Journal of International Arbitration* 735.

Chapter five will build on the considerations advanced in the previous chapter to discuss how regulatory norms are created in this field. After having established in chapter four that states are not able to – or at least have largely decided not to – create detailed rules to oversee arbitrators' behaviour, this chapter will argue that a unique system of norm creation takes place in regard to international arbitrators. The hypothesis developed and explored in this chapter is that the community members have a self-interest in helping develop rules of behaviour, leading the community to have de facto mechanisms of producing normative content. Sometimes, the way the community creates 'norms' is easy to identify, such as when arbitral institutions and associations of lawyers produce ethical codes. Other times, such a role in the creation of norms is more subtle, such as the role of the community in developing over time a 'culture of arbitration' – ie, the social norms and expectations shared between those who participate in the arbitration community.[54]

Chapter six proceeds from the previous chapter to discuss the content of the norms produced. More than a descriptive account of these norms, this chapter will contextualise what kind of issues the arbitral community addresses and how. If in chapter five it was shown that there are strong incentives for the community to produce 'norms', the open question is whether such regulation is just a pointless set of initiatives only intended to gather members of the community or instead effectively addresses the most concerning issues within the arbitral community. This chapter will show that compliance with some professional obligations is intrinsically more problematic than with others, as sometimes incentives for deviation are considerably high. This chapter will put forward the idea that there seems to be a higher level of self-regulatory interest in these more problematic areas, such as conflicts of interest and disclosure duties.

Chapter seven will, in turn, dedicate itself to the question of why arbitrators comply with their professional obligations. In doing so, this chapter will explore a number of related topics. First, and on the basis of chapter three, it will show that following these rules is the dominant market strategy adopted by arbitrators despite the inexistence of clearly defined formal sanctions. It will further explore how the arbitration market and arbitral community pre-select those who enter the arbitration market and how the characteristics of those selected may contribute to compliance. A key idea here is that, despite arbitration lacking formal licensing or educational requirements, it still filters out those not committed to the field. Finally, it will also analyse how the long process of entering into the arbitration community helps members learn and internalise these rules, arguably also contributing to compliance.

Chapter eight will complete the analysis presented in chapter seven by analysing how certain institutions, namely arbitral institutions, professional associations, national courts, and criminal investigation authorities, contribute to the enforcement of these obligations. This part analyses how these institutions provide incentives for arbitrators to comply with professional rules and how these interrelate with market and community forces. Significant attention will be paid to how some of these mechanisms, namely civil liability suits and criminal investigations, have more limited usage in the arbitral context. This discussion will show, however, how the actions undertaken by these institutions provide a system of

[54] See Tom Ginsburg, 'The Culture of Arbitration' (2003) 36 *The Vanderbilt Journal of Transnational Law* 1335, 1337.

checks that allows recourse when the underlying grid of incentives is insufficient to lead arbitrators to comply with their obligations.

Chapter nine will conclude the book by tying in the analysis provided in the previous chapters with the discussions currently being undertaken within the arbitral community. First, it will analyse whether the current transformations in the market – such as the increase in the number and diversity of practitioners – will disrupt the self-regulatory framework in place. From there, it will analyse whether the 'professionalisation' of international arbitrators is to be encouraged. With this aim, it will first analyse which actors could bring such transformations into fruition, analysing the role that states could play in this regard, changing parties' preferences, arbitral institutions and the arbitral community itself. Finally, it will consider the arguments for and against such transformations and how such changes would affect the incentives currently leading to the creation and enforcement of professional norms.

2

The Emergence of International Commercial Arbitration and the Modern Arbitrator

The success of arbitration, as well as its current regulatory issues, were not inevitable. The growth of arbitration and its transformation into a global industry resulted from a conscious effort of several players to create the legal infrastructure through international treaties and domestic legislation that has made the progress of arbitration possible. These efforts moved arbitration from a merchant-driven alternative mode of dispute resolution in niche markets to a flourishing legal industry. At the same time, they represented an inevitable shift in the type of problems and risks associated with arbitration and the systems of formal and informal control of arbitrators.

To contextualise how the current issues discussed around arbitration have emerged, this chapter focuses on two significant, largely still recent, modifications to this field. First, it explores how international arbitration developed into an increasingly technocratic and quasi-judicial system of solving disputes, with arbitrators acting in ways increasingly akin to national judges. Second, it notes how, at the same time, arbitration evolved into a fully-fledged for-profit industry, with different actors developing increasingly complex commercial strategies. This is important as it helps to establish how arbitrators have come to conduct themselves with market goals in mind. At the same time, arbitrators are still expected to play a 'public role'[1] and ensure that the proceedings they preside over respect basic principles of procedural fairness.[2] Both are key premises which the following chapters will be built upon.

This chapter will start by reviewing the development of international commercial arbitration. It will focus on how an initially reasonably small community of practitioners, spearheaded by the International Chamber of Commerce (ICC), transformed arbitration into a well-functioning system capable of producing enforceable awards across borders. It will further explore how this led to a dramatic increase in the number of proceedings and the financial gains that could be obtained from providing services in this area. The chapter will then review the transformations that took place in the arbitral 'profession' by establishing how arbitrators' profiles adapted to the changes in the arbitration field.

[1] See Catherine A Rogers, 'The Vocation of the International Arbitrator' (2004) 20 *American University International Law Review* 957, 1016.

[2] See Susan D Franck, 'The Role of International Arbitrators' (2005) 12 *ILSA Journal of International and Comparative Law* 499, 505.

I. The Development of International Commercial Arbitration and its Transformation into a Distinct Market

A first step to understanding international commercial arbitration, its market and the regulation of arbitrators demands contextualising its deep transformation over the past century. An abridged introduction to the modern history of international arbitration demands selecting key facts and actors that illustrate the main events leading to the current status quo. While any such selection is necessarily incomplete, there were a few actions and trends since the First World War that were paramount to the construction of the system of international commercial arbitration.[3] These include the arbitration reform movement in the 1920s, the signing of the New York Convention in the 1950s, the approval of pro-arbitration statutes throughout the 1970s and 1980s, and the rapid expansion in the number of cases and service providers since the 1990s.

A. Arbitration Prior to the Twentieth Century: A Markedly Distinct Institution

It is commonplace in texts of international commercial arbitration to note the centuries-old origins of international commercial arbitration.[4] Often, it is noted that arbitration predates court litigation, with historical examples dating back to the great ancient civilisations.[5] It is important to note that arbitration in this historical context worked markedly differently from what we think of today as arbitration. Importantly, it lacked the enforceability that is usually associated with international commercial arbitration nowadays. Rather, it strived to achieve solutions that both parties could voluntarily comply with.[6] It further relied on reputation and the threat of ostracism to persuade parties to comply with an arbitrator's decision.[7]

[3] While noting that a full historical account of arbitration largely remains unwritten, for a more thorough introduction to the history of arbitration, see Gary Born, *International Commercial Arbitration*, 2nd edn (Alphen aan den Rijn, Wolters Kluwer Law & Business, 2014) 7. Also, Roebuck's prolific work should be noted. See, eg, Derek Roebuck and Bruno De Fumichon, *Roman Arbitration* (Oxford, The Arbitration Press 2004); Derek Roebuck, *Early English Arbitration* (Oxford, The Arbitration Press 2008); Derek Roebuck, *Mediation and Arbitration in the Middle Ages: England 1154 to 1558* (Oxford, Holo Books, The Arbitration Press, 2013); Derek Roebuck, *The Golden Age of Arbitration: Dispute Resolution Under Elizabeth I* (Oxford, Holo Books, The Arbitration Press, 2015); Derek Roebuck, *Arbitration and Mediation in Seventeenth-Century England* (Oxford, Holo Books, The Arbitration Press, 2017); Derek Roebuck, Francis Calvert Boorman and Rhiannon Markless, *English Arbitration and Mediation in the Long Eighteenth Century* (Oxford, Holo Books, The Arbitration Press, 2019). Equally worth noting is the more recent Mikaël Schinazi, *The Three Ages of International Commercial Arbitration* (Cambridge, Cambridge University Press, 2021).

[4] See, amongst others, Born (n 3) 6; Mauro Rubino-Sammartano, *International Arbitration Law and Practice*, 3rd edn (New York, Juris Publishing, Inc 2014) 51.

[5] See J Martin and H Hunter, 'Arbitration Procedure in England: Past, Present and Future' (1985) 1 *Arbitration International* 82; Andrea M Steingruber, *Consent in International Arbitration* (Oxford, Oxford University Press, 2012) 11; Born (n 3) 7; Frances Kellor, *American Arbitration: Its History, Functions and Achievements* (Washington, Beard Books, 1948) 3.

[6] Alec Stone Sweet and Florian Grisel, *The Evolution of International Arbitration: Judicialization, Governance, Legitimacy* (Oxford, Oxford University Press, 2017) 39.

[7] ibid.

While arbitration was, in this sense, successful in solving disputes between established traders that, due to the nature of their transactions, were heavily dependent on their reputation, it was poorly equipped to deal with disputes outside well-connected, closely-knit trading communities. While never extinguished, arbitration was, to an extent, superseded by court litigation. By the sixteenth century, national courts had become the typical way of solving disputes, relegating arbitration to a secondary role in most western jurisdictions.[8] For example, in England, by the nineteenth century, national judges, likely motivated by a self-interested desire to increase their number of commercial cases and consequently the fees received, had determined to have jurisdiction even in the cases for which the parties had determined an arbitration clause.[9]

B. From the Foundation of the ICC to the Signing of the Geneva Conventions

The rise of national courts as the dominant system of solving commercial disputes also brought several difficulties that would ultimately allow a rebirth of arbitration. Indeed, national courts proved over time to be inadequate fora for international commercial disputes. Although international private law could theoretically provide the tools to allow national courts to address international disputes, it was often clear that courts could not provide truly effective dispute resolution for international disputes.[10] In particular, there were: i) problems with consistently selecting and applying national laws regarding transnational contracts; ii) inexperience with the problems arising with complex transnational transactions; iii) difficulties with enforcing foreign court judgments; and iv) apprehensions regarding the neutrality of national courts when one of the disputants was a foreign party.

i. The ICC and the Changing Framework at the International Level

Against this background, international arbitration began its revival in the aftermath of the First World War.[11] This was a period marked by an internationalist movement looking increasingly into arbitration as a key to solving international disputes.[12] It was also an age of progressively open global commerce, needing newer approaches to dispute resolution. It was also in this context that the International Chamber of Commerce (ICC) emerged. It would prove to be one of the key players in developing the modern international commercial arbitration system. Founded in 1919 by prominent members of the business

[8] ibid; Thomas Hale, *Between Interests and Law: The Politics of Transnational Commercial Disputes* (Cambridge, Cambridge University Press, 2015) 27. See also Born (n 3) 12.

[9] Martin and Hunter (n 5) 84. See also Bruce L Benson, 'An Exploration of the Impact of Modern Arbitration Statutes on the Development of Arbitration in the United States' (1995) 11 *Journal of Law, Economics, & Organization* 479, 483.

[10] See Stone Sweet and Grisel (n 6) 40.

[11] See Kellor (n 5) 9; Imre S Szalai, 'Modern Arbitration Values and the First World War' [2007] *The American Journal of Legal History* 355, 363.

[12] See Szalai (n 11) 363.

communities of Belgium, France, Italy, the UK, and the US,[13] the ICC aimed to facilitate business transactions and strived to be a 'world parliament of business'.[14]

This revival of international arbitration is, to an extent, indissociable from the role played by the ICC.[15] Soon after its creation, the ICC identified the need to provide a reliable dispute resolution mechanism for international commercial disputes as key to the development of international commerce.[16] With this aim, it established, in 1923, its International Court of Arbitration. This Court, against a fee, organised arbitral proceedings and indicated, when necessary, arbitrators to solve a dispute. While not the first arbitral institution,[17] it rose at one point to be the absolute dominant arbitral institution for international disputes,[18] helping to lead the preference over time for 'institutionalised' arbitration – ie, arbitral proceedings organised within an arbitral institution.

Finally, to guarantee that arbitration clauses and arbitral awards would be complied with, the ICC further worked with the League of Nations in the elaboration of the Geneva Protocol of Arbitration Clauses of 1923 and the Geneva Convention on the Execution of Foreign Arbitral Awards of 1927.[19] By the first Protocol, contracting states agreed to recognise the validity of foreign arbitration agreements and that their tribunals, when facing a dispute covered by the scope of an arbitration clause, would refer the parties to arbitration. By the 1927 Convention, contracting states agreed that arbitral awards should be recognised as binding and be enforced if the award was not contrary to the public policy or to the principles of the law of the country in which it was sought to be relied upon.

ii. Changes at the National Level and the Shifting Perception of International Arbitration

The transformations of the legal framework did not occur only at the international level. Contemporaneous to the global changes described above were transformations in domestic arbitration acts that would foster arbitration. The most iconic of these transformations was the passage of the Federal Arbitration Act (FAA), signed into law by President Coolidge in 1925 and still in force today. In the case of the FAA, the role of the American Bar Association (ABA) and its Committee on Commerce, Trade and Commercial Law should be particularly highlighted since it prepared the original draft of the Bill that Congress enacted into law with only minor amendments.[20]

[13] Eric A Schwartz and Yves Derains, *Guide to the ICC Rules of Arbitration*, 2nd edn (Alphen aan den Rijn, Kluwer Law International, 2005).

[14] Lyman Cromwell White, *International Non-Governmental Organizations: Their Purposes, Methods, and Accomplishments* (New Brunswick, Rutgers University Press, 1951) 250.

[15] See, on the role of the ICC in developing arbitration, Schinazi (n 3).

[16] See Florian Grisel, 'Treaty-Making between Public Authority and Private Interests: The Genealogy of the Convention on the Recognition and Enforcement of Foreign Arbitral Awards' (2017) 28 *European Journal of International Law* 73, 76; Katherine L Lynch, *The Forces of Economic Globalization: Challenges to the Regime of International Commercial Arbitration* (Alphen aan den Rijn, Kluwer Law International, 2003) 114.

[17] For example, the London Court of Arbitration (LCIA), initially named The City of London Chamber of Arbitration, had its origin in 1892.

[18] Richard J Graving, 'The International Commercial Arbitration Institutions: How Good A Job Are They Doing?' (1989) 4 *American University International Law Review* 319, 330.

[19] See Lynch (n 16) 128; Simon Greenberg, Christopher Kee and J Romesh Weeramantry, *International Commercial Arbitration: An Asia-Pacific Perspective* (Cambridge, Cambridge University Press, 2011) 7.

[20] Christopher R Drahozal, 'In Defense of Southland: Reexamining the Legislative History of the Federal Arbitration Act' (2002) 78 *Notre Dame Law Review* 101, 125.

It is also important to note that the US business community's strong and well-organised lobbying efforts fuelled the passage of the FAA.[21] In this sense, it is possible to identify that this period of development of domestic arbitration in the US mirrors that of arbitration at the international level. If the international business community, through the ICC, had spearheaded the creation of the international legal framework that would support arbitration, American corporate power expressed its support for a new domestic arbitration law through the lobbying efforts of the New York Chamber of Commerce and the Arbitration Society Association, beyond the aforementioned ABA. Underlying both movements, one could see identification with broader ideals of free enterprise and business 'self-regulation'.[22]

Also, in regard to content, the FAA covered the main issues addressed by the Geneva Protocol of 1923 and the Geneva Convention of 1927. Following previous legal acts at the state level, the FAA established arbitration agreements to be enforceable and irrevocable,[23] whereas before, arbitration agreements were generally considered revocable at will and, therefore, unenforceable in a court of law.[24] It further established arbitral awards to be enforceable, determining only a limited amount of circumstances where parties could seek to have the arbitral award annulled by a judicial court.[25] This was important, as American courts, following English courts' views, traditionally regarded arbitration with hostility.[26] This previous hostility was an attitude that the passage of the FAA and pro-arbitration statutes at the state level would help change.[27]

Changes could also be observed in other jurisdictions. In England, a movement to modernise commercial dispute resolution had already started in the late nineteenth century, expressed through the approval of the Arbitration Act (1889), the foundation of the London Court of International Arbitration (1892) and the establishment of the Supreme Court's Commercial Court (1895).[28] In the 1920s and 1930s, further changes were established, namely through the Arbitration Clauses (Protocol) Act 1924, which gave effect within England to the Geneva Protocol of 1923 and by the Arbitration (Foreign Awards) Act 1930, which gave effect to the Geneva Convention of 1927. This new background was complemented by a change in attitude by English judges who were increasingly prepared to construe generously the powers and autonomy given to arbitrators.[29]

Also, a similar movement of increased support for arbitration can be observed in France.[30] Before the twentieth century, the restrictions imposed by the Napoleonic Code of Civil Procedure of 1806 and by the dominant case law determined that French nationals

[21] Szalai (n 11) 380; Jérôme Sgard, 'A Tale of Three Cities: The Construction of International Commercial Arbitration' in Gregoire Mallard and Jerome Sgard (eds), *Contractual Knowledge* (Cambridge, Cambridge University Press, 2016) 167.

[22] Eric George, 'A Historical Reflection on Arbitration and the Corporation as an Object of Economic Governance' (2017) 39 *Western New England* 557, 563.

[23] See Federal Arbitration Act 1925, §2–4.

[24] See Szalai (n 11) 356.

[25] See Federal Arbitration Act 1925, §201–208.

[26] See Jennifer Schulz, 'Arbitrating Arbitrability: How the U.S. Supreme Court Empowered the Arbitrator at the Expense of the Judge and the Average Joe Comment' (2010) 44 *Loyola of Los Angeles Law Review* 1269, 1270.

[27] Noting, however, that arbitration was well established and growing rapidly, long before these statutes were passed, see Benson (n 9).

[28] See V Veeder and Brian Dye, 'Lord Bramwell's Arbitration Code 1884–1889' (1992) 8 *Arbitration International* 329.

[29] See Gershon Ellenbogen, 'English Arbitration Practice' (1952) 17 *Law and Contemporary Problems* 656, 658.

[30] For a detailed account of these transformations, see Schinazi (n 3) 67.

who were parties to a domestic contract could not agree to arbitrate future disputes, seriously limiting the availability of arbitration for internal disputes.[31] This state of affairs started to change with a legislative act in 1925, which legalised compromissory clauses in certain specified commercial cases, yet again mirroring the transformations that had been brought by the Geneva Protocol of 1923.[32]

It is important to note that the changes in commercial arbitration did not affect only the legal or institutional framework. The interwar period also significantly transformed how arbitration as a legal institution was perceived. As an American lawyer writing in 1934 explained:

> We cannot ignore the fact, for example, that the nature of arbitration has changed in recent years. To the Middle Age merchant, and in fact up to the time of our modern arbitration acts, the process was more or less a friendly method of settlement of disputes. Awards were compromises and arbitrators were agents whose authority in effect was limited to securing a settlement which both sides would willingly accept. To compel 'arbitration' as used in that sense borders on the grotesque. But arbitration as visualised by modern proponents of the movement, arbitration such as results when an entire industry agrees that disputes should be thus settled, arbitration by which one pre-empts his right to secure court disposition of any possible dispute which may thereafter arise between the parties, is no longer a simple agency-compromise, it is a substitute for the courts, termed quasi-judicial by its proponents; which probably means judicial in result, judicial in its nature, non-judicial in its judges.[33]

By the interwar period, the notion that national courts were poorly equipped to deal with commercial disputes, particularly transnational ones, had gained traction.[34] This led to a revival of a profoundly different arbitration. Arbitration had, by this time, stopped being an amicable method of dispute resolution between traders akin to conciliation. Instead, it started working as a genuine alternative to the national court systems, providing awards of a true adjudicatory nature. Based on a specific international legal framework, arbitration, albeit dependent on national courts' supervision and sometimes enforcement, was beginning to be shaped as an alternative self-enforcing system, semi-independent of national jurisdictions and national judicial forums.

C. From the New York Convention to the UNCITRAL Model Law and a Wave of Arbitral Reform

Although the interwar period saw an increase in popularity, the nascent modern international commercial arbitration was still mostly ad hoc and used in a small number

[31] Born (n 3) 39. It should be noted that in regards to international arbitration, French courts' approach had always been more amicable. See on this point Thomas E Carbonneau, 'The Elaboration of a French Court Doctrine on International Commercial Arbitration: A Study in Liberal Civilian Judicial Creativity' 55 (1980) *Tulane Law Review* 1.

[32] See Carbonneau (n 31) fn 6; Lynden Macassey, 'International Commercial Arbitration – Its Origin, Development and Importance' (1938) 24 *American Bar Association Journal* 518. See also Born (n 3) 68.

[33] Philip G Phillips, 'A Lawyer's Approach to Commercial Arbitration' (1934) 44 *The Yale Law Journal* 31, 35.

[34] See George (n 22) 564.

of enclaves, such as disputes related to the international trade of commodities.[35] In these markets, the close-knit nature of the community of traders, which would repeatedly trade amongst themselves, and the strong power of trade associations to blacklist non-complying traders, led parties to voluntarily comply with arbitral decisions.[36] Outside these situations, international commercial arbitration was not as successful. Indeed, while noteworthy, the number of cases at the ICC at the time was incomparably lower than it would become.[37]

i. The New York Convention as the Catalyst for a New Era of International Arbitration

Part of the difficulties of arbitration at the time related to the obstacles of enforcing foreign arbitral awards in a court of law, even in the aftermath of the Geneva Conventions. This derived from the 1927 Geneva Convention, in its Article 4(2), determining that a party, in order to enforce an award abroad, had to supply, among other things, documentary evidence to prove that the award has become final in the country where it was made.[38] This gave rise to the so-called 'double-exequatur' system, as according to the dominant interpretation, it demanded a party first to initiate proceedings at the seat of the arbitration (to obtain a declaration that the award was indeed final) and after at the place of enforcement (to enforce the award and seize assets located in that country). This significantly lengthened the process of enforcing an award.[39]

Reforming this cumbersome system was a priority for international arbitration advocates. The ICC would again play a paramount role in the next step of advancing the international commercial arbitration agenda: the signing of the New York Convention in 1958 – which would substitute the Geneva Protocol and the Geneva Conventions. Indeed, it was the ICC, under the initiative of its chairman, who first offered a draft of a new Convention.[40] This draft was then presented to the United Nations Economic and Social Council, which presented a modified version to an international conference held at the United Nations headquarters.[41]

In summary, the New York Convention covered two main issues. It first placed an obligation upon the courts of contracting states to respect arbitral agreements by determining that a court, when seized of a matter in respect of which the parties have made an arbitration agreement, must, at the request of one of the parties, refer them

[35] Detailing that, in the pre-war period, the London Corn Trade Association was reported to have handled about 20,000 cases annually, the Incorporated Oil Seed Corporation about 7,000 and the London Jute Association about 1,000, see Morris S Rosenthal, 'Arbitration in the Settlement of International Trade Disputes' (1946) 11 *Law and Contemporary Problems* 808, 825.

[36] Sgard (n 21) 159.

[37] From 1923 to 1939 the ICC had reportedly arbitrated a total of around 700 cases. See Rosenthal (n 35) 829.

[38] See Herbert Kronke, 'The Role of Private International Law: UNIDROIT and the Geneva Conventions on Arbitration' in Michel Erpelding, Burkhard Hess and Hélène Ruiz Fabri (eds), *Peace Through Law* (Baden-Baden, Nomos Verlagsgesellschaft mbH & Co KG, 2019) 191.

[39] Grisel (n 16) 77.

[40] See Julian DM Lew, Loukas A Mistelis and Stefan Kröll, *Comparative International Commercial Arbitration* (Alphen aan den Rijn, Kluwer Law International, 2003) 21.

[41] Pieter Sanders, 'The Making of the Convention', *Enforcing arbitration awards under the New York Convention: experience and prospects* (UN 1999) 3.

to arbitration.[42] Second, it determined that contracting states are obligated to recognise arbitral awards as binding and to enforce them, with the parties seeking enforcement of a foreign award needing to supply only the arbitral award and the arbitration agreement.[43] Courts within the contracting states are then only able to refuse enforcement if one of the limited grounds recognised within the Convention applies.[44]

Unlike the Geneva Conventions, the New York Convention was a resounding success, leading some within the community to simply summarise that 'it works'.[45] Its success may be attributed to a range of factors. First, as mentioned previously, eliminating the double exequatur system was a major step towards a pro-enforcement system.[46] Second, the New York Convention was more widely adopted than the Geneva Convention of 1927, having been ratified within its first 30 years of existence by 79 parties.[47] Finally, and equally important, has been the tendency of national courts across jurisdictions to interpret the New York Convention relatively uniformly and in a pro-enforcement fashion, leading to arbitration working as a predictable system of solving disputes.[48]

Therefore, with the New York Convention, the idea that arbitral awards were final was enshrined into the international legal order, becoming one of the cornerstones of the success of modern international arbitration. It inaugurated a trend of a non-interventionist approach[49] by national courts, which emphasised the idea that national courts should undertake no merit review.[50] The easier enforcement of arbitral awards in comparison with judicial decisions across borders, due to the effect of the New York Convention, is a particular in-built advantage in the context of international dispute resolution, which, to this day, gives arbitration an edge over other dispute resolution methods.[51]

ii. Competition between Jurisdictions and the Birth of the Modern Arbitral Market

While the New York Convention was a key step in allowing arbitration to flourish as a dispute resolution mechanism, it only covered a small part of the entire canvas of international

[42] See New York Convention, Art II, para 3. For an in-depth analysis of the New York Convention, see, eg, Reinmar Wolff (ed), *New York Convention on the Recognition and Enforcement of Foreign Arbitral Awards: A Commentary* (Munchen, CH Beck, 2019); Herbert Kronke, Patricia Nacimiento and Dirk Otto, *Recognition and Enforcement of Foreign Arbitral Awards: A Global Commentary on the New York Convention* (Alphen aan den Rijn, Kluwer Law International BV, 2010).

[43] See New York Convention, Art IV.

[44] See New York Convention, Art V.

[45] Linda Silberman, 'The New York Convention After Fifty Years: Some Reflections on the Role of National Law' (2009) 38 *Georgia Journal of International & Comparative Law* 25, 26.

[46] Emmanuel Gaillard, 'International Arbitration as a Transnational System of Justice' in Albert Jan Van Den Berg (ed), *Arbitration – The Next Fifty Years* (Alphen aan den Rijn, Kluwer Law International, 2012) 72.

[47] Including the US and the Soviet Union which had not ratified the Geneva Convention of 1927.

[48] See Silberman (n 45) 26.

[49] Some jurisdictions, most notably England, still maintain as a default mechanism the possibility of, to a small extent, re-evaluating the arbitral award. These are, however, in most jurisdictions, not intended as to allow relitigating the issues addressed in the arbitration proceedings. See English Arbitration Act 1996, s 69.

[50] See Emmanuel Gaillard, *The Review of International Arbitral Awards* (New York, Juris Publishing, Inc, 2010) 2.

[51] In turn, the benefits in terms of speed, cost, and to some extent, neutrality, are largely contextual. They depend on the specific characteristics of the dispute, the arbitral tribunal and institutions involved, and the judicial system being compared. See Alessandra Casella, 'On Market Integration and the Development of Institutions: The Case of International Commercial Arbitration' (1996) 40 *European Economic Review* 155, 162.

arbitration. It was still upon states to define many vital issues, including the scope of arbitrability, ie, the kind of disputes that may be referred to arbitration; the extent of court support to arbitration in regards, for example, to taking evidence; and the powers of the arbitral tribunal, in regards for example, to decree provisional measures. Therefore, the subsequent transformation of the international arbitration system would take place at the national legislation level, addressing many of these issues in a pro-arbitration fashion.

Two movements should be noted. First, at the international level, the creation of the UNCITRAL Model Law was a key move. This initiative by UNCITRAL, a part of the United Nations family, was designed to assist states in reforming and modernising their arbitration laws. This was at a time when many jurisdictions still held what was considered outdated and fragmentary legislation as relevant issues were not addressed.[52] The Model Law was intended to help solve these issues, presenting itself as a 'modern' pro-arbitration legislation template to be adopted with or without modifications by Member States. In doing so, the goal was to harmonise practices between different jurisdictions, as significant differences between local legislations were perceived to hinder a predictable system of international arbitration.[53]

The second movement to be noted was a string of arbitration laws supporting generally pro-arbitration solutions.[54] The late 1970s and the 1980s would witness, amongst others, new acts in England and Wales (1979), France (1981), Italy (1983), the Netherlands (1986), the Federal Republic of Germany (1986), and Switzerland (1988). This drive, whose start predated the Model Law, illustrated an increased tendency of states to present themselves as arbitration-friendly jurisdictions in a bid to attract arbitral proceedings.[55] These inaugurated a legislative movement that has continued to this day, by which numerous jurisdictions would cyclically approve revised arbitral statutes, many of which were inspired by the Model Law, that would incorporate increasingly 'modern' and 'pro-arbitration' features.[56]

The combination of the New York Convention with an increasingly arbitration-friendly set of statutes at the domestic level was essential in crystalising many of the advantages that would propel arbitration to be the dominant method of solving transnational commercial disputes. By this time, the principle of party autonomy had become an indisputable aspect of modern arbitration. With it, it became almost universally accepted that parties could not only define the procedural rules applicable to their proceedings but also decide broader aspects, including the seat of the arbitration,[57] the

[52] See Explanatory Note by the UNCITRAL Secretariat on the 1985 Model Law on International Commercial Arbitration, para 6. See also Gerold Herrmann, 'UNCITRAL's Work Towards a Model Law on International Commercial Arbitration' (1984) 4 *Pace Law Review* 537, 543.

[53] See ibid.

[54] See Casella (n 51) 160.

[55] See Steven J Stein and Daniel R Wotman, 'International Commercial Arbitration in the 1980s: A Comparison of the Major Arbitral Systems and Rules' (1983) 38 *The Business Lawyer* 1685, 1686.

[56] See Christopher R Drahozal, 'Regulatory Competition and the Location of International Arbitration Proceedings' (2004) 24 *International Review of Law and Economics* 371.

[57] This allows parties to select, to an extent, the level of oversight they want their arbitral proceedings to be subject to. Since it is primarily upon the courts of the seat of the arbitration to review the award and it is upon the parties to decide where the seat of arbitration is, parties can, in effect, define whether they want to opt for a jurisdiction where awards and arbitrators' behaviour is more thoroughly scrutinised or not.

arbitral institution (if any) organising their proceedings,[58] and the arbitrators that would decide the proceedings.[59]

The ability to undertake these decisions would be an important catalyst for the development of different markets within arbitration. The ability to select arbitrators was increasingly presented as a selling point of arbitration,[60] allowing, at least in theory, parties to select those with the needed skills and expertise.[61] In practice, this gave rise to increasingly more strategic approaches by parties in selecting arbitrators and, therefore, a marketplace where arbitrators compete to be selected.[62] Also, the possibility of selecting an arbitral institution opened another market, with a key characteristic of the emergent arbitration environment being the increasing competition between arbitral institutions to attract disputes.[63] Finally, the possibility for parties to select the seat where arbitral proceedings take place opened an avenue for competition between different jurisdictions,[64] leading some to note the emergence of a regulatory market within arbitration.[65]

Still, it is important to note that the transformations around this time were not only legal or institutional in nature. Attitudes towards this legal institution also changed. The 1980s saw international arbitration develop into a fully-fledged service industry with the opportunity to obtain large sums of money now available to all service providers in this market. Michael Mustill, a well-known English judge and arbitrator at the time, encapsulated the new perspective on arbitration, writing in 1989:

> [A]rbitration is now a service industry, and a very profitable one at that. The arbitral institution, the arbitrators, the lawyers, the expert witnesses and the providers of ancillary services all charge fees on a scale which would quite literally have been inconceivable thirty years ago. Hotel bills alone may now surpass what would then have been the entire cost of an arbitration. Of course, in one sense there is nothing wrong with charging what the market will stand. But in another, the recognition that this is what those concerned are doing demonstrates how far commercial arbitration has come from its former roots.[66]

[58] It is important to note that parties have at their disposal two sets of possible arrangements to undertake commercial arbitration. First, they may refer a dispute to an ad hoc arbitral tribunal to be composed in accordance with the parties' agreement and the applicable national statutes. Alternatively, parties may refer a dispute to an arbitral institution. In this instance, an arbitral tribunal will be constituted pursuant to the arbitral institution rules. In institutional arbitrations, the arbitral institution will play a multitude of roles, including constituting the arbitral tribunal, fixing the arbitrators' compensation, and providing help with the logistics of the hearing. For an overview of the role of arbitral institutions, see Gary Born, *International Arbitration: Law and Practice* (Alphen aan den Rijn, Kluwer Law International, 2012) 26.

[59] The idea of the 'party appointed-arbitrator' has accompanied arbitration throughout history being presented by some as its cornerstone. See Douglas Pilawa, 'Sifting through the Arbitrators for the Woman, the Minority, the Newcomer Notes' (2019) 51 *Case Western Reserve Journal of International Law* 395, 404.

[60] Applicable laws and arbitral institutional rules typically allow parties to agree on the arbitrator(s) deciding the dispute. Further, in case, of a three-member panel, these rules usually allow each party to appoint an arbitrator to the panel.

[61] See Christian Bühring-Uhle, Lars Kirchhoff and Gabriele Scherer, *Arbitration and Mediation in International Business* (Alphen aan den Rijn, Kluwer Law International BV, 2006) 64.

[62] See Sam Luttrell, *Bias Challenges in International Commercial Arbitration: The Need for a 'real Danger' Test* (Alphen aan den Rijn, Kluwer Law International, 2009) 138. See also Pilawa (n 59) 405.

[63] See Barbara Alicja Warwas, *The Liability of Arbitral Institutions: Legitimacy Challenges and Functional Responses* (The Hague, TMC Asser Press, 2017) 43.

[64] See Lynch (n 16) 274.

[65] Christopher R Drahozal, 'Regulatory Competition and the Location of International Arbitration Proceedings' (2004) 24 *International Review of Law and Economics* 371.

[66] Michael John Mustill, 'Arbitration: History and Background' (1989) 6 *Journal of International Arbitration* 43.

By the 1980s, arbitration was indeed notably a distinct institution. With an international and national legal framework that heavily facilitated the usage and enforcement of arbitral proceedings, all pieces were in place for a burst in the number of arbitral proceedings. The explosion in the number of cases[67] made arbitration judicial-like and business-like, leading to changes in the approach of the different players in the field. The big Anglo-American law firms entered the field, partly leading to the importation of the adversarial stance dominant in common law litigation.[68] Arbitrators relied increasingly on a technocratic and legalistic approach in their decision-making[69] and arbitral institutions, in a landscape still dominated by the ICC, professionalised and expanded their activities.[70]

D. Arbitration from the 1990s Onwards: The Explosion of Cases and the Move East and South

If the 1980s saw all the institutional pieces finally in place, the 1990s and the first decade of the twenty-first century would witness an explosion in the number of arbitral proceedings taking place around the world. By this time, international commercial arbitration had transformed into an undisputed major legal market, representing a relevant source of income for law firms, senior lawyers, and arbitrators, representing a key opportunity for these service providers to internationalise their services. From the 1990s onwards, further changes would accelerate this movement, as arbitration would gain prominence, globalise to previously unexplored markets, and become the dominant method of solving international (and many domestic) disputes.

The first change to be noted was the spectacular rise of international investment arbitration in the 1990s. If, until the early 1990s, investment arbitration was a discreet and somewhat exotic sub-branch of international public law, mostly relegated to academic discussions, it would rapidly thrive in that decade and the first decade of the twenty-first century. Following the growing international investment and the increasing number of bilateral investment treaties providing for arbitration, a wave of international disputes between investors and, most often, developing states emerged.[71] This growth would give rise to another profitable legal market. This space was quickly occupied by many of the same

[67] The caseload from the ICC offers a good benchmark of the spectacular rise in the number of cases. From 1922 to 1976 the ICC had roughly 3,000 cases filed. From 1977 to 1988 another 3,000 cases were filed. See Jacques Werner, 'International Commercial Arbitrators: From Merchant to Academic to Skilled Professional' (1997) 4 *Dispute Resolution Magazine* 22.

[68] See Yves Dezalay and Bryant G Garth, *Dealing in Virtue: International Commercial Arbitration and the Construction of a Transnational Legal Order* (Chicago, University of Chicago Press, 1996) 48; Elena V Helmer, 'International Commercial Arbitration: Americanized, Civilized, or Harmonized' (2003) 19 *Ohio State Journal on Dispute Resolution* 35.

[69] See Dezalay and Garth (n 68) 34.

[70] This was notably the case of the London Court of Arbitration, which after some earlier success, had by the 1950s became '*essentially a prostrated institution with an almost empty docket*'. See Sgard (n 21) 166. It remerged, fully reformed, in the 1980s with a new name (London Court of International Arbitration), eventually rising to be a key player in the international arbitration market.

[71] From the 1950s to 1989 there was a single investor-state dispute settlement arbitration case. From 1990 to 2007 there were 291. See UNCTAD, 'World Investment Report 2015: Reforming International Investment Governance', 121.

key law firms, senior lawyers and arbitrators that populated commercial arbitration, giving firms and arbitrators a new source of work that would allow the sizeable practices typically found today.[72]

Equally important in the globalisation of arbitration was the contemporary movement of arbitration expansion outside its traditional venues. As the 1980s came to a close, arbitration remained an institution primarily used in the western world. However, as the 1990s and beyond unfolded, this began to change. Suddenly, new hubs for arbitration were emerging in Asia, shifting away from the traditional centres of Paris, Geneva, and London.[73] Hong Kong and Singapore, in particular, emerged as vital arbitral seats. Helped by local governments interested in fostering a dispute resolution industry in those jurisdictions, local institutions such as the Hong Kong International Arbitration Court (HKIAC) and the Singapore International Arbitration Court (SIAC) would become leading institutions.[74] Around these institutions, law practices, often branches of British and American international law firms, flourished.

At the same time, emergent new markets also provided increased demand and developed their own approaches to arbitration.[75] China, for example, took its first steps to enter the global international arbitration community by joining the New York Convention in 1986 and passing a domestic arbitral law in 1994. While maintaining many peculiarities compared to international practice,[76] Chinese parties would increasingly use arbitration, becoming a key source of work for the new arbitration centres in Hong Kong and Singapore. Brazil, where until the late 1990s arbitration was virtually inexistent, would, following an arbitration law in 1996 and a 2001 Supreme Federal Court decision upholding the constitutionality of arbitration, see arbitration thrive against the background of an often inadequate judicial system.[77] India would also inaugurate a slow process for arbitral reform and development in 1996 through the passage of its new arbitration law.[78]

Arbitration would, therefore, become globalised in the 2000s. From North America to sub-Saharan Africa, arbitration started being used as the dispute mechanism for most major international transactions and many domestic disputes. This era was also, however, a time of backlash. The increasing 'judicialisation' of arbitration – ie, the increasingly formalistic and

[72] See Charles N Brower, 'W(h)Ither International Commercial Arbitration? The Goff Lecture 2007' (2008) 24 *Arbitration International* 181, 191.

[73] Neil Kaplan, writing in 1996, describes how 'a mere 15 years ago, Hong Kong would never have been thought of, let alone mentioned, in the context of international arbitration'. The author further indicates that the members of the Hong Kong Branch of The Chartered Institute of Arbitrators numbered fewer than 50; by the mid 1990s they numbered in the region of 1,100. See Neil Kaplan, 'The History and Development of Arbitration in Hong Kong Symposium: Financial Law in Hong Kong and South-East Asia' (1996) 1 *Yearbook of International Financial and Economic Law* 203.

[74] In 1990, HKIAC had been established for five years and its docket consisted of 54 cases. See Brower (n 72) 181. In 2020, a total of 483 cases were submitted to HKIAC.

[75] See Fernando Dias Simões, 'A Dispute Resolution Center for the Brics?' in Rostam J Neuwirth, Alexandr Svetlicinii and Denis De Castro Halis (eds), *The BRICS-Lawyers' Guide to Global Cooperation* (Cambridge, Cambridge University Press, 2017).

[76] Most notably there are severe limitations on Chinese parties to have recourse to international forums in domestic disputes. For an overview, see Kun Fan, *Arbitration in China: A Legal and Cultural Analysis* (Oxford, Hart Publishing, 2013) 26.

[77] For an overview of the evolution of arbitration in Brazil, see Joaquim T de Paiva Muniz and Ana Tereza Palhares Basílio, *Arbitration Law of Brazil: Practice and Procedure* (New York, Juris Publishing, Inc, 2006) 3.

[78] See Sumeet Kachwaha, 'The Arbitration Law of India: A Critical Analysis' (2005) 1 *Asian International Arbitration Journal* 105.

legalistic approach taken by arbitral tribunals instead of a more 'amicable' approach once dominant – created significant concerns.[79] At this time, complaints about the rising costs, slowness of arbitral proceedings, and the inadequacy of arbitration to solve issues outside strictly commercial matters were increasingly being noted.[80]

Indeed, by this time, many practitioners started noting that international arbitral proceedings, especially those with significant amounts at stake, often devolved into complex, expensive and long-drawn-out affairs. International arbitration crystallised its own set of distinctive procedural techniques,[81] with parties and their counsel, against the background of an increasingly adversarial culture, often trying to use tactics to delay and derail proceedings.[82] Complaints against the nature of modern arbitral proceedings covered several issues, from the usage of lengthy submissions and evidence production to extensive document discovery. Also, community members complained against the frequent recourse to national courts in attempts to unwarrantedly challenge arbitrators and awards.[83]

Also, at this time, as concerns regarding gender and racial equality within the legal profession became more mainstream, questions regarding representation became a hot topic within arbitration circles. At the core of these discussions were calls to end potentially underlying discriminatory attitudes in regard to arbitral appointments, with most conversations centred around the systematic gender imbalance.[84] Closely linked to this were concerns that appointments, proceedings and decisions lacked transparency and accountability, with calls for reform becoming louder, especially in the context of investment arbitration.[85]

Still, by the 2010s, arbitration was beating all-time highs, with many predicting arbitration to continue dominating international dispute resolution.[86] It had become a fully mature market, filled with a thriving community of practitioners and academics. It also became a new environment where arbitral institutions would more aggressively pursue marketing strategies and enter new territories, law firms' arbitral teams would increase, and states would quickly reform arbitral laws. Arbitrators would also evolve and become

[79] See, eg, Lucy Greenwood, 'The Rise, Fall and Rise of International Arbitration: A View from 2030' (2011) 77 *Arbitration* 435.

[80] See Michael McIlwrath and Roland Schroeder, 'Transparency In International Arbitration: What Are Arbitrators And Institutions Afraid Of?' in Arthur W Rovine (ed), *Contemporary Issues in International Arbitration and Mediation: The Fordham Papers (2010)* (Leiden, Brill | Nijhoff, 2011) 334.

[81] One of the most well-known examples of a procedural instrument specific to international arbitration is the usage of the so called 'Redfern Schedule', a form, named after well-known arbitrator Alan Redfern, used to streamline document requests in arbitration. For an example of the format, see Nathan D O'Malley, *Rules of Evidence in International Arbitration: An Annotated Guide* (Abingdon, Taylor & Francis, 2013) 52.

[82] See Catherine A Rogers, *Ethics in International Arbitration* (Oxford, Oxford University Press, 2014) 26.

[83] In this context, discussions around the concept of 'guerrilla tactics', ie, strategies used by counsel and parties to delay and disrupt arbitral proceedings, emerged. For an overview, see Günther J Horvath and Stephan Wilske, *Guerrilla Tactics in International Arbitration* (Alphen aan den Rijn, Kluwer Law International, 2013).

[84] See, eg, Lucy Greenwood and Mark Baker, 'Getting a Better Balance on International Arbitration Tribunals' (2012) 28 *Arbitration International* 653.

[85] Changes most notably spearheaded by the European Commission and its Multilateral Investment Court project. For an overview, see Julian Scheu (ed), *Creation and Implementation of a Multilateral Investment Court* (Baden-Baden, Nomos, 2022).

[86] See Jean E Kalicki and Mohamed Abdel Raouf (eds), 'Personal Reflections from Leading Arbitrators: Transcript of Luncheon Panelists' Remarks' in *Evolution and Adaptation: The Future of International Arbitration* (Alphen aan den Rijn, Kluwer Law International, 2019) 163.

significantly distinct from the arbitrators of 100 years before. How this transformation took place will be analysed next.

II. The Evolution of the Arbitral Profession from a Socio-legal Perspective

Parallel to the evolution of international arbitration described above, there were profound transformations in the role and characteristics of the arbitrator. As arbitration evolved from an amicable system into an increasingly major legal market where players act increasingly as entrepreneurs, arbitrators also adapted. In this sense, arbitrators evolved from merchants to legal experts and from there to legal entrepreneurs, adapting their approach to the changing expectations of parties. All these happened without, in most circumstances, fully professionalising into a full-time occupation. At the same time, the 'profession' grew and became more open and competitive. These transformations will be explored next.

A. The Traditional Vision of the Arbitrator: An Honorary Appointment of a Merchant

Until the transformations that took place in the 1950s, arbitrators were deeply distinct from arbitrators today. Indeed, by the turn of the nineteenth to the twentieth century, arbitrators were most often still 'merchants' themselves, in the sense that arbitrators were recruited amongst those within the industries where the dispute took place. In London's commodities associations, where arbitration was widely used to solve international commercial disputes, arbitrators were most often participants in the same trade association as the disputing parties.[87] In continental Europe, during the first couple of decades of the ICC, engineers, businesspeople, corporate executives and members of trade federations were a considerable percentage of the arbitral appointments within this institution – a profile that would quickly transform.[88]

In the dominant arbitration environment at the time, arbitrators were expected to solve disputes in a way acceptable to both parties – ie, there was a preference for a consensual approach to arbitration. In this sense, persuasion, industry knowledge and status in relation to the disputing parties were key attributes for the arbitrators. Trust was a critical factor in the selection of arbitrators. Conversely, proficiency in the applicable legal rules was perceived as unnecessary,[89] even counterproductive. This was a time when arbitrators often decided disputes in accordance with the trade usages, ie the practices and expectations

[87] For an overview of arbitration at the English trade associations, see Sgard (n 21) 157.

[88] For a detailed description of these changes, see Eduardo Silva Romero, Emmanuel Jolivet and Florian Grisel, 'Aux origines de l'arbitrage commercial contemporain : l'émergence de l'arbitrage CCI (1920-1958)' [2016] *Revue de l'arbitrage* 403.

[89] In the context of US domestic commercial arbitration, in the early 1950s, a survey by the AAA showed that only 21% of commercial arbitrators were lawyers. See Sylvain Gotshal, 'Arbitration and the Lawyer's Place in the Business Community' (1956) 11 *The Business Lawyer* 52, 57.

within a specific industry.[90] Arbitrators were expected to decide cases as 'businessmen', not bound by state legal norms.

This was also a time when an arbitrator's appointment was often unpaid. As indicated in the 1922 ICC Arbitration rules, while the arbitrators were 'entitled to reimbursement of all expenses', they should 'render their services gratuitously' except for those industries and countries that customarily provided fees for arbitrators, in which the ICC Court could determine, at its discretion, to allow arbitrators' fees to be included in the costs of arbitration.[91] This trend of gratuity in arbitrators' performance derived from the belief that an appointment's honorific nature was sufficiently rewarding.[92] However, this approach to arbitrators' pay would quickly change, with the 1934 rules already establishing the power of the ICC Court to fix arbitrators' fees.[93]

B. International Commercial Arbitrators from the 1950s to the 1970s: The 'Grand Old Men'

From the 1950s to the 1970s, as the New York Convention inaugurated a new era of international commercial arbitration, the characteristics of international commercial arbitrators were already clearly distinct. It should be noted that the particular sociological makeup of the arbitral community at this time has become well-known due to Dezalay and Garth's seminal work *Dealing in Virtue*.[94] The authors provided an account of how an earlier generation of 'Grand Old Men' was partially displaced in the 1980s and 1990s by a new generation of arbitration 'technocrats'. According to this narrative, such transformations in the social makeup of arbitrators were due to the transformations taking place in the arbitration field itself, namely its increasingly technical complexity.

This account described how arbitration from the 1950s to 1970s was dominated by 'Grand Old Men' – ie, a group of mostly western men who had risen to the top of their national legal professions but had not specialised in arbitration. These men (there were virtually no women) relied on their accomplishments outside arbitration as a platform to enter the restricted group of people considered for the role of arbitrators. They were, primarily, a small number of great professors or high judges of Continental Europe and, more rarely, senior barristers, Queen's Counsels (QCs), and partners at law firms from the Anglo-American system.[95] It has been noted, however, that arbitral appointments in the ICC, in reality, often favoured those with strong transnational profiles, though they were not necessarily leading figures within their jurisdictions.[96]

[90] See Stone Sweet and Grisel (n 6) 56. See also Romero, Jolivet and Grisel (n 88) 412.

[91] See Rules of Procedure for Arbitration of the International Chamber of Commerce of 1922, Art XIX, e).

[92] See Stone Sweet and Grisel (n 6) 91.

[93] See ibid.

[94] Dezalay and Garth (n 68). See also Yves Dezalay and Bryant G Garth, 'Merchants of Law as Moral Entrepreneurs: Constructing International Justice from the Competition for Transnational Business Disputes' (1995) 29 *Law & Society Review* 27.

[95] Dezalay and Garth (n 68) 35.

[96] For a detailed analysis of ICC arbitral appointments at the time, see Florian Grisel, 'Competition and Cooperation in International Commercial Arbitration: The Birth of a Transnational Legal Profession' (2017) 51 *Law & Society Review* 790.

Independently of the best description of the background of arbitrators at the time, it is clear that, by this time, knowledge and a career in law were almost indispensable to accede the small circle of arbitrators surrounding the ICC.[97] Albeit not necessarily lawyers or law professors, almost all key arbitrators had a degree and knowledge in law.[98] Still, a technocratic legal approach was not often undertaken. Many disputes were solved without delving into the particularities of national laws, often resorting to reasoning following, sometimes loosely defined, transnational legal rules and principles encompassed under the term *lex mercatoria*.[99] The informal setting, small number of arbitrators, and close relationships inspired an environment where many decisions were compromise-oriented exercises between the panels.[100]

It should be noted that, by this time, arbitral appointments were already paid. In ICC arbitrations, by 1950, arbitrators were expected to receive around 1 per cent of the amount in dispute.[101] From 1955 onwards, the ICC started publishing fee schedules that would indicate percentages bands of how much arbitrators' fees would amount to, a practice that many of the other major arbitral institutions would emulate. Arbitrators often treated being an arbitrator not as an entrepreneurial venture but more as a part-time duty derived from their accomplishments in their legal careers.[102] Entrance into the arbitral club was, however, still mostly in the hands of a small number of jurists who frequented closed circles around the ICC and the leading European arbitral capitals.

C. International Commercial Arbitrators from the 1980s to the Late 1990s: The 'Technocrats'

By the 1980s and 1990s, the makeup of international commercial arbitrators had already changed again. By this time, a younger generation which had become specialised in the field of international arbitration, often through experiences at international law firms or within arbitral institutions, took over the elite position within arbitration.[103] This younger generation relied on its technical expertise regarding an increasingly complex body of rules applicable to international arbitration to climb to the top of the arbitral world. The more 'judicial-like' approach to decision-making resulted in more meticulously reasoned awards

[97] This was, however, not necessarily the case in more specialised sub-sets of domestic arbitration. Flood and Caiger present an interesting socio-legal account of the competition between lawyers and non-lawyers in the field of construction arbitration occurring in the early 1990s. See John Flood and Andrew Caiger, 'Lawyers and Arbitration: The Juridification of Construction Disputes' (1993) 56 *The Modern Law Review* 412.

[98] See Grisel (n 96) 799.

[99] Catherine A Rogers, 'Transparency in International Commercial Arbitration' (2006) 54 *Kansas Law Review* 1301; Dezalay and Garth (n 68) 89.

[100] Rogers (n 99).

[101] See Stone Sweet and Grisel (n 6) 91.

[102] As Glossner stated in 1982, channelling the dominant view at the time: 'To be an arbitrator is to exercise an honourable function. It is no profession […]. To be an arbitrator is a noble task which challenges the whole personality.' See Ottarndt Glossner, 'Sociological Aspects of International Commercial Arbitration' (1982) 10 *International Business Lawyer* 311, 311.

[103] Dezalay and Garth (n 68) 37.

expressly based on the law selected by the parties,[104] a requirement of increasingly sophisticated and highly advised commercial entities.[105]

The preference for arbitrators with more specialised knowledge in international arbitration should also be understood in the context of a more adversarial attitude within arbitral proceedings. As large Anglo-American law firms started entering the market, it was increasingly common to see parties willing to challenge arbitrators and awards.[106] At the same time, they also imported antagonistic approaches previously reserved for court ligation.[107] As the number of cases increased and parties were increasingly willing to resist enforcement (albeit most often unsuccessfully) through recourse to national courts, it became increasingly important for arbitrators to be aware of and engage with arbitral practice and the technicalities of producing enforceable awards.

At the same time, it should be noted that potential gains from acting as an arbitrator were also on the rise. As the 1980s and 1990s progressed, very large arbitral cases became more common. As the amount in dispute strongly correlates with arbitrators' fees, an appointment for these cases could amount to significant gains for those selected.[108] In this context, it was clear that both an increase in the level of specialisation of international arbitrators and a more aggressive pursuit of appointments were occurring.[109] Also, the increased number of cases gave rise to an increased pool of arbitrators and would-be arbitrators.[110] Still, the dominance of western, old, white and male arbitrators was an oft-noted characteristic, contributing to a still 'homogeneous' group of elite members.[111]

D. International Commercial Arbitrators from the 2000s Onwards: The 'Corporatisation' of Arbitrators

In the 2000s, the ever-increasing usage of international commercial arbitration accelerated transformations in the characteristics of international arbitrators. As the number of arbitral centres increased, the arbitral community metastasised into different regional communities, not only around the traditional European 'arbitral capitals' but also in the

[104] Still, it should be noted that in arbitration circles it is often emphasised that arbitrators are frequently better prepared to take in consideration the particularities of the dispute and the disputing parties and the practical consequences of a solution vis-à-vis national judges. See Jan Paulsson, *The Idea of Arbitration* (Oxford, Oxford University Press, 2013) 8.

[105] Rogers (n 99).

[106] See Luttrell (n 62) 252.

[107] See Helmer (n 68) 46.

[108] Showing the sharp contrast, Austrian arbitrator Werner Melis reminisces how in the early 1960s, in the beginning of his career as an arbitrator, the fees received from his first ICC case as an arbitrator were only enough to 'invite a friend to a good fish restaurant in Paris for dinner'. See Werner Melis, 'The Role of Individuals in International Arbitration' in Patricia Shaughnessy and Sherlin Tung (eds), *The Powers and Duties of an Arbitrator: Liber Amicorum Pierre A. Karrer* (Alphen aan den Rijn, Kluwer Law International, 2017) 226.

[109] See Catherine A Rogers, 'Regulating International Arbitrators: A Functional Approach to Developing Standards of Conduct' (2005) 41 *Stanford Journal of International Law* 53, 64.

[110] See ibid 62; Franck (n 2) 519.

[111] See Susan D Franck, 'Empirically Evaluating Claims About Investment Treaty Arbitration' (2007) 86 *North Carolina Law Review* 1, 75.

burgeoning Asian arbitral capitals, namely Hong Kong and Singapore. Different regional communities emerged, establishing their own networks, where members mainly interacted with members of the same community. Arbitrators started to specialise not only in arbitration generally but to focus their practice along national and regional lines or in subsets of arbitral disputes.

This is, therefore, a growing market with an increased number of participants. Albeit still often described as a 'closed shop',[112] the number of arbitrators and arbitration practitioners had in many jurisdictions, and certainly at many of the arbitration 'capitals', grown beyond the point where members of this community personally knew each other. An interesting development around this time was the appearance of new ways of establishing and communicating hierarchies. With the expansion of the market, service providers who rate, advertise and inform about arbitrators, often compiling lists indicating the most preeminent and in-demand arbitrators and arbitral practices, appeared and increased in visibility,[113] allowing insiders and outsiders a handy summary of those most well-known within each particular jurisdiction.

At the same time, a select few arbitrators became fully international providers, with some of the most accomplished arbitrators becoming true 'brands', providing services across multiple jurisdictions and in different types of arbitrations. Also, around this time, discussions about arbitrators' practice of delegating tasks to staff, including the preparation of hearings, issuing procedural orders, and even writing awards, became more prominent.[114] The acceptability of such practices became hotly debated,[115] as it became clear that at least some arbitrators played an increasingly 'managerial' role, delegating many tasks in increasingly larger support teams.[116]

As some have argued, international commercial arbitration could be witnessing the rise of a third generation of arbitrators,[117] where arbitrators act increasingly as heads of structures that heavily support their work and career development. Indeed, such structures not only help arbitrators provide services but also accomplish tasks that allow them to obtain visibility in the market, namely through writing and participation in community gatherings. While any definitive trends are still not fully clear, it may be possible to anticipate that arbitration services are moving to develop some primitive corporate features, where services,

[112] See, eg, Rogers, (n 1) 967.

[113] Examples of such publications include Chambers and Partners, Who's Who Legal (WWL) and Legal 500 that produce international rankings for the legal industry and have started organising specialised rankings for arbitration. Also, the GAR 100, started in 2008, and specialising in ranking law firms arbitration capabilities, is worth noting.

[114] Gabrielle Kaufmann-Kohler and Antonio Rigozzi, *International Arbitration: Law and Practice in Switzerland* (Oxford, Oxford University Press, 2015) 404–405.

[115] A particular point of contention is the role to be played by arbitral secretaries (usually junior lawyers who assist the arbitral tribunal in the performance of their arbitral mandates) For a discussion, see Constantine Partasides, 'The Fourth Arbitrator? The Role of Secretaries to Tribunals in International Arbitration' (2002) 18 *Arbitration International* 147.

[116] As Schultz and Kovacs concluded from a survey of lawyers and arbitrators engaged in international arbitration: 'Sixty-five per cent of participants responded that they did not mind if an arbitrator delegated the arbitrator's preparation for hearings, issuing procedural orders and even writing the award. Brutally simplified, this seems to be an indication that arbitrators are seen as managers today, only responsible for the product, with no mandate to do the work themselves.' See Thomas Schultz and Robert Kovacs, 'The Rise of a Third Generation of Arbitrators? Fifteen Years After Dezalay and Garth' (2012) 28 *Arbitration International* 161, 171.

[117] ibid.

while still very linked to a specific person, are, in reality, supplied by increasingly complex structures.[118]

A parallel, more recent phenomenon is a tendency from some leading arbitrators to establish small- or medium-sized arbitration boutiques upon leaving or retiring from larger law firms.[119] While several factors may contribute to this tendency, increasingly strict rules regarding conflicts of interest, which leads to many of the partners of large law firms being barred from accepting arbitral appointments, is likely to be one of the most relevant factors.[120] However, even these practitioners are rarely fully professionalised into full-time arbitrators, as most of these boutique firms serve as platforms for their partners to act as arbitrators and counsel specialising in arbitration. Arbitrators, therefore, still retained their hybrid nature as arbitral providers – often operating simultaneously as lawyers, academics and arbitrators.[121]

Still, even as arbitration became increasingly market-driven, arbitrators did not see themselves as profit-seeking entrepreneurs who provided a service against payment of a sum. Instead, arbitrators increasingly perceive themselves as quasi-judicial neutral adjudicators with special obligations to uphold a public role and an important public function. The fulfilment of this role is an essential assumption of the legitimacy of international arbitration as a whole and of each arbitrator taken individually.[122] The tension between the notion that arbitrators are private market actors and that, at the same time, they are bound to public obligations will be a key theme of the following chapters.

[118] On this topic, see João Ilhão Moreira and Riccardo Vecellio Segate, 'The 'It' Arbitrator: Why Do Corporations Not Act as Arbitrators?' (2021) 12 *Journal of International Dispute Settlement* 525.

[119] For example, out of 25 'elite' arbitrators identified in the Who's Who 2016 survey, a professional directorate listing most in demand arbitrators, 14 operated as either independent arbitrators or within small- to medium-sized law firms.

[120] Also, the per hour potential earnings as counsel in a leading international law firm often outstrips the per hour earnings as an international arbitrator. This leads these firms to often require their partners to focus in working as counsel as this proves to be more profitable for the firm. See Gerald Aksen, 'Taming the Twin Dragons of International Arbitration: Cost and Delay' in Patricia Shaughnessy and Sherlin Tung (eds), *The Powers and Duties of an Arbitrator: Liber Amicorum Pierre A. Karrer* (Alphen aan den Rijn, Kluwer Law International, 2017) 3.

[121] See Grisel (n 96) 813.

[122] See Franck (n 2) 504.

3

International Commercial Arbitration as a Market

The previous chapter explored how the significant success of international commercial arbitration, coupled with the hefty fees charged by arbitrators, lawyers, arbitral institutions, and other service providers, has led to an increased awareness of the market-like features of international commercial arbitration.[1] While the idea that arbitration should not be too profit-driven for a long time held sway amongst most traditional sections of the arbitral community,[2] it has become clear that many arbitral institutions, and at least part of the arbitral community, often pursue strategies to increase demand for their services, raise their market share, and increase their income.[3] As will be highlighted in this chapter, this is, however, a very unique market.

Underlying the current arbitration system there is a *sui generis* service contract[4] through which arbitrators perform an adjudicatory function against payment of – often very substantial – monetary compensation. Against this background, market mechanisms are very much in play and, therefore, are an essential determinant of behaviour in this field. Still, the specific method by which arbitrators and arbitral institutions are selected and prices are formed separates commercial arbitration from other markets. As will be argued in the following chapters, this is important as many of the regulatory specificities of the

[1] See, Joanna Jemielniak, *Legal Interpretation in International Commercial Arbitration* (London, Ashgate Publishing Ltd, 2014) 100; Katherine L Lynch, *The Forces of Economic Globalization: Challenges to the Regime of International Commercial Arbitration* (Alphen aan den Rijn, Kluwer Law International, 2003) 112; Thomas Clay, 'El Mercado Del Arbitraje' (2014) 7 *Arbitraje: revista de arbitraje comercial y de inversiones* 15.

[2] Paulsson explains that: 'Although arbitrators can expect to receive fees for their work, the prospect of financial rewards is doubtless a less motivating factor than non-specialists might imagine. For occasional arbitrators, the income is unsteady. Arbitrators who are much in demand are likely to have the ability and the opportunity to earn at least equal rewards in other endeavours. The important attractions of the job are, therefore, perhaps less tangible. Lawyers like to judge, and believe they do it well. Undeniably, appointment as arbitrator satisfies the ego in more or less admirable ways.' Jan Paulsson, 'Ethics, Elitism, Eligibility' (1997) 14 *Journal of International Arbitration* 13, 14.

[3] See Jacques Werner, 'Competition within the Arbitration Industry' (1985) 2 *Journal of International Arbitration* 5, 6.

[4] The nature of this service contract was discussed in great detail in the well-known case of *Jivraj v Hashwani* [2011] UKSC 40. In this case, The Supreme Court ruled that arbitrators are not 'employees' under UK employment discrimination law. Lord Clarke held that 'though an arbitrator may be providing services for the purposes of VAT and he of course receives fees for his work, and although he renders personal services which he cannot delegate, he does not perform those services or earn his fees for and under the direction of the parties […] He is rather in the category of an independent provider of services who is not in a relationship of subordination with the parties […] Agreeing on this point, Lord Mance quoted from the German Reichsgericht: 'It does not seem permissible to treat the arbitrator as equivalent to a representative or an employee or an entrepreneur. His office has … an entirely special character, which distinguishes him from other persons handling the affairs of third parties.'

arbitral profession are a result of the market adaptations undertaken by arbitrators, would-be arbitrators and arbitral institutions.

With the aim of understanding how these agents behave in the market, this chapter will first provide an overview of the market's current structure at both the arbitral institution and arbitrator levels. From there, it will summarise the mechanics of selecting these service providers and the establishment of their remuneration. Next, the determinants underlying the selection of arbitrators will be detailed. Finally, this chapter will explore arbitral institutions and arbitrators' strategies to maintain and expand their market share. As will be seen, many of the characteristics of the arbitral community that will be relevant to understanding the regulation of arbitrators, such as the strong interconnection and continuing efforts of its members to increase their reputation and visibility, are adaptions to the dominant market characteristics.

I. The Current Structure of International Commercial Arbitration Markets

Understanding the interplay between market forces and the regulation of arbitration advises analysing two markets separately: a market for arbitral institutions' services and a market for arbitrators' services. Indeed, international arbitration has evolved not only a market for arbitrators' services but also one for arbitral institutions' services; both significantly influence how arbitrators are regulated. Some of the fundamental notions necessary to understand how the international commercial arbitration market interplays with the regulation of the field include the following ideas: i) in practice, arbitral institutions operate in an oligopolistic market; ii) these institutions are not fully entrepreneurial, and many of the critical positions inside it are occupied by senior members of the arbitral community; and iii) becoming an arbitrator demands not only obtaining an elite status within the legal profession but also making inroads within the arbitral community. These ideas will be explored below.

A. The Market Structure at the Institutional Level

A key decision for all users of international commercial arbitration is whether to undertake arbitration through an arbitral institution or in an ad hoc setting. While the advantages and disadvantages of institutional arbitration in relation to ad hoc arbitration are a topic frequently discussed in the literature,[5] there are no reliable ways of definitively determining the relative usage of these two methods.[6] Still, some data and anecdotal evidence seem

[5] Gary Born, *International Commercial Arbitration: Commentary and Materials* (Alphen aan den Rijn, Kluwer Law International, 2001) 12; Anne Véronique Schlaepfer and Christian Girod, 'Institutional vs. Ad Hoc Arbitration' in Gabrielle Kaufmann-Kohler and Blaise Stucki (eds), *International Arbitration in Switzerland: A Handbook for Practitioners* (Alphen aan den Rijn, Kluwer Law International, 2004); Alan Redfern and Martin Hunter, *Law and Practice of International Commercial Arbitration* (London, Sweet & Maxwell, 2004).

[6] To this effect Naimark reported: 'I have been doing an informal word-of-mouth survey of lawyers who specialize in international commercial arbitration. The question I ask them is very simple, 'compared to the

to corroborate the idea that, over time, institutional arbitration has become the preferred method of arbitrating a commercial dispute.[7]

In theory, parties wishing to undertake institutional arbitral proceedings may choose from an ever-growing list of arbitral institutions.[8] At a glance, these arbitral institutions may seem similar. They proclaim similar goals, such as promoting efficient and agile dispute resolution systems for business enterprises, and display similar arbitral rules, generally giving the arbitral institution similar powers in the organisation of arbitral proceedings. However, the level of sophistication, experience, and geographical reach of these different institutions varies widely. Therefore, the current market structure at the institutional level is stratified, with different arbitral institutions catering to different subsets of the arbitration market.

A convenient rough distinction between national and international arbitral institutions may be drawn to understand the market of institutional arbitration services.[9] While often displaying strong national connections, international arbitral institutions tend to feature: i) members coming from different countries; ii) the arbitrators chosen and the administrative staff are of different nationalities; and iii) the disputes solved often display strong transnational components. On the other hand, national institutions are those which tend to: i) operate within a single jurisdiction; ii) with administrative staff and arbitrators drawn primarily from that country; and iii) with most of the cases handled relating to contracts performed or otherwise substantially linked to that jurisdiction.

While, in practice, a significant number of institutions will fit between the two concepts, in the current market, only a handful of arbitral institutions are prepared logistically and in terms of experience to deal with a large number of truly international disputes. While often proclaiming ambitious goals, most arbitral institutions deal mostly with domestic arbitrations and are generally avoided by parties in large international transactions.[10] It is thus possible to identify a small number of leading institutions that dominate the market in what concerns large-sized international disputes. This list includes the International Chamber of Commerce (ICC), the London Court of International Arbitration (LCIA), The Hong Kong

institutionally conducted arbitrations, how many ad hoc cases are taking place every year?' A number of attorneys have said that there were just a few of these cases, with most of the cases going through institutions; others have said that there were a significant number of ad hoc cases and estimated that the number might approximate the number of institutional cases; and two attorneys told me that they thought there were far more ad hoc cases taking place around the world each year than all the arbitral institutions put together.' Richard W Naimark, 'Building a Fact-Based Global Database-The Countdown' (2003) 20 *Journal of International Arbitration* 105, 106. See also Jemielniak (n 1) 89.

[7] To this effect, the 2008 QMUL / PwC's survey reported that '86% of awards were rendered by arbitration institutions rather than through ad hoc arbitrations.' See '2008 International Arbitration Study – Corporate Attitudes and Practices: Recognition and Enforcement of Foreign Awards' 4 www.arbitration.qmul.ac.uk/docs/123294.pdf accessed 8 March 2016. See also Loukas Mistelis, 'International Arbitration – Corporate Attitudes and Practices – 12 Perceptions Tested: Myths, Data and Analysis Research Report' (2004) 15 *American Review of International Arbitration* 525, 559.

[8] Barbara Alicja Warwas, *The Liability of Arbitral Institutions: Legitimacy Challenges and Functional Responses* (The Hague, TMC Asser Press, 2017) 45.

[9] On the distinction between national and international arbitral institutions, see Philippe Fouchard and others, *Fouchard Gaillard Goldman on International Commercial Arbitration* (Alphen aan den Rijn, Kluwer Law International, 1999) 159.

[10] See Karl-Heinz Böckstiegel, 'Do Institutions Really Add Value to the Arbitral Process?' in Bernard Hanotiau and Alexis Mourre (eds), *Dossier IX Players' Interaction in International Arbitration* (ICC Publishing SA 2012).

International Arbitration Centre (HKIAC) and the Singapore International Arbitration Centre (SIAC).[11]

A review of these institutions allows for the identification of several shared features. Arbitral institutions are usually not-for-profit entities,[12] being instead often organised as independent bodies of a chamber of commerce or incorporated as non-profit companies that frequently offer institutional arbitration services with the stated goal of encouraging and facilitating international commerce.[13] Structure-wise, while the details of their internal organisation may vary significantly, their senior management and internal consulting bodies are often filled by well-known arbitrators and highly accomplished practitioners in this field.[14] Further, these institutions have internal teams, often composed of full-time internal lawyers, which deal with the day-to-day aspects of managing the institutions' proceedings. Commonly, those working within these case management positions often transit to and from positions as arbitration counsel in law firms.

A few further notes are warranted. Despite usually possessing a non-profit nature, ample information supports the idea that these arbitral institutions compete to attract more proceedings and expand their market quota.[15] It is, therefore, possible to, at least partially, equate the behaviour of arbitral institutions to that of commercial entities.[16] Still, arbitral institutions do not possess the corporate governance structure, which usually ensures that their behaviour aligns with the profit motive of its shareholders. Therefore, a more apt comparison would be perhaps with non-profit enterprises, such as the ones common in the field of education, research and the arts, which have been noted to have a

[11] Naturally, even these institutions do not show a uniform global presence, often being more popular in specific regions of the world or in relation to certain types of disputes. To this effect, eg, the HKIAC highlights in its website its role as '*experts in China-Related Disputes*'.

[12] See, Ilias Bantekas, *An Introduction to International Arbitration* (Cambridge, Cambridge University Press, 2015) 26; Christopher R Drahozal, 'Commercial Norms, Commercial Codes, and International Commercial Arbitration' (2000) 33 *Vanderbilt Journal of Transnational Law* 79, 123. An exception to the non-profit model is the Judicial Arbitration and Mediation Services (JAMS) a for-profit arbitral institution with a sui-generis structure. It is owned by its (full-time) neutrals and management.

[13] See, eg, foreword to ICC's 2014 'Arbitration Rules/Mediation Rules' available at <www.iccwbo.org/> accessed 14 March 2016, 1.

[14] In the case of the ICC, a strong structural dichotomy between bodies composed by experienced members of arbitral community and internal staff is readily identifiable. The ICC is composed primarily by the Court, which in turn consists of a President, 17 Vice-Presidents, and members and alternate members largely drawn from the top of the legal arbitral profession and academia. The Court functions include: i) confirming, appointing, and replacing arbitrators; ii) deciding on any challenges filed against arbitrators; and iii) scrutinising and approving arbitral awards. In its work the Court is assisted by the Secretariat, which is composed of full-time lawyers and support staff.

Similarly, the LCIA is also composed by the LCIA Court and by the Secretariat. The LCIA Court is composed of 35 members, plus representatives of associated institutions, and former Presidents. Similarly to the ICC Court, the LCIA Court is composed of leading practitioners in commercial arbitration. The LCIA Court is the final authority for the proper application of the LCIA rules. Its principal functions include appointing tribunals, determining challenges to arbitrators, and controlling costs. Similarly to the ICC secretariat, the LCIA secretariat is responsible for the day-to-day administration of disputes referred to the LCIA.

[15] See Warwas (n 8) 38. Arbitral institutions, however, also sometimes cooperate by developing common initiatives and sharing resources. Mohamed Abdel Raouf, 'Emergence of New Arbitral Centres in Asia and Africa: Competition, Cooperation and Contribution to the Rule of Law' in Stavros L Brekoulakis, Julian DM Lew and Loukas A Mistelis (eds), *The Evolution and Future of International Arbitration* (Alphen aan den Rijn, Kluwer Law International, 2016) 327.

[16] Gerhard Wagner, 'Dispute Resolution as a Product: Competition between Civil Justice Systems' in Horst Eidenmüller (ed), *Regulatory Competition in Contract Law and Dispute Resolution* (London, Bloomsbury Publishing, 2013) 390; Drahozal (n 12) 123.

broad spectrum of entrepreneurial motivations, including personal/professional development of the members of the organisation, belief in a cause, or a desire to gain power and prestige.[17]

It should also be noted that while there are no significant regulatory barriers to entry,[18] it is possible to identify a trend of stability. Indeed, the same institutions have largely maintained their place at the top of the international commercial arbitration market in the last couple of decades:

Figure 3.1 Breakdown of arbitral institutions' international arbitral cases[19]

	2000	**2002**	**2004**	**2006**	**2008**	**2010**	**2012**	**2014**	**2016**	**2018**	**2020**
CIETAC	543	468	461	442	548	418	331	387	483	522	739
HKIAC	298	320	280	394	602	624	456	477	460	521	483
ICC	541	593	561	593	663	793	759	791	966	842	946
ICDR	510	672	614	586	703	888	996	1052	1050	993	704
LCIA	87	88	87	133	213	237	265	277	303	317	407
SIAC	37	34	39	47	71	140	235	222	343	402	1080
SCC	66	50	45	64	74	91	92	94	103	76	105
Total	2082	2225	2087	2259	2874	3191	3134	3300	3708	3673	4464

An analysis of these statistics shows ICC, ICDR and, more recently, SIAC as displaying the highest number of international commercial arbitrations in recent years. While in some years trailing behind SIAC and ICDR in the number of cases, the ICC is often perceived as the market leader and referred to as the arbitral institution with the most global reach.[20]

[17] Cristoph Badelt, 'Entrepreneurship in Nonprofit Organizations: Its Role in Theory and in the Real World Nonprofit Sector' in Helmut K Anheier and Avner Ben-Ner (eds), *The Study of Nonprofit Enterprise: Theories and Approaches* (New York, Springer Science & Business Media, 2003) 143. An interesting observation that is found in the literature on non-profit firms and that may be applicable to arbitral institutions relates to the mechanisms incentivising their commitment to their core goals. Despite a theoretical tendency of non-profit organisations to be less pressured to be efficient due to governance issues, the need for non-profits to compete in product markets and in the market for donations keeps organisations in line. See Edward L Glaeser (ed), *The Governance of Not-for-Profit Organizations* (Chicago, University of Chicago Press 2006) 40.

[18] Warwas (n 8) 44.

[19] Where possible, the numbers presented indicate only international arbitral cases and exclude domestic arbitrations. This is a particularly relevant feature in CIETAC which would otherwise be the most widely used arbitral institution worldwide. It is relevant to note that the ICDR defines 'international' cases in an ample manner to include cases which involve US-based subsidiaries of non-US companies who prefer arbitration to the US court system, as well as cases in which one, or both, parties are from overseas. This explains in part the large numbers presented by the ICDR. Also, the numbers presented for HKIAC include all cases submitted to the institution including domestic disputes and domain name disputes. Sources: International Arbitration institutions websites, Markus Altenkirch and Nicolas Gremminger, 'Parties' International Arbitration Statistics 2018 – Another busy year for Arbitral Institutions' (Global Arbitration News, 5 August 2015) globalarbitrationnews.com/ accessed 30 May 2020; James Nicholson and Howard Rosen, 'Trends in International Arbitration' www.fticonsulting.com/ insights/fti-journal/trends-in-international-arbitration accessed 15 March 2016.

[20] Giuditta Cordero-Moss, *International Commercial Arbitration: Different Forms and Their Features* (Cambridge, Cambridge University Press, 2013) 205; Julian DM Lew, Loukas A Mistelis and Stefan Kröll, *Comparative International Commercial Arbitration* (Kluwer Law International 2003) 38; Thomas Hale, *Between Interests and Law: The Politics of Transnational Commercial Disputes* (Cambridge University Press 2015) 20; Sam Luttrell, *Bias Challenges in International Commercial Arbitration: The Need for a 'real Danger' Test* (Alphen aan den Rijn, Kluwer Law International, 2009) 88.

However, the ICC has long lost what was at one point its quasi-monopolistic position in the market.[21] Indeed, the last few decades have seen a consistent rise of other competitors not only in the western world but also in Asia, where the HKIAC and the SIAC have risen in prominence.

Figure 3.2 Total number of international arbitral cases in the major arbitral institutions

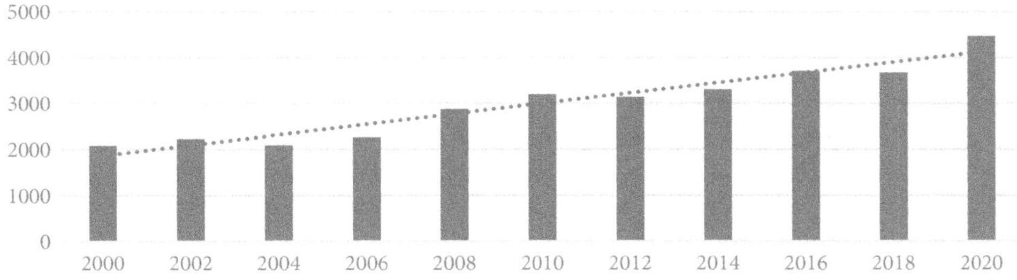

On a macro level, analysis of the available statistics shows a sharp increase in the total number of cases at the institutions mentioned above over the last 20 years. This increase is not a recent trend. An analysis of the number of cases in the major institutions between 1992 and 2012 showed an increase of circa 400 per cent in several institutions.[22] This growth is not, however, representative of the fate of all international arbitral institutions. Other arbitral institutions do not show significant increases in caseload or have been unsuccessful in getting off the ground in a meaningful way.[23] As will be seen in the following chapters, this dominance of some arbitral institutions has significant consequences for the regulation of arbitrators, as the well-established nature of some of these arbitral institutions gives them a pivotal role in creating and enforcing professional norms.[24]

B. The Market Structure at the Arbitrator Level

At the arbitrator level, the market presents itself more atomised in the sense that there is a much larger pool of potential service providers. While the exact number of people who have acted as arbitrators is not possible to determine, there are today a considerable number of practitioners and academics who have acted as arbitrators in international commercial disputes and an even larger number of those interested in being appointed to this

[21] Yves Dezalay and Bryant G Garth, *Dealing in Virtue: International Commercial Arbitration and the Construction of a Transnational Legal Order* (Chicago, University of Chicago Press, 1996) 45.

[22] Gary Born, *International Arbitration: Law and Practice* (Alphen aan den Rijn, Kluwer Law International, 2012) 16.

[23] Leading practitioners Paulsson, Rawding and Reed summarise the issue as a 'vicious circle'. '[P]arties do not insert clauses providing for arbitration under a new institution's rules due to the absence of practical experience or fear of lack of permanence; consequently the institution is unable to acquire the practical experience and a viable caseload necessary to ensure its permanence'. Jan Paulsson, Nigel Rawding and Lucy Reed, *The Freshfields Guide to Arbitration Clauses in International Contracts* (Alphen aan den Rijn, Kluwer Law International BV, 2011) 62.

[24] See, in particular, ch 5, section III and ch 8, section I.

function.[25] Still, identifying common social-professional traits amongst the people selected for this role establishes a clearer picture of possible behavioural incentives, social interconnections, and underlying shared values. As will be seen, there are some characteristics typical between arbitrators, such as their high elite status, average age, and previous experiences, which may yield relevant consequences regarding norm compliance.[26]

It should be noted that the high number of arbitrators, different geographic origins, and different levels of commitment to the role of arbitrator make any generalisations regarding the profession unreliable. Still, arbitrators are generally portrayed as a small group of talented, multilingual individuals drafted from the higher echelons of the legal profession.[27] Typically, arbitrators are, previously to being appointed, already successful in their legal career, mostly as practitioners and also, more rarely, as academics or in the judiciary. It is also clear that they are usually educated at some of the world's most prestigious universities and display high levels of academic achievement.[28] On the other hand, at least at its higher levels, the arbitral profession has been criticised as lacking diversity and being dominated by an elite group of mainly old, male, and white arbitrators.[29]

While some – likely most – arbitrators, especially the most prominent, are specialists in arbitration law and have built their careers around international arbitration, others may act as arbitrators only once or twice and will have no long-lasting relevant connections to the field.[30] It is also important to note that while a few practitioners seem to engage in the market primarily as arbitrators, most potential arbitrators combine this activity with other professional endeavours, most commonly working as counsel for parties in arbitration.[31] Indeed, many of the most well-known names in international arbitration interact with each other, playing interchanging roles. In one dispute, 'A' may play the role of arbitrator and interact with 'B' while he is playing the role of counsel; in the following dispute, roles may be reversed, with 'A' playing the role of counsel and 'B' playing the role of arbitrator.

The lack of published awards and difficulties in assessing the reliability of the wide number of profiles of arbitrators publicly available do not allow a full description of the makings of the community. Nevertheless, an analysis of arbitrators' professional careers, as described in professional directorates such as Chambers and Partners, confirms that arbitrators have four main professional origins: i) partners, or former partners, of often large and international law firms; ii) academics, often specialising in arbitration or in related areas such as international private law, who usually combine their academic career with work as practitioners; iii) highly regarded barristers with a special interest in arbitration

[25] It is important to note that, while there is no census on the size of the arbitral community, it is clear that the number of participants has been growing exponentially. Diego P Fernández Arroyo, 'Soft Law and Arbitral Procedure: A Conditioned But Inescapable Couple' (2018) 7 *European International Arbitration Review* 71.

[26] See, in particular, Section ch 7, section II.B.

[27] Catherine A Rogers, 'The Vocation of the International Arbitrator' (2004) 20 *American* University *International Law Review* 957, 958; Joshua DH Karton, *The Culture of International Arbitration and The Evolution of Contract Law* (Oxford, Oxford University Press, 2013) 23.

[28] Rogers (n 27) 958; Karton (n 27) 23.

[29] See, among others, V Veeder, 'Who Are the Arbitrators?' in Albert Jan van den Berg (ed), *Legitimacy: Myths, Realities, Challenges, ICCA Congress Series, Volume 18* (Alphen aan den Rijn, Kluwer Law International, 2015).

[30] Karton (n 27) 23.

[31] See Thomas Clay, 'Qui Sont Les Arbitres Internationaux? : Approche Sociologique' in Rosell (ed), *Les arbitres internatonaux* (Société de législation comparée, 2005) 31.

or commercial law; and iv) legal practitioners who have developed a career within arbitration institutions, often holding relevant positions within the same.[32]

It should be noted, however, that the background of most arbitrators, instead of neatly fitting into any of the above categories, displays composite features of the different backgrounds. Indeed, many arbitrators who have developed their careers within law firms display strong academic links, often undertaking teaching duties and publishing academic pieces related to arbitration. Conversely, many academics who act as arbitrators have past or present relevant associations with law firms. Also, a few of today's elite arbitrators have started their careers or spent relevant time amongst the internal teams of arbitral institutions. Many have held relevant executive or advisory roles within (sometimes several of) the world's leading arbitral institutions.

An interesting recent phenomenon is the tendency of some leading arbitrators to form small- or medium-sized arbitration boutiques upon leaving or retiring from larger law firms. Out of 47 'Most in Demand Arbitrators' identified in the Chamber and Partners 2023 survey, 43 operated as sole practitioners, as part of small- to medium-sized law offices or integrated with chambers. While several factors may contribute to this tendency, increasingly stricter rules regarding conflicts of interest[33] are likely one of the most relevant factors. These rules lead to partners of large law firms being often barred from accepting appointments. Most of these boutique firms do, however, serve as platforms for their partners to act both as arbitrators and counsel specialising in arbitration.

Finally, the dominance of 'western' arbitrators at the top of their arbitral profession should also be noted. An analysis of the nationalities of the 47 leading arbitrators of the Chamber and Partners 2023 survey and the nationalities of arbitrators most common in ICC arbitrations show that most elite arbitrators come from the UK, the US, France and Switzerland. Further, the dominance of male arbitrators is also confirmed, with 79 per cent of these leading arbitrators identified in the survey as male. This imbalance is a well-identified trend among empirical studies of international arbitration[34] and available data from arbitral institutions.[35]

Figure 3.3 Leading nationalities amongst the Chambers 2023 Survey

Nationality	*N.º*	%
US	12	26
British	8	17
French	5	11
Swiss	4	9

[32] See also Karton (n 27) 23.

[33] See, eg, IBA's 2014 Guidelines on Conflicts of Interest in International Arbitration.

[34] Susan D Franck, 'Empirically Evaluating Claims About Investment Treaty Arbitration' (2007) 86 *North Carolina Law Review* 1; Susan D Franck and others, 'The Diversity Challenge: Exploring the Invisible College of International Arbitration' (2014) 53 *Columbia Journal of Transnational Law* 429.

[35] To this effect, ICC reported that the percentage of women sitting in ICC arbitral tribunals reached 23.4% in 2020. In turn, LCIA's Registrar's report 2020 indicates that 33% of arbitrators appointed were female.

Figure 3.4 Leading nationalities in ICC arbitrations in 2020

Nationality	*N.º*	%
British	220	14
US	153	10
Swiss	135	9
French	101	7

The apparent lack of diversity in the current roster of international arbitrators denotes gaps which are often still present across the higher echelons of the legal profession.[36] Since reaching the position of arbitrator is often linked with reaching the top of the legal profession, there are good reasons to expect the arbitral profession to reflect, perhaps with some delay, the socio-demographic features of the legal profession elite. In any case, the lack of diversity in the arbitral profession has been a concern of many within the field, with arbitral institutions, in particular, driving an effort for a more diverse background of arbitrators.

The relatively similar background between arbitrators also shows a reasonably homogeneous community, which gives preference to already well-established members of the legal profession. This similarity results from a framework which leads agents to take a conservative approach regarding selecting service providers in this market. In this sense, the difficulties faced by those wanting to enter the market as arbitrators are often noted. Indeed, there is an overwhelming preference for well-established arbitral institutions and arbitrators. The reasons leading to this will become clearer through exploring the mechanics of selecting arbitral institutions and arbitrators as well as the factors underlying these choices. The mechanics of these choices will be explored next.

II. How Service Providers are Selected in International Commercial Arbitration

A. The Methods of Selecting an Arbitral Institution

Selecting an arbitral institution does not pose legal difficulties. In most jurisdictions, parties are free to choose an arbitral institution to supervise and organise their proceedings if all disputing parties have agreed to it. Parties can determine an arbitral institution to oversee their proceedings after a dispute has arisen or pre-establish the chosen institution by incorporating an arbitration clause into a contract where they pre-define the arbitral institution. While the exact wording of these clauses may vary, parties are generally recommended to establish the specified institution by using a template clause.[37] Due to understandable

[36] Sharon C Bolton and Daniel Muzio, 'Can't Live with 'Em; Can't Live without 'Em: Gendered Segmentation in the Legal Profession' (2007) 41 *Sociology* 47; Leah V Durant, 'Gender Bias and Legal Profession: A Discussion of Why There Are Still So Few Women on the Bench' (2004) 4 *University of Maryland Law Journal of Race, Religion, Gender & Class* 181.

[37] Most arbitral institutions provide recommended ready-made arbitration clauses with the purpose of avoiding problematic drafting and as a marketing tool to facilitate adherence to the arbitral institution.

difficulties in establishing agreements after a dispute has arisen, the selection of the arbitral institution usually takes place while a contract is negotiated between the parties.[38]

B. The Methods of Selecting Arbitrators

The legal issues arising from the appointment of arbitrators are, on the other hand, more complex than those arising from the selection of arbitral institutions. Arbitration acts, institutions' rules, and soft law provisions all provide a mixture of mandatory and subsidiary rules regarding the appointment of arbitrators. While these norms are not entirely consistent, there are still trends across legal systems and institution rules that allow a description of a general legal framework for selecting arbitrators. As will be described below, this analysis also allows an identification of the main players driving the selection of arbitrators.

i. An Overview of Institutional Arbitral Rules and National Statutes

Across legal systems, the constitution of an arbitral tribunal is subject to the principle of parties' autonomy – ie, parties are largely free to agree on how their disputes are to be resolved, subject only to such safeguards as are necessary for safeguarding basic notions of procedural fairness and the public interest.[39] The vast majority of national statutes allow parties to establish the number of arbitrators that will constitute the arbitral tribunal (almost without exception, parties choose a panel of three arbitrators or a single arbitrator) and the identity or the method to be utilised for selecting the specific arbitrators that will solve the dispute.[40]

In practice, parties often establish a specific method of appointment by reference to institutional arbitral rules that detail procedural rules regarding arbitrators' appointments. One of the most often cited advantages of institutional arbitration is precisely providing secure and predictable methods of arbitrators' appointments,[41] with the ability to select, when needed, a capable arbitrator being one of the most important roles of an arbitral institution. While specific arbitral institutional rules vary, reviewing the major arbitral institutions' rules allows for identifying some trends regarding the most common methods of arbitrators' nomination in an arbitral setting. Most arbitral rules establish that:

(i) Where the parties have agreed that three arbitrators shall resolve the dispute, each party nominates one arbitrator. If a party fails to nominate an arbitrator, the arbitral institution will make the appointment. The third arbitrator, depending on the institution,

[38] See, Francisco Cabrillo and Sean Fitzpatrick, *The Economics of Courts and Litigation* (Cheltenham, Edward Elgar Publishing, 2008) 212.

[39] English Arbitration Act 1996, s 1(b).

[40] See for all, Gary Born, *International Commercial Arbitration*, 2nd edn (Alphen aan den Rijn, Wolters Kluwer Law & Business 2014) 1653. For practical reasons parties rarely identify a specific arbitrator within their arbitration clause. Emilia Onyema, 'Drafting an Effective Arbitration Agreement in International Commercial Contracts' (2003) 7 *Vindobona Journal of International Commercial Law & Arbitration* 277, 283. Since it is not possible to determine when a dispute will take place, selecting a specific arbitrator in advance is often not feasible as he/she may not be available at the necessary time.

[41] See Born (n 40) 170; Gabrielle Kaufmann-Kohler and Blaise Stucki, *International Arbitration in Switzerland: A Handbook for Practitioners* (Alphen aan den Rijn, Kluwer Law International, 2004) 12.

is either chosen by the two arbitrators already selected or, alternatively, selected directly by the institution.[42]

(ii) Where the parties have agreed that a sole arbitrator shall resolve the dispute, they may, by agreement, appoint the sole arbitrator. The institution appoints the sole arbitrator if the parties fail to nominate the arbitrator.[43]

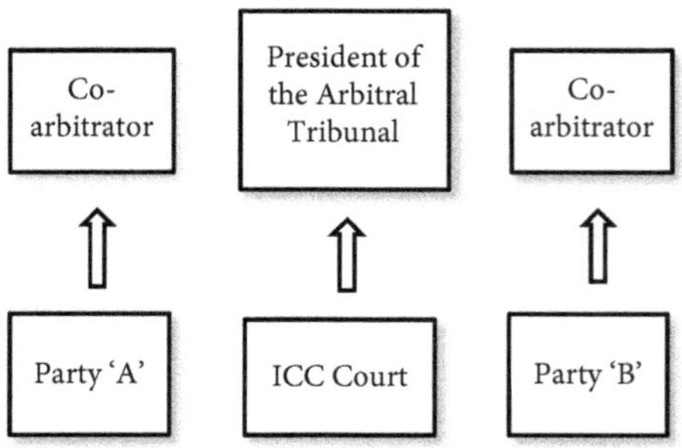

Figure 3.5 Procedure for composition of 3-arbitrator tribunals under the ICC Rules

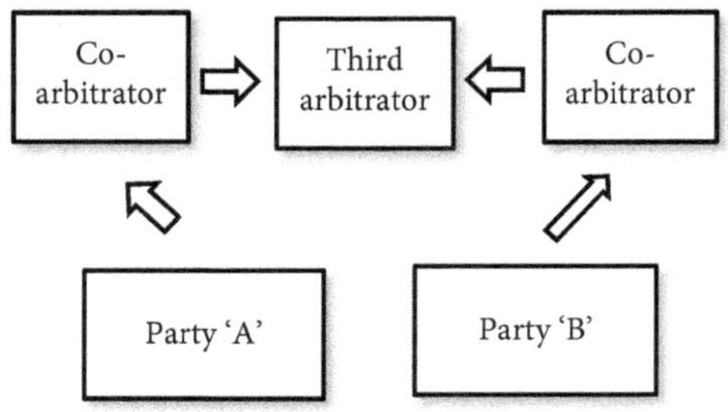

Figure 3.6 Procedure for composition of 3-arbitrator tribunals under the UNCITRAL Model Law

In ad hoc arbitrations, national arbitration statutes also provide default rules for selecting arbitrators when parties fail to agree on a specific method for their appointment or the parties fail to appoint the arbitrators per the applicable norms.[44] According to most rules, with a sole arbitrator, if the parties are unable to agree on the arbitrator, they shall be appointed by the competent national court;[45] in an arbitration with three arbitrators, each party shall appoint one arbitrator, and the two arbitrators thus appointed shall appoint the third arbitrator; if a party fails to appoint its arbitrator or if the two arbitrators fail to agree on the third arbitrator, the appointment shall be made, upon request of a party, by the competent court.[46]

ii. The Relative Weight of the Different Actors in the Selection of Arbitrators

From the description above, it results that several actors may, in different circumstances, appoint arbitrators. Namely, i) parties to arbitral proceedings; ii) co-arbitrators; iii) arbitral

[42] See Art 12(4) and 12(5) ICC 2021 Arbitration Rules, Art 17(4) 2023 SCC Rules, Art 8 2018 HKIAC Administered Arbitration Rules and Art 11 2016 SIAC Rules. ICC 2021 Rules, SCC 2023 Rules and 2016 SIAC Rules determine that, absent agreement of the parties to the contrary, is upon the institution to nominate the third arbitrator of the panel. The HKIAC's 2018 rules provide that the two arbitrators appointed by the parties shall designate a third arbitrator.

[43] See Art 12(3) ICC 2021 Arbitration Rules, Art 17(3) 2023 SCC Rules, Art 7 2018 HKIAC Administered Arbitration Rules, Art 10 2016 SIAC Rules.

[44] For an detailed analysis of the different possible scenarios, see Emilia Onyema, *International Commercial Arbitration and the Arbitrator's Contract* (London, Routledge, 2010) 84.

[45] See, among others, UNCITRAL Model Law, Art 11(3), English Arbitration Act 1996, s 16(3), French Code of Civil Procedure, Art 1452(1).

[46] See, among others, UNCITRAL Model Law, Art 11(3), English Arbitration Act 1996, s 16(5), French Code of Civil Procedure, Art 1452(2).

institutions; and iv) courts may all play a role in selecting arbitrators. While it is not possible to fully deconstruct the relative weight of these different actors throughout the whole system, ICC statistics provide some insight that may be representative of larger trends:

Figure 3.7 Breakdown of the appointments made in 2020 by type of arbitrator and method of designation in ICC Arbitrations[47]

	Nominations by parties (confirmed by the ICC)	**Nominations by co-arbitrators (confirmed by the ICC)**	**Appointments by the ICC (upon proposal of a national committee or directly by the ICC Court)**	**Appointment by another entity than the ICC Court**	**Total**
Sole arbitrator	84	–	212	2	298
Co-arbitrators in three-members' tribunals	782	–	38	0	820
Presidents in three-members' tribunals	40	227	135	0	402
	906	227	385	2	1520

While only partial, these figures indicate that parties are responsible, in ICC-administered arbitrations, for just over 50 per cent of the nominations. To the same effect, LCIA's 2022 statistics indicate that parties accounted for 50 per cent of the nominations.[48] Even in the context of ad hoc arbitrations, while no available aggregated data exists, it is to be expected that the selection of at least one or more members of a tribunal often will not be undertaken by the parties but instead by a third appointing authority – typically by the other members of the arbitral tribunal regarding the third arbitrator or the national courts where parties fail to appoint an arbitrator.

The fact that actors beyond the disputing parties often select arbitrators has significant implications for the international commercial arbitration market. It means that arbitrators must consider not only how they will be perceived by potential disputing parties, but also by other actors such as arbitral institutions, other arbitrators, and national courts. This multitude of actors taking a role in appointing arbitrators allows the arbitral community an important say on who becomes successful in the field. The relevance of the community as a driver of appointments will be picked up again at the end of this chapter[49] when discussing the strategies undertaken by arbitrators to improve their position in the market and again, in more detail, in chapter seven.

[47] ICC, '2020 ICC Dispute Resolution Statistics' (2021).

[48] LCIA, 'Registrar's Report 2022' (2022) 19, www.lcia.org/LCIA/reports.aspx.

[49] See ch 3, section V.B.

III. The Mechanics of Establishing the Remuneration of Arbitral Institutions and Arbitrators

Another particularity of the international commercial arbitration market derives from its price formation mechanisms. Indeed, remuneration of arbitrators, and to a lesser extent arbitral institutions, does not follow the same procedures as in regard to the purchase of most other services. Again, it should be noted that there are also considerable differences between institutional arbitrations and ad hoc arbitrations regarding the remuneration of services. Therefore, these two situations will be analysed in turn.

In institutional arbitrations, parties must remunerate the arbitral institution and the arbitrators. For this reason, each arbitral institution establishes its own rules regarding the payment of its services and the services of the arbitrators.[50] In practical terms, parties adhere to these rules by selecting the relevant institution when negotiating the underlying contract to the dispute, with little to no availability from institutions to accept negotiated alterations to their established provisions and schedule of costs.[51]

While rules vary from institution to institution, general trends can be identified. Most arbitral institutions remunerate their services and the services of arbitrators according to a pre-defined scale of costs based on the monetary value of the claims. These institutions usually attribute a small percentage of the value at stake in the arbitral proceedings to both the arbitrators and the arbitral institution. Such a percentage will typically decrease as the values claimed increase.[52] Other institutions remunerate services based on time spent by the arbitrators and the arbitral institution's personnel on the case.[53] Independently of the method by which arbitrators' remuneration is defined, many arbitral institutions reserve some discretion regarding the exact values they charge.

Regarding ad hoc arbitrations, parties will have to negotiate with arbitrators on how their remuneration is calculated.[54] If no agreement is reached, but the arbitrators still perform their mandate, it is usually upon the arbitrators themselves to determine their fees.[55] Arbitrators and parties often, as in institutional arbitrations, agree to calculate arbitrators' remuneration as a percentage of the amount in dispute or on the basis of time spent. In practice, it is not uncommon for arbitrators and parties to look into the fees of a relevant arbitral institution as a guide to the establishment of the arbitral tribunal's remuneration.[56] It is, however, possible in most jurisdictions to request a review of the fees established by an arbitral tribunal to the competent court or other competent authority.[57]

[50] Lew, Mistelis and Kröll (n 20) 285; Mauro Rubino-Sammartano, *International Arbitration Law and Practice*, 3rd edn (New York, Juris Publishing Inc, 2014) 518.

[51] ICC, eg, establishes in Appx III, Art 2(4) of its 2017 Rules that: 'The arbitrator's fees and expenses shall be fixed exclusively by the Court as required by the Rules. Separate fee arrangements between the parties and the arbitrator are contrary to the Rules.'

[52] This is the case of, among others, the ICC, SIAC and the SCC.

[53] This is the case of, among others, the LCIA and, when parties do not agree on other method, the HKIAC. The ICDR establishes a hybrid system where arbitrators are to be paid on the basis of a daily or hourly rate and the institution's fees on the basis of a fixed value calculated from the amount at stake.

[54] Lew, Mistelis and Kröll (n 20) 285; Onyema (n 44) 133.

[55] Lew, Mistelis and Kröll (n 20) 285; Rubino-Sammartano (n 50) 518.

[56] Onyema (n 44) 133.

[57] See, to this effect, eg, English Arbitration Act 1996, s 28(2).

Figure 3.8 Proportion of costs between party costs, arbitrators' fees, and administrative costs in ICC arbitrations in 2012

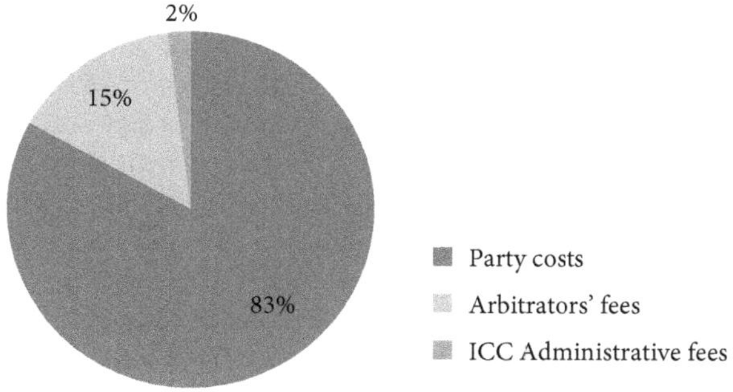

In any case, it should be noted that the costs related to arbitrators' and administrative fees usually represent only a fraction of litigating a dispute. As an illustration, ICC administrative fees and arbitrators' fees represent, on average, respectively, 2 per cent and 15 per cent of the total arbitration costs borne by the parties, with the remaining being party costs, most notably lawyer and expert witness fees and expenses.[58] Finally, it should be further noted that while not all arbitral institutions and arbitration acts establish exactly the same rules, it is common practice for tribunals to allow the successful party to recover its reasonable costs – ie, arbitration often works based on a mitigated 'loser pays' system.[59]

The particularities of how prices are established in international commercial arbitration have important implications for the regulation of international commercial arbitrators. In institutional and ad hoc arbitrations, arbitrators have minimal benefit from competing on prices. As it will be picked up again at the end of this chapter,[60] this leads arbitrators to mostly compete through 'quality' displays and networking. Before analysing these implications, it will be important to provide an overview of the reasons underlying the choice of one service provider over another in this market. This analysis will be undertaken next.

IV. The Determinants of Service Providers' Selections in International Commercial Arbitration

A. Factors Determining the Choice of an Arbitral Institution

While the mechanics of choosing an arbitral institution are relatively straightforward, the reasons underlying any such choice are more difficult to pinpoint. Deciding on an arbitral institution requires the negotiated consent of two different parties. Further, the internal process of decision-making in each of the parties may follow different paths and determine the intervention of different internal and external counsel. Therefore, determining

[58] ICC, 'Decisions on Costs in International Arbitration' (2015) 3.
[59] ibid.
[60] See ch 3, section V.B.

the reasons underlying the choice of an arbitral institution through an inquiry of former or prospective users faces limitations.

Still, some surveys have been carried out and allow some light to be shed on the determinants of choosing an arbitral institution. Perhaps the most well-known of these surveys is the annual survey conducted by QMUL.[61] Their 2015 survey of 763 senior in-house counsel, senior representatives of arbitral institutions, academics, and arbitrators asked respondents: 'Why are certain institutions selected the most?'. Presented with a set of different options, respondents selected as their top two considerations 'reputation and recognition' and 'previous experience of the institution', which were chosen by 62 per cent and 52 per cent of respondents, respectively. The same study questioned, 'What are the four most important reasons for preference for certain institutions?' Respondents' top three answers were: 1) high level of administration (including proactiveness, facilities, quality of staff); 2) neutrality/'internationalism'; and 3) global presence/ability to administrate arbitrations worldwide/high level of administration.

Several aspects may be hypothesised to justify the centrality of reputation and experience in the arbitral institution market. First, as in other professional service markets, reputation provides buyers with a surrogate for quality,[62] providing an ex-ante indicator of the level of service to be expected. In the case of international arbitration, since the decision to enlist the services of an arbitral institution requires the common consent of at least two different parties, the well-established status of the institution may be an important factor in allowing both parties to agree to the same service provider. Conceivably, larger and more well-established institutions will be less likely to be 'captured' by one of the disputants as, typically, any single user does not represent a significant source of business for the institution.[63]

Second, parties and their counsel may display a tendency for risk-averse behaviour in choosing a dispute resolution mechanism. In-house and external counsel likely have an incentive to recommend conservative approaches to dispute resolution clauses since an unenforceable contract or an inoperative dispute resolution clause may damage the company and harm the counsel's position within the structure.[64] Further, since disputes may arise considerably after the parties agree on an arbitration clause, a well-established institution might give greater assurance that it will be able to provide the service when needed.[65]

Finally, counsel will likely display a preference, even if subconsciously, for arbitration rules and arbitral institutions they are familiar with. For practical purposes, counsel may feel uncomfortable litigating under arbitral rules they might not be familiar with or dealing with arbitral institutions whose staff or way of operating are unknown to them.[66] Other practical considerations, such as the ability to provide services in the parties' language or

[61] QMUL, '2015 International Arbitration Survey: Improvements and Innovations in International Arbitration', www.arbitration.qmul.ac.uk/docs/164761.pdf, accessed 17 October 2015.

[62] See, Richard L Abel, *American Lawyers* (Oxford, Oxford University Press, 1989) 183; Harris H Kim, 'Market Uncertainty and Socially Embedded Reputation' (2009) 68 *American Journal of Economics and Sociology* 679.

[63] See Stephen J Choi, 'The Problem with Arbitration Agreements' (2003) 36 *Vanderbilt Journal of Transnational Law* 1233, 1237.

[64] Noting that in-house and external counsel are often perceived in the business world as excessively risk-averse, see Steven L Lovett, 'The Employee-Lawyer: A Candid Reflection on the True Roles and Responsibilities of In-House Counsel' (2015) 34 *Journal of Law and Commerce* 113, 146.

[65] See, Paulsson, Rawding and Reed (n 23) 62.

[66] Noting that here is a 'comfort' element in arbitrating within a well-established institution, see Mistelis (n 7) 563.

to arrange facilities for hearings in a location convenient to the parties, also play a role in the selection.

B. Factors Determining the Choice of an International Arbitrator

A detailed account of the reasons underlying the choice of a specific arbitrator in international arbitration is challenging. As highlighted above, distinct actors choose arbitrators in various contexts and are motivated by different goals. Further, even the same type of players lack homogeneity in their decision-making processes as they may face different grids of incentives and may show different social and cultural attachments. Still, a primary understanding of the forces determining preference for some arbitrators above others is essential to determine which behaviours by arbitrators are rewarded and which behaviours are 'punished' in the market. With this goal in mind, the motivations influencing the selection of arbitrators from the perspective of each type of player with the power to make appointments will be analysed next.

i. Parties' Selection of Arbitrators

Assuming that parties try to maximise their gains from participating in arbitral proceedings, it is fair to assume that they will strive to appoint the arbitrator that will yield the most positive outcome of the arbitral proceedings to that party.[67] However, the strategy to achieve this goal is far from straightforward and depends on a complex set of considerations, including the number of arbitrators in the panel, the likely interactions amongst the panel, and the specific facts and legal questions that arise from the case. Further practical considerations, such as prospective arbitrators' language skills and availability, will also play a role in the selection of arbitrators.[68]

Facing the impossibility of predicting all the influencing factors of arbitrators' decision-making, parties can do no better than, with the aid of internal and external counsel and, through instinct and experience, attempt to determine the most advantageous arbitrator. Parties might, therefore, look for arbitrators who hold doctrinal views most favourable to their case. At the same time, in a three-panel arbitrator setting, parties might look to appoint a highly regarded arbitrator[69] amongst their peers, calculating that, through their senior position, they may yield some clout over the remaining members of the panel.[70]

A few further points are important to note. First, if unbounded by ethical and legal constraints, parties could theoretically try to develop a pure agency relationship with their chosen arbitrator. A party could, therefore, appoint the arbitrator that would be prepared

[67] See Juan Fernandez-Armesto, 'Salient Issues of International Arbitration' (2012) 27 *American University International Law Review* 721, 724.

[68] C Leaua, 'Factors Taken into Consideration by the Parties When Appointing an Arbitrator' (2012) 33 *Procedia – Social and Behavioral Sciences* 925, 926.

[69] Mistelis empirically notes how corporations typically look for arbitrators with a solid reputation in the arbitration community and, in addition, display common sense and relevant industry/geographic expertise. See Mistelis (n 7) 576.

[70] See Carlos A Matheus López, 'Practical Criteria for Selecting International Arbitrators' (2014) 31 *Journal of International Arbitration* 795, 799.

to most openly favour their position.[71] Any such strategy could, however, prove detrimental. Arbitrators perceived as biased, dishonest, or insincere by the rest of the panel might be less likely to influence the final decision. As noted by a leading practitioner:

> When I am representing a client in arbitration, what I am really looking for in a party-nominated arbitrator is someone with the maximum predisposition towards my client, but with the minimum appearance of bias.[72]

Therefore, the dominant strategy appears to be to appoint the arbitrator who will be most prone towards the position of the party[73] and that, through his argumentation, gravitas and perceived independence, may nudge the panel's position towards the position of the appointing party. It should, however, be noted that while the dominant attitude is that all members of the arbitral panel, including party-appointed arbitrators, should be impartial,[74] how much advocacy from a party-appointed arbitrator is accepted still varies across jurisdictions.[75]

Finally, the possible relevance of principal-agent problems between parties and counsel in the context of selecting arbitrators should also be taken into consideration.[76] Frequently, parties will lack the necessary information to evaluate the best arbitrator for their case and will, therefore, rely on the advice of external counsel to appoint their arbitrator. This situation may create an opportunity for counsel to choose, consciously or unconsciously, an arbitrator in accordance with its own goals and values. Counsel may, for example, use this opportunity to push for arbitrators who conform to their own normative understanding of behaviour in arbitral proceedings.

On the other hand, counsel, especially in the context where they also act in the market as a potential arbitrator, may use their influence on the arbitral appointment process in a specific proceeding to advance their career as an arbitrator. Counsel may appoint a certain arbitrator hoping – or even agreeing – to be appointed by that same person in a future

[71] This is not to say that open advocacy of a co-arbitrator does not happen in practice. Recalling one such incident but indicating that in his view this 'was someone, in short, who should never have been acting as arbitrator', see Ugo Draetta, 'The Dynamics of Deliberation Meetings in Arbitration: Some Personal Considerations' (2011) *International Business Law Journal* 219, 225.

[72] Martin Hunter, 'Ethics of the International Arbitrator' (1987) 53 *Arbitration* 219, 223.

[73] See Simon Greenberg, Christopher Kee and J Romesh Weeramantry, *International Commercial Arbitration: An Asia-Pacific Perspective* (Cambridge, Cambridge University Press, 2011) 263; Doak Bishop and Lucy Reed, 'Practical Guidelines for Interviewing, Selecting and Challenging Party-Appointed Arbitrators in International Commercial Arbitration' (1998) 14 *Arbitration International* 395, 396.

[74] Greenberg, Kee and Weeramantry (n 73) 283.

[75] Indeed, in the US, the traditional default understanding, at least in domestic arbitrations, was that party-appointed arbitrators did not need to be neutral. This understanding seems, however, to have changed in the last decades. A survey undertaken in the early 2000s found that a majority of US in-house lawyers favoured the notion that party-appointed arbitrators should not agree to be anything but neutral when serving on a panel. See, Douglas Earl Mclaren, 'Party-Appointed vs List-Appointed Arbitrators: A Comparison' (2003) 20 *Journal of International Arbitration* 233. See also, Christopher R Drahozal, 'Arbitration by the Numbers: The State of Empirical Research on International Commercial Arbitration' (2006) 22 *Arbitration International* 291, 303.

[76] Indicating that the knowledge-intensiveness of conflict resolution generates power in favour of law professionals, who may, therefore, overpower their clients and take control of the agency relationship, see Adrian Borbély, 'Agency in Conflict Resolution as a Manager–Lawyer Issue: Theory and Implications for Research' (2011) 4 *Negotiation and Conflict Management Research* 129, 131. Principal-agent problems while arguably a relevant consideration to understand choices in the context of international arbitration have been, however, largely overlooked in the literature. See, Wagner (n 16) 407.

arbitral proceeding.[77] Still, competition amongst law firms and legal and ethical bounds will limit, at least partially, the opportunities for counsel to deviate significantly from their clients' interests.

ii. Co-arbitrators' Selection of Arbitrators

In practical terms, the selection of a third arbitrator by co-arbitrators is a negotiated procedure where the co-arbitrators often consider several names to ultimately agree on a third-panel member that is acceptable to both.[78] During this selection process, it is considered acceptable, at least in some circles, that party-appointed arbitrators consult with their appointing parties regarding the identity of the third arbitrator.[79] Further, in the context of institutional arbitrations, it is also possible that even when the co-arbitrators appoint the chairperson, the institute offers input by, for example, providing the co-arbitrators with a list of potential appointees.[80]

In these circumstances, it seems reasonable to assume that the co-arbitrators' decision regarding whom to appoint will be subject to the same incentives that underlie their remaining decisions. It is, therefore, to be expected that arbitrators, when selecting the presiding arbitrator, will make a decision that will best allow them to accomplish their goals and conform to what they consider appropriate behaviour. To this effect, arbitrators will undoubtedly consider how the choice of the third arbitrator will reflect on the quality of the work produced by the arbitral tribunal and how it will bear on the perceived quality of the arbitrators themselves. Due to the collegial nature of the work to be undertaken, it is natural that selections will fall over members that co-arbitrators trust and respect.[81]

iii. Arbitral Institutions' Selection of Arbitrators

Assuming arbitral institutions endeavour to improve their position in the market, and that they grow their position in the market by increasing their reputation and by having a track record of successfully managed arbitrations, arbitral institutions will tend to appoint arbitrators that will guarantee an efficacious proceeding and an enforceable award. Further, to reinforce their legitimacy – and, subsequently, their reputation amongst the community of businesses and lawyers that ultimately are responsible for selecting arbitral institutions – these institutions will likely aim to strive to appoint independent and impartial arbitrators.[82]

[77] Less directly, counsel may use their influence on the process to curry favour with the most relevant members of the arbitral community and raise their profile within the community.

[78] Noting, however, this process to be, in his experience, in most cases, rather fast, see Ugo Draetta, 'Cooperation among Arbitrators in International Arbitration' (2016) 5 *Indian Journal of Arbitration Law* 107, 114.

[79] See, James H Carter and John Fellas, *International Commercial Arbitration in New York* (Oxford, Oxford University Press, 2010) 128.

[80] ibid 129.

[81] See Draetta (n 78) 114.

[82] Stephen Bond, former Secretary General of the ICC, explains that 'The arbitral institutions are [...] not only conscious of their responsibility to satisfy as best they can the legitimate expectations of the parties, but that failure to do so places in jeopardy their own reputation and perhaps that of international arbitration as a means of dispute resolution.' Stephen R Bond, 'The International Arbitrator: From the Perspective of the ICC International Court of Arbitration' (1991) 12 *Northwestern Journal of International Law & Business* 1.

It is important to note that arbitral institutions' selection of arbitrators may give rise to possible agency problems. There is, at least in theory, the possibility of members of institutions appropriating the decision to advance their own interests, especially taking into consideration that this decision is often made by the chairperson of the institution or special boards, positions often occupied by relevant members of the community themselves. Again, the possibility of informal trading of nominations may arise. It should also be considered that arbitral institutions, not being truly commercial corporations, may not possess the strong governance mechanisms that usually control managerial decisions in for-profit organisations.

Still, in the context of imperfect competition between arbitral institutions, its decision-makers may not be able to significantly deviate from the interests of the arbitral institution without damaging the market position and reputation of the institution they are linked to. Further, in a context where high-profile positions within institutions attract attention to the position holders, inappropriate decision-making may subject that member to criticism, leading to a decrease in their value in the eyes of the community and consequentially lower long-term returns from their participation in the arbitral market.

iv. National Courts' Selection of Arbitrators

Finally, national courts' underlying motivations in selecting arbitrators should be mentioned. Typically, their involvement in the process of appointing arbitrators is residual – ie, they typically only intervene in appointing an arbitrator when the main appointment method has failed to work properly, such as in situations where parties failed to reach an agreement on a sole arbitrator, failed to make an appointment or the primary appointing authority (typically an arbitral institution) failed to appoint.[83] As judicial authorities have less experience and are usually less knowledgeable about the arbitration market, their decisions might be less informed than those taken by parties, co-arbitrators and arbitral institutions. In this sense, depending on the jurisdiction and the circumstances, appointments have been noted to range between parochial choices of local legal figures when such choices were likely not advisable to well-measured selections of experienced members of the arbitral community.[84]

V. Markets Participants' Strategies for Expanding their Presence and Influence in the Market

Due to the above-described market structure and the specific method through which arbitral institutions and arbitrators are selected, many of the market strategies used by those in the field diverge from other elite service markets. In a market where many of the selections are undertaken by members of the community – for example, counsel advising on the selection of a specific arbitral institution or arbitral institutions selecting an arbitrator – many of the strategies adopted by the different actors are directed to improve the agent's position

[83] See UNCITRAL Model Law. Art 11(3) and (4).

[84] See Born (n 40) 1713 and 1727.

inside the community. A general picture of how these agents look to improve their position in this market will allow an understanding of how the behaviour within the community helps shape the regulation of the field. With this goal in mind, the strategies taken by arbitral institutions and arbitrators to improve their position will be analysed in turn.

A. Strategies Developed by Arbitral Institutions

The environment where arbitral institutions compete is unique for a few reasons. First, arbitral institutions, as discussed above, are not usually for-profit enterprises and, therefore, are not necessarily profit-maximising. Second, with few exceptions, arbitral institutions are often linked with a particular jurisdiction where they might dominate the market. At the international level, there is an oligopoly of sorts, with a small number of institutions leading the market. Third, the decisions taken by parties when selecting arbitral institutions do not seem to be very price-sensitive but instead driven by the prestige, familiarity and proximity with the arbitral institution. Some of the ways that arbitral institutions 'compete' in this environment will be discussed next.

i. Well-established Arbitral Institutions Undertake Limited Price-competition

A value often emphasised by arbitral institutions is their 'cost-effectiveness', with the institutions sometimes presenting data where they look to illustrate the advantages of the institution over their rivals.[85] It is important to note that this has not equated to aggressive price competition by arbitral institutions, nor do they seem to engage in other forms of more aggressive commercial practices such as discounting or direct price agreements with parties. While major arbitral institutions seem to consider the price positioning of their more direct competitors, they have not looked to actively undercut each other in terms of pricing.[86] While some newer institutions position their prices purposely below more established competitors, such strategies by themselves seem to have limited success in guaranteeing a relevant number of cases to an institution.

It is important to note that arbitral institutions, in reality, show a strong variance in prices due to widely different schedules and methods of calculating fees.[87] The way their fees' schedules are designed means that a certain arbitral institution may be very competitive for a dispute of a specific size but not competitive at all for disputes of other sizes. Also, when selecting an arbitral institution in a contract for future disputes, the actual size of a

[85] See as examples, ICDR, *International Centre for Dispute Resolution (ICDR) Arbitration Report: Time and Cost* available at www.icdr.org/sites/default/files/document_repository/AAA241_ICDR_Time_and_Cost_Study.pdf, last accessed 11 March 2020; LCIA, *Facts and Figures: Cost and Duration 2013–2016*, available at www.lcia.org// media/download.aspx?MediaId=596 last accessed 11 March 2020.

[86] To this effect, Alexis Mourre, President of the ICC International Court of Arbitration, has indicated in interviews that he does 'not think that the costs of the institution are a major driver in the choice of an arbitral institution'. HSF, Inside Arbitration: An interview with Alexis Mourre, President ICC International Court of Arbitration, 7 February 2019 available at www.herbertsmithfreehills.com/latest-thinking/inside-arbitration-an-interview-with-alexis-mourre-president-icc-international-court last accessed 11 March 2020.

[87] See Warwas (n 8) 50.

future fee is not always easy to establish. All this further complicates 'shopping around' for an arbitral institution on a price basis.[88] Altogether, this market's oligopolistic and sui generis nature helps explain why arbitral institutions have not engaged in aggressive price competition, focusing instead on forms of 'quality' competition.[89] Still, the trend for arbitral institutions to more directly compare their fees to their competitors should be noted, perhaps signifying that parties have become more cost-conscious over time.

ii. Arbitral Institutions Emphasise their Experience and Neutrality as Ways of Attracting Parties

In this context, further to their cost-effectiveness, arbitral institutions emphasise other values as distinguishing features. As detailed above, reputation as an independent and impartial institution and a track record of successfully organising arbitrations appear to be the leading reasons underlying the choice of an arbitral institution. Assuming that arbitral institutions intend to expand their position, they will behave in a way that will lead them to be perceived as independent and impartial and able to support the arbitral tribunals in performing their functions satisfactorily. Reputation is also important for parties because reputed institutions may see their awards have a greater likelihood of being enforced in national courts.[90]

In this environment, it is natural to expect arbitral institutions to focus on establishing a strong reputation, experience, and proven track record in the market for the services of international arbitration institutions. Anecdotal evidence seems to corroborate the idea that international arbitral institutions perceive the importance of reputation and experience as core values to communicate externally. On its webpage, the ICC, under the heading 'ten good reasons to choose ICC arbitration',[91] indicated reputation as the first reason to choose its arbitral proceedings; AAA-ICDR highlights its 'long history and experience in the field of alternative dispute resolution',[92] and SCC stresses its status 'as one of the most important and frequently used arbitration institutions worldwide'.[93]

Further, arbitral institutions can undertake 'quality' competition by providing different service levels. Not all arbitral institutions provide the same functions, with some arbitral institutions having a more hands-on approach in guaranteeing that arbitral awards are produced efficiently and fairly and are enforceable in a court of law. Perhaps one of the most

[88] Noting that 'there is no clear-cut formula for identifying the most attractive institutional regime regarding the costs of institutional arbitration from the perspective of its users', see ibid 53.

[89] As noted in an interview with Marek Krasula, Director of Arbitration and ADR in North America for the ICC International Court of Arbitration: 'As you all know, there are lots of different arbitration service providers and there are some international commercial courts out there also open to resolving international commercial disputes. So, there's really a race to the top. Some people may think this is kind of a race to the bottom. We can offer the cheaper, quicker service, but the race is really kind of upwards: who can provide the best quality services? And that ties in with what needs to be our focus going forward.' James Plotkin, Ozge Yazar and Marek Krasula, 'YCAP and CJCA Interview of Marek Krasula Features' (2021) 2 *Canadian Journal of Commercial Arbitration* 92, 99.

[90] See Thomas E Carbonneau, 'The Exercise of Contract Freedom in the Making of Arbitration Agreements' (2003) 36 *Vanderbilt Journal of Transnational Law* 1189, 1207.

[91] www.iccwbo.org/Products-and-Services/Arbitration-and-ADR/Arbitration/Introduction-to-ICC-Arbitration/Ten-good-reasons-to-choose-ICC-arbitration/ last accessed 16 October 2015.

[92] www.adr.org/aaa/faces/s/about/ last accessed 16 October 2015.

[93] www.sccinstitute.com/about-the-scc/ last accessed 16 October 2015.

well-known examples of the distinction in the level of service provided is ICC's practice of 'scrutinising' awards – a multiple-step process through which different people within the institution and, finally, ICC's Court review the awards' 'quality'.[94] This review, aimed at ensuring a higher likelihood that the award will be enforceable in a court of law, as other institutions do not generally undertake it, allows ICC, an institution usually perceived to be on the pricier side, to separate itself from its competitors.[95]

iii. Arbitral Institutions Focus on Expanding Links and Connections to the Wider Arbitral Community

The efforts of an arbitral institution to increase its profile and compete are not limited to fulfilling its activities in an independent and impartial fashion. In the context of a still reasonably small community of arbitrators and practitioners, the reputation of these arbitral institutions is very much derived from the opinions of the arbitration 'insiders' upon the 'quality' of the different arbitral institutions. Not only can practitioners and those within the community influence the general perception regarding that institution, but they can also direct parties to the institution by advising it as a good choice for their clients and contacts. Therefore, much of the business development efforts undertaken by arbitral institutions are directed precisely towards the arbitral community itself.

Arbitral institutions can establish these bridges and connections with the arbitral community in different ways. For example, arbitral institutions often incorporate members of the community in executive and advisory boards. Some institutions also organise lists of arbitrators from which they then draw appointments. While these selections are primarily made to improve the performance of the arbitral institution, approaching and engaging with the arbitral community in this fashion conceivably links arbitrators and arbitral institutions. On the one hand, it allows the arbitral institution to develop a closer relationship with selected members of the community. Further, it conceivably allows the arbitral institution to rely on the arbitrators' reputation to increase its own reputation.

Arbitral institutions also relate with members of the arbitral community in other relevant ways. Major and minor arbitral institutions undertake efforts to organise frequent events of varying sizes, such as conferences, courses, and symposia dedicated to arbitration.[96] Some of these events, such as the 'Joint Colloquium on International Arbitration' co-organised by ICSID, AAA, and ICC every year, may gather hundreds of participants from all over the world, including much of the arbitral elite and provide a forum for discussing complex arbitral topics and opportunities to network for members of the community.[97] Other events may only be attended by a few dozen participants and have a more introductory approach to arbitration.

It is important to note that this connection between arbitral institutions and the arbitral community is very much a two-way street. Arbitral institutions and those connected to

[94] See Art 33 ICC 2017 Arbitration Rules. See also Thomas H Webster and Dr Michael Buhler, *Handbook of ICC Arbitration: Commentary, Precedents, Materials* (London, Sweet & Maxwell, 2014) 497.

[95] Eric A Schwartz and Yves Derains, *Guide to the ICC Rules of Arbitration*, 2nd edn (Alphen aan den Rijn, Kluwer Law International, 2005) 312.

[96] See Warwas (n 8) 48.

[97] See Emmanuel Gaillard, 'Sociology of International Arbitration' (2015) 31 *Arbitration International* 1, 13.

them often look to arbitration practitioners as the key players that will help divulge and increase the usage of that arbitral institution. As will be discussed below, for practitioners, especially those also participating or intending to participate in the market as arbitrators, having a working relationship with an arbitral institution can be relevant as arbitral institutions are important sources of appointments and visibility within the community. In this environment, it is possible to observe a sort of 'revolving door' between positions in arbitral institutions and private practice, with many key members rotating or cumulating positions in arbitral institutions and law firms or arbitration studios.

iv. Arbitral Institutions' Engagement with the Business Community and Governments

The efforts of arbitral institutions to improve their position in the market do not only involve establishing links with the community of established arbitrators and practitioners. Arbitral institutions are often connected with chambers of commerce and are primarily designed to serve the interests of a business community. Therefore, arbitral institutions often engage with the business community to promote arbitration in general and the arbitral institution in particular. In this effort, arbitral institutions make a special effort to divulge ready-made, standardised arbitration clauses that parties can easily incorporate into their contracts.

To better serve parties and the business community at large, arbitral institutions often update their rules and produce related documents such as guidelines and reference works. These changes are often primarily directed to better adapt to the dispute resolution needs of business parties and improve the quality of proceedings. Further, these changes and assorted documents also help to promote the arbitral institution, offering a way of 'advertising' the arbitral institutions' commitment to modernise and align their activities with the concerns of the arbitral community. As will be discussed in chapter five, such works are often the object of review within specialised literature and divulged in websites, newsletters, and other mediums dedicated to arbitration, helping further publicise the arbitral institution.

Finally, the relationship between arbitral institutions and governments merits a reference. Governments can be important supporters of arbitral institutions, offering funding or cooperating in strategies to develop a certain jurisdiction as an arbitration hub.[98] Government support can be especially important for nascent arbitral institutions as, through funding and institutional support, supported institutions have a better chance of overcoming the difficulties of entering the international arbitration market.[99] However, typically, governments do not meddle in the day-to-day internal affairs of the arbitral institutions that intend to be selected for international disputes. This lack of intervention is to be expected.

[98] One of the most iconic of examples of government support for the development of arbitration has been the extensive efforts of the Dubai government in the establishment of arbitration as part of the Dubai International Financial Centre (DIFC) project. For an overview, see R Mohtashami and S Tannous, 'Arbitration at the Dubai International Financial Centre: A Common Law Jurisdiction in the Middle East' (2009) 25 *Arbitration International* 173.

[99] Denoting the importance of the local government in supporting the development of HKIAC, see Neil Kaplan, 'The History and Development of Arbitration in Hong Kong Symposium: Financial Law in Hong Kong and South-East Asia' (1996) 1 *Yearbook of International Financial and Economic Law* 203, 222.

The perception that an arbitral institution might be influenced in its operations by external forces would undermine its ability to attract parties to voluntarily select that arbitral institution.

B. Strategies Developed by Arbitrators

Turning now to the strategies undertaken by international arbitrators to enter and improve their position in the market, it is important to note that this market is also quite unique for the reasons explained above. Therefore, the strategies undertaken by arbitrators are distinct from those undertaken in other professional services markets. Two key ideas will be explored. First, arbitrators usually develop a primary career prior to assuming a role as arbitrators and then invest heavily in activities that allow them to network and obtain exposure within the community. Second, arbitrators compete by projecting images of technical expertise and independence, especially amongst their peers.

i. Strategies to Enter the Market: Primary Occupations, Networking and Visibility

A first point to note is that becoming an arbitrator is notoriously difficult, even for well-accomplished individuals, with a first appointment often being described as 'elusive'. Without a clear career path to guarantee entry into the world of the select few who routinely act as arbitrators,[100] reaching such status most often involves first achieving a high level of accomplishment within the legal profession or the academic world, with a strong preference for those achieving such feats within the arbitration field.[101] Obtaining such positions gives practitioners visibility and connections that can facilitate their recruitment into the arbitral elite.

Given the conservative approach to appointments and the inability of more junior community members to undercut incumbents through charging lower prices, realistically, most arbitrators only access this position after building a successful primary career. As discussed above, an analysis of the profile of arbitrators shows that most arbitrators combine working in this function with other professional endeavours, most commonly working as counsel, but also in academia or the judiciary. This first career is essential for a prospective arbitrator to build the profile and expertise necessary to be considered for these appointments. Not only may professional success serve as a proxy to their ability as an arbitrator, but it may also lead them to be considered valuable members of the community, offering them the visibility in the field necessary to advance in their careers.

However, building a primary career is not the only activity those wishing to participate in the field undertake. In a context where many appointments are made or at least influenced by practitioners and arbitral institutions, arbitrators invest heavily in creating connections

[100] See Rémy Gerbay, "How Does a New Arbitrator Get Their First Appointment?', A Q&A Session with Remy Gerbay (Interview Given to Lexis PSL Arbitration)' (Social Science Research Network 2014) SSRN Scholarly Paper ID 2519505.

[101] See Thomas Schultz and Robert Kovacs, 'The Rise of a Third Generation of Arbitrators?' (2012) 28 *Arbitration International* 161, 170.

with other members and raising their profile within the community.[102] To this effect, arbitrators and prospective arbitrators often attend conferences and arbitration events where, beyond opportunities for members to signal their knowledge and commitment to the field, they have the occasion to connect and network.[103] Further, they often participate in professional arbitral associations and arbitral institutions and assume positions within them.[104]

Beyond this, arbitrators and those looking to act as arbitrators may pursue different activities to signal their technical proficiency and ability to be appointed as arbitrators. A common approach is to undertake speaking engagements and produce academic writing related to arbitration where they display their knowledge and commitment to the field.[105] More recently, many within the field also opted to develop an online presence where they note their experience within arbitration and connect with other community members and prospective parties. Still, the cumulation of visibility and markers of expertise only accounts for part of the competition that takes place amongst arbitrators.

ii. Continuing Market Competition: Projecting Images of 'Expertise' and 'Virtue'

After an arbitrator manages to enter the market, despite the relatively closed nature of the arbitration ranks, a degree of competition between those within the field continues to take place. In this aspect, arbitrators must continue to maintain and develop relationships with members of the arbitral community and ensure that those making appointments will continue considering that arbitrator for future appointments. Assuming that the dominant strategy by parties, counsel, arbitrators, and arbitral institutions is to select an arbitrator perceived as experienced, knowledgeable and impartial, potential arbitrators will, therefore, assume strategies that will lead them to be perceived as displaying these characteristics.

Beyond the above-discussed steps, the most straightforward way for an arbitrator to be perceived as possessing such qualities is to demonstrate them in arbitral proceedings and accrue a reputation as a competent professional over time. Despite the often-confidential nature of proceedings, due to the well-connected nature of the international arbitration community, information travels between members of the community, allowing effective arbitrators to be known within the field. The important point to note is that it is more relevant for arbitrators to build a general reputation among the community than to develop a relationship with a particular party or even a specific law firm. Given the limitations derived from conflict of interest rules, an arbitrator may not be successively appointed by the same party or law firm, leading arbitrators to focus instead on how the market generally perceives them.

[102] See Marc J Goldstein, 'A Career in International Commercial Arbitration' in Salli Swartz (ed), *Careers in International Law* (American Bar Association, 2008) 105.

[103] Noting the number of players attending these events as being 'larger and larger', see Gaillard (n 97) 13.

[104] A well-established arbitrator indicates that becoming involved with groups such as local bar associations, the ABA, and International Bar Association committees were 'the way I got to develop my practice and meet so many people'. Adam R Martin, Edna Sussman and Maxi Scherer, 'Success in International Arbitration: No Shortcuts' (2014) 21 *Dispute Resolution Magazine* 27, 28.

[105] See Peter B Rutledge, 'Toward a Contractual Approach for Arbitral Immunity' (2004) 39 *Georgia Law Review* 151, 164; Mistelis (n 7) 574.

In summary, a successful arbitrator will often need to attain a successful career prior to achieving nominations and establish a web of personal and professional connections amongst the arbitral community. From there, an arbitrator must continue to develop a standing image as an effective and trustworthy arbitrator. Establishing a reputation as a reliable and technically proficient member of the community and cultivating connections with arbitral institutions and other key members of the community in the many forums reserved for such social engagements appears to be the dominant strategy amongst elite arbitrators and those wishing to achieve such status.

The cumulative effect of a high number of arbitrators assuming the behaviours described above has relevant consequences for their 'regulation'. The practical impossibility of arbitrators competing on price leads to an exacerbated need for arbitrators to distinguish themselves by adopting the above-described strategies. How, in turn, these lead to an environment which steers the members of the arbitral community to create norms that regulate their behaviour and fulfil their socially relevant role will be discussed, respectively, in chapters five and seven. How the particularities of the market have helped shape the different evolution of the regulation of international arbitrators will be discussed in the next chapter.

4

The Unique 'Regulation' of International Commercial Arbitrators

The previous two chapters argued that international commercial arbitration has transformed into a complex marketplace where a multitude of actors offer services in an increasingly competitive market. However, as it was described, the market for international commercial arbitrators has many peculiarities. The way arbitrators are chosen, the way prices are established, and the mechanisms through which competition takes place separate arbitration from most other elite service providers. As discussed, these characteristics lead arbitrators to adapt to this market by investing in strong displays of technical proficiency, such as producing academic work and networking. This chapter will discuss how these characteristics have profound consequences for the regulatory preferences of the arbitral community, namely, leading to a preference for a 'non-interventionist' approach.

A good starting point for analysing how the regulation of arbitrators differs from other fields is reviewing how the evolution of organised professions and their associated regulatory frameworks have taken place.[1] Examining these evolutions allows us to identify patterns in how many service providers are regulated.[2] In particular, it allows for identifying how professional groups tend to organise themselves according to predictable patterns and develop similar legal frameworks intended to protect members of the profession, consumers and third parties.[3] As will be seen, by comparison, the regulation of arbitrators has not developed similar structures.[4]

With this in mind, this chapter will start by evaluating how the evolution of certain professional fields has typically meant a predictable transformation in their regulatory framework. From there, this chapter will explore the attitude of different actors in regard to the regulation of international commercial arbitrators. In particular, the approach of three main actors will be explored. First, the approach of states will be explored, noting how,

[1] For a review of literature on professions, see Andrew Abbott, *The System of Professions: An Essay on the Division of Expert Labor* (Chicago, University of Chicago Press, 1988) 3; Eliot Freidson, 'The Theory of Professions: State of the Art' in Robert Dingwall and Philip Lewis (eds), *The Sociology of the Professions: Lawyers, Doctors and Others* (Quid Pro, LLC, 2014).

[2] See Andrew Abbott, 'The Order of Professionalization: An Empirical Analysis' (1991) 18 *Work and Occupations* 355, 356.

[3] The discussion whether 'professionalisation' as a phenomenon and the legal framework usually associated with the profession have as a primary effect protecting the clients and the public or are, instead, aimed at excluding outsiders is one of the key contentious points in the sociology of professions' literature. See ibid; Rosemary Crompton, 'Professions in the Current Context' (1990) 4 *Work, Employment and Society* 147.

[4] Noting that arbitrators have however developed some of the markers of professionalism, see Catherine A Rogers, 'The Vocation of the International Arbitrator' (2004) 20 *American University International Law Review* 957, 977.

under the current framework, regulatory competition makes creating the same systems found in other fields difficult to achieve. Second, the attitude of the arbitral community towards the regulation of arbitration will be discussed, noting how the characteristics of the arbitration market lead the community to be less interested in procuring the same sort of protection from competition found in other professions. Finally, the attitude of arbitration users and the public will be explored, ultimately noting the lack of external public pressure to further regulate arbitrators.

I. The Regulation of Professions: Different Paths Leading to Different Models of Regulation

The regulation of professional services has been a hot topic that has produced profoundly different views on how and why the existing regulations have emerged.[5] These academic analyses have often aimed to find patterns in what unites the regulation of professions; however, they disagree on what ultimately motivated the appearance of these regulations. It is true that the paths that have led certain occupations to rise to the level of fully regulated professions have not been identical.[6] Different professions in different countries see much variance in how they have evolved and what regulatory arrangements they are subjected to. Still, it is possible to identify trends in how occupations evolve into fully-fledged professions and the rules that preside in offering services in these fields.[7]

Before addressing the particularities of the international commercial arbitrators' regulatory regime, the following two sub-sections will explore: i) the process through which certain occupations evolve into distinct professions with well-established legal and regulatory frameworks; and ii) what characteristics the regulation of these professions usually acquires over time. This will establish the groundwork to discuss the particularities of the regulation of commercial arbitrators and the attitudes of different actors towards the existing regulatory framework in the second part of this chapter.

[5] See, amongst many others, Eliot Freidson, *Profession of Medicine: A Study of the Sociology of Applied Knowledge* (Chicago, University of Chicago Press, 1988); Richard L Abel, *The Making of the English Legal Profession* (Beard Books, 1998); Wai-Fong Chua and Stewart Clegg, 'Professional Closure: The Case of British Nursing' (1990) 19 *Theory and Society* 135; Norman K Denzin and Curtis J Mettlin, 'Incomplete Professionalization: The Case of Pharmacy' (1968) 46 *Social Forces* 375; William J Goode, 'The Librarian: From Occupation to Profession?' (1961) 31 *The Library Quarterly* 306.

[6] A full review of the numerous different theories from the fields of economics, sociology and political science that look to provide explanations for these tendencies is well outside of the scope of this text. On broad simplistic terms, two main accounts have been advanced to explain the support of organised professions for increased state regulation, and, in particular, state-backed self-regulation, of their profession. Some highlight that these efforts are mostly the result of practitioners looking to earn supra-competitive profits, stifle competition, and protect incumbency. See George Stigler, 'The Theory of Economic Regulation' (1971) 2 *Bell Journal of Economics* 3; Richard A Posner, 'Theories of Economic Regulation' (1974) 5 *Bell Journal of Economics and Management Science* 335. Others prefer to emphasise that these mechanisms of regulation are efficient ways of reducing information asymmetry, reducing the costs of enforcement, and avoiding negative externalities resulting from malpractice. See Anthony Ogus, 'Rethinking Self-Regulation' (1995) 15 *Oxford Journal of Legal Studies* 97, 97.

[7] See, Mark Neal and John Morgan, 'The Professionalization of Everyone? A Comparative Study of the Development of the Professions in the United Kingdom and Germany' (2000) 16 *European Sociological Review* 9.

A. The Evolution from 'Occupation' to 'Profession': Patterns Leading to Separate Professional Regulation

In modern societies, many service activities have evolved from occupations to professions – ie, areas of labour which, due to the perception of needing special expertise and dealing with sensitive public interests, are held not to be simply business ventures or trades. In this sense, professions are those occupations which have developed a body of specific knowledge transmitted through means of formal education (often demanding graduate studies), supported by a body of professional literature and with the professionals often viewing themselves as working for some aspect of the good of society.[8] This process, which started for some professions as early as the Middle Ages, has today extended to many fields as diverse as doctors, building engineers, and patent lawyers.[9]

In one of the most well-known studies on the evolution of professions, Wilensky proposed in 1964 a typical sequence through which professions established themselves in the US.[10] In broad terms, Wilensky proposed that in order for a profession to establish itself: i) an occupation starts to be undertaken full-time by at least a subset of practitioners; ii) specialised training schools start to develop either inside or outside of universities; iii) a professional association is formed; iv) persistent political agitation requesting protection for those participating in the profession takes places; and v) rules to eliminate the unqualified and unscrupulous, reduce internal competition, protect clients and emphasise the service ideal are organised into a formal code of ethics.

While Wilensky developed his hypothesis based on a study of the history of 18 occupations in the US, studies focusing on other countries also describe somewhat similar processes. In the UK context, for example, a typical route to professionalisation included: i) the occupation becoming 'full-time'; ii) the establishment of an articles system; iii) the formation of a professional association; iv) the introduction of qualifying examinations; v) the undertaking of political agitation for legal protection of specific work areas and Royal Charter establishment; vi) the creation of academic routes to qualification in co-operation with higher education authorities; and vii) the introduction of rules to ensure continuous professional development.[11]

It is important to note that the models described above may oversimplify more complex processes[12] and may not necessarily fit well with all jurisdictions and professions.[13]

[8] See Thomas Donaldson, 'Are Business Managers "Professionals"?' (2000) 10 *Business Ethics Quarterly* 83, 84; Howard S Becker, *Sociological Work: Method and Substance* (London, Routledge, 1976) 88. For a discussion on the highly contentious concepts of 'profession' and 'professionalism' see, amongst many others, Freidson (n 1); Abbott (n 1) 9.

[9] See Neal and Morgan (n 7). See also Beth Redbird, 'The New Closed Shop? The Economic and Structural Effects of Occupational Licensure' (2017) 82 *American Sociological Review* 600, 600.

[10] Harold L Wilensky, 'The Professionalization of Everyone?' (1964) 70 *American Journal of Sociology* 137. Prior to Wilensky, Caplow's work in this field is worth noting, Theodore Caplow, *The Sociology of Work* (Minneapolis, University of Minnesota Press 1954).

[11] See Neal and Morgan (n 7).

[12] Wilensky's work has not been without critics. Noting the model proposed by Wilensky to be 'seriously flawed' and presenting professionalisation as a more 'complex, contagious, multilevel process', see Abbott (n 2) 380.

[13] The concept of 'profession' itself is sometimes problematic outside the Anglo-Saxon world, often without an exact correspondence in other languages. See David Sciulli, 'Continental Sociology of Professions Today: Conceptual Contributions' (2005) 53 *Current Sociology* 915.

Countries in continental Europe and the 'non-western' world have unique patterns, often involving a stronger impulse of the state in creating and regulating many professions.[14] For example, in Germany, local licensing and the introduction of academic degrees as requirements were more the outcome of local and governmental intervention than professional self-regulation.[15] Still, overall, the main idea that stands out is that over time, some occupations, under the impulse of their own members, the state, or both, establish separate regulatory frameworks and become regulated professions.

B. Characteristics of the 'Regulated Profession': Different Models in Different Jurisdictions

As it is possible to detect patterns of evolution to an occupation becoming a profession in different jurisdictions, it is also possible to identify some patterns regarding how professions are regulated. To this effect, in the Anglo-Saxon world, professions were traditionally largely self-regulated. Professional standards were (and still are to a large extent) developed by professional associations that retain considerable levels of self-determination. Further, professional associations retain some level of responsibility for professional education. In continental Europe, as seen above, with sometimes the exception of the more high-status professions, states usually took a more hands-on approach to regulation, with state bureaucracies playing the role usually reserved for professional associations in the Anglo-Saxon world.[16]

Over time, the traditional distinction between continental and Anglo-Saxon approaches to regulation has largely subsided. Many occupations find themselves regulated by a mixture of government statutory regulation and self-regulation.[17] Some literature strands, in particular, highlight how professions are regulated by a mixture of: i) self-regulation, usually induced by a professional association to which all members have to belong; ii) 'rational-legal' regulation, induced more directly by states through the use of mandatory legal norms; and iii) market pressures, induced by consumer clients and employers' preferences.[18] The emergence of supranational entities, such as the EU, also created both a new level of regulation affecting these professions and a tendency to render uniform regulation in their respective spheres of influence.[19]

[14] See Carlos Wing-Hung Lo and Ed Snape, 'Lawyers in the People's Republic of China: A Study of Commitment and Professionalization' (2005) 53 *The American Journal of Comparative Law* 433, 437. See, also Sciulli (n 13); Anna Buchner-Jeziorska and Julia Evetts, 'Regulating Professionals: The Polish Example' (2016) 12 *International Sociology* 61.

[15] See Neal and Morgan (n 7) 19; James R Faulconbridge and Daniel Muzio, 'Professions in a Globalizing World: Towards a Transnational Sociology of the Professions' (2012) 27 *International Sociology* 136, 140.

[16] See Buchner-Jeziorska and Evetts (n 14); James R Faulconbridge and Daniel Muzio, 'Legal Education, Globalization, and Cultures of Professional Practice Symposium: Empirical Research on the Legal Profession: Insights from Theory and Practice' (2009) 22 *Georgetown Journal of Legal Ethics* 1335, 1342.

[17] Many jurisdictions also establish so called 'co-regulation' mechanisms through which states incorporate professional associations or other self-regulating organisations in establishing the regulatory framework to assist with both the detailed rule-making and the administration of the regulatory regime.

[18] Eliot Freidson, 'The Changing Nature of Professional Control' (1984) 10 *Annual Review of Sociology* 1. See also Buchner-Jeziorska and Evetts (n 14).

[19] Faulconbridge and Muzio (n 15) 141.

Still, in broad terms, similarities can be found regarding the regulation of professions across jurisdictions and professions. First, the regulation of these types of services often involves carving out a legal monopoly over a professional activity.[20] This means, in practice, that legal rules determine that only members of a particular profession may provide that specific category of services. Closely related to this idea, regulation of the profession also often includes licensing and certification requirements – ie, members of the profession, to engage in the market legally, are obligated to first obtain an authorisation from the relevant authority.[21] It also often includes some form of mandatory education, most commonly at the university level, and mandatory apprenticeship programmes.[22]

Second, rules regarding how services must be provided are also commonly established. Often, these are encapsulated in ethical codes, some with the nature of mandatory law, others appearing as 'soft law'.[23] These rules may establish protection for the consumers, third parties, the public in general or the professionals themselves. In achieving these goals, rules are introduced to cover several topics, including how the service provider must act and which goals it must adhere to, how advertisements can be made, how clients can be acquired and, more rarely, how prices should be defined.[24] On a more sceptical view, some argue that these rules also have the effect (and sometimes the primary intent) of curbing competition.[25]

Finally, specialised organisations are typically established to oversee and regulate a profession. Most typically, especially high-level professions, are organised around local, regional or national professional associations with mandatory membership. They characteristically express a form of self-regulation in the sense that the members of the profession often play a role in selecting amongst their own who will take the leadership of such organisations. Such organisations also often play a key role in creating and implementing entrance requirements and the content of regulatory rules. The role of these professional organisations is often complemented by public entities that also take a role in regulating the provision of professional services.[26]

II. The Lack of Command-and-Control State-backed Regulation of the Arbitral Community

One of the most interesting aspects of the evolution of international commercial arbitration is that arbitrators have not evolved a regulation structure similar to that of other apparently

[20] See Frank Parkin, *Marxism and Class Theory: A Bourgeois Critique* (New York, Columbia University Press, 1983) 57.

[21] It should be noted that occupational closure has extended much beyond the historically privileged professions. See Redbird (n 9) 600.

[22] See Richard L Abel, 'Comparative Sociology of Legal Professions: An Exploratory Essay' (1985) 10 *American Bar Foundation Research Journal* 5, 10.

[23] On the different types of professional ethical codes, see Mark S Frankel, 'Professional Codes: Why, How, and with What Impact?' (1989) 8 *Journal of Business Ethics* 109, 110.

[24] Those advocating that the regulation of professions is driven primarily as a process to monopolise a certain service market have been quick to argue that many of these limitations are in reality thinly disguised attempts to stop competition. For example, noting that limitations on advertising are often driven by a fear of price competition, see Abel (n 22) 32.

[25] See, eg, the highly influential Magali S Larson, *The Rise of Professionalism: A Sociological Analysis* (Berkeley, University of California Press, 1977).

[26] Noting different types of relationship between States and regimes of self-regulation, see Julia Black, 'Constitutionalising Self-Regulation' (1996) 59 *The Modern Law Review* 24, 27.

similar 'elite' service providers. As discussed in chapter three, being an arbitrator has never truly become a full-time occupation, with most engaging in the market on a part-time basis, cumulating their appointments with another more primary occupation, most often as a lawyer specialising in dispute resolution. Several reasons may help explain why most arbitrators do not engage in this function full-time. As discussed, holding other occupations, especially high-level positions in the legal industry or academia, facilitates entering the arbitration market and acquiring appointments.[27]

In this sense, one could even question if arbitrators can be classified as professionals in the stricter sense of the word.[28] Arbitrators have not exhibited as a socio-professional group all the identifying markers most professions display.[29] First, while many, if not all, arbitrators have undertaken tertiary education, often to very advanced levels, there are usually no legally mandated educational, apprenticeship, or even licensing requirements.[30] Indeed, one of the most notable aspects of the arbitration market is that, despite often being described as a closed circle, there are usually no legal limitations to entering into this market.[31] Also, while some institutions provide arbitration training,[32] many arbitrators have not undertaken formalised training on arbitration; rather, they generally build experience and knowledge by learning the practice of arbitration in their primary occupation.

Finally, closely related to the ideas above is the distinct nature of the regulatory institutions governing arbitrators. While many arbitral associations exist, these are not professional associations, at least in the traditional sense. They usually include many members who are not arbitrators but practitioners, and their activities are not directed to oversee the profession as much as they are to advance arbitration. Similarly, while playing a fundamental role in directing the market, arbitral institutions do not play regulatory functions similar to those of professional associations or regulatory agencies. As will be seen in more detail in chapters five and seven, while arbitrators are indeed regulated, this often occurs through mechanisms distinct from those that regulate other fields.

III. Attitudes Towards the Regulation of Arbitration: States, the Arbitral Community and the Users of Arbitration

Beyond its characteristics, the regulatory framework applicable to arbitrators is unique in the way that the main actors that can influence it decide to approach the regulation of this field. To this effect, states, the arbitral community and the users of arbitration all seem

[27] See ch 3, section V.B.

[28] For an analysis, see João Ilhão Moreira, 'Arbitration Vis-à-Vis Other Professions: A Sociology of Professions Account of International Commercial Arbitrators' (2022) 49 *Journal of Law and Society* 48.

[29] See, however, Rogers (n 4) 977.

[30] See ibid.

[31] See Gary Born, *International Commercial Arbitration*, 2nd edn (Alphen aan den Rijn, Wolters Kluwer Law & Business, 2014) 2047.

[32] Most notably CIArb that provides training which, when completed, allows candidates access to different levels of membership within the organisation. See Júlio César Bettencourt and Tony Marks, 'The Chartered Institute of Arbitrators' in JDM Lew and others (eds), *Arbitration in England: With Chapters on Scotland and Ireland* (Alphen aan den Rijn, Kluwer Law International, 2013) 80.

inclined to support a non-interventionist approach to the arbitral market. It is important to note that this preference for not transforming the regulation of arbitrators into a system more in line with the ones found in other fields is the result of the specific legal framework within which arbitration operates and the incentives these actors face. How the existing institutions and incentives shape the attitudes of States, the arbitral community and the users of arbitration will be discussed next.

A. Transnational Regulation and Regulatory Competition in International Arbitration

As noted above, states have usually taken little to no steps to establish the same kind of regulations that oversee other professions. This approach is primarily the result of the intrinsically transnational nature of arbitration, which shapes the way that states interact with this field. As will be seen, under the current system of international arbitration, it is not easy for states to regulate international commercial arbitrators individually due to the framework provided by the New York Convention. Two key ideas are important to note in this regard: i) regulation of international commercial arbitrators cannot truly be undertaken unilaterally by a single state; and ii) in practice, some states compete to attract arbitrations to their jurisdiction and, therefore, show little interest in advancing stringent regulation of arbitrators.

i. The Limits to the Ability of States to Regulate within the System Established by the New York Convention

International commercial arbitration's intrinsically transnational nature, combined with the ability of parties to delocalise the arbitration seat, leads to the fact that heightened regulation within a single jurisdiction would have a limited effect on the actual regulation of international commercial arbitrators. As discussed in chapter two, parties can easily choose under what set of rules they want to operate and what regulatory regime will apply.[33] If no parties choose a particular jurisdiction as their seat, its arbitration law will rarely apply in arbitral proceedings. Combined with the highly mobile nature of arbitrators and proceedings, this opens an avenue for regulatory competition, where cases will tend to flow to the jurisdictions most in line with the preferences of parties and their counsel.

To understand how this competition works, one should note that parties can determine that their arbitration will take place under a certain jurisdiction by simply establishing in their contract that the arbitral seat will be in place '*x*'. While this selection has significant legal consequences, namely by determining which courts will have powers to oversee the proceedings, this is, at the same time, essentially a formal choice as it does not mandate that the arbitral hearings take place in said jurisdiction.[34] Therefore, parties can select

[33] See ch 2, section I.C. See also Horst Eidenmüller, 'The Transnational Law Market, Regulatory Competition, and Transnational Corporations' (2011) 18 *Indiana Journal of Global Legal Studies* 707, 723.

[34] See UNCITRAL Model Law, Art 20(2).

jurisdiction '*x*', even if none of the parties or arbitrators have any link with that jurisdiction or even if no part of the arbitral proceedings actually takes place in that jurisdiction. Within the system instituted by the New York Convention, states are then bound to enforce these arbitral awards unless the strict exceptions provided for by the Convention apply.

States that would wish to impose stricter regulatory requirements to international arbitral awards would have to stay outside the New York Convention framework or limit the ability of their own national companies to adhere to international arbitration agreements, arguably putting them at a disadvantage and discouraging investment and trade with foreign companies. While some legal alternatives may be found to secure the interests of contracting parties and investors, companies from states that have not ratified the New York Convention may be held to be less reliable since any awards against such companies might be more challenging to enforce. Also, states not prepared to enforce foreign arbitral awards may be perceived as investment destinations where the business is more difficult to undertake.[35]

This all means that if a state were to individually try to create regulatory burdens to the development of international commercial arbitration, it would be largely ineffective. Any regulatory measure taken by a state in an uncoordinated fashion, if unaccepted by parties and legal counsel, would result in said jurisdiction being shunned. Any attempts to further regulate how arbitral services can be provided would need coordinated action by states, most likely through amending the New York Convention or creating a new and widely accepted international treaty. Any such multilateral international regulatory action is largely unrealistic as it would demand many countries to agree on the detailed regulation of a market. However, as it will be seen next, many states instead compete to fine-tune their legislation to attract arbitrations to their jurisdiction.

ii. States Compete to Bring Arbitrations to their Jurisdictions by Adapting their Legislation

Another important point to note is that the ability of parties to select an arbitral seat leads to an element of competition between jurisdictions.[36] Under the current system, domestic legislatures are pressured through a system of regulatory competition, often driven by the arbitral community itself, not to over-regulate behaviour in international commercial arbitration.[37] Indeed, a string of increasingly pro-arbitration statutes, such as those that increase the realm of arbitrable disputes or limit the possibility for national courts to disrupt arbitral proceedings, have been approved in the last few decades in several jurisdictions.[38]

[35] See Koffi Annan, 'Opening address commemorating the successful conclusion of the 1958 United Nations Conference on International Commercial Arbitration', in *Enforcing Arbitration Awards under the New York Convention Experience and Prospects* (New York, United Nations Publications, 1999) 2.

[36] See Christopher R Drahozal, 'Regulatory Competition and the Location of International Arbitration Proceedings' (2004) 24 *International Review of Law and Economics* 371. Interestingly, this competition might not exist to the same extent in intra-domestic legislative efforts. Noting that US states have not engaged in significative efforts to attract domestic interstate arbitration business, see Erin O'Hara O'Connor and Peter B Rutledge, 'Arbitration, the Law Market, and the Law of Lawyering' (2014) 38 *Unlocking the Law: Building on the Work of Professor Larry E. Ribstein* 87, 104.

[37] See Filip De Ly, 'The Place of Arbitration in the Conflict of Laws of International Commercial Arbitration: An Exercise in Arbitration Planning' (1991) 12 *Northwestern Journal of International Law & Business* 48.

[38] See Drahozal (n 36) 373.

These alterations appear to signal a convergence of attitudes regarding international commercial arbitration for less stringent state intervention in arbitral proceedings.

It should be noted, however, that despite states engaging in some level of regulatory competition, this does not mean that a regulatory 'race to the bottom' has been observed. On the contrary, parties and their lawyers seem to prefer to conduct their arbitrations in places where there is a well-established legal framework and trusted national courts that the parties can rely on as a safety mechanism in case arbitral proceedings do not develop in accordance with acceptable principles of procedural fairness.[39] Conversely, jurisdictions providing no national court oversight or an insufficiently developed framework may be avoided. In this sense, providing an optimal amount of oversight seems to be the dominant approach, meaning that parties, while desiring an autonomous and flexible system of arbitration, also want a level of control and support by the courts of the selected jurisdiction.

To illustrate this point, the modifications trialled in Belgium in 1985 show how states that pursue an extreme 'non-interventionist' policy may end up attracting fewer international arbitrations.[40] At the time, Belgium took the largely unprecedented step of determining that if neither party were nationals or resided in Belgium, they would not be able to apply to set aside an arbitral award made in Belgium in Belgium courts. The move, which planned to attract more international arbitrations to Belgium, operated instead as a deterrent, as parties were, in all probability, uncomfortable with not having a means of reacting to a decision in the jurisdiction where the arbitration took place.[41]

In any case, the fact that different jurisdictions seem interested in competing to attract international arbitrations is itself a revealing phenomenon.[42] While the direct economic advantages for a country in hosting international commercial arbitration may be negligible in absolute terms,[43] special interest groups – mainly local arbitration lawyers, local arbitrators, and local arbitral institutions – have a strong interest in developing pro-arbitration statutes aimed at attracting arbitrations.[44] It is plausible that this indicates the arbitral community, through their specific technical expertise, holds significant sway over legislative changes in this field.[45] This, coupled with the lack of interest of the arbitral community itself in state regulation of arbitrators, may help explain the lack of interest of states in regulating arbitrators.

[39] See Joshua DH Karton, *The Culture of International Arbitration and The Evolution of Contract Law* (Oxford, Oxford University Press, 2013) 70.

[40] Alan Redfern and Martin Hunter, *Law and Practice of International Commercial Arbitration* (London, Sweet & Maxwell, 2004) 329.

[41] See Bernard Hanotiau and Guy Block, 'The Law of 19 May 1998 Amending Belgian Arbitration Legislation' (1999) 15 *Arbitration International* 97, 97.

[42] Some states, in supporting arbitration, go much beyond providing arbitration friendly legislations. Noting that in the case of Singapore, a host of measures, including tax-breaks and heavy support for the local institution, were implemented, see Elizabeth MacArthur, 'Regulatory Competition and the Growth of International Arbitration in Singapore' (2018) 23 *Appeal: Review of Current Law and Law Reform* 165, 172.

[43] Drahozal (n 36) 373. Drahozal ultimately concludes that while 'a country which enacts a new or revised arbitration statute experiences a statistically significant increase in the number of ICC arbitration proceedings [...] [i]n absolute numbers, the estimated increase is small'.

[44] See Christopher R Drahozal, 'Arbitrator Selection and Regulatory Competition in International Arbitration Law' in Christopher R Drahozal and Richard W Naimark (eds), *Towards a Science of International Arbitration: Collected Empirical Research* (Alphen aan den Rijn, Kluwer Law International, 2004) 167; Ly (n 37) 49.

[45] See Katherine L Lynch, *The Forces of Economic Globalization: Challenges to the Regime of International Commercial Arbitration* (Alphen aan den Rijn, Kluwer Law International, 2003) 94; Ralf Michaels, 'Roles and Roles

B. The Approach of the Arbitral Community to the Regulation of the Field

As mentioned above, in many markets, those offering services often support the development of regulation that insulates them from competition. The kind of regulatory barriers to entry that may be taken with this aim vary widely but typically include, in the context of professional services, licensing and educational requirements and mandatory participation in professional organisations. In contrast, international commercial arbitration, so far, has not developed similar rules.[46] Indeed, arbitrators do not seem to organise to lobby the state in order to acquire legal protection in the market.[47] On the contrary, examples can be found of arbitrators and arbitral organisations actively opposing regulatory interventions that would make their regulation more akin to that of other professions.[48]

Three likely explanations can help elucidate this unique state of affairs. First, the kind of characteristics that the market demands of arbitrators operate as de facto barriers to entry into the market, meaning that those already established would not benefit from regulatory barriers. Second, a lack of price competition between arbitrators leads the community to feel less pressure to avoid increased competition. Third, many – or at least the most elite members of the profession – would be worse off if states were to establish disjointed requirements to exercise the profession since that would restrict the potential to offer services across jurisdictions. These ideas will be discussed in more detail next.

i. Preferences in the Selection of Arbitrators Lead to a Lack of Incentives for Arbitrators to Push for Regulation

In relation to the first idea, it should be noted that incumbent arbitrators face less competitive pressure from would-be market entrants. As detailed in chapter three, arbitrators' prior experience and existing reputation within the arbitral community are key factors

Perceptions of International Arbitrators' in Walter Mattli and Thomas Dietz (eds), *International Arbitration and Global Governance: Contending Theories and Evidence* (Oxford, Oxford University Press, 2014) 52.

[46] Interestingly this may not fully apply to the market of arbitral institutions. Notably, Alexis Mourre, ICC's International Court of Arbitration former president, argued that an institutional self-regulation through a common framework to consider 'best practices and international standards' would be preferable to 'free competition' to weed out institutions that do not deserve the trust of users. See GAR, 'Mourre calls for institutions to join forces', 9 March 2018, available at globalarbitrationreview.com/article/1166513/mourre-calls-for-institutions-to-join-forces, last accessed 11 March 2020.

[47] Other professions' regulatory interests sometimes influence the arbitral regulatory framework. Spain established in its 1988 Arbitration Law that when the dispute is to be settled by de jure arbitration, the arbitrators had to be practising lawyers. This uncommon requirement was maintained, although only in relation to domestic arbitrations, in the 2003 Spanish arbitration law reform. Some saw this as the result of corporatist pressure by the legal profession. See, Marta Gonzalo Quiroga, 'Reflexiones y Propuestas Prácticas a La Luz Del Arbitraje Internacional En La Ley 60/2003' (2006) 3 *Revista Brasileira de Arbitragem* 71, 80.

[48] This was the case in Brazil where several proposals, such as Draft-Law 4.891/05 and Draft-Law 3293/2021, intended to regulate the profession were received with significant opposition by the Brazil arbitration community. See, regarding Draft-Law 4.891/05, Cbar, 'Profissão de árbitro: Projeto de Lei n. 4.891/05', available at cbar.org.br/site/wp-content/uploads/2018/04/Projeto-de-Lei-n.-4.891-2005-Silvia.pdf, last accessed 4 December 2023. See, regarding Draft-Law 3293/2021, CIArb, 'Nota Técnica do CIArb Brasil sobre o Projeto de Lei nº 3293/2021', available at www.ciarb-brazil.org/wp-content/uploads/2022/01/220110_NotaTecnicaPL3293-2021_01a-1.pdf, last accessed 4 December 2023.

in their selection by parties and arbitral institutions.[49] Arbitrators already installed in the market, through their acquired technical expertise and prior established relationships in the community, have a strong advantage over new entrants. As many practitioners note, the market almost always heavily prefers those that already have experience as arbitrators or otherwise leading legal or technical experts with many years of experience.[50]

The strong incumbency advantages and elite status of international commercial (and domestic) arbitrators may partially explain arbitrators' lack of interest in advancing an agenda for, for example, licensing or educational mandatory requirements. Their incumbent position is often already protected by the market in a way that makes such requirements unnecessary. While mandatory licensing or educational requirements are barely existent, the market's strong preference for highly qualified individuals plays the same role, making such regulatory interventions to maintain their position largely unnecessary.

ii. Limited Price Competition Leads to a Lack Of Incentives for Arbitrators to Push for Regulation

Closely related to this idea, it should be noted that price competition is not a key driver of competition among arbitrators. As discussed in more detail in chapter three,[51] both in the context of institutional arbitrations and ad hoc arbitrations, arbitrators are not heavily pressured to compete on price. In institutional arbitrations, prices are most often defined by arbitral institutions and an arbitrator being willing to work at a lower price than that established by the institution does not lead to an increased number of appointments. The way fees are established in ad hoc arbitrations, typically through negotiation with the two disputing parties, usually only after the arbitrators are selected, with the arbitral tribunal often retaining the power to establish their own fees, also does not incentivise strong price competition.

This separates them from most other service providers. In most circumstances, an increase in the number of potential suppliers leads to a decrease in the price. While sometimes elite members of a profession – such as specialised, highly-regarded doctors or senior lawyers – may be more insulated from competition pressures, many often have an interest in restricting entrance to keep prices high. However, arbitrators are not in a fully equivalent position since incumbent arbitrators mostly do not have to charge lower fees if more potential arbitrators are willing to enter the market due to the way fees are set and the strong preference for previous experience. Therefore, they are also conceivably less incentivised to procure regulatory barriers to protect their position and keep their fees at a higher level.

iii. Disjointed Regulatory Systems would Lead Arbitrators to be in a Worse Position

Further to this, the fact that many arbitrators provide their services across jurisdictional lines should also be noted. This is another aspect that differentiates arbitration from many

[49] See Fernando Dias Simões, *Commercial Arbitration Between China and the Portuguese-Speaking World* (Alphen aan den Rijn, Wolters Kluwer Law & Business, 2014) 74.

[50] See Rogers (n 4) 967.

[51] See ch 3, section V.B.i.

other professional fields. Indeed, most professions are traditionally regulated along national lines, with most professionals offering their services in a single locality and subject to the norms of a single jurisdiction.[52] Arbitrators, on the other hand, at least in regard to international arbitration, typically work on proceedings seated in different jurisdictions. Elite arbitrators, in particular, often act in multiple jurisdictions at the same time, with multiple concurrent cases taking place in many of the most important arbitral seats. Arbitrators are, therefore, potentially subject to different regulatory jurisdictions.

If different jurisdictions developed their own unique regulatory rules, for example, by creating unique licensing systems, this would make offering arbitral services across borders more challenging. The need to comply with these multiple regulatory frameworks could significantly burden arbitrators. This likely discourages arbitrators, especially the most elite ones, from pushing for such developments. Such regulatory developments could harm even arbitrators offering their services in a single jurisdiction, as an idiosyncratic regime could conceivably make that jurisdiction less attractive and lead parties to delocalise their proceedings.

C. Attitudes of the Users of Arbitration to the Regulation of the Field

In addition, it should be noted that due to its particular characteristics, international commercial arbitration has been subjected to little external pressure to heighten state regulation. Indeed, no other stakeholders have forced significant changes in the regulation of international commercial arbitrators so far. In this regard, three key ideas should be highlighted. First, the particularities of the users of international commercial arbitration lead them to be less exposed to the kind of asymmetric information that justifies regulatory intervention. Second, commercial arbitration has been able to present itself as an elective alternative to the use of national courts. Finally, international commercial arbitration seems not to have been marred by important scandals that force a re-evaluation of the system. These ideas will be explored in turn.

i. The Characteristics of the Users of International Commercial Arbitration

The first idea that helps explain the attitude of the users of arbitration to the regulation of the field relates to the fact that the users of international commercial arbitration are likely to perceive themselves as not needing protection. While sometimes individuals are parties to commercial arbitration proceedings, international commercial arbitration has been mostly used by companies with a reasonable level of economic power and sophistication and, most often, in a context where they are supported by either in-house or outside counsel. Indeed, commercial arbitration is mostly designed to deal with high-level disputes. Further, the high

[52] It should be noted, however, that, in regards to many professions, globalisation processes have led to a recalibrated role by state entities and local professional associations regarding professional closure regimes, with supra-national governance playing an increased role in regulating these services. See Faulconbridge and Muzio (n 16) 1344.

costs of arbitration and the practical need of including a written arbitration clause prior to the emergence of an actual dispute have also helped lead arbitration not to become a mass-market method of dispute resolution.[53]

In this sense, the parties and arbitrators' relationship is subject to different concerns in comparison to other fields. In many fields, professionals provide services to users who are often unable to determine the quality of the service provider. This often leads to the creation of 'floor regulation' – ie, regulation to ensure that all service providers guarantee minimum quality standards. Since the users of arbitration are usually sophisticated companies operating in a transnational setting, they are arguably in a better position to identify the underlying quality of the services of arbitrators and arbitral institutions. This, in turn, conceivably makes interventions in the arbitrators' market unnecessary, as the consumers of the services are understood to be in a position to make these selections and to have the means to identify and react against deviations.

Closely relating to this idea, it should also be considered that international commercial arbitration, while an important legal phenomenon, stays mostly outside the spotlight partially due to the lack of mass adoption. While the number of proceedings has been increasing, in absolute terms, it is still reasonably low, with most ordinary people having little to no contact with commercial arbitration and international commercial arbitration in particular. Equally, the confidential nature of most arbitration proceedings might lead arbitration to have less public exposure than court litigation. This arguably leads to less public pressure and media interest in the area and less pressure to intervene in this market. In this aspect, investment arbitration, where increased public attention has been accompanied by discussions to fundamentally change the regulation of the field, provides a good contrasting example.[54]

ii. International Commercial Arbitration as an 'Alternative' Dispute Resolution Mechanism

Regarding the second idea, it is important to note that international commercial arbitration is an option that parties might use as an alternative to the default dispute resolution system: litigation at a national court. In reality, due to the difficulties of enforcing foreign court decisions in some contexts, arbitral proceedings are, on occasion, such an advantageous method of solving international disputes that parties systemically introduce arbitration clauses of a transnational nature in contracts.[55] Still, parties are perceived as having the possibility of recourse to national courts instead of arbitration if they so choose in their contractual dealings.

[53] See, on this topic, João Ilhão Moreira, 'The Limits to Voluntary Arbitration in Establishing a Fair, Independent and Accessible Dispute Resolution Mechanism Outside Large Contractual Disputes' in Leonardo de Oliveira and Sara Hourani (eds), *Access to Justice in Arbitration: Concept, Context and Practice* (Alphen aan den Rijn, Kluwer Law International, 2020).

[54] Putting forth a theory explaining domestic backlash against international investment law by connecting media coverage, specifically the bias in the news media's selection of international disputes, to public opinion formation towards international agreements, see Ryan Brutger and Anton Strezhnev, 'International Investment Disputes, Media Coverage, and Backlash Against International Law' (2022) 66 *Journal of Conflict Resolution* 983.

[55] Indicating the usage of arbitration clauses in 88% of international joint-venture agreements, see Christopher R Drahozal and Richard W Naimark, *Towards a Science of International Arbitration: Collected Empirical Research* (Alphen aan den Rijn, Kluwer Law International BV, 2005) 59.

In this sense, commercial arbitration is usually perceived as an 'alternative' dispute resolution mechanism – ie, a system that parties expressly opt-in and where party autonomy is understood to be a key principle.[56] In this sense, arbitration is often presented as more of an extension of a right to freely contract between two parties than a service that parties acquire from a service provider. This might arguably lead legislators and public opinion to be less interested in the regulation of the inner workings of commercial arbitration. From another perspective, the common public-private divide often used to categorise fields helps contextualise these differences in attitude. In this sense, courts are perceived to be part of the public sphere, while, by opposition, arbitral proceedings are perceived essentially as part of the private sphere. Therefore, arbitrators' regulation is seen as a concern primarily of the disputing parties, practitioners, and arbitral institutions, not something demanding public intervention.

iii. The General Perception that International Commercial Arbitration Works

Finally, it should be noted that a key reason why the international commercial arbitration market has not been more thoroughly regulated relates to a general perception that international commercial arbitration has been accomplishing its main goal: providing an efficient and trustworthy dispute resolution for highly complex contractual arrangements, in particular those with a transnational element.[57] While other fields of arbitration, such as investor-state arbitration and labour arbitration, have faced repeated calls for reform from those outside the field, commercial arbitration specifically has been less controversial.[58]

Several explanations may help explain this perception. First, in relation to commercial arbitration, there is a lack of an organised effort by countervailing forces. Judges, whom one could perhaps imagine would be natural competitors to arbitrators, often instead welcome commercial arbitration. Indeed, commercial arbitration in many jurisdictions helps move judges' dockets by freeing them from highly complex litigation cases.[59] In some jurisdictions, it further offers a career for judges post-retirement.[60] Second, despite a few cases that will be discussed at the end of chapter eight,[61] arbitration has not been marred by high-profile scandals or cases that have put into question its legitimacy as a dispute resolution system,

[56] See Julian DM Lew, Loukas A Mistelis and Stefan Kröll, *Comparative International Commercial Arbitration* (Alphen aan den Rijn, Kluwer Law International, 2003) 4.

[57] As noted by Caselle: 'it is clear that the enforcement power is lent by the national courts, and the latitude allowed to arbitration depends on explicit provisions made by the law-makers or the courts. Presumably the currently liberal legislation would be revoked if there were perceptions of abuse'. Alessandra Casella, 'On Market Integration and the Development of Institutions: The Case of International Commercial Arbitration' (1996) 40 *European Economic Review* 155, 161.

[58] For example, Van Harten notes that his criticism of investment in arbitration is not 'directed at the usage of arbitration in other contexts, especially the commercial context, where it does not generally raise the same concerns'. See Gus van Harten, 'Perceived Bias in Investment Arbitration' in Michael Waibel and others (eds), *The Backlash Against Investment Arbitration: Perceptions and Reality* (Alphen aan den Rijn, Kluwer Law International, 2010).

[59] See, however, describing the relationship of judges with the finality of arbitration awards as a 'love-hate' relationship, Amy J Schmitz, 'Ending a Mud Bowl: Defining Arbitration's Finality through Functional Analysis' (2002) 37 *Georgia Law Review* 123, 134.

[60] See Robert Coulson, 'Will the Growth of Alternative Dispute Resolution (ADR) in American Be Replicated in Europe' (1992) 9 *Journal of International Arbitration* 39, 40.

[61] See ch 8, section V.B.

nor has it been seen to jeopardise the public at large. In this sense, it has not attracted the attention of political groups intending to change the system.

This last point is particularly salient. Commercial arbitration has largely not seen situations that have led users, legislators or the general public to distrust the system.[62] In this sense, with every year that goes by without commercial arbitration being challenged by news reports that undermine trust in its ability to fairly solve disputes, it further entrenches itself in legal life. By extension, arbitrators' legal status tends to be maintained. The interesting point here is that the tendency of arbitration and arbitrators to fulfil their goals does not seem to be merely accidental. Indeed, despite the lack of similar regulatory arrangements that govern other professions, the particular characteristics of international arbitration have led to unique regulatory arrangements that steer arbitrators to compliance with a predefined set of professional norms. These arrangements will be analysed in the next chapters.

[62] Roger summarises: 'International commercial arbitration has not itself been entirely free from issues regarding arbitrator bias and conduct. The number of challenges to arbitrators has risen sharply in recent years, and there is lively debate about standards for disclosure and challenge. These issues, however, have largely percolated within the system without creating an externally perceptible crisis of legitimacy.' Catherine A Rogers, 'The Arrival of the "Have-Nots" in International Arbitration' (2007) 8 *Nevada Law Journal* 371, 376.

5

The Creation of Professional Norms Applicable to Arbitrators

This chapter analyses how different actors interact to create the professional norms that regulate commercial arbitrators. In this analysis, the role of states, courts, arbitral institutions, professional associations, and members of the international arbitration community themselves will be examined.[1] Beyond a discussion of how these different forces contribute to the regulation of arbitrators, this chapter sheds light on the incentives that lead each actor to participate in these processes. This analysis will provide the backdrop for more general ideas regarding the formation of arbitrators' professional norms. In the last section, this chapter will argue that: i) boundaries between legal norms and soft law applicable to arbitrators are blurred; ii) a mixed process of state intervention and self-regulation can be observed; and iii) the particularities of the market incentivise strong community participation in normative creation processes.

I. The Role of State Legislators in Establishing Professional and Ethical Norms for Commercial Arbitrators

Chapter four examined why states do not intervene in the regulation of international commercial arbitrators in the same way that they intervene in most other professions.[2] However, they still play a key role in international commercial arbitration, particularly in sketching out the fundamental obligations that arbitrators must comply with. It is important to note that arbitration, as we understand it today, can only exist with the support of states.[3] Without the support of states' legal institutions and coercive instruments, arbitration could not operate as a quasi-judicial resolution system of easily enforceable awards. Therefore, the obligations defined by states' authorities are particularly relevant as they manifest the key goals that commercial arbitration must achieve to continue to enjoy wide state support.

[1] It has been noted that the area of ethical standards is 'the most fractured area of international arbitration'. James Ng, 'When the Arbitrator Creates the Conflict: Understanding Arbitrator Ethics through the IBA Guidelines on Conflict of Interest and Published Challenges' (2015) 2 *McGill Journal of Dispute Resolution* 23, 24. See also Katia Fach Goméz, *Key Duties of International Investment Arbitrators: A Transnational Study of Legal and Ethical Dilemmas*, 1st edn (Cham, Springer Berlin Heidelberg, 2018) 12.

[2] See ch 5, section III.A.

[3] Identifying eleven roles that the state takes in relation to arbitration, see Neil Kaplan, 'The Role of the State in Protecting the System of Arbitration' (2015) 81 *Arbitration* 452.

To further explore how states influence the creation and development of normative standards within the international arbitration community, this section will focus on three key ideas. First, it will analyse how states contribute to defining and strengthening the basic principles that arbitrators must follow through international treaties and national legislation. Second, it will highlight how state interventions in the regulation of arbitrators take place almost exclusively through the use of open-ended legal principles, such as impartiality and independence, separating the regulation of international commercial arbitrators from that of other professions. Finally, this section will review how the international commercial arbitration community plays a decisive role in shaping states' efforts in creating norms for international commercial arbitrators.

A. International Treaties and National Arbitration Legislation as a Source of Arbitrators' Obligations

States regulate international commercial arbitration through two main kinds of legal norms. First, states establish international arbitration treaties where they establish common rules regarding arbitration. These treaties focus on two specific areas: the mutual recognition of arbitration agreements and the enforcement of international arbitral awards. Second, they establish domestic legal acts regarding, amongst other issues, the validity of arbitration agreements, the conduct of arbitral proceedings, and the recognition and enforcement of arbitral awards. While these legal instruments are not primarily designed to regulate arbitrators' behaviour, from them, transpire several duties that arbitrators are expected to follow.

The New York Convention provides the most important example by far of the kind of international conventions that states establish to regulate international commercial arbitration.[4] It is important to note that the Convention does not establish directly any obligations for arbitrators. Instead, it establishes only the conditions under which contracting states must recognise and enforce arbitration agreements and arbitral awards. Still, in doing so, the Convention indirectly imposes obligations on international arbitrators. For example, the Convention determines that the recognition and enforcement of an award may be refused if a party is 'unable to present his case'.[5] By establishing this standard, the Convention contributes to the idea that an arbitrator must uphold procedural fairness within arbitral proceedings.

At the domestic level, states establish further details regarding arbitrators' professional and ethical obligations. Sometimes, national arbitration acts use language that directly establishes generic obligations upon the arbitral tribunal. For example, the English Arbitration Act 1996 determines that the arbitral tribunal must 'act fairly and impartially as between the parties, giving each party a reasonable opportunity of putting his case'[6] and

[4] Other major arbitral treaties include the 1975 Inter-American Convention on International Commercial Arbitration (usually known as the 'Panama Convention') and the European Convention on International Commercial Arbitration of 1961. The practical relevance of these conventions is relatively small when compared to the New York Convention.

[5] New York Convention, Art V 1(b).

[6] English Arbitration Act 1996, s 33, 1(a).

avoid 'unnecessary delay or expense'.[7] Also, the French arbitration law establishes that: 'irrespective of the procedure adopted, the arbitral tribunal shall ensure that the parties are treated equally and shall uphold the principle of due process'.[8]

At other times, arbitration legislation establishes obligations not to the arbitral tribunal as a whole but instead directly to the arbitrators themselves. For example, many Model Law-inspired legislations establish that 'arbitrators must disclose any circumstances likely to give rise to justifiable doubts as to their impartiality or independence'.[9] Also, some arbitration acts have defined more general principles directed to arbitrators. To this effect, for example, the Spanish Arbitration Act 2003 establishes in general terms that arbitrators must 'be and remain independent and impartial throughout the arbitration'.[10] In the same vein, the Swedish Arbitration Act 2019 establishes that 'An arbitrator shall be impartial and independent'.[11]

Like the New York Convention, national arbitration acts also make clear the applicability of these generally held norms even when not establishing obligations directly upon arbitrators. Most jurisdictions will establish, for example, that an arbitrator may be challenged 'if circumstances exist that give rise to justifiable doubts as to his impartiality or independence'[12] or that an arbitral award may be set aside if 'the award is in conflict with the public policy'[13] of the state. These rules, while not directly establishing obligations to arbitrators, reflexively reinforce the key values and norms applicable in this field.

It is important to note that all major jurisdictions contain provisions within their national legislation that clarify the importance of certain fundamental principles that dominate commercial arbitration. In particular, legal principles such as the obligation of the arbitral tribunal to be impartial and that the arbitrators should respect basic principles of due process are universally present across arbitral legislation.[14] Even if such obligations are often not neatly expressed by arbitral legislation in a systematic fashion, they are referred to directly and indirectly consistently throughout the acts either as general principles to be applied or by determining ways for the parties to react if such principles are violated.

B. Light-touch Regulation and the Usage of Open-ended Concepts as the Dominant Approach to the Regulation of Arbitrators

The combination of the New York Convention with national legislation is the bedrock of the legal framework that arbitrators must adhere to. It should, however, be noted that the commands established by the New York Convention and national legislations do not establish detailed rules and usually refer only to open-ended concepts. In this sense,

[7] English Arbitration Act 1996, s 33, 1(b).
[8] French Code of Civil Procedure, Art 1510.
[9] UNCITRAL Model Law, Art 12(1). See also, among others, French Code of Civil Procedure, Art 1456 and Spanish Arbitration Act 2003, Art 17(2).
[10] Spanish Arbitration Act 2003, Art 17(1).
[11] Swedish Arbitration Act 2019, s 8.
[12] See, eg, UNCITRAL Model Law, Art 12(2).
[13] See, eg, UNCITRAL Model Law, Art 34(2) (b) (i).
[14] See Gary Born, *International Commercial Arbitration*, 2nd edn (Alphen aan den Rijn, Wolters Kluwer Law & Business, 2014) 1810.

references to ideas of independence, impartiality, or due process as guiding principles for arbitrators are common. However, arbitration acts usually offer no substance to the meaning of these concepts.[15] Equally, most arbitration acts establish no requirements concerning mandatory legal qualifications or training nor demand a minimum of arbitral experience.[16] This is especially the case with regard to international arbitrations.

These arrangements contrast deeply with other professions. Take auditors, for example, who usually are expected to maintain a level of independence from the companies they audit. In most jurisdictions, they face not only general legal demands of independence but also detailed binding legal rules prohibiting auditors and audit firms from establishing certain kinds of arrangements with the firms they audit.[17] While the exact details of regulations will vary from jurisdiction to jurisdiction, auditors will also have mandatory requirements concerning training and education, often having to sit licensing exams and accumulate a certain number of hours working within the profession.[18]

The striking differences between the regulation of auditors and arbitrators in the US may help to exemplify how much the state regulation of arbitrators may be considered 'light touch'. In regard to arbitrators, little to no direct regulation of the profession can be found. The Federal Arbitration Act 1925 does not even expressly require arbitrators to be independent or impartial (albeit there is general agreement that an arbitral tribunal has to be impartial). It instead establishes simply that the competent court may make an order vacating the award 'where there was evident partiality or corruption in the arbitrators'.[19] In the text of the law itself, no details are given regarding what is meant by 'evident partiality' or what conflict of interests could give rise to a vacatur of the award.[20]

By comparison, in the US, auditors and audit firms are also expected to be independent in the performance of professional services. However, beyond establishing these more general principles expressly as a matter of law, several legally binding instruments provide detailed rules to preserve such independence. Most notably, the Sarbanes-Oxley

[15] A few jurisdictions do offer guidance on the meaning of these concepts. For example, Brazil determines that arbitrators are precluded to act in the same situations that judges would be in accordance with the Brazilian Civil Procedure Code. See Brazilian Arbitration Law 1996, Art 14.

[16] A few exceptions outside the most used seats of arbitration should, however, be noted. The most relevant of these exceptions can be found in the Chinese Arbitration Law, which determines requirements of professional experience or education namely, amongst other routes, that an arbitrator must have been engaged in arbitration work for at least eight years or have worked as a lawyer or a judge for eight years. These requirements are applicable only to domestic arbitrations. See, Chinese Arbitration Law 1994, Art 13. See also, Jingzhou Tao, 'Arbitration Law of the PRC' in *Concise International Arbitration*, 2nd edn (Alphen aan den Rijn, Kluwer Law International, 2015). Other exceptions include Indonesia, see Indonesian Arbitration Law 1999, Art 12(1), Vietnam, see Vietnamese Law on Commercial Arbitration, Art 20(1) and Colombia, see Colombian Arbitration Law 2012, Art 7. Also, notably, Latvia heavily regulates arbitrators, see Latvian Arbitration Law 2014.

[17] See, Directive 2006/43/EC of the European Parliament and of the Council of 17 May 2006 on statutory audits of annual accounts and consolidated accounts, Art 22 in particular, and also Sarbanes–Oxley Act of 2002, ss 201–209 in particular. See also, Niels Philipsen, 'Recent Developments in the Regulation of Auditors: An Economic Perspective' in Niels Philipsen and Guangdong Xu (eds), *The Role of Law and Regulation in Sustaining Financial Markets* (London, Routledge, 2014).

[18] See, for all, Directive 2006/43/EC of the European Parliament and of the Council of 17 May 2006 Arts 6 and 7.

[19] US Federal Arbitration Act 1925, s 10(a)(2).

[20] For a brief description of how courts in New York approach this provision, see John VH Pierce, Janet R Carter and David N Cinotti, 'Challenging and Enforcing International Arbitral Awards in New York' in James H Carter and John Fellas (eds), *International Commercial Arbitration in New York*, 2nd edn (Oxford, Oxford University Press, 2016) 490.

Act of 2002 prohibits auditors from providing a number of other services contemporaneous to the audit, including bookkeeping, management functions, investment advice, investment banking services, and legal services.[21]

The unique status of arbitrators is not only noticeable when they are compared to auditors. Most professions with a strong public interest element are regulated by state legislations or other legally binding instruments that provide detailed rules regarding licensing, ethical issues, and conflict of interests. Amongst many other professions, lawyers, doctors, or engineers will find detailed binding rules regarding these issues. In turn, when looking at national legislation, arbitrators are usually only bound to the sort of open-ended rules described above.

This does not mean that arbitrators are not bound to (sometimes very detailed) norms regarding similar issues, namely conflicts of interest and standards of independence and impartiality. However, these are found by connecting other sources of regulatory norms such as court decisions, arbitral institutions' rules, soft law, and academic and non-academic writing. Before discussing how these rules are created, it is important to note how the arbitral community heavily influences the development of arbitral legislation.

C. The Influence of the Arbitral Community on the Development of Arbitral Legislation

In international commercial arbitration, while state legislators formally hold the power to legislate, in practice, many of these legislators do not truly drive innovative regulatory efforts in this area. Two main considerations are important in this regard. First, many states simply import wholly or partially the UNCITRAL Model Law on International Commercial Arbitration instead of developing their own regulatory framework. Second, even when the states develop their own arbitral legislative framework, they often do it under the influence of a local arbitral community. These ideas will be further illustrated in the sections below.

i. The UNCITRAL Model Law and the Influence of the Arbitral Community on its Development

With regard to the first point raised, it bears explaining that the UNCITRAL Model Law works as a highly influential effort towards harmonisation of national legislatures in the field of international arbitration. Developed by the United Nations Commission on International Trade Law (UNCITRAL), it was first adopted in 1985 by a resolution of the UN General Assembly and amended in 2006. While not mandatory, the Model Law is designed to be adopted by national legislatures. It has since been adopted, albeit in some cases with considerable changes, by around 70 states and 100 jurisdictions.[22]

[21] Sarbanes–Oxley Act of 2002, s 201.

[22] J Ole Jensen, 'Setting Aside Arbitral Awards in Model Law Jurisdictions: The Singapore Approach from a German Perspective' (2015) 4 *European International Arbitration Review* 55.

The adoption of the Model Law has been touted to have several advantages by its proponents.[23] First, it allows states to implement a well-drafted and internally coherent arbitration legislative text. Second, its wide usage provides a level of familiarity to the users of international arbitration, even if they would otherwise not be familiar with that particular jurisdiction. Therefore, states often incorporate the Model Law into their national legislation to attract international arbitral proceedings and promote the usage of arbitration as a means of solving disputes within that jurisdiction.[24] Equally, local practitioners and arbitrators often refer to the Model Law as an example of the best legislative practices to be followed and as a way to further develop arbitration in that jurisdiction.[25]

The development of the Model Law text itself is an interesting example of how the community of arbitrators and practitioners is involved in the development of state arbitral legislation. While the Model Law was developed by the United Nations Commission on International Trade Law, the decision to commence work on the Model Law followed a consultative meeting in Paris in September 1978, which included representatives of the ICC, the leading arbitral institution, and the International Council for Commercial Arbitration (ICCA), an NGO composed mainly by arbitration specialists.[26] The Model Law text was then discussed by representatives of different states, some of whom were well-known figures within the arbitral community.[27] Further, several arbitral organisations participated as observers in the discussions.[28]

ii. The Influence of the Arbitral Community in the Development of National Arbitration Acts

The influence of the arbitral profession on legislation is perhaps even more notable when looking at the way arbitrators and arbitral practitioners provide impulses to the creation and development of arbitral legislation within many jurisdictions. This was, for example, the case of the passage of the England and Wales Arbitration Act 1996, where a ministerially appointed Departmental Advisory Committee on Arbitration Law (DAC) largely drove the legislative effort.[29] Comprising a veritable 'who's who' of English arbitration at the time, the DAC presented a proposal for a modern, arbitration-friendly legislative framework. The UK Parliament quickly adopted the proposal, with the new legislation significantly contributing to cementing London as a key seat in international arbitration.

[23] See David Cairns, 'The Spanish Application of the UNCITRAL Model Law on International Commercial Arbitration' (2006) 22 *Arbitration International* 573, 573.

[24] See, amongst others, Pedro Galindo Gil, 'Ley de Arbitraje, Artículo 1 [Ámbito de Aplicación]' in Carlos González-Bueno (ed), *Comentarios a la Ley de Arbitraje* (Madrid, Consejo General del Notariado, 2014) 15.

[25] See, amongst others, Christopher R Seppälä, 'Why Finland Should Adopt the UNCITRAL Model Law on International Commercial Arbitration' (2017) 34 *Journal of International Arbitration* 585.

[26] Eric A Schwartz, 'The ICC Arbitration Rules and the UNCITRAL Model Law' (1993) 9 *Arbitration International* 231.

[27] This was for example the case for Sir Michael Mustill (UK) and Prof. Dr Heinz Strohbach (German Federal Republic) both leading arbitration figures in their respective jurisdictions.

[28] This was the case for the Chartered Institute of Arbitrators and the ICC.

[29] See, amongst others, V Veeder, 'La Nouvelle Loi Anglaise Sur l'arbitrage de 1996: La Naissance d'un Magnifique Éléphant' [1997] *Revue de l'Arbitrage* 3; Claude Reymond, 'L'Arbitration Act, 1996 – Convergence et Originalité' [1997] *Revue de l'Arbitrage* 45; Julian DM Lew and Melissa Holm, 'Development of the Arbitral System in England' in Julian DM Lew and others (eds), *Arbitration in England: With Chapters on Scotland and Ireland* (Alphen aan den Rijn, Kluwer Law International, 2013).

The influence of the arbitral community members in the development of arbitration is by no means a phenomenon restricted to England. Similar interventions by the arbitral community can be identified in many other jurisdictions, including France,[30] Germany,[31] and Sweden.[32] Indeed, every well-established national arbitral community continuously evaluates their arbitral legislation as well as legislative proposals, comparing them with those of other jurisdictions. In these efforts, members of the arbitral community push for so-called pro-arbitration legislation – ie, arbitration acts that comply with tenets of international arbitration, such as allowing a great degree of party autonomy or establishing easily enforceable arbitral awards.

The fact that members of the arbitral community spend so much effort on helping to develop legislative standards and publicly analysing those legislative acts is itself a telling reflection of the strategies undertaken by the community members to progress within the profession. Arbitrators benefit from legislation that increases the usage of arbitration.[33] However, most uniquely to the arbitral profession, the participation of arbitrators in these processes allows them to raise their profile and network with similarly minded community members. The link between the need to raise a profile within the community and success in the profession might explain the level of involvement of members of the arbitral community in this process. This idea will be discussed again at the end of this chapter.[34] First, however, it will be important to review the role played by other institutional actors. The role of national courts will be analysed next.

II. National Courts as a Source of Regulatory Norms for International Commercial Arbitrators

In a context where most states' legislatures do not provide detailed guidance on the specific requirement for becoming an arbitrator or the content of arbitrators' obligations, national courts have played an important role in developing the norms that are usually considered binding on arbitrators. In exploring how this process takes place, this section focuses on two key ideas. First, it will discuss how, through ad hoc approaches, courts have helped to clarify, crystallise, and sometimes create normative understandings in this field. Second, it will discuss how this process is not necessarily straightforward and how a feedback loop

[30] See Guido Carducci, 'The Arbitration Reform in France: Domestic and International Arbitration Law' (2012) 28 *Arbitration International* 125.

[31] Böckstiegel, a key figure on the German arbitration circles, reported his own role and efforts in the development of the 1998 Arbitration Law reform. See, Karl-Heinz Böckstiegel, 'An Introduction to the New German Arbitration Act Based on the UNCITRAL Model Law' (1998) 14 *Arbitration International* 19.

[32] See 'The Draft New Swedish Arbitration Act: The 'Presentation' of June 1994 Preface' (1994) 10 *Arbitration International* 407; Kaj Hobér, 'Arbitration Reform in Sweden' (2001) 17 *Arbitration International* 351.

[33] For empirical support of the idea that local arbitrators see an increased number of appointments following the enactment of a new or a revised arbitration law, see Christopher R Drahozal, 'Arbitrator Selection and Regulatory Competition in International Arbitration Law' in Christopher R Drahozal and Richard W Naimark (eds), *Towards a Science of International Arbitration: Collected Empirical Research* (Alphen aan den Rijn, Kluwer Law International, 2004) 167.

[34] See ch 5, section VI.C.

process with the arbitral community determines that only certain court decisions effectively enter the normative understandings of the arbitral community.

A. Courts' Role in Developing and Crystallising the Content of Arbitrators' Professional and Ethical Norms

The idea that judges, in practice, 'create' legal rules is by no means a particularity of the regulation of arbitrators. Despite being bound by institutional and legal constraints, judges make new 'law' by applying or extending established rules to novel circumstances and by altering the content of legal rules in accordance with changed economic and social circumstances.[35] Naturally, the level of influence that jurisprudence has in developing a particular legal framework will depend on a large number of factors, including the historical particularities of that specific jurisdiction, the level of detail that applicable legislative rules have, how many novel questions courts face, and how judges perceive their own role as law-makers.

In the context of arbitration, where legislation often offers mostly open-ended concepts and rules, the role of national courts is particularly important. National courts have numerous opportunities to engage with arbitral proceedings. Amongst other functions, national courts might be called upon to decide challenges raised against arbitrators, set aside arbitral awards, or recognise and enforce awards. These operations often involve evaluating the conduct of arbitrators during the arbitral proceedings. Through applying general legal standards to these situations, courts: i) reinforce and develop interpretations that are, over time, incorporated into the canon of norms applicable to arbitrators; and ii) sometimes present novel understandings that shift the dominant understandings of a particular issue.

To this effect, classic court decisions such as *Commonwealth Coatings Corp. v Continental Cas. Co.* illustrates how this process takes place. In this case, the US Supreme Court evaluated the conduct of an arbitrator who failed to disclose that he had provided previous engineering consultancy services to one of the parties, ultimately concluding that the award should be vacated on the ground of evident partiality under FAA section 10(a)(2).[36] In doing so, the Supreme Court reinforced the idea that arbitrators are bound to obligations of impartiality and independence from which an obligation to disclose any dealings which might create an impression of possible bias arises.[37] From this key idea, several federal courts have derived a variety of standards, all determining that the failure to disclose a relationship or conflict constitutes evident partiality.[38]

It should be noted that in most circumstances, court decisions do not represent radical departures from the understandings dominant within the arbitral community.

[35] Ronald Sackville, 'Why Do Judges Make Law: Some Aspects of Judicial Law Making' (2001) 5 *University of Western Sydney Law Review* 59, 59.

[36] In this case from 1968, the Supreme Court held that since previous engineering consultancy services provided by the arbitrator to one of the parties were not disclosed, the award could be vacated under s 10 of the FAA.

[37] See Born (n 14) 716.

[38] José Carlos Fernández Rozas, 'Clearer Ethics Guidelines and Comparative Standards for Arbitrators' in Bernardo María Cremades, Miguel Angel Fernández-Ballesteros and David Arias Lozano (eds), *Liber Amicorum Bernardo Cremades* (Madrid, La Ley, 2010) 421.

On the contrary, national courts often rely on the arbitral community's soft law[39] and academic works when considering arbitrators' professional and ethical obligations.[40] Exceptionally, court decisions have produced important transformations of the practices within the community. The well-known *Dutco* decision of the French Cour de Cassation provides an example of a court decision serving as a catalyst of significant changes in how arbitral institutions and parties dealt with appointments of arbitrators in multi-party arbitrations, determining that in these types of arbitrations, all parties must be afforded equal rights in the appointment process.[41]

Importantly, when deciding how to interpret the dominant arbitral standards, some courts seem to consider how their decisions will affect the perception of their jurisdiction on the international arbitration market. To this effect, for example, in *Halliburton Company v Chubb Bermuda Insurance Ltd*, the UK Supreme Court noted that:

> the duty on all arbitrators to act fairly and impartially is enshrined in section 33 of the 1996 Act. Lord Grabiner submits that London is the premier seat for international arbitration. He points to a survey of international arbitration which Queen Mary University of London carried out in 2018 which reveals that the main reasons why parties in international arbitration choose to arbitrate in England are the reputation of London and that the English legal system guarantees neutrality and impartiality. It is therefore important that English law upholds rules which support the integrity of international arbitration.[42]

B. The Relative Importance of Different National Courts and the Feedback Loop between the Arbitral Community and Courts

If it is true, as seen above, that courts influence how arbitrators' obligations are construed, it should be said that not all national courts have the same impact on the development of these normative standards. Some courts see their decisions widely quoted by commentators in arbitration-related books, articles, and conferences.[43] In turn, decisions from other jurisdictions may be more or less ignored outside that particular jurisdiction. While all national courts help generate the norms that frame arbitration, courts from key arbitral seats – such as England, France, the US, and Switzerland – likely display a much more important role in this process than others, at least in the international arena.

[39] A particular work to be noted in this respect is the ICCA's Guide to the Interpretation of the 1958 New York Convention prepared with assistance of the Permanent Court of Arbitration and intended as a handbook 'to give guidance to judges determining applications under the Convention as to its scope, interpretation and application'.

[40] Noting that courts defer increasingly to the IBA Guidelines on Conflicts of Interest, see Gabrielle Kaufmann-Kohler, 'Soft Law in International Arbitration: Codification and Normativity' (2010) 1 *Journal of International Dispute Settlement* 283, 296; Felix Lüth and Philipp K Wagner, 'Soft Law in International Arbitration – Some Thoughts on Legitimacy' [2012] *StudZR* 409, 418.

[41] For an analysis of the Dutco case Jean-Louis Delvolvé, 'Multipartism: The Dutco Decision of the French Cour de Cassation' (1993) 9 *Arbitration International* 197. For an overview of the transformations in arbitration practice following the case, see Thomas Bevilacqua and Ricardo Ugarte, 'Ensuring Party Equality in the Process of Designating Arbitrators in Multiparty Arbitration: An Update on the Governing Provisions' (2010) 27 *Journal of International Arbitration* 9.

[42] *Halliburton Company v Chubb Bermuda Insurance Ltd (Formerly known as Ace Bermuda Insurance Ltd)* [2020] UKSC 48, para 63.

[43] See as an example the appendix of cases to Born (n 14).

The level of importance given to certain jurisdictions over others will be linked to several factors such as: i) the importance perceived of a certain jurisdiction due to the number of international cases it handles; ii) the reputation of the court and their judges; iii) how easily available those court decisions are; and iv) how widely read the language used by the court is. Naturally, even within the same jurisdiction, not all decisions will have the same influence over the 'canon' of professional and ethical norms that govern international arbitrators. In this sense, the most relevant and original decisions will usually be more publicised and, therefore, more influential in the regulation of the arbitral community.

It should be further said that not all court judgments are accepted by the arbitral community. In particular, court decisions perceived as inconsistent with international practice are often criticised by the community in online forums, blogs, or academic publications.[44] In such circumstances, judges are sometimes criticised for their 'lack of understanding' of arbitration. Conversely, court decisions that uphold a 'pro-arbitration' stance, namely by respecting arbitrators' autonomy, are usually praised as 'modern' and 'moving in the right direction'.[45] In this sense, members of the arbitration community filter and mediate the understandings produced by courts, favouring those that better coincide with the community's interests.[46]

III. Arbitral Institutions as a Source of Professional and Ethical Obligations

In addition to state legislators and national courts, arbitral institutions are also key players in the development and practice of international commercial arbitration. In practice, their role extends far beyond organising the arbitral proceedings. They play a key role in regulating the behaviour of parties and arbitrators. While their importance as regulatory agents is perhaps more automatically evident as an enforcer of regulatory norms,[47] arbitral institutions are also an important source of professional and ethical norms applicable to arbitrators. Their contribution to the development of the normative environment occurs mainly through: i) the enactment of arbitral institutional rules; and ii) the development of guidelines and other soft law texts.

A. Arbitral Institutional Rules as a Source of Professional and Ethical Obligations

Arbitral institutional rules, while only directly applicable in institutional arbitrations, are vital to the normative groundwork applicable to commercial arbitrations. They primarily

[44] Examples of such publications and forums include the Global Arbitration Review (GAR), the Kluwer Arbitration Blog and the OGEMID mailing list, amongst many others.

[45] See, eg, Chiann Bao lauding Hong Kong courts for undertaking 'persistent and proactive crafting of pro-arbitration policy that has enabled Hong Kong to remain a top reliable seat for arbitration.' Chiann Bao, 'Hong Kong Courts: International Arbitration Law in the Making' [2019] *Belgian Review of Arbitration* 615, 628.

[46] See also ch 5, section V.

[47] See ch 8, section I.

define mandatory pre-established rules and procedures that frame the arbitral proceedings organised within a certain arbitral institution. Arbitral rules determine such issues as: i) how to initiate arbitral proceedings; ii) how to constitute the arbitral tribunal; or iii) how the arbitral tribunal shall make the award. However, institutional arbitral rules also contribute to the normative framework in which arbitrators operate. They do so by: i) emphasising principles applicable to arbitrators, such as impartiality and efficiency; and ii) creating obligations that arbitrators must follow within institutional arbitral proceedings.

To this effect, institutional arbitration rules contribute to reinforcing generally held principles arbitrators are expecting to accomplish by declaring, for example, that 'every arbitrator must be and remain impartial and independent of the parties involved in the arbitration'[48] or that 'the arbitral tribunal [...] shall make every effort to conduct the arbitration in an expeditious and cost-effective manner'.[49] In this respect, arbitral rules do not typically contain provisions that establish different principles from those often found in national legislation statutes. In fact, the formulations used in national legislation statutes and arbitral rules in this regard are often of a similar nature. Still, by incorporating such principles, arbitral institutions signal their commitment to these values, reinforcing their paramount role in arbitration.

Further to incorporate principles, institutional arbitral rules also create more tangible obligations to arbitrators. They might determine that an arbitrator must: (i) 'disclose in writing [...] any facts or circumstances to call into question the arbitrator's independence in the eyes of the parties, as well as [...] the arbitrator's impartiality';[50] (ii) 'render its final award in [X] months';[51] or (iii) 'state the reasons upon which [the award] is based'.[52] In this sense, arbitral institutions sometimes provide specific ways to operationalise these obligations. This is the case, for example, when arbitral institution rules establish how arbitrators must communicate a possible conflict of interest and how these are to be decided. At other times, arbitral institutions merely restate well-established principles of behaviour, such as when they establish a general obligation of the arbitrators to be impartial.[53]

In any case, the development, update, and discussion of their arbitral rules is one of the most relevant tasks undertaken by arbitral institutions. As explored in chapter three, having arbitral rules perceived as appropriate, modern, and generally conducive to cost-efficient, well-run proceedings and enforceable awards is an important element of an arbitral institution's success.[54] Further, arbitral institutions may benefit from the 'free' publicity that is

[48] Art 11(1) ICC 2021 Arbitration Rules. See also Art 5(3) LCIA 2020 Arbitration Rules and Art 11(1) 2018 HKIAC Administered Arbitration Rules.

[49] Art 22(1) ICC 2021 Arbitration Rules. See also Art 13(5) 2018 HKIAC Administered Arbitration Rules.

[50] Art 11(2) ICC 2021 Arbitration Rules. See also Art 5(4) LCIA 2020 Arbitration Rules and 11(4) 2018 HKIAC Administered Arbitration Rules.

[51] Eg, 6 months in ICC, see Art 31(1) ICC 2021 Arbitration Rules.

[52] Art 32(2) ICC 2021 Arbitration Rules. See also Art 26(2) LCIA 2020 Arbitration Rules and Art 35(4) 2018 HKIAC Administered Arbitration Rules.

[53] Indeed, arbitral institutions tend not to particularise the meaning of concepts such as 'independence' and 'impartiality'. See Susan D Franck, 'The Role of International Arbitrators' (2005) 12 *ILSA Journal of International and Comparative Law* 499, 514.

[54] See ch 3, section V.A.

generated by the discussion around the changes to their rules. It is, therefore, unsurprising that all major arbitral institutions frequently update their rules. In this sense, the increased rhythm of changes to arbitration rules may perhaps be a reflection of the increased competitiveness between arbitral institutions.[55]

B. Arbitral Institutions as a Source of Soft Law Norms Applicable to International Commercial Arbitrators

Arbitral institutions do not contribute only to the regulatory environment applicable to arbitrators through their arbitration rules. In addition, arbitral institutions create other texts that sometimes offer more detail regarding what arbitrators are expected to accomplish and how they are expected to act. Such texts come under different names, such as ethical codes or practice notes, but share a common goal: providing information regarding how arbitrators, parties, and counsel should act in proceedings, how arbitral rules should be interpreted, and how arbitral institutions will carry out their functions. These texts, however, are not intended to be binding for the parties or arbitrators but instead are designed to provide guidance.

The growing number of these soft law texts must be understood in the context of arbitral institutions' strategy to enhance the transparency and predictability of the arbitration process in the eyes of their users.[56] Several transformations in the arbitral market may help explain the increased usage of these texts by arbitral institutions: i) the growing heterogeneity and number of arbitrators and arbitrations linked to each arbitral institution makes the need for uniform proceedings and understandings more palpable;[57] and ii) the growing competition between arbitral institutions pressures these institutions to tackle issues that may be seen as problematic, such as conflicts of interests or rising costs in international arbitration. The development of these 'soft law' texts is an attractive way of showing users the commitment of the institution to tackle these issues and, at the same time, 'advertise' the work undertaken by the institution.[58]

[55] The ICC, eg, first established its first arbitration rules in 1922, subsequently amending them in 1927, 1928, 1932, 1934, 1939, 1947, 1955, 1975, 1998, 2012, 2017 and 2021. The LCIA, in turn, adopted revised rules in 1981 and again in 1985, 1998, 2014 and 2020. HKIAC passed its first administered rules in 2008 and revised them in 2013 and again in 2018. SIAC first rules were developed in 1991 and revised in 1997, 2007, 2010, 2013 and 2016. In the same fashion, almost all other major arbitral centres have reviewed their arbitral rules over the last few years.

[56] Noting that 'while efficient case administration remains the core activity of arbitral institutions, institutions increasingly assume related roles […] including participate in developing arbitration laws and best practices through issuing guidelines and practice notes', see Mohamed Abdel Raouf, 'Emergence of New Arbitral Centres in Asia and Africa: Competition, Cooperation and Contribution to the Rule of Law' in Stavros L Brekoulakis, Julian DM Lew and Loukas A Mistelis (eds), *The Evolution and Future of International Arbitration* (Alphen aan den Rijn, Kluwer Law International, 2016) 325.

[57] See William Park, 'The Procedural Soft Law of International Arbitration: Non-Governmental Instruments' in Loukas A Mistelis (ed), *Pervasive Problems in International Arbitration* (Alphen aan den Rijn, Kluwer Law International, 2006) 150.

[58] See Barbara Alicja Warwas, *The Liability of Arbitral Institutions: Legitimacy Challenges and Functional Responses* (The Hague, TMC Asser Press, 2017) 46.

IV. Professional Organisations' Soft Law as a Source of Arbitrators' Professional and Ethical Norms

Another particular aspect of international commercial arbitration is the multitude of professional organisations dedicated to the profession. Some of these, such as the Chartered Institute of Arbitrators (CIArb) or the ICCA International Council for Commercial Arbitration (ICCA), have a global reach with thousands of members across multiple jurisdictions.[59] Others have national ambitions, aggregating arbitrators and arbitral practitioners from a particular jurisdiction. Others still aim to gather arbitrators working within particular areas of law or arbitrators or practitioners typically perceived as having backgrounds, often regarding gender[60] and age,[61] that put them at a disadvantage when entering the market. Importantly, some professional organisations not directed solely to arbitration practitioners pay particular attention to arbitration and count significant numbers of arbitration practitioners amongst their ranks.

The popularity of membership within these professional organisations must be understood in a context where arbitrators often look to expand their networks. While the levels of activity within these organisations vary greatly, they most frequently organise events and social gatherings and provide promotional opportunities. Some provide training and education to their members. Further, and importantly for the purpose of understanding the normative environment where arbitrators operate, some of these professional organisations also develop professional and ethical codes as well as practical notes to guide how arbitrators should operate in a number of situations.[62]

These texts work not only as a 'codification' of existing practices but, in some circumstances, also display truly original normative solutions.[63] They, therefore, represent one of the clearest examples of the 'soft normativity' that dominates international arbitration.[64] Often involving elite members of the arbitral community in their creation, the popularity of some of these texts over others may result from two factors: i) the 'borrowed authority'

[59] CIArb, while initially an UK-based association, has today membership that expands across more than 100 countries and has more than 12,000 professionally qualified members around the world. See Júlio César Bettencourt and Tony Marks, 'The Chartered Institute of Arbitrators' in JDM Lew and others (eds), *Arbitration in England: With Chapters on Scotland and Ireland* (Alphen aan den Rijn, Kluwer Law International, 2013) 75. For an overview on the ICCA, see V Veeder, 'Gala Dinner Address: Memories from ICCA's First Fifty Years' in AJ van den Berg (ed), *Arbitration: The Next Fifty Years* (Alphen aan den Rijn, Kluwer Law International, 2012).

[60] These include associations such as ArbitralWomen and initiatives such as Equal Representation in Arbitration ('the Pledge').

[61] These include different branches directed to 'young' practitioners either sponsored by arbitral institutions, such as the ICC's Young Arbitrators Forum (YAF) or LCIA's Young International Arbitration Group (YIAG), or arbitral organisations such as CIArb's Young Members Group (YMG).

[62] See, eg, the ethical codes provided by CIArb (Code of Professional and Ethical Conduct – 2009). the American Bar Association (Code of Ethics for Arbitrators in Commercial Disputes 1977, revised in 2003), Club Espanõl del Arbitraje (Code of Good Arbitral Practices 2005, which has the particularity of being primarily designed as a code of practice for arbitral institutions). See also the guidelines provided by CIArb (notably its 2016 Arbitration Practice Guidelines, covering best practices regarding issues such as terms of appointment including remuneration and drafting awards).

[63] This is, eg, the case of the IBA Guidelines on Conflicts of Interest which in their definition of situations that constitute conflicts of interests or create a duty of disclosure develops a creative element. See Kaufmann-Kohler (n 40) 9.

[64] See Kaufmann-Kohler (n 40).

of the institutions they emanate and the members who develop these texts; and ii) the need for the normative solutions that the particular text addresses.

Indeed, the importance of these texts and the extent to which they are relied upon varies widely. While some of these texts seem to be rarely relied upon, others have undoubtedly reached a central stage in international arbitration practice. Texts like the IBA Guidelines on Conflicts of Interest in International Arbitration or the IBA Rules on the Taking of Evidence in International Arbitration have become key normative sources within the community. Given their importance, these texts are often the focus of debate, review, and sometimes dissent. While not all of these texts deal primarily with professional and ethical norms, they reinforce key principles and detail obligations that arbitrators must follow.

Again, the heavy participation in the committees that develop these documents must be understood in the context of the professional development strategies undertaken by community members. More directly, participating in developing these documents is an opportunity to increase that particular member's visibility within the community and network with other relevant members. More indirectly, by addressing perceived problems that may affect the legitimacy of international commercial arbitration, members of the community help secure its usage and reinforce the position of arbitration as the main method of solving international commercial disputes.[65]

V. Academic and Non-academic Writing as Sources of Arbitrators' Professional and Ethical Obligations

Another particularity of international commercial arbitration is the importance of academic and non-academic writing in the development of arbitration and its legal framework. While much could be said about the functions of academic writing in relation to the development of arbitrators' professional and ethical obligations, this section will focus on two main ideas: i) academic and non-academic writing plays a key role in organising and disseminating professional and ethical norms; and ii) academic and non-academic writing in international arbitration is largely dominated by those practising in the field, which arguably influences how these shape the content of these norms. These ideas will be analysed in turn.

A. The Importance of Academic Writing and Non-academic Writing in Systematising and Communicating Professional and Ethical Norms

It should be said that the de facto importance of the academic community as an influence on the development and interpretation of the law is by no means exclusive to international

[65] As Goméz states: 'It is clear that if arbitrators comply with their duties, regardless of how and where they are set out in writing, this benefits not only the arbitrators' careers, but also the entire arbitration collective, the institution managing the arbitration, and ultimately all participant stakeholders.' Fach Goméz (n 1) 14.

commercial arbitration.[66] However, the transnational nature of international commercial arbitration and the numerous competing sources of norms exacerbate the role played by the academic community in this field.[67] In international commercial arbitration, members of a somewhat diverse community, coming from different jurisdictions and working across boundaries, need a common basis of understanding and a set of rules and principles they can rely upon.[68]

Widely read and relied upon academic works about arbitration play this role. Major works, such as Gary Born's 'International Commercial Arbitration', Fouchard, Gaillard, Goldman on International Commercial Arbitration, or Redfern and Hunter on International Arbitration, among many others, summarise, 'codify', and describe the complex legal framework in ways which are intelligible across borders, providing common ground for the different members of the community.[69] Familiarity with key arbitration authors and their works is a necessary part of participating in international commercial arbitration at any relevant level, making these texts known and accepted by virtually all members of the arbitral community.

It should be noted that in the complex normative environment of international arbitration, where there is no centralised legislative power, the role of academic work in codifying these norms is especially relevant. Given that many legislative acts, national court decisions, and soft law texts can potentially project obligations on international arbitrators, the numerous books, articles, and texts produced by the members of the arbitral community play a role in selecting which of these sources are to be relied upon and how are they to be interpreted. This process often involves critically evaluating the quality of these texts in order to determine if they are useful as reference points. Arguably, legislative acts, national court decisions, and soft law texts quoted frequently and presented in a positive light within the texts of the community might see their relevance increased.

Further to these roles of selecting and codifying the norms, the vast number of academic works (and, increasingly, blogs and other online forums) dedicated to arbitration play an important role in communicating developments in the field throughout the community. Information regarding new arbitral acts and legislative alterations in relevant jurisdictions, changes to the rules and developments in the lives of arbitral institutions, as well as important court decisions, are therefore quickly disseminated through the community.[70] Furthermore, a small but increasingly visible specialised international

[66] For a discussion on the influence of legal scholarship, see, amongst others, William Twining and others, 'The Role of Academics in the Legal System' in Mark Tushnet and Peter Cane (eds), *The Oxford Handbook of Legal Studies* (Oxford, Oxford University Press, 2005).

[67] See Paola Catenaccio, 'Cultural Variation in Arbitration Journals: The International Court of Arbitration Bulletin and the Arbitration Journal Compared' in Vijay Kumar Bhatia, Christopher Candlin and Maurizio Gotti (eds), *Discourse and Practice in International Commercial Arbitration: Issues, Challenges and Prospects* (London, Ashgate Publishing Ltd, 2012) 164.

[68] See Park (n 57) 150.

[69] In the words of Ginsburg: 'Like the grand civil-law tradition, it is scholarly commentary that produces the law and technique of arbitration.' Tom Ginsburg, 'The Culture of Arbitration' (2003) 36 *The Vanderbilt Journal of Transnational Law* 1335, 1340.

[70] In divulging the developments within the arbitral community, the role of blogs such as Kluwer Arbitration blog, a publication of Kluwer Law International, and law firm organised newsletters, such as Herbert Smith Arbitration Notes, a news blog organised by the law firm Herbert Smith Freehills, have been particularly relevant.

press on international arbitration focuses on these issues.[71] This media focus allows any relevant changes to arbitrators' obligations to be quickly informed and discussed across the community.[72]

As discussed throughout this chapter, the community constantly evaluates the norms that are part of the arbitral regulatory framework. In this process, these innovations are often analysed through the prism of whether said development is positive or negative to the development of arbitration. Legislative alterations that are perceived as promoting the use of arbitration and attracting international arbitrations to that jurisdiction are usually praised. Reforms which do not achieve this goal are usually considered 'missed opportunities'. In the same vein as discussed above, national court decisions that are perceived as upholding the 'values' of arbitration and as helping to maintain arbitration as a functional method of solving disputes are lauded. Court decisions that are perceived as doing the opposite are usually received with concern.[73]

B. The Particularities of the Arbitral Academic/Practitioner Community and its Influence on the Content of Norms

To understand the process through which academic and non-academic writing influences the creation of regulatory norms in this field, one should note that this process has important particularities. First, arbitration exhibits arguably less of a 'division of labour' between practitioners and academics than other fields of law.[74] As explored in chapter three, academic writing and teaching in arbitration possibly: i) offer academics a platform that facilitates entry into the market; and ii) offer practitioners visibility and provide an opportunity to show prowess and understanding of the technical aspects of international commercial arbitration. Therefore, it is very common for there to be an overlap between the people participating in both activities.[75]

This also means that in international commercial arbitration, policy analysis is primarily undertaken by people who participate in the industry as service providers. In theory, this could lead to a systematic predilection for sub-optimal regulatory decisions – ie, scholarship in this area may display a tendency to favour policy solutions that benefit service providers.[76] This might help explain the common tendency to see pro-arbitration

[71] Launched in 2006, Global Arbitration Review (GAR) is perhaps the most well-known of these publications.

[72] See Paula Hodges, 'The Arbitrator and the Arbitration Procedure, The Proliferation of 'Soft Laws' in International Arbitration: Time to Draw the Line?' in Christian Klausegger and others (eds), *Austrian Yearbook on International Arbitration 2015* (Wien, Manz'sche Verlags, 2015) 206.

[73] See, amongst many others, Edward Torgbor, 'Overview of the Disposition of Courts Towards Arbitration in Africa' in Emilia Onyema (ed), *Rethinking the role of African national courts in arbitration* (Alphen aan den Rijn, Kluwer Law International, 2018) 50; Johannes Koepp and Agnieszka Ason, 'An Anti-Enforcement Bias? The Application of the Substantive Public Policy Exception in Polish Annulment Proceedings' (2018) 35 *Journal of International Arbitration* 157.

[74] See Catenaccio (n 67) 164.

[75] See Hodges (n 72) 206; Ginsburg (n 69) 1340.

[76] See Stephen K Huber, 'State Regulation of Arbitration Proceedings: Judicial Review of Arbitration Awards by State Courts' (2009) 10 *Cardozo Journal of Dispute Resolution* 509, 512.

solutions being lauded in arbitral academic writing. At the same time, as is apparent in many texts, there is a concern with the long-term legitimacy and improvement of international arbitration.[77] Ultimately, increased legitimacy and usage of international arbitration will benefit those who offer services in this area, arguably producing an incentive for those operating in the area to defend regulatory solutions that maintain the legitimacy of the field.

Closely related to the idea above is the notion that within the field of international arbitration, there are strong incentives for participation in academic production. Practitioners and academics know that participating in this process is a key step in evolving their careers. As one commentator quipped:

> much scholarship on international commercial arbitration is difficult to distinguish from advertising.[78]

At the same time, it is clear that authors are conscious of how the opinions they express about the field will influence how the community perceives them.[79] This state of affairs leads to one notable particularity of international commercial arbitration. While often displaying high levels of expertise, academic and non-academic writings and speeches in international commercial arbitration rarely deviate significantly from the ideological foundations of arbitration. Ideas, such as arbitration is a worthy enterprise that should be pursued as an efficient alternative to state-based adjudication and that its autonomy should be protected, are almost always explicitly or implicitly present in the texts produced.[80]

This, in turn, might influence how arbitrators' professional obligations are interpreted and developed through academic scholarship. Speculatively, there is perhaps a tendency of the community to start from 'optimistic' assumptions regarding arbitrators' behaviour. Arbitrators are usually assumed to be trustworthy, well-intentioned and able to deal with complex legal questions effectively. These assumptions, therefore, might help explain the implied 'laissez-faire' perspective – ie, a preference for limited state intervention in the arbitration market – that underlies most of the writings in international arbitration.

[77] See, eg, Neil Andrew's address 'Improving Arbitration: Responsibilities and Rights – Roebuck Lecture 2017' available at: www.ciarb.org/docs/default-source/ciarbdocuments/events/flagship/events/roebuck-lecture/roebuck-lecture-2017.pdf?sfvrsn=4.

[78] Ralf Michaels, 'Dreaming Law without a State: Scholarship on Autonomous International Arbitration as Utopian Literature' (2013) 1 *London Review of International Law* 35, 37.

[79] In this regard, an article by Stephen Huber indicates how an author is often conscious that opinions outside the mainstream might put him or her at odds with the community: '[…] expanding state court review of arbitration awards offers a promising route for those who believe that arbitration needs to be checked – both in the sense of limiting arbitration and in quality control of arbitral awards. For this heresy, I expect to become a pariah among persons associated with the organized arbitration community, which consistently opposes any suggestion that courts do anything with respect to arbitration awards other than confirm them'. Huber (n 76) 512.

[80] This is not to say that the members of the community do not sometimes present criticisms to the status quo or spearhead calls for reform. But even when they do, attachment to the dominant goals of the community can still be found. For example, Paulsson's well publicised criticism of the party-appointed arbitrator system was, as per the author, ultimately rooted in the need to defend arbitral values such as independence and impartiality of the adjudicators. Jan Paulsson, 'Moral Hazard in International Dispute Resolution' (2010) 25 *ICSID Review* 339.

VI. The Creation of Regulatory Norms for International Commercial Arbitrators as a Unique Process

By way of conclusion, there are three main takeaways regarding the production of professional and ethical norms in international commercial arbitration. First, the creation of the regulatory norms applicable to international commercial arbitrators is the result of a composite of general legal principles, concrete judicial decisions, and internal discussions that are permanently ongoing within the arbitral community. Second, the development of these norms is the result of a unique mixed system where states establish the fundamental principles which arbitrators must adhere to and where the arbitral community develops and details them. Third, the particularities of the arbitration market explain the high-level participation in the process of creating and developing norms by the community members. These ideas will be addressed in turn.

A. A Diffuse Process of Norm Creation where Boundaries between Legal Norms, Soft Law and Merely Expected Behaviour are Blurred

In international commercial arbitration, it is possible to find arbitrators as both operating in an ethical no man's land or suffering from a bout of 'legislitis'.[81] On the one hand, state-backed 'hard law' often offers little more than open-ended demands regarding how an arbitrator should act.[82] As seen above, states' legislatures often do not indicate much more than an arbitrator must be 'independent' and 'impartial' or that, for example, the fees charged must be 'reasonable'.[83] On the other hand, arbitrators operate in an environment where, in practice, they are expected to observe many written and unwritten norms arising from a wide number of sources, from detailed ethical codes with varying degrees of enforceability to unprinted cultural expectations about how an arbitrator should act, talk, and behave.[84]

[81] See on the one side, Catherine A Rogers, 'Fit and Function in Legal Ethics: Developing a Code of Conduct for International Arbitration' (2001) 23 *Michigan Journal of International Law* 341, 342. On the other hand, warning against the risks of over-regulation see Ugo Draetta, 'The Transnational Procedural Rules for Arbitration and the Risks of Overregulation and Bureaucratization' (2015) 33 *ASA Bulletin* 327. See also Toby Landau and Romesh Weeramantry, 'A Pause for Thought' in AJ van den Berg (ed), *International arbitration: the coming of a new age?* (Alphen aan den Rijn, Kluwer Law International, 2013).

[82] In this sense, as one commentator has summarised: '… barbers and taxidermists are subject to far greater regulation than [arbitrators]'. See, Richard C Reuben, 'Constitutional Gravity: A Unitary Theory of Alternative Dispute Resolution and Public Civil Justice' (1999) 47 *UCLA Law Review* 949, 1013.

[83] Regarding independence and impartiality of arbitrators, see amongst others the English Arbitration Act 1996, s 1(a) and the Spanish Arbitration Act 2003, Art 17(1). Regarding the 'reasonableness' of fees see, amongst others, the English Arbitration Act 1996, s 64(1). These concepts will be further explored in ch 6.

[84] Michael Kerr, who served as a Lord Justice of Appeal and acted as an arbitrator, noted in his autobiography, that a 'successful arbitrator' should beyond 'total integrity and impartiality as both go without saying' also display an 'absence of any eccentricity or arrogance'. Michael Kerr, *As Far as I Remember* (Oxford, Hart Publishing, 2002) 326.a.

For the reasons set out in chapter four, the regulation of international arbitrators has not evolved in the same way as other professions. International commercial arbitration has not evolved organised institutions with the power to establish legally binding professional standards and generally applicable ethical rules.[85] That does not mean, however, that well-established rules of behaviour do not bind international commercial arbitrators. As in other professions, there are mechanisms for creating these norms that often evolve into rather detailed commands which determine issues such as what kind of disclosures arbitrators are expected to do in relation to an appointment or when arbitrators are supposed to refuse an appointment.

Due to the lack of centralised governing bodies with mandatory authority over these issues, determining the exact answer to many practical questions demands puzzling together different legal statutes, jurisprudence, soft norms, academic texts, and accepted practices within this community. Within this environment, it is often difficult to determine precisely where binding legal rules and social practices start and end. Many of the tenets that regulate international arbitrators do not have a single well-defined source but, instead, result from a process where certain principles and rules crystalise over time.

In this regard, arbitrators are different from judges, practising lawyers, or other organised professions. Often, arbitrators will not find a well-defined set of institutions that will state their function and determine their exact role within a given jurisdiction. Instead, regulatory norms are developed in community-dominated phenomena that operate across borders. While this does not mean that there is a universally accepted set of detailed legal obligations and ethical standards that arbitrators must comply with uniformly across the world,[86] this normative environment has been capable of producing universally accepted principles arbitrators are obligated to follow.

Therefore, within the international commercial arbitration community, it seems more apt to think of their regulation as being governed by several key principles to which many different sources contribute.[87] As discussed in the next chapter, some of these have developed into detailed rules, while others have remained vague. What is important to note is that arbitrators are more often regulated through universally accepted and oft-repeated concepts and formulas such as an 'arbitrator must be impartial and independent' or 'an arbitrator must conduct proceedings diligently' than steadfast precise rules. While detailed rules increasingly appear within international arbitration, they are almost always the result of the work of the arbitral community and are often not legally binding.

[85] As argued by Gaillard, in the context of an enlargement of the number of service providers and the geographical spaces where arbitration takes place, few actors have the legitimacy to generate norms that will be accepted by all relevant players. See Emmanuel Gaillard, 'Sociology of International Arbitration' (2015) 31 *Arbitration International* 1, 16.

[86] While there has been a strong tendency for standards and practice to be growingly uniform in the field of arbitration, some geographical and sector communities maintain sometimes specificities. The most traditional example of this distinction has been the acceptance in the US of 'partisans' co-arbitrators in the domestic arbitration context.

[87] See Fach Goméz (n 1) 11. See also William Park, 'Rectitude in International Arbitration' (2011) 27 *Arbitration International* 473, 512.

B. A Mixed Process of Creating Professional Norms: State Intervention and 'Self-regulation'

Further to the idea above, it should be noted that the regulation of international commercial arbitrators does not work: i) as a system of top-down imposition, where an external regulatory force imposes regulatory norms on a professional community; or ii) as a system of mandatory self-regulation where the members of the profession establish compulsory professional standards for all the members of the community.[88] Instead, there is a sui generis system of creating professional norms derived from the transnational nature of commercial arbitration where community consensus-building is central. In this sense, there is a division of regulatory power between the state and the arbitral community.

In broad terms, states establish the blueprint for international arbitration and arbitrators' obligation, often through a consensus approach expressed in international conventions such as the New York Convention and through national legislation, which most often establishes a high level of autonomy to arbitration. States then delegate to the arbitral community the responsibility to develop the few key principles established in their legislation into actual, meaningful commands.[89] This is made increasingly through the usage of soft law rules that, while not legally binding, are often highly influential in practice. These processes are aided by a mix of academic and non-academic writing from community members, which offers guidance on the applicable principles and rules, and offers prescriptive criticism on current practices.

As noted in this chapter, the arbitral community plays a dominant role in setting these regulatory frameworks.[90] However, the arbitral community's grasp over the normative environment that regulates international commercial arbitration takes place through different mechanisms than those usually associated with regulatory 'capturing'. Instead of traditional lobbying activities, the influence of the arbitral community takes place through: i) a quasi-monopoly on the production of the dominant understandings of what arbitration is and ought to be – in this sense, operating a sort of 'cognitive' capture of the regulatory process; ii) a strong commitment by the members of the community in participating directly and indirectly in the process of creating these norms; and iii) collectively rejecting as much

[88] See the qualification of 'self-regulation' in four types proposed by Black: mandated self-regulation, in which a collective group, an industry or profession for example, is required or designated by the government to formulate and enforce norms within a framework defined by the government, usually in broad terms; sanctioned self-regulation, in which the collective group itself formulates the regulation, which is then subjected to government approval; coerced self-regulation, in which the industry itself formulates and imposes regulation but in response to threats by the government that if it does not the government will impose statutory regulation; and voluntary self-regulation, where there is no active state involvement, direct or indirect, in promoting or mandating self-regulation. Julia Black, 'Constitutionalising Self-Regulation' (1996) 59 *The Modern Law Review* 24, 27.

[89] In this process, despite typically not being the drivers of these initiatives, sometimes the users of arbitration have some input in the content of these soft-law texts, with the views of general counsel in large corporations, in particular, being considered by members of the community. See, eg, Otto de Witt Wijnen, Nathalie Voser and Neomi Rao, 'Background Information on the IBA Guidelines on Conflicts of Interest in International Arbitration' (2004) 5 *Business Law International* 433, 436.

[90] Kaufmann-Kohler (n 40) 13. It is important to note that this is by no means a particularity of the arbitral community. In reality, '[l]iittle legislation relating to any profession is passed without being largely shaped by that profession.' William J Goode, 'Community Within a Community: The Professions' (1957) 22 *American Sociological Review* 194, 195.

as possible the jurisdictions, courts, or institutions that do not conform to their view of arbitration, forcing them to make changes if they intend to obtain any relevant role in the international commercial arbitration world.

C. The 'Collective Action Problem' of Creating Regulating Norms and the Arbitral Market

A final idea regarding the incentives for regulatory norm creation should be noted. The strong commitment of the members of the arbitral community to participating in this regulatory process is not an accident. Underlying the strong participation in the production of these normative standards by the community, one can find powerful individual market incentives. For arbitrators and practitioners, participating in the process allows visibility, networking opportunities, and showing proficiency within the community, which ultimately influences who succeeds in the profession.[91] For arbitral institutions, involvement in the process of creating and influencing the creation of norms of behaviour is a form of projecting commitment to the dominant values and increasing its visibility and reputation.

It should be noted that the creation of general welfare-oriented regulatory norms has, in a way, the nature of a 'public good' – ie, 'goods' for which consumption is both non-excludable and non-rivalrous and therefore may be 'underprovided' by the 'market'. In the case of professional regulation specifically, the activity of creating professional and ethical norms cannot be 'charged' to those who benefit from the activity as it is not feasible to negotiate a price with those who extract utility from this activity. In most cases, regulation, therefore, has to be undertaken by public entities or, alternatively, by private entities which are financed: i) by mandatory contributions of those regulated or others; or ii) by voluntary donations of time and money from those who are regulated or other parties.

In the context of the regulation of international commercial arbitrators, the bulk of regulatory work has been undertaken by arbitrators, practitioners, and arbitral institutions on a voluntary basis. As seen above, members of the arbitral community and arbitral institutions 'donate' their time to, among other activities: i) propose, shape, and review legislation passed in different jurisdictions; and ii) participate in associations, committees, and other groups that develop soft law. The high level of participation is, however, not only derived from a commitment to the profession's values but also from the fact that this participation is sometimes part of a business development strategy.

This feature of the international commercial arbitration market allows the defeat of the collective action problem that otherwise would make such widespread creation of norms

[91] In a typical example of how participation in community initiatives may benefit participants, well-known Austrian arbitrator Werner Melis describes how the negotiations for the UNCITRAL Arbitral Rules 1976: 'gave the opportunity to become acquainted with persons working in this field and to establish personal relationships and even friendships which were very helpful for the work in the professional field'. Werner Melis, 'The Role of Individuals in International Arbitration' in Patricia Shaughnessy and Sherlin Tung (eds), *The Powers and Duties of an Arbitrator: Liber Amicorum Pierre A. Karrer* (Alphen aan den Rijn, Kluwer Law International, 2017) 226.

unattainable.[92] Without the existence of direct and indirect advantages for the ones who participate in these processes, it would be difficult to understand the high number of normative creation initiatives and the high level of participation across the community in these projects. The participation across jurisdictions of elite members of the professions seems to indicate that members of the community perceive their costs of participating in this process (most importantly, their time invested in it) as lower than the benefits they ultimately obtain from these interactions.

[92] On the concept of the 'collective action problem' see Mancur Olson, *The Logic of Collective Action: Public Goods and the Theory of Groups* (Cambridge, MA, Harvard University Press, 1971) 11–16.

6

The Regulatory Norms Applicable to International Commercial Arbitrators

Chapter five explored the different sources contributing to the development of arbitrators' professional obligations. As discussed, states rarely provide details regarding the content of the professional norms applicable to arbitrators. Despite this, there is general agreement regarding the fundamental duties that are imposed upon arbitrators.[1] Arbitrators are far from being expected to be simple 'hired guns' who should comply with the request of producing an award.[2] Arbitrators are bound to special professional and ethical obligations, most importantly guaranteeing a fair adjudicative dispute resolution process.[3] While the application of these principles to actual real-life situations is often not evident, nor are those principles universally understood in the same way, the arbitral community has gone to great lengths to develop guidance regarding many of the practical issues that most commonly arise.[4]

This chapter will focus on four of the arbitrators' key professional obligations that illustrate how different issues have been addressed by the arbitral community: i) to be independent and impartial and disclose conflicts of interests; ii) to guarantee parties' due process rights; iii) to efficiently solve the dispute; and iv) to guarantee that substantive public policy considerations are not violated.[5] More than providing a thorough description of the content of these duties, this analysis intends to illustrate how, in regard to certain obligations, there are underlying incentives that make deviation more or less likely and how the international arbitration community has addressed these issues. This analysis allows insight into the heterogeneous set of regulatory responses given to different professional issues and how the level of regulatory detail can be linked to how problematic the underlying issue is.

[1] See Paula Hodges and Joanne Greenaway, 'Duties of Arbitrators' in JDM Lew and others (eds), *Arbitration in England: With Chapters on Scotland and Ireland* (Alphen aan den Rijn, Kluwer Law International, 2013) 317.

[2] See Alexis Mourre, 'Arbitration and Criminal Law: Reflections on the Duties of the Arbitrator' (2006) 22 *Arbitration International* 95, in particular 114.

[3] See Susan D Franck, 'The Role of International Arbitrators' (2005) 12 *ILSA Journal of International and Comparative Law* 499, 502. See also QMUL's 2015 International Arbitration Survey which indicates that participants mention speed and cost within the three most valuable characteristics of international arbitration in only 10% and 2% of the responses respectively. Neutrality is, in turn, mentioned by 25% of respondents. QMUL, '2015 International Arbitration Survey: Improvements and Innovations in International Arbitration', www.arbitration.qmul.ac.uk/docs/164761.pdf last accessed 17 October 2015.

[4] See Katherine L Lynch, *The Forces of Economic Globalization: Challenges to the Regime of International Commercial Arbitration* (Alphen aan den Rijn, Kluwer Law International, 2003) 94.

[5] This is not an exhaustive list of arbitrators' obligations. Other obligations such as, eg, the duty of maintaining the confidentiality of proceedings and completing the arbitrator's mandate exist. For a blackletter analysis of arbitrators' obligations, see Gary Born, *International Commercial Arbitration*, 2nd edn (Alphen aan den Rijn, Wolters Kluwer Law & Business, 2014) 1986; Hodges and Greenaway (n 1) 317.

I. Arbitrators' Obligation to be Independent and Impartial and to Disclose Conflicts of Interest

Arbitration has developed a set of detailed rules on when to disclose conflicts of interest based on the basic principles of independence and impartiality. These offer a prime example of how the arbitral community built detailed ethical duties on the basis of very general principles. National legislators,[6] courts,[7] arbitral institutions,[8] and leading commentators[9] all express directly and indirectly that the arbitrators – or at least the arbitral tribunal as a whole – must always be independent and impartial and consequently disclose any conflicts of interest they might have. The idea of the arbitral tribunal as a neutral decider has not only become one of the key selling points of international commercial arbitration[10] but also, perhaps, the bedrock of the argument for the legitimacy of international arbitration.[11]

Still, legislative texts do not define the exact meaning of these concepts and how they should be interpreted. Instead, it has been up to the arbitral community to establish their meaning through commentary and, most importantly, soft law texts. An analysis of how these obligations have been crystallised allows an illustration of a number of interesting points, specifically that: i) the regulatory norms applicable to international arbitrators have demonstrated a tendency to become institutionalised; and ii) the international arbitration community seems to respond to areas where incentives for non-compliance are higher by upping the level of detail of its rules. However, before turning to these points, it will be necessary to review the concept and meaning of independence and impartiality and why the duty of disclosure is a particularly sensitive topic in arbitration. This will be discussed next.

A. The Concepts of Independence, Impartiality, and the Duty of Disclosure Imposed on Arbitrators

In conceptual terms, independence and impartiality are sometimes used to refer to two closely related but different ideas. Some authorities regard independence as concerned only with objective, external matters involving the question as to whether an arbitrator has connections or relationships with a party (or its counsel) which render them – at least

[6] To this effect, eg, the English Arbitration Act establishes that 'the object of arbitration is to obtain the fair resolution of disputes by an impartial tribunal'. English Arbitration Act 1996, s 1(a). Similarly, the Spanish Arbitration Act establishes that: '[a]ll arbitrators must be and remain independent and impartial throughout the arbitration.' Spanish Arbitration Act 2003, Art 17(1).

[7] As Lord Clarke highlighted in Jivraj v Hashwani: '[t]he dominant purpose of appointing an arbitrator is the impartial resolution of dispute between the parties in accordance with the terms of the agreement'. *Jivraj v Hashwani* [2011] UKSC 40.

[8] See, amongst others, ICC 2021 Rules, Art 11(1); 2018 HKIAC Administered Arbitration Rules, Art 11(1); 2016 SIAC Rules, Art 13(1).

[9] See, amongst others, Born (n 5) 1759; Julian DM Lew, Loukas A Mistelis and Stefan Kröll, *Comparative International Commercial Arbitration* (Alphen aan den Rijn, Kluwer Law International, 2003) 255.

[10] See, amongst others, Lew, Mistelis and Kröll (n 9) 6.

[11] See, Stephan Schill, 'Conceptions of Legitimacy of International Arbitration' in David Caron and others (eds), *Practising Virtue: Inside International Arbitration* (Oxford, Oxford University Press, 2015) 118.

apparently[12] – dependent on the party. In contrast, impartiality is said to be concerned with subjective biases and predispositions involving the dispute before the arbitrator.[13] In practical terms, however, independence and impartiality are terms often used together to refer generically to the idea that an arbitrator must be objectively and subjectively able to decide a dispute neutrally and fairly.

This general obligation of independence and impartiality creates several practical duties for the arbitrators. First, an arbitrator has a duty to decline to serve in a proceeding if they are not fully satisfied that they can serve impartially. Equally, an arbitrator should refuse to serve in an arbitral tribunal if they have a material connection to the parties, their counsel, or the dispute, which would lead the arbitrator not to be independent.[14] In the same vein, even if the arbitrator believes they could be independent and impartial, when, from the point of view of a reasonable third person, there are circumstances which give rise to justifiable doubts, the arbitrator also has a duty to decline the appointment.[15] Further, an arbitrator also has a duty to disclose any information to the parties that may give rise to doubts as to the arbitrator's impartiality or independence, even if they consider that such circumstances do not disqualify them from accepting the appointment.[16]

These obligations comprise an element of personal self-regulation imposed upon the arbitrators and the parties. In the first instance, it is left to the arbitrators to evaluate a possible conflict of interest according to their understanding of the applicable norms. Based on the information disclosed by the arbitrator and the information they can independently obtain about the arbitrator, parties must then determine whether they are satisfied with their independence and impartiality. In instances where they are not, they may challenge the appointee.[17] While rules may vary, the challenge of an arbitrator's independence and impartiality will then be decided by the arbitral institution or the arbitral tribunal as a whole – ie, the challenged arbitrator and remaining arbitrators if existing.[18] If the challenge is refused, parties will then usually have the right to escalate the matter to the competent national court.

Operating in an adversarial system, parties have an incentive to investigate whether arbitrators are independent and impartial. Deciding to challenge is often a strategic decision, with parties calculating the benefits, risks, and costs of undertaking a challenge. In the first moment, the decision is kept within the community by being taken by the panel or the arbitral institution. Still, if the challenge is not accepted, recourse to national courts is possible, allowing for an external review of that more self-regulatory approach. It should be noted that if parties do not present an objection to the arbitration in a

[12] See, IBA Rules of Ethics for International Arbitrators 1987, s 3(2). For a discussion, see Gary Born, *International Commercial Arbitration*, 2nd edn (Alphen aan den Rijn, Wolters Kluwer Law & Business, 2014) 1762.

[13] Gary Born, *International Commercial Arbitration: Commentary and Materials* (Alphen aan den Rijn, Kluwer Law International, 2001) 734–735. See also, Sam Luttrell, *Bias Challenges in International Commercial Arbitration: The Need for a 'real Danger' Test* (Alphen aan den Rijn, Kluwer Law International. 2009) 21.

[14] See IBA Guidelines on Conflicts of Interest in International Arbitration (IBA Guidelines), Standard 2(a). See also Margaret L Moses, *The Principles and Practice of International Commercial Arbitration* (Cambridge, Cambridge University Press, 2012) 136.

[15] See IBA Guidelines, Standard 2(b).

[16] See IBA Guidelines, Standard 3(a).

[17] See UNCITRAL Model Law, Art 13(2); ICC Arbitration Rules, Art 14.

[18] See UNCITRAL Model Law, Art 13(3).

timely manner, any subsequent challenge regarding the information disclosed might be unsuccessful.[19]

B. The Tension between Arbitrators' Short-term Self-interest and the Community Interest

An arbitrator's decision to refuse an appointment or disclose a potential conflict of interest is one of the thorniest issues arbitrators face. By declining to serve or deciding to disclose a connection to one of the parties, the arbitrator often foregoes considerable payment and, sometimes, valuable opportunities to advance their careers. At the same time, as will be discussed in more detail in chapter seven,[20] the arbitrator will also have to consider how failing to comply with this duty may jeopardise their position in the market.[21] Further, as will be discussed in the next chapter, the decisions to refuse or disclose are influenced by personal moral codes of conduct and social pressures from professional peers.

Further, it is worth considering how each arbitrator's decision to accept or refuse an appointment and disclose or not disclose connections affects the community. As the success of voluntary commercial arbitration is ultimately linked to the belief that arbitrators produce unbiased decisions, violations of these obligations have the potential to affect not only those who break the norms but also other members of the community.[22] Conversely, arbitrators' compliance with these obligations positively impacts other community members who benefit from the increased legitimacy of international arbitration.[23]

In this sense, the legitimacy of international arbitration depends on arbitrators voluntarily complying with the requirements of independence, impartiality, and disclosure obligations, spurring the community as a whole to be interested in compliance.[24] As explained in chapter five, this creates an incentive for the arbitral community to deal with this issue by addressing it in soft law regulation and, due to the strong incentives for individual involvement in community initiatives, for members of the community to participate in these regulatory efforts. The IBA Guidelines on Conflicts of Interest represent one of the clearest examples of the community identifying and addressing an issue through a set of common rules. The Guidelines will be discussed in more detail next.

[19] Karel Daele, *Challenge and Disqualification of Arbitrators in International Arbitration* (Alphen aan den Rijn, Kluwer Law International, 2012) 120.

[20] See, ch 7, section I.B.

[21] See Herman Verbist and Erik Schäfer, *ICC Arbitration in Practice*, 2nd edn (Alphen aan den Rijn, Kluwer Law International, 2015) 67. See also Paula Hodges, 'Equality of Arms in International Arbitration: Who Is the Best Arbiter of Fairness in the Conduct of Proceedings?' in Andrea Menaker (ed), *International arbitration and the rule of law: contribution and conformity* (Alphen aan den Rijn, Kluwer Law International, 2017) 628.

[22] See Hodges (n 21) 603.

[23] See James H Carter, 'The Culture of Arbitration and the Defense of Arbitral Legitimacy' in David D Caron and others (eds), *Practising Virtue: Inside International Arbitration* (Oxford, Oxford University Press, 2015) 102.

[24] See Will Sheng Wilson Koh, 'Think Quality Not Quantity: Repeat Appointments and Arbitrator Challenges' (2017) 34 *Journal of International Arbitration* 711, 713; Nathalie Allen and Daisy Mallett, 'Arbitrator Disclosure – No Room For The Colour Blind' (2011) 7 *Asian International Arbitration Journal* 118, 119.

C. The IBA Guidelines on Conflicts of Interest as an Example of the Tendency to Institutionalise Professional and Ethical Rules

As discussed in the previous chapter, professional and ethical obligations in international commercial arbitration have been crystallised into different texts in the last few decades. In a context where arbitrators may sometimes have strong, short-term incentives to deviate from their obligations, but the community generally has a strong interest in compliance, significant attention has been paid to the issues of impartiality, independence and disclosure. The community has addressed these issues by establishing a widely used text: the IBA Guidelines on Conflicts of Interest in International Arbitration. This represents one of the most effective instances of arbitral self-regulation, with the community successfully developing, spreading and largely self-accepting a set of norms.[25]

i. The Structure and Originality of the IBA Guidelines on Conflicts of Interest

One of the most interesting aspects of the IBA relates to its innovation and practical nature as a regulatory text within arbitration. Indeed, the Guidelines not only establish general standards regarding impartiality, independence, and disclosure but also provide lists of practical applications of these general standards. They do so by providing a so-called 'traffic light system' – ie, red (waivable and non-waivable), orange and green lists describing possible circumstances arbitrators may face.[26] While the situations described are not an exhaustive list, they are intended to provide an overview of the circumstances where arbitrators should refuse an appointment or disclose a connection to the parties, as well as situations in which such disclosure is not necessary.[27]

Situations described in the red list are either: i) serious enough to warrant that an arbitrator can only accept their nomination if the parties, being aware of the conflict of interest situation, expressly state their willingness to have such a person act as arbitrator (waivable list); or ii) so serious that even if both parties, fully aware of the circumstances, expressly accept that arbitrator, they may not act in that case. An example of the first situation is an arbitrator who is a lawyer in the same law firm as the counsel to one of the parties.[28] An example of the second is an arbitrator who, at the same time, acts as a manager or director or is a member of the supervisory board of one of the parties.[29]

Situations described in the orange list may or may not give rise to doubts about the arbitrator's impartiality or independence, depending on the full circumstances of the case.[30]

[25] See Hodges (n 21) 604; Gabrielle Kaufmann-Kohler, 'Soft Law in International Arbitration: Codification and Normativity' (2010) 1 *Journal of International Dispute Settlement* 283, 296; Diego P Fernández Arroyo, 'Soft Law and Arbitral Procedure: A Conditioned But Inescapable Couple' (2018) 7 *European International Arbitration Review* 71, 75.

[26] See Hodges (n 21) 602.

[27] See Luttrell (n 13) 201.

[28] See IBA Guidelines, 2.3.3. It is worth noting that this IBA Guidelines have significant consequences for the participation of partners of law firms in arbitral proceedings as arbitrators, especially for those working in large law firms. See Jean-François Poudret and Sébastien Besson, *Comparative Law of International Arbitration* (London, Sweet & Maxwell, 2007) 349.

[29] See IBA Guidelines, 1.2.

[30] See Otto de Witt Wijnen, Nathalie Voser and Neomi Rao, 'Background Information on the IBA Guidelines on Conflicts of Interest in International Arbitration' (2004) 5 *Business Law International* 433, 434.

They should, however, be disclosed by the arbitrator to the parties, who then can decide whether they want to challenge the arbitrator in the appropriate forum: the arbitral tribunal itself, the arbitral institutions or the competent national court. Examples of situations covered in the orange list include an arbitrator who has served as counsel for one of the parties within the past three years or the arbitrator having publicly advocated a position on the case.[31]

Finally, the IBA Guidelines' green list also covers situations in which the arbitrator neither has a duty to disclose nor can the situation be used as the basis for a challenge to the arbitrator. Examples of these situations include: i) the arbitrator teaching in the same faculty or school as another arbitrator or one of the counsel to one of the parties; ii) the arbitrator holding an insignificant number of shares in one of the parties if such party is publicly listed; or iii) the arbitrator having a relationship with one of the parties or its affiliates through a social media network.[32] This green list has, as an objective, the clarification that some links between arbitrators and the parties or counsel should not serve as the basis of contention, an important goal in a context where some parties have been seen as misusing challenging mechanisms.[33]

ii. The Popularity and Success of the IBA Guidelines as a Regulatory Initiative of the Arbitral Community

Different codes of ethics, guidelines of behaviour and codes of conduct directed to both international arbitrators and counsel have been developed with different degrees of acceptance and influence. As mentioned above, it is arguable that none of these texts have been more influential than the IBA Guidelines.[34] Albeit subject to criticism from some who see these Guidelines as inappropriate in particular markets, it has been nonetheless widely adopted by arbitral tribunals and arbitrators and has often been referred to by national courts.[35] An interesting, albeit difficult to fully answer, question relates to knowing why some texts, such as the IBA Guidelines, have been accepted while others have largely been ignored.[36] While it is not easy to fully identify the reasons that explain this text's wide acceptance, some factors can be recognised as contributing to its popularity.

The first reason for the popularity of the Guidelines may derive from the fact that independence and impartiality are complex, open-ended concepts that need some level of development.[37] Since state legislatures usually do not detail the type of situations that would lead arbitrators not to be independent or impartial, the need to establish some common ground between agents was clear. Without the emergence of a text generally accepted in the community, participants in the international commercial arbitration would be forced to either navigate a complex repository of national case law they might not always be

[31] See IBA Guidelines, 3.1.1 and 3.5.2.

[32] See IBA Guidelines, 4.3.3, 4.4.2 and 3.5.2.

[33] See Born (n 5) 1842.

[34] Luttrell, eg, argues that the IBA Guidelines are so widely used they are part of *lex mercatoria*. Luttrell (n 13) 27. See also Allen and Mallett (n 24) 121.

[35] See Kaufmann-Kohler (n 25) 14; Hodges (n 21) 212; Luttrell (n 13) 195.

[36] See Hodges (n 21) 576.

[37] See Kaufmann-Kohler (n 25) 14.

familiar[38] with or rules of thumb that might not be universally accepted inside or outside the community.

A second reason for the popularity of the Guidelines may also be related to its eminently practical nature and, in this context, the original labelling system. The system of red, orange and green lists has been praised as providing an accessible but, at the same time, flexible approach to the most common situations an arbitrator may face. In a context where arbitrators increasingly come from different jurisdictions and legal cultures, the IBA guidelines provide a simple and accessible reference tool to which arbitrators and parties may refer as guidance. Also, albeit not often updated – only once in 2014 – the IBA Guidelines have also been able to incorporate new realities, such as the emergence of third-party funders within international arbitration or the usage of social media, into their guidelines.

A final notable reason that helps explain the popularity of the IBA Guidelines relates to the standing and reputation of its authors. The IBA Guidelines were developed initially in 2004 by 19 very well-known members of the international arbitration community. In a similar fashion, the subcommittee responsible for its 2014 revision was also composed of key figures from the arbitral world. Likely, the standing of its authors lent prestige to the Guidelines. Further, the involvement of leading figures, selected amongst those routinely appointed to high-profile arbitral tribunals, conceivably led to visibility and facilitated the use of the Guidelines. Still, it should be noted that the involvement of leading figures in the creation of a soft law text in international arbitration does not guarantee wide adoption.[39]

II. Arbitrators' Obligation to Guarantee the Procedural Fairness of the Arbitral Proceedings

Closely related to the idea that an arbitrator must be independent and impartial is the notion that an arbitral proceeding must respect basic notions of procedural justice. International conventions, legal statutes, institutional rules, and leading commentators all point to the existence of clear obligations by arbitrators to guarantee procedural fairness.[40] Exploring this obligation will allow uncovering a different regulatory approach from the established regarding the disclosure of conflicts of interest. As will be seen, regarding parties' procedural rights, the arbitral community produced less guidance, giving more latitude to arbitral tribunals to address these issues as they see fit. It is worth noting that in regard to guaranteeing procedural rights to the parties, there is less tension between arbitrators' self-interest and their obligations. These ideas will be explored next.

[38] See Luttrell (n 13) 27.

[39] See, eg, the case of the IBA Guidelines on Party Representation in International Arbitration which also involved many key members of the arbitral community in its elaboration. Despite some relevance, it has not achieved the same widespread adoption as the IBA Guidelines on Conflicts of Interest in International Arbitration.

[40] See, for all, Fabricio Fortese and Lotta Hemmi, 'Procedural Fairness and Efficiency in International Arbitration' (2015) 3 *Groningen Journal of International Law* 110.

A. The Concepts of Due Process and Procedural Fairness

Under the current legal arrangements, parties are reasonably free to establish the rules that will apply to the solution of their dispute. They can, amongst other issues, decide the number of arbitrators that will decide the dispute, how and when parties shall present their submissions, and how and when hearings will take place. The parties can do so by expressly defining these issues by agreement or by referring to institutional arbitral rules that will often regulate these issues. Typically, the procedural questions not addressed by the parties' agreement or the applicable rules will be solved by the arbitral tribunal, which is usually granted by the applicable laws and rules' broad discretion and flexibility in the conduct of arbitral proceedings.[41]

While great latitude is given to the parties and the arbitrators to establish the procedural rules that will guide the functioning of the arbitral tribunal, certain basic principles, such as the right to present their case and the principle of equality of treatment between the parties, must be respected independently of what rules the parties agreed upon.[42] These principles create obligations for arbitrators. These include the idea that the arbitral tribunal must allow each party a fair opportunity to present its evidence and arguments, offer due notice of the start of any proceeding and of the time and place of any hearing and, where appropriate, ensure that the parties are informed of the procedural aspects of the process.[43]

B. The Underlying Incentives for Compliance with Obligations Relating to Due Process

It was noted above that in regard to their obligation to be independent and impartial, arbitrators sometimes have to balance their own short-term interest of increasing their income by accepting an appointment and their obligation to comply with impartiality and independence. Such tension does not exist in the same way in regard to the obligation of arbitrators to guarantee procedural fairness. In most situations, respecting procedural fairness does not represent a significant loss to an arbitrator. Complying with a party's request to present documents, make a written submission, or correctly notify the parties does not often entail direct significant costs beyond a possible increase in the arbitral tribunal workload.

On the other hand, not respecting these rules may displease at least one of the parties and open the arbitral award to the possibility of being annulled or refused enforcement in a court of law, consequences arbitrators generally would want to avoid.[44] In the current framework, incentives seem to lead arbitrators to comply with parties' procedural rights in most circumstances. In fact, this underlying incentive structure may help explain a tendency for what some have perceived as an over-protection of parties' procedural rights. Indeed,

[41] See Philipp Habegger, 'Saving Time and Costs in Arbitration' in Manuel Arroyo (ed), *Arbitration in Switzerland: The Practitioner's Guide*, 2nd edn (Alphen aan den Rijn, Kluwer Law International, 2018) 2595.

[42] See, amongst others, English Arbitration Act 1996, s 33.

[43] See CIArb's Code of Professional and Ethical Conduct for Members (October 2009), Rule 5. See also CRP's Code of Ethics for Arbitrators in Commercial Disputes, Cannon IV.

[44] See Klaus Peter Berger and J Ole Jensen, 'Due Process Paranoia and the Procedural Judgment Rule: A Safe Harbour for Procedural Management Decisions by International Arbitrators' (2016) 32 *Arbitration International* 415, 420.

some have protested that arbitrators too often entertain dilatory requests by parties, leading proceedings to drag more than would otherwise be necessary.[45] This idea will be picked up again when discussing arbitrators' efficiency obligation.[46]

C. Soft Law as a Bridge between Different Legal Cultures

Regulatory soft law in international commercial arbitration can be seen as having paid less attention to ideas of 'procedural fairness' when compared, for example, to the level of detail found regarding arbitrators' independence and impartiality obligations. In particular, there is less development regarding what is meant by concepts such as parties' equality or a right to a fair hearing. That is, however, not to say that no rules exist relating to how parties' procedures should be conducted. The goal of such texts, however, does not seem primarily to be to guarantee parties' procedural rights. Instead, they seem directed at bridging different understandings of how arbitral proceedings should be conducted, a particular concern when parties come from different legal cultures.

i. The IBA Rules as Another Example of a Widely Adopted Regulatory Initiative of the Arbitral Community

The most well-known of these soft-law texts are the IBA Rules on Taking of Evidence in International Arbitration, a soft-law text which parties and arbitrators often adopt to govern their proceedings and is influential even when not expressly agreed upon.[47] Its origin can be traced back to the 1983 Supplementary Rules Governing the Presentation and Reception of Evidence in International Commercial Arbitration, its current form having been developed in 1999 by a working group of the IBA and revised in 2010 to deal with perceived transformations in arbitration. As with the IBA Guidelines on Conflicts of Interest, key figures of the arbitration world developed the IBA Rules on Taking of Evidence, with some of the most well-known practitioners and arbitrators participating in either their creation or revision.[48]

The IBA Rules tackle several different issues, including document production, witness statements, expert witnesses, and evidentiary hearings. To a great extent, rather than creating obligations upon the arbitral tribunal, it directs parties on how to present their evidence, allowing the arbitral tribunal extensive powers and discretion in how to conduct the proceedings. Still, some obligations are imposed on the arbitral tribunal, particularly regarding the admissibility and assessment of the evidence. An example of such obligations can be found in Article 9.2(b). This provision determines that the arbitral tribunal shall, at the request of a party or on its own motion, exclude evidence covered by legal impediment or privilege under the legal or ethical rules that the arbitral tribunal determines to be applicable.

[45] See ibid 418.

[46] See ch 6, section III.

[47] Qualifying the IBA Guidelines as a 'commonly accepted standard', see Detlev Kühner, 'The Revised IBA Rules on the Taking of Evidence in International Arbitration' (2010) 27 *Journal of International Arbitration* 667.

[48] See Michael McIlwrath and John Savage, *International Arbitration and Mediation: A Practical Guide* (Alphen aan den Rijn, Kluwer Law International, 2010) 289.

ii. The IBA Rules as an Example of Regulatory Competition between Different Legal Cultures?

As with the IBA Guidelines on Conflicts of Interest, the IBA Rules have not been unanimously praised. Criticism of the IBA Rules has focused on the idea that, despite the collaboration of members of different jurisdictions in their elaboration, these Rules have increasingly led arbitration proceedings to assume an adversarial nature more akin to the 'common law' litigation tradition.[49] In particular, there have been concerns that the IBA Rules may allow requests for document production that are too extensive, a practice – sometimes analogous to the maligned discovery proceedings of US litigation – that has been criticised as leading to increased costs and delays in arbitral proceedings.[50]

Beyond these apprehensions, it is also possible to speculate that some of those apprehensions betray an underlying market competition between legal cultures. Some from a civil law background may perceive the evolution of arbitration that increasingly relies on cross-examination, written witness statements, and document production to favour Anglo-American law firms and those trained in a common law background where such litigation techniques are more common than in civil law jurisdictions. It should, however, be noted that: i) even among 'civil law' practitioners, many favour the application of IBA Rules;[51] and ii) this divide between 'civil law'/'common law' practitioners over the IBA Rules has not really extended to discussions over other soft law texts.[52]

Indeed, despite a few flares of tension between arbitral practitioners of different jurisdictions, the practice seems to indicate a globalisation of approaches to arbitral proceedings techniques and how arbitrators are supposed to act.[53] In this sense, arbitration has become increasingly insulated from local litigation approaches. Again, the arbitral community can find a competitive edge in separating arbitral proceedings' techniques from litigation in national courts. The more distinct arbitral proceedings are from domestic litigation, the more those who practise it are shielded from the potential competition of the large number of lawyers who practise court litigation.[54]

[49] See David W Rivkin, 'The Revised IBA Rules on the Taking of Evidence' in Arthur W Rovine (ed), *Contemporary Issues in International Arbitration and Mediation* (Leiden, Brill Academic Publishers, 2012) 212; See also the Draft Prague Rules (Draft 1 September 2018): 'From a civil law perspective, the IBA Rules are still closer to common law traditions, as they follow a more adversarial approach regarding document production, fact witnesses and Party-appointed experts. In addition, the parties' entitlement to cross-examine witnesses is almost being taken for granted. These factors contribute greatly to the costs of arbitration, while their efficiency is sometimes rather questionable.'

[50] Noting the fears but concluding, in his experience, that the IBA rules allow to streamline arbitral proceedings, see Rivkin (n 49) 251.

[51] It should be noted that in regards to the IBA Guidelines on Taking of Evidence, even its critics admit it has become an unavoidable tool for international arbitration tribunals and counsel alike. See Matthias Scherer, 'Limits of the IBA Rules on the Taking of Evidence: Document Production Based on Contractual or Statutory Rights' (2010) 13 *International Arbitration Law Review*; Rivkin (n 49) 212.

[52] See Klaus Peter Berger, 'Common Law vs. Civil Law in International Arbitration: The Beginning or the End?' (2019) 36 *Journal of International Arbitration* 295, 303.

[53] See McIlwrath and Savage (n 48) 225; Elena V Helmer, 'International Commercial Arbitration: Americanized, Civilized, or Harmonized' (2003) 19 *Ohio State Journal on Dispute Resolution* 35, 37.

[54] See Tom Ginsburg, 'The Culture of Arbitration' (2003) 36 *The Vanderbilt Journal of Transnational Law* 1335, 1344.

III. Arbitrators' Obligation to be Diligent, Cost-efficient, and Respecting Reasonable Timeframes

Closely interlinking with due process duties is the arbitrators' duty to be cost-efficient, diligent and respect reasonable timeframes for concluding arbitral proceedings. These obligations have become increasingly relevant due to the perception that arbitral proceedings' total costs have escalated and proceedings have become lengthier.[55] Partially, this may be explained by the increased tendency of arbitrators to guarantee parties the ability to present their cases fully. Other factors, however, also seem to play a role. Before analysing this issue and the regulatory approaches in this area, it will be first necessary to review what obligations arbitrators are expected to accomplish under these principles.

A. The Concept of Efficiency in Arbitration

As with the obligations to be independent and impartial and respect due process, the obligation to be 'efficient' can be found in national legislation,[56] arbitration rules,[57] soft law,[58] and the texts of leading commentators of international arbitration.[59] To this effect, the English and Wales Arbitration Act 1996 emphasises in its section 1 that, as a general principle, 'the object of arbitration is to obtain the fair resolution of disputes by an impartial tribunal without unnecessary delay or expense'. In this sense, these two ideas of timely decisions and keeping costs reasonable can be seen as the core of the efficiency duty that arbitrators must comply with. These two notions are worth analysing in more detail.

In regard to the idea of avoiding 'unnecessary delay', it is often highlighted that a well-functioning system of international commercial arbitration demands that arbitrators provide their award in reasonable time frames. In a context where international commercial arbitration has, to an extent, lost its edge as a time-saving dispute resolution mechanism,[60] the goal of increasing efficiency has been the focus of arbitral institutions and the community as a whole.[61] This is, in fact, one of the rare areas where several institutional arbitral rules and a few arbitral legislations provide clear substantive guidance on what metrics should be accomplished. For

[55] See Philipp Habegger, 'The Arbitrator's Duty of Efficiency: A Call for Increased Utilization of Arbitral Powers' in Patricia Shaughnessy and Sherlin Tung (eds), *The Powers and Duties of an Arbitrator: Liber Amicorum Pierre A. Karrer* (Alphen aan den Rijn, Kluwer Law International, 2017) 123.

[56] See, eg, UNCITRAL Model Law, Art 14(1), determining the possibility of terminating an arbitrator's mandate if he fails to act with undue delay.

[57] See, eg, UNCITRAL Arbitral Rules, Art 17(1).

[58] See, eg, Canon I, para F of the American Bar Association, Code of Ethics for Arbitrators in Commercial Disputes.

[59] See William K II Slate, 'Cost and Time Effectiveness of Arbitration' (2010) 3 *Contemporary Asia Arbitration Journal* 182; Rémy Gerbay, 'Is the End Nigh Again? An Empirical Assessment of the 'Judicialization' of International Arbitration' (2014) 25 *American Journal of International Arbitration* 223, 224.

[60] See Franck (n 3) 500; Hermann Bietz, 'On the State and Efficiency of International Arbitration – Could the German `Relevance Method` Be Useful or Not?' (2014) 12 *SchiedsVZ* 121, 122.

[61] See ICC, 'ICC Arbitration Commission Report on Techniques for Controlling Time and Costs in Arbitration' (2012).

example, the ICC, HKIAC and SCC provide a soft (in the sense that it can be extended under some circumstances) time limit of six months for the arbitral award to be produced.

It is important to highlight that this obligation is not only thought of as to determine that the arbitrators should not protract their own activity unnecessarily. Instead, it is also increasingly understood as creating an obligation for arbitrators to control the behaviour of the parties that may result in an unwarranted delay to the proceedings. This will include a duty to limit parties' over-extension of submissions and extensive unfocused evidence production. Also, and perhaps more critically, arbitrators are particularly expected to guarantee the conclusion of the arbitral proceedings in due time when one of the parties – usually a respondent who considers it likely that they will lose the case – is not interested in a swift decision and repeatedly tries to stall the arbitral proceedings.

In regard to the obligation of avoiding 'unnecessary cost', it is also possible to see it from a double perspective. On the one hand, the arbitral tribunal is obligated to charge only 'reasonable' fees and expenses,[62] a special concern when it is upon the arbitral tribunal to determine its own fees and costs. On the other hand, this also creates an obligation for the arbitral tribunal to control the parties' behaviour. Increasing emphasis is being put on the idea that an arbitral tribunal should not allow practices that unnecessarily increase the cost of the arbitral proceedings.[63] These are often expressed as an encouragement for arbitrators to conduct proceedings in a way that avoids repeated extensive submissions and document production, unnecessary translation costs, and reliance on costly experts' reports, amongst similar concerns.

Finally, a different, albeit, connected obligation has also started to be emphasised: the idea that arbitrators are mandated to prepare proceedings and the award themselves and should not delegate their obligations to non-members of the arbitral tribunal.[64] Indeed, several different actors have expressed that arbitrators must 'prepare appropriately for the dispute resolution process concerned'[65] and 'devote the time and attention to its completion that the parties are reasonably entitled to expect'.[66] These concerns are ultimately linked with the perception that some arbitrators accept too many cases or cumulate the acceptance of appointments with too many other professional commitments, leading them to either not discharge their obligations in a timely fashion or subdelegate tasks that should be carried out directly by the arbitrators in either a tribunal secretary or a 'foreign' member to the tribunal.[67]

B. The Underlying Incentives for Compliance and Deviation in Relation to the Obligations of Efficiency and Diligence

The concern with 'efficiency' is a particularly thorny issue due to the dynamics of the arbitration market. In most markets, competitive pressures often lead providers to offer goods

[62] See English Arbitration Act 1996, s 64(1).

[63] See Habegger (n 55) 126.

[64] The exact limits to what constitute acceptable and non-acceptable delegation remains, however, controversial. See Felix Dasser and Emmanuel O Igbokwe, 'The Award and the Courts, Efficient Drafting of the Arbitral Award: Traditional Ways Revisited – Lesson Learned from the Past?' in Christian Klausegger and others (eds), *Austrian Yearbook on International Arbitration 2019* (Wien, Manz'sche Verlags-und Universitätsbuchhandlung, 2019) 306.

[65] See CIArb's Code of Professional and Ethical Conduct for Members 2009, Rule 7.

[66] See AAA's Code of Ethics for Arbitrators in Commercial Disputes 2003, Cannon I(b).

[67] See Constantine Partasides, 'The Fourth Arbitrator? The Role of Secretaries to Tribunals in International Arbitration' (2002) 18 *Arbitration International* 147.

and services at the lowest cost and highest quality to obtain an edge over competitors. However, the particularities of the arbitration market lead this process to not play in the same way in relation to arbitrators. As discussed in more detail in chapters three and seven, arbitrators are selected for reasons beyond the price and quality – in the sense of diligence – of the services they provide. In fact, as discussed in those chapters, strategic decisions regarding which arbitrator will most advance the parties' interests can play a decisive role in the arbitrators' selection.

That is not to say that there are no incentives for arbitrators to be proactive, timely, keep costs down and be diligent. Many selections often favour the most competent arbitrators in the sense that those who prove capable of solving disputes quickly and fairly will likely build a strong reputation in the market. Still, countervailing incentives should be considered. First, as discussed above, arbitrators often seem to be particularly sensitive to guaranteeing parties' procedural rights, leading them to accept unnecessary submissions, evidence production and procedural requests under pressure to ensure parties' 'right to be heard' – a phenomenon that some have dubbed 'due process paranoia'.[68] The underlying calculation by some arbitrators seems to be that the reputational cost of undertaking longer and more expensive arbitral proceedings is lower than that of not allowing parties to present their cases fully.[69]

Second, arbitrators also seem to have incentives to deviate from their obligation to not over-accept nominations. Here, the underlying calculation by some arbitrators seems to be that monetary and visibility gains from being appointed in a high number of proceedings trump the long-term reputational 'cost' of not being fully available for every proceeding.[70] Lack of transparency regarding arbitrators' past performance and availability can exacerbate these issues. It must also be said that this situation seems to result from the preference to select primarily seasoned practitioners, an expectable choice, as discussed in chapter three, in the context of a risk-averse and low-price competitive environment.[71]

In any case, a situation akin to the discussion regarding the obligation of independence and impartiality emerges. While some arbitrators may have an individual incentive to deviate from their obligations of efficiency and diligence by undertaking too many appointments, the arbitral community as a whole benefits from compliance in the sense that if most arbitrators are diligent, arbitration will see greater usage and legitimacy. Growing discontent with rising costs and long timeframes has been seen as a potential threat to users' trust in the international arbitration system.[72] Therefore, the arbitral community has an advantage if it can create the conditions to deliver awards within short timeframes and with competitive costs.

[68] See Berger and Jensen (n 44) 418.

[69] In the context of decisions to set aside or not enforce an award being rare, making cautious procedural decisions has been compared to paying an insurance premium against an unlikely, but extremely damaging, event. See, Robin Oldenstam, 'Due Process Paranoia or Prudence?' in Patrik Schöldström and Alex Calissendorff (eds), *Stockholm Arbitration Yearbook 2019* (Alphen aan den Rijn, Kluwer Law International, 2019) 126.

[70] Noting the temptation by many arbitrators to accept all, or at least too many, appointments, see Karl-Heinz Böckstiegel, 'Arbitrator's Case Management:Experiences and Suggestions' in Gerald Aksen and others (eds), *Global reflections on international law, commerce and dispute resolution : liber amicorum in honour of Robert Briner* (ICC, 2005) 127.

[71] See ch 3, section IV.B.

[72] See William Park, 'Arbitration in Autumn' (2011) 2 *Journal of International Dispute Settlement* 287, 288.

C. The Transfer of Powers to the Arbitral Tribunal as a Strategy to Increase Efficiency

The idea that arbitrators must be diligent and proceedings be conducted efficiently has found its way to many of the codes of ethics, arbitral rules and other texts that detail arbitrators' professional obligations. To this effect, for example, Canon I, paragraph F of the American Bar Association, Code of Ethics for Arbitrators in Commercial Disputes, establishes that: 'An arbitrator should conduct the arbitration process so as to advance the fair and efficient resolution of the matters submitted for decision. An arbitrator should make all reasonable efforts to prevent delaying tactics.' In a more tangible obligation, the IBA Rules determine that 'the Arbitral Tribunal shall exclude from evidence or production any Document, statement, oral testimony or inspection' for compelling 'considerations of procedural economy'.[73]

Two points should be highlighted. First, it should be noted that the normative approach in regard to these obligations seems incidental, in the sense that instead of a detailed approach detailing procedures to reduce costs or time, mentions of 'efficiency' are added to texts that do not primarily address this question. Typically, mentions of notions such as 'availability', 'reasonable costs' and 'procedural economy' can commonly be found in arbitral rules, guidance notes and other similar texts. However, these are usually presented as broader goals that an arbitral tribunal is expected to achieve, not detailed rules on how proceedings should be organised. Some exceptions, such as the ICC Arbitration Commission Report on Techniques for Controlling Time and Costs in Arbitration, should, nonetheless, be noted.

Second, the practical considerations of making proceedings more efficient seem to have been a primary concern of arbitral institutions.[74] As evidenced by the work of some arbitral institutions to benchmark the costs and duration of their proceedings against competitors, arbitral institutions appear to consider keeping costs and duration of proceedings at a competitive level to be an important element of their goals.[75] However, rather than establishing more detailed procedural instruments, the dominant approach seems to be to transfer more powers to the arbitral tribunal to organise the proceedings coupled with an increased reference to the importance of 'efficiency'. Sometimes, arbitral institutions use more blunt instruments, such as making arbitrators' fees partially dependent on the time taken to complete the proceedings. These will be discussed further in chapter eight.[76]

IV. Arbitrators' Obligation to Uphold Fundamental Principles of Transnational Public Policy

One last obligation of arbitrators is important to note: the idea that arbitrators are expected to play a role as guardians of the legal order.[77] As will be seen, it is certainly the most

[73] See IBA Rules on the Taking of Evidence in International Arbitration, Art 9, para 2 g).

[74] See Michael Polkinghorne and Benjamin A Gill, 'Due Process Paranoia: Need We Be Cruel to Be Kind?' (2017) 34 *Journal of International Arbitration* 935, 941.

[75] See, eg, LCIA, *Facts and Figures: Cost and Duration 2013–2016*, page 21 available at www.lcia.org//media/download.aspx?MediaId=596, last accessed 11 March 2020.

[76] See ch 8, section I.A.ii.

[77] See Pierre Lalive, 'Transnational (or Truly International) Public Policy and International Arbitration' in Pieter Sanders (ed), *Comparative Arbitration Practice and Public Policy in Arbitration* (Alphen aan den Rijn, Kluwer Law and Taxation Publishers, 1987) 273.

intangible of all the obligations mentioned. The key underlying idea is reasonably straightforward, however. An arbitrator's role is akin to that of a judge, leading them to hold in practice considerable powers that can affect not only the parties to the dispute but also third parties both directly and indirectly. Two major concerns are at play here: first, that arbitral proceedings can be used to contravene dominant moral values – such as aid and abet the enforcement of corruption schemes – or, second, put at risk the regulatory agenda of states – such as being used to avoid competition law rules.

It has emerged that arbitrators are, at least under some circumstances, expected not to allow parties to use arbitral proceedings in these ways. It should be said that, conversely, what arbitrators are expected to do when faced with these situations – whether they should refuse an appointment, declare the underlying contract null and void or contact the relevant authorities – is less clear and an area where guidance is largely not available. Still, a brief analysis of these questions allows for identifying some of the thorniest ethical and legal dilemmas that arbitrators may have to deal with. Also, a complex set of incentives can be uncovered. An analysis of these will be undertaken next.

A. The Concepts of 'International Public Policy' and 'Transnational Public Policy'

In conceptual terms, the notions of 'international public policy' and 'transnational public policy' are a good starting point to identify the professional obligations arbitrators may face. International public policy is one of the key concepts within international commercial arbitration, often used in the discussions around the enforcement of arbitral awards. The New York Convention establishes that recognition and enforcement of an arbitral award may be refused if 'recognition or enforcement of the award would be contrary to the public policy of that country'.[78] Also, national legislative acts typically allow national courts to set aside or refuse enforcement of arbitral awards when 'the award would be contrary to the public policy' of the relevant state.[79]

While a notoriously elusive legal concept, international public policy is usually used in simplistic terms to refer to the small set of a jurisdiction's mandatory norms which cannot be derogated from – even if a foreign legal system was selected by the parties as the applicable law (in this sense opposing itself to a broader concept of 'domestic public policy').[80] Despite a repeated preference in arbitration-related literature for a restrictive interpretation of the concept of 'international public policy',[81] courts from different jurisdictions have very

[78] See New York Convention, Art V(2) b).

[79] See UNCITRAL Model Law, Arts 34(2) b)(ii) and 36(2) b)(ii).

[80] See Lalive (n 77) 259; Pierre Mayer, 'Effect of International Public Policy in International Arbitration?' in Loukas A Mistelis (ed), *Pervasive Problems in International Arbitration* (Alphen aan den Rijn, Kluwer Law International. 2006) 61.

[81] In conceptual terms, public policy is potentially a very open-ended concept, allowing, in theory, national courts a large margin of discretion to not enforce arbitral awards. Commentators and national courts, particularly those with a more 'pro-arbitration' approach in their decisions, emphasise the need to interpret this clause in a restrictive way. This narrative plays an important role in guaranteeing that the international commercial arbitration operates smoothly. Arbitration advocates are particularly concerned with the idea that if interpreted too broadly, the concept of 'public policy' may be used as a basis to re-open the litigation of cases at national courts and, therefore, defeating the advantages of international arbitration. See Born (n 5) 3654.

different views on how this concept should be interpreted.[82] Still, for reference, 'international public policy' may include, for example, situations where a party looks to enforce an illegal smuggling contract, contracts that contravene EU competition law, or decisions that seriously affect certain basic principles of contract law.[83]

In arbitration-related literature, another concept emerged: the notion of 'transnational public policy' (also sometimes referred to as 'truly' international public policy). This even narrower notion is used to refer to a purported set of principles which are widely accepted across most legal systems and are so fundamental and unanimous across legal orders that they cannot be derogated by the parties or not applied by the arbitral tribunal independently of the law applicable to the dispute.[84] Again, the exact content of this concept is not undisputed. Transnational public policy would certainly determine that a contract that would uphold a situation of slavery is unenforceable.[85] Arguably, it could also determine, in a situation that has been increasingly addressed in arbitral proceedings, that at least under specific circumstances, a contract obtained through corruption will not be enforceable.[86]

B. The Practical Duties Arbitrators are Expected to Fulfil by Reference to their Role as 'Guardians of the International Public Order'

As a reflection of these ideas of 'international public policy' and 'transnational public policy', it is clear that arbitrators have obligations that go beyond solving the dispute in accordance with the parties' specifications.[87] Although it may sometimes be unclear as to what extent such obligations bind arbitrators, there seems to have emerged some consensus around the idea that arbitrators are under a duty to produce an enforceable award, even if this involves tackling issues that parties do not raise. In this sense, arbitrators may, for example, raise questions of EU competition law on their own initiative, even if parties have not raised such issues with the arbitral tribunal.[88] This will be particularly the case if the arbitrator considers that not addressing such questions would lead the arbitral award to be set aside or unenforceable in the relevant jurisdictions.

Obligations will be heightened when the arbitral tribunal faces a question that it may consider running against basic principles of law, namely those that may be considered transnational public policy. This is the case with corruption issues affecting the disputing parties' contractual relationship. An argument can be made that arbitrators have a duty not only to

[82] See Sormeh Bouzarjomehri and Eisa Amini, 'Public Policy as Ground for Refusal of International Arbitral Awards – A Comparison Between Different Judicial Practices' (2016) 9 *Journal of Politics and Law* 81, 84.

[83] Such as the principle of good faith, *pacta sunt servanda* or the prohibition of *venire contra factum proprium*, that, if seriously violated, may lead a court not to enforce an award. See Gabrielle Kaufmann-Kohler and Antonio Rigozzi, *International Arbitration: Law and Practice in Switzerland* (Oxford, Oxford University Press, 2015) 494.

[84] See Mark A Buchanan, 'Public Policy and International Commercial Arbitration' (1988) 26 *American Business Law Journal* 511, 514.

[85] See Mayer (n 80) 67.

[86] See Carolyn B Lamm, Hansel T Pham and Rahim Moloo, 'Fraud and Corruption in International Arbitration' in Miguel Angel Fernandez-Ballester; and David Arias Lozano (eds), *Liber amicorum Bernardo Cremades* (Madrid, Wolters Kluwer España, 2010) 728.

[87] See Mourre (n 2) 115.

[88] See Robert B Von Mehren, 'The Eco-Swiss Case and International Arbitration' (2003) 19 *Arbitration International* 465, 468.

raise corruption issues but also to investigate *sua sponte* and require the parties' cooperation, even if both parties are uninterested in exploring such issues or the applicable substantive laws have less stringent requirements than international practice.[89] However, whether arbitrators have a duty to communicate suspected corruption to the relevant authorities is less clear, as confidentiality obligations may be at play.[90]

Arbitrators' obligations are even more explicit in more extreme situations. It is unanimous that arbitrators are under a duty not to collaborate with so-called 'sham arbitrations' – ie, arbitral proceedings that, while in appearance intend to solve a dispute, in reality, intend to achieve an illegitimate purpose.[91] A particular risk is that the arbitral process is hijacked to further a criminal purpose or to escape the application of a certain regulation.[92] A possible example of the first situation would be having arbitration used to abet money laundering: parties may, for example, undertake a fraudulent dispute in order to justify an illicit increase in assets.[93] An example of the second situation would be parties using fake arbitral proceedings to circumvent capital control regulations.

C. The Underlying Incentives for Compliance and Non-compliance with Considerations of Public Policy

Arbitrators' incentives to address questions of public policy present a peculiar grid. On the one side, there are incentives for arbitrators to comply with their obligations to guarantee that arbitral proceedings are not used for nefarious purposes. Getting involved in such arbitral proceedings might lead to a reputational cost and, in some of the most egregious cases, contend with the moral values of the arbitrator. However, there may be a concern that this sort of incentive, although leading arbitrators not to get involved in these cases, may not lead to the optimal approach from a public interest point of view. For example, it is possible to imagine cases where incentives may lead arbitrators to simply refuse or withdraw from an appointment even if the 'optimal' course of action from a societal point of view would be in that particular case to, for example, declare the underlying contract null and void and report it to the relevant authorities.

[89] See Domitille Baizeau and Tessa Hayes, 'The Arbitral Tribunal's Duty and Power to Address Corruption Sua Sponte' in Andrea Menaker (ed), *International Arbitration and the Rule of Law: Contribution and Conformity*, vol 19 (Alphen aan den Rijn, Kluwer Law International, 2017).

[90] See Vladimir Pavic, 'Bribery and International Commercial Arbitration – The Role of Mandatory Rules and Public Policy' (2012) 43 *Victoria University of Wellington Law Review* 661, 671. See also Pierre Heitzmann, 'Arbitration and Criminal Liability for Competition Law Violations in Europe' in Gordon Blanke and Phillip Landolt (eds), *EU and US Antitrust Arbitration: a Handbook for Practitioners*, vol 1 (Alphen aan den Rijn, Kluwer Law International, 2011) 1276.

[91] See Heitzmann (n 90) 1285.

[92] It's worth noting that, in the words of Caron: 'In general, the arbitration community avoids discussion of the possibility that criminal activity somehow takes advantage of the arbitration framework. In significant part, this is because such criminal activity is the rare exception.' See David D Caron, 'Light and Dark in International Arbitration: The Virtues, Risks and Limits of Transparency' in Hong Kong International Arbitration (ed), *International Arbitration: Issues, Perspectives and Practice: Liber Amicorum Neil Kaplan* (Alphen aan den Rijn, Kluwer Law International, 2019) 230.

[93] See Andrew de Lotbiniere McDougall, 'International Arbitration and Money Laundering' (2004) 20 *American University International Law Review* 1021, 1023; Hodges and Greenaway (n 1) 304.

Another concern relates to the particular case of sham arbitral proceedings discussed above.[94] In this case, parties will not necessarily use arbitrators or arbitral institutions operating in the market. If there is no genuine underlying dispute between parties, there is no advantage for parties to appoint 'real' arbitrators beyond, perhaps, giving the sham arbitration a veneer of respectability. If parties select someone not related to the field and not intending to operate in the market as an arbitrator, reputational mechanisms will not play a relevant role in determining compliance. The particular situation of one-off arbitrators will be discussed in more detail in chapter seven.[95]

D. The Lack of 'Soft Law' Regarding the Duties of Arbitrators in Relation to Public Policy

An interesting aspect of the role of arbitrators concerning public policy is, at least until recently, the lack of soft regulatory norms addressing these issues.[96] This contrasts with other professional and ethical questions where, as discussed above, the arbitral community undertook significant work to develop and organise standards. Several reasons may help explain why such regulatory texts have not emerged in relation to these sorts of questions. First, some of the questions discussed above have been perceived more as academic matters rather than actual issues arbitral tribunals face on a frequent basis.[97] Also, the heterogeneity of possible issues makes guidance in regard to these issues challenging to produce. Finally, in the particular case of 'sham arbitrations,' this sort of soft law guidance would have little persuasive power.

This trend of lack of guidance regarding these issues is perhaps changing. As arbitrability – ie, the range of issues that arbitral tribunals can decide – has increased to allow arbitrators to deal with issues previously reserved to national courts, questions of public policy have appeared more often. Two issues, in particular, have risen in prominence. First, the question of contracts obtained through corruption has been a particular concern against the background of larger alarm with the effects of these practices.[98] Second, the question of money laundering, also a growing concern inside and outside legal circles, has been raised.[99] Both issues have been addressed in an increasing number of doctrinal articles

[94] It is worth noting that, from the discussions with members of the community, the perception seems to be that these situations are, in practice, very rare. See also Heitzmann (n 90) 1285.

[95] See ch 7, section I.C.ii.

[96] See Stephan Wilske, 'International Arbitration and Its Dark Sides, in Particular Corruption: What Arbitral Institutions Could and Should Do to Tackle Such Unwelcome Issues' (2019) 12 *Contemporary Asia Arbitration Journal* 147, 160.

[97] Noting that discussions around the concepts of domestic, international and transnational public policy are more often found in academic discussions that in actual practice: see Buchanan (n 84) 531.

[98] See Michael Hwang and Kevin Lim, 'Corruption in Arbitration: Law and Reality' (2012) 8 *Asian International Arbitration Journal* 1.

[99] See Kristine Karsten, 'Money Laundering: How It Works and Why You Should Be Concerned' in Kristine Karsten and Andrew Berkeley (eds), *Arbitration: money laundering, corruption and fraud* (ICC, 2003). See also Fabian Teichmann, Sonia Ruxandra Boticiu and Bruno S Sergi, 'Compliance Issues in Arbitration Proceedings – Bribery, Money Laundering and Other Abuses' (2023) Ahead of Print, *Journal of Financial Crime*.

that, despite being academic in nature, have practical advice on how arbitrators should deal with this issue.[100]

Overall, such changes seem to indicate that when issues that bring the legitimacy of international commercial arbitration to question arise, the community intervenes by creating regulatory norms to address the topic through the mechanisms and due to the incentives analysed in chapter five. International commercial arbitration competition with other dispute resolution alternatives is dependent on states – and more specifically national courts – enforcing arbitral awards and arbitration agreements without creating excessive burdens. Naturally, any systematic deference of states and state courts to commercial arbitration is dependent on a general trust regarding the ability of arbitrators to guarantee that arbitration proceedings are not used for nefarious prospects.[101] How the current market steers arbitrators to uphold these regulatory norms will be explored in the next chapter.

[100] Noting the proliferation of articles and studies on the appearance of issues of corruption (bribery in particular) before arbitration tribunals, see Pavic (n 90). Also, a recent soft law text entitled '*Corruption and Money Laundering in International Arbitration: A Toolkit for Arbitrators*' prepared by the Basel Institute on Governance should be noted.

[101] See Alessandra Casella, 'On Market Integration and the Development of Institutions: The Case of International Commercial Arbitration' (1996) 40 *European Economic Review* 155, 161.

7

Arbitrators' Compliance with Professional Norms

One of the most salient features of the arbitral profession is the inexistence of the deterrent mechanisms found in other apparently similar professions to guarantee compliance with professional norms.[1] Many, if not almost all, 'liberal professions' – such as lawyers, doctors or accountants – find that states typically enforce professional rules by resorting to some public agency which oversees behaviour in the field or by delegating powers to a state-backed professional self-regulatory body.[2] Serious sanctions such as banishment of the profession are often proposed. Arbitrators, however, do not have a central institutional framework responsible for monitoring and promoting compliance, nor do they face the threat of specific professional sanctions similar to those of other professions.[3]

This chapter proposes that compliance by arbitrators with professional norms – such as the ones discussed in chapter six – is mostly left to a complex set of economic forces and social interactions. These regulatory mechanisms are then bolstered by a number of ad hoc legal mechanisms and institutional interventions that add a layer of protection against arbitrators' misconduct. These mechanisms will be the subject of analysis in chapter eight but are not often used overall. Indeed, the low number of arbitral awards annulled,[4] the low success rate in the challenges to arbitrators[5] and the extremely few cases of criminal investigations into arbitrators' conduct[6] also seem to support the general impression that serious deviations by arbitrators are rare.

Against this background, this chapter proposes that this level of compliance results from arbitrators being provided with strong incentives to abide by applicable norms and the selection of arbitrators favouring a population more inclined to comply. In order to clarify

[1] For a discussion on the concept of deterrence, see Christopher Hodges, *Law and Corporate Behaviour: Integrating Theories of Regulation, Enforcement, Compliance and Ethics* (Oxford, Hart Publishing, 2015) 47.

[2] For a definition of 'liberal profession' and a discussion of the role of professional bodies in the European context, see Tinne Heremans, *Professional Services in the EU Internal Market : Quality Regulation and Self-Regulation* (Oxford, Hart Publishing, 2012) ch 1.

[3] The most approximate mechanism is CIArb's *'Complaints against Members'* system. However, participation in CIArb is not mandatory and CIArb lacks the power to de facto prohibit an individual to act as an arbitrator. Despite its large membership, CIArb only includes a small fraction of those acting as arbitrators. See also, ch 8, section II.A.

[4] See, eg, Richard W Naimark and Stephanie E Keer, 'Post-Award Experience in International Commercial Arbitration' in Christopher R Drahozal and Richard W Naimark (eds), *Towards a Science of International Arbitration: Collected Empirical Research* (Alphen aan den Rijn, Kluwer Law International BV, 2005) 263, where out of a sample of 153 international arbitration awards conducted by the AAA/ICDR only one was overturned in a court of law. See also Robin Oldenstam, 'Due Process Paranoia or Prudence?' in Patrik Schöldström and Alex Calissendorff (eds), *Stockholm Arbitration Yearbook 2019* (Alphen aan den Rijn, Kluwer Law International, 2019) 125.

[5] See ch 8, section I.A.

[6] See ch 8, section V.

these two factors, this chapter explores four interrelated forces: i) how the market provides incentives for arbitrators to comply; ii) how the particularities of entering the market help arbitrators become familiar with their professional obligations and pre-select a complying population; iii) how the arbitral community plays a role by rewarding and sanctioning members and transmitting information regarding compliance; and iv) how these forces contribute to an 'internalisation' of norms by arbitrators.

I. The Key Role of Market Incentives in 'Regulating' Behaviour of International Commercial Arbitrators

Under the current system of international arbitration, market forces are an essential determinant of arbitrators' behaviour.[7] As explored in chapter three, arbitrators and arbitral institutions seem to act, at least partially, in a commercial fashion.[8] Indeed, considerable evidence shows that they adapt their behaviour to attract new business and maintain their market share.[9] As a first step to understanding the particularities of the enforcement of professional and ethical obligations amongst arbitrators, it is necessary to explore how the arbitration market and existing legal structures in arbitration operate differently from other professions. From there, it will be possible to determine when market incentives lead arbitrators to respect the ethical and professional obligations discussed in chapter six.

A. The Lack of Control of Parties Over the Arbitrator they Appoint

Before advancing a discussion on how the market provides an incentive for an arbitrator to comply with the applicable norms, it is important to understand how the particularities of the market and the legal framework in arbitration separate arbitrators from other professions. In this regard, the key vital aspect to note is that parties – ie, the 'final consumers' – have limited to no control over the behaviour of 'their' arbitrator. A party usually lacks repeated interactions with a particular arbitrator that would allow it to 'capture' them. How the long-term interactions that an arbitrator establishes with the 'paying consumer' are distinct from the ones taking place in other fields of professional practice will be explored next.

i. The Tension between Complying with Professional Standards and Keeping the 'Client' Happy

In many professions, there is often an underlying opposition between having to follow professional standards and the dependency on a client's repeated business.[10] The need

[7] See, Joanna Jemielniak, *Legal Interpretation in International Commercial Arbitration* (London, Ashgate Publishing Ltd, 2014) 100; Katherine L Lynch, *The Forces of Economic Globalization: Challenges to the Regime of International Commercial Arbitration* (Alphen aan den Rijn, Kluwer Law International, 2003) 112; Thomas Clay, 'El Mercado Del Arbitraje' (2014) 7 *Arbitraje: revista de arbitraje comercial y de inversiones* 15.

[8] See ch 3, section I.A.

[9] Jacques Werner, 'Competition within the Arbitration Industry' (1985) 2 *Journal of International Arbitration* 5, 6.

[10] For a discussion, see Hugh P Gunz and Sally P Gunz, 'Client Capture and the Professional Service Firm' (2008) 45 *American Business Law Journal* 685.

to satisfy their clients may provide perverse incentives that may lead these professionals to infringe on their professional and ethical obligations.[11] Regulatory intervention is, therefore, often needed to provide counter-incentives and shape the market to guarantee that these professionals comply with their professional obligations. External auditors and lawyers illustrate how these tensions operate and provide an interesting counterpoint to the position arbitrators are in. A brief reference to their regulation will allow a good starting point to understand better why and how enforcement of professional norms among arbitrators is different.

a. The Example of the External Auditor: From Financial Scandals to Heightened Regulation

Auditors provide a well-known example of how professional ethical standards often conflict with the economic interests of the professional.[12] On the one hand, auditors are expected to serve the public by being objective and acting with integrity in providing examinations of financial statements. On the other hand, auditors will sometimes be pressured to forego their integrity in order to sustain the economic bond with the client. A typical case will be the situation of management pressuring the external auditor to confirm a financial statement which overstates the value of the company. As noted by a commentator:

> the audit contract suffers from the 'a dog will not bite the hand that feeds him' problem.[13]

It should be noted that there are strong underlying economic and legal incentives for auditors to comply with their obligations. By not accurately reporting financial information, auditors may suffer a reputational cost or open themselves to possible litigation by third parties who rely on the information provided.[14] Still, these inbuilt deterrents are often not sufficient to guarantee that auditors correctly report financial information. This is a particular concern, as shown by empirical research, when the audited firm represents a relevant source of ongoing income to the auditor firm.[15]

The difficult equilibrium described has prompted a different mixture of legislative and self-regulatory interventions, often heightened when serious financial scandals arise. For example, following a widely-publicised string of accounting and auditing frauds in the early 2000s, regulatory interventions in the US and later in Europe aimed to shape the incentives of auditors by creating, amongst other interventions: i) rules regarding disclosure of conflicts of interest; and ii) rotation of auditors. Together, these interventions limit the possibility of the service 'consumer' – ie, the audited firm – 'capturing' the service provider – ie, the auditing firm.

[11] See Hugh P Gunz, Sally P Gunz and Ronit Dinovitzer, 'Professional Ethics: Origins, Applications, and Developments' in Laura Empson and others (eds), *The Oxford Handbook of Professional Service Firms* (Oxford, Oxford University Press, 2015) 125.

[12] See Jonathan R Macey and Hillary A Sale, 'Observations on the Role of Commodification, Independence and Governance in the Accounting Industry' (2003) 48 *Villanova Law Review* 1167.

[13] Hollis Ashbaugh, 'Ethical Issues Related to the Provision of Audit and Non-Audit Services: Evidence from Academic Research' (2004) 52 *Journal of Business Ethics* 143, 144.

[14] Noting that at one time such reputation mechanisms were sufficient to induce high quality financial reporting, see Macey and Sale (n 12) 1168.

[15] Providing support for the idea that larger firms have greater power to persuade their auditors to approve erroneous or misleading financial statements, see Theodore Eisenberg and Jonathan R Macey, 'Was Arthur Andersen Different? An Empirical Examination of Major Accounting Firm Audits of Large Clients' (2004) 1 *Journal of Empirical Legal Studies* 263.

On top of these ex-ante interventions, the option of public or quasi-public oversight agencies to discipline accounting firms should also be highlighted. These agencies, such as the US Securities and Exchange Commission (SEC), the Public Company Accounting Oversight Board (PCAOB) or the Financial Reporting Council (FRC), have the power to impose considerable penalties on auditors and auditing firms who violate the applicable regulations. Such fines often run into the millions.[16] It is important to note that such blunt deterrents do not exist regarding commercial arbitrators or arbitral institutions.

b. The Example of Lawyers: From the Regulation of Traditional Professionals to a Legal Industry

A variation of the same problem can be found regarding the members of the legal profession. While the exact contours of professional ethics and regulation vary considerably from jurisdiction to jurisdiction, most legal systems recognise a public function for the members of the legal profession. To this effect, in England and Wales, barristers are not only agents of their clients but also 'officers of the court', and solicitors are expected to 'uphold the rule of law and the proper administration of justice'.[17] In France, *avocats* are considered to represent not only their client's interests but also '*auxiliaires de justice*'.[18] These ideas are often complemented with other more tangible ethical obligations such as confidentiality duties and avoiding conflicts of interest.[19]

In this regard, lawyers are in a situation somewhat akin to that of auditors. On the one hand, their presence in the market often depends on maintaining their accounts, giving their clients some theoretical ability to pressure the legal professionals they hire.[20] On the other hand, their professional obligations might mandate them to refuse to take unethical acts on behalf of their clients, such as misleading a court or unduly obstructing legal proceedings. Further, lawyers are sometimes in a position to explore the strong information asymmetries between themselves and their clients to engage in opportunistic behaviour, taking advantage of their client's inability to evaluate the quality of the service provided.[21]

As in relation to auditors, in the legal profession, practitioners' self-interest can, to some extent, provide countervailing forces to the need of satisfying clients. In a market where quality is often difficult to observe, reputation is often a surrogate for quality.[22] Members of the legal profession, especially those in areas of practice where reputation is particularly relevant, may want to avoid being involved in actions that will diminish their

[16] In the UK context, a list of cases is available at www.frc.org.uk, last accessed 9 February 2019.

[17] See Legal Services Act 2007, s 1(1). For an overview on the impact of the act, see Andrew Boon, 'Professionalism under the Legal Services Act 2007' (2010) 17 *International Journal of the Legal Profession* 195.

[18] See Christophe Jamin, 'Services juridiques : la fin des professions?' (2012) 1 *Pouvoirs* 33.

[19] See Solicitors Regulation Authority (SRA) Code of Ethics chs 3 and 4. See also Réglement Intérieur National de la Profession d'Avocat, Arts 2 and 4.

[20] Another variation of this problem can be found in regards to 'in-house' lawyers. On this topic, see Hugh P Gunz and Sally P Gunz, 'Hired Professional to Hired Gun: An Identity Theory Approach to Understanding the Ethical Behaviour of Professionals in Non-Professional Organizations' (2007) 60 *Human Relations* 851.

[21] Camille Chaserant and Sophie Harnay, 'Self-Regulation of the Legal Profession and Quality in the Market for Legal Services: An Economic Analysis of Lawyers' Reputation' (2015) 39 *European Journal of Law and Economics* 431, 431.

[22] See ibid 433.

standing amongst their peers and the legal community due to pure long-term economic interests.[23] In many other situations, however, self-interest will not be sufficient, needing reinforcement by other sets of incentives.

In most jurisdictions, enforcement of lawyers' ethical obligations has traditionally mostly relied on self-regulatory bodies composed of members of the profession that hold powers to discipline behaviour and apply sanctions, including the power to forbid someone from practising the profession.[24] Social pressures amongst peers and internalisation of certain understandings of their special role have also historically played a role in the regulation of the profession.[25] With the increasing business-like features of the legal industry, there has been an increasingly flexible interpretation of some traditional tenets of being a lawyer in many jurisdictions.[26] In particular, notions of independence of a lawyer regarding the client have often waned with the modernisation of the legal profession.

ii. How Arbitrators Differ: The Lack of Leverage of a Particular 'Consumer' Over the Arbitrator

In certain ways, similarities can be found between the position of an arbitrator and an auditor. All these agents are 'competing' within their specific markets with other highly specialised members of their field to be selected for what are often very profitable assignments. At the same time, they are expected to follow a number of ethical obligations that may not allow them to follow what the consumer of the service commands. In the case of auditors and, to an extent, of lawyers, they are expected to guarantee the interests not only of whoever hires them but also of third parties and the public at large by maintaining a level of independence from their clients. Arbitrators are expected to remain independent from the parties who appoint them and comply with a set of professional obligations discussed in chapter six, such as assuring due process, conducting proceedings efficiently, and guaranteeing that basic public policy principles are respected.

However, it is important to note that international commercial arbitrators are in a considerably different position from external auditors and lawyers. After a party has appointed an arbitrator, that party has few mechanisms to influence the behaviour of the arbitrator. This derives from the fact that, as discussed in chapters five and six, the arbitral practice has evolved to determine that the same company or group of companies cannot successively appoint the same arbitrator.[27] These rules are not the result of centralised legislative interventions or imposed by state-backed professional bodies, but instead emerged from the combined effect of court decisions and the work of the arbitral community and arbitral professional associations.

[23] See W Bradley Wendel, 'Nonlegal Regulation of the Legal Profession: Social Norms in Professional Communities' (2001) 54 *Vanderbilt Law Review* 1953, 1959.

[24] See Chaserant and Harnay (n 21) 432.

[25] See Michael Burrage, *Revolution and the Making of the Contemporary Legal Profession: England, France, and the United States* (Oxford, Oxford University Press, 2006) 32.

[26] See Christopher J Whelan and Neta Ziv, 'Privatizing Professionalism: Client Control of Lawyers' Ethics Colloquium: Globalization and the Legal Profession' (2011) 80 *Fordham Law Review* 2577.

[27] See, inter alia, IBA Guidelines Orange List 3.1.3. For a discussion see Gomez-Acebo, *Party-Appointed Arbitrators in International Commercial Arbitration* (Alphen aan den Rijn, Kluwer Law International, 2016) ch 5.

While a party is most often not strictly forbidden to appoint an arbitrator whom it has previously nominated in other cases, the arbitrator might be under an obligation to disclose the previous appointments and refuse the appointment.[28] If an arbitrator does not fulfil these obligations, they might be open to challenges by the other party[29] which leads the award to be annullable or non-enforceable.[30] Further, as will be discussed below, they might be perceived as untrustworthy and dishonest by the other members of the arbitral panel and, more broadly, by the arbitral institutions and the arbitral community at large.[31] This is particularly important as arbitrators are dependent on their reputation to continue finding work in the field.[32]

Since there are, in practice, severe limitations on a party's ability to appoint the same arbitrator in future arbitrations,[33] arbitrators know that keeping the particular party that nominated them content with their behaviour is not a high priority to guarantee future appointments.[34] This effect is compounded by the fact that, as described in chapter three, a considerable number of appointments are not undertaken by parties but rather by other actors, such as co-arbitrators and arbitral institutions. As such, an arbitrator will often find it in its best long-term interest to display allegiance to the arbitral community – ie, maintain and develop their position as a respected member of the community – rather than unwavering loyalty to their appointing party.

A second point to be noted is that parties have limited influence on the amount the arbitrator will receive for the proceedings. The fees to be paid are often regulated ex-ante within the rules of an arbitral institution or pre-determined before the start of the arbitral proceedings or ultimately defined by the arbitral tribunal itself.[35] Again, this separates the relationship between arbitrators and parties from the relationship established by an auditor or a lawyer with their clients. Lawyers and auditors can typically negotiate rates and terms of payment with clients. This, at least in theory, allows the client some leverage over the lawyer and auditor to shape their behaviour. On the contrary, in arbitration, a party cannot dangle a promise of increased payment or the 'threat' of decreased remuneration to influence the arbitrators' behaviour since prices are usually pre-determined or finally fixed by the arbitrators.

[28] Further to ch 6 and the references therein, see also, specifically regarding the duty to disclose, Dominique Hascher, 'Independence and Impartiality of Arbitrators: 3 Issues' (2011) 27 *American University of International Law Review* 789.

[29] See, inter alia, 2021 ICC Rules, Art 14; UNCITRAL Model Law, Art 12.

[30] See, inter alia, UNCITRAL Model Law, Art 34. See also Gary Born, *International Arbitration: Law and Practice* (Alphen aan den Rijn, Kluwer Law International, 2012) §16.03.

[31] See also Lucy Greenwood and Mark Baker, 'Are Challenges Overused in International Arbitration?' (2013) 30 *Journal of International Arbitration* 101, 111.

[32] See Yu Jin Tay, 'Reflections on the Selection of Arbitrators in International Arbitration' in AJ van den Berg (ed), *International Arbitration: The Coming of a New Age?*, vol 17 (Alphen aan den Rijn, Kluwer Law International, 2013) 126.

[33] To this effect, the IBA Guidelines on Conflicts of Interest, para 3.1.3. establish that situations where '[t]he arbitrator has, within the past three years, been appointed as arbitrator on two or more occasions by one of the parties, or an affiliate of one of the parties' are in its 'orange list', ie, create a duty of disclosure and may give raise to doubts about an arbitrators' independence and impartiality.

[34] A relevant complication derives from the possibility of counsel 'concentrating' appointments – ie, sizeable law firms leveraging the fact that they participate in numerous arbitrations to credibly influence arbitral behaviour. Limitations on the possibility of the counsel of the parties to repeatedly select the same arbitrators limits the possibility of these being 'captured' by law firms on behalf of the parties. See, in this particular, the IBA Guidelines on Conflicts of Interest, para 3.3.8.

[35] See Michael McIlwrath and John Savage, *International Arbitration and Mediation: A Practical Guide* (Alphen aan den Rijn, Kluwer Law International, 2010) 267.

Altogether, this means that a party has limited capability of steering an arbitrator to perform an action that contravenes the dominant rules in the field by tacitly or expressly promising future appointments. That is to say that arbitrators face the difficult equilibrium of satisfying the client and respecting 'professional norms' to a lesser extent than other professions have to deal with. Instead of trying to cultivate a relationship with particular clients, arbitrators must often pursue a strategy of developing networks within the community and, within this, displaying technical expertise and commitment to the dominant 'ethical' and professional norms. This idea and how this framework provides an effective incentive for compliance with both professional and ethical norms will be explored next.

B. How Arbitrators' Market Strategies Lead them to Comply with Professional Rules

In analysing the role of market forces as a regulator of the behaviour of international commercial arbitrators, this section will focus on how the particularities of the international commercial arbitration market influence the regulation of international arbitrators by leading them to compete by projecting an image of being credible, impartial and efficient. Since, as seen above, parties do not have a credible system of 'controlling' arbitrators, arbitrators will be less pressured to forego allegiance to the dominant understanding of what constitutes ethical behaviour in this field. From there, the grid of economic gains and losses an arbitrator faces when deciding to comply or not with their professional obligations will be analysed.

i. The Benefits of Complying with Professional Obligations

Arbitrators are not pure rational agents looking to maximise their long-term self-interest. Still, given that arbitrators operate in a competitive market, it is important to note that adhering to the community rules and expectations offers clear benefits for arbitrators. As noted by a member of the arbitral community:

> A good arbitrator is one who imposes his ethical values, fully aware that this will affect his reputation and that his professional future will be benefited by conducting himself according to these values and not bending to the demands of a particular case.[36]

In this sense, the market incentives for arbitrators to comply with their professional duties are relatively straightforward. Deciding procedural and substantial issues efficiently, disclosing possible conflicts of interest, and correctly addressing public policy issues help arbitrators build their reputation as competent. In turn, an increased reputation increases the value of the arbitrator within the community, possibly leading to more appointments and other working opportunities within the legal profession.[37]

[36] José Carlos Fernández Rozas, 'Clearer Ethics Guidelines and Comparative Standards for Arbitrators' in Bernardo María Cremades, Miguel Angel Fernández-Ballesteros and David Arias Lozano (eds), *Liber Amicorum Bernardo Cremades* (Madrid, La Ley, 2010) 414.

[37] See Richard A Posthuma, James B Dworkin and Maris Stella Swift, 'Arbitrator Acceptability: Does Justice Matter? Arbitrator Acceptability' (2000) 39 *Industrial Relations: A Journal of Economy and Society* 313; Yongkyun Chung and Hong-Youl Ha, 'Arbitrator Acceptability in International Commercial Arbitration: The Trading Firm Perspective' (2016) 27 *International Journal of Conflict Management* 379.

The link between reputation and future increased appointments ultimately derives from the dynamics of selecting an arbitral panel.[38] Parties who have to agree on a single arbitrator will find an arbitrator they believe to be in favour of the other party unacceptable. In most circumstances, therefore, this means that parties can find only agreement on an arbitrator which they both perceive as competent and not biased in favour of the other party. Also, co-arbitrators or arbitral institutions have strong incentives to choose 'compliant' arbitrators when they have to make selections. Since their reputation would be negatively affected if they participated in or organised arbitral tribunals that would not act in accordance with expectations, there are reasons to believe they are usually motivated to select 'norm-compliant' arbitrators.

Finally, it should be said that reputation may also increase the probability of an arbitrator being selected as a party-appointed arbitrator.[39] An arbitrator's 'value' to a party is partially dependent on their ability to persuade the remaining members of the arbitral tribunal.[40] This ability is itself dependent on the arbitrator's perceived legal expertise, independence and neutrality.[41] While some predisposition towards the appointing party's arguments is, to a degree, considered acceptable behaviour, open partisanship will most often result in the co-arbitrator's positions being disregarded by the rest of the panel.[42] Hence, arbitrators, at least those who intend to act long-term in the market, have a long-term incentive to pursue an image of neutrality and technical proficiency in most circumstances.[43]

ii. The Costs of Complying with Professional Obligations

Two further ideas are important to note. First, it should be highlighted that complying with dominant values often has no significant costs for the arbitrators. For example, complying with the obligations of guaranteeing parties' procedural rights, confidentiality and respecting time-frames has low to no costs for the arbitrator. In these circumstances, arbitrators have very few incentives not to comply. However, a key exception relates to the duty of independence and impartiality. In some cases, arbitrators' obligation to disclose information and eventually refuse an appointment where a conflict of interest arises may carry a considerable cost for the arbitrator – in this case, the risk of not being appointed.

An abstract example helps to understand the sort of market incentives an arbitrator faces when deciding to comply with the rules described in chapter six. For example,

[38] See Dolores Bentolila, *Arbitrators as Lawmakers* (Alphen aan den Rijn, Wolters Kluwer, 2017) 151.

[39] See ibid.

[40] As Professor Martin Hunter explains 'when I am representing a client in arbitration, what I am really looking for in a party-nominated arbitrator is someone with the maximum predisposition towards my client, but with the minimum appearance of bias'. Martin Hunter, 'Ethics of the International Arbitrator' (1987) 53 *Arbitration* 219, 223.

[41] See Günther Horvath, 'Guerrilla Tactics in Arbitration, an Ethical Battle: Is There Need for a Universal Code of Ethics?' in Christian Klausegger and others (eds), *Austrian Yearbook on International Arbitration 2011* (Wien, Manz'sche Verlags-und Universitätsbuchhandlung, 2011) 311.

[42] See Charles N Brower and Charles B Rosenberg, 'The Death of the Two-Headed Nightingale: Why the Paulsson – van Den Berg Presumption That Party-Appointed Arbitrators Are Untrustworthy Is Wrongheaded' (2013) 29 *Arbitration International* 7, 14.

[43] See William Park, 'Arbitrator Integrity' in Michael Waibel and others (eds), *The Backlash Against Investment Arbitration: Perceptions and Reality* (Alphen aan den Rijn, Kluwer Law International, 2010) 280.

in a dispute between party '*a*' and party '*b*', arbitrator '*x*', whom parties were considering appointing for the case, has a connection to party '*a*', such as a previous contractual engagement for the provision of consulting services. In deciding to disclose this connection, arbitrator '*x*' has to consider that: i) disclosing the conflict of interests might result in not being appointed and therefore not being able to receive the fees from this one arbitration; but ii) such a serious violation of a well-established obligation of declaring conflicts of interest could jeopardise its reputation amongst the community and risk further appointments in the future.[44]

Overall, in the dominant market conditions, arbitrators, therefore, find an incentive to provide 'high-quality' instead of 'low-cost' services; ie, arbitrators are incentivised to act in a way that conforms to the generally accepted professional and ethical rules and also satisfies counsel, arbitral institutions, and the wider community of peers instead of competing in prices. In situations where there are strong individual incentives for deviation, reputational mechanisms are significant deterrents of unethical behaviour. Also, as it will be explored in chapter eight, awards that do not conform to professional and ethical rules are more likely to be annulled or not enforced, which may damage an arbitrator's reputation.[45]

The collection of individual decisions taken by the arbitral community, which tends to favour experience and 'good standing' within the community, acts as a filter which leads to a reasonably closed profession.[46] Assuming that parties, counsel and, more generally, the community members prefer arbitrators who show commitment to their professional and ethical obligations, markets will, in most circumstances, provide incentives for arbitrators to fulfil their role. This, however, does not mean that arbitrators' strict economic self-interest will provide enough incentives to avoid deviating from the dominant professional and ethical rules in all circumstances. This will be explored next.

C. The Limits of Markets in Providing Incentives for Arbitrators to Act in Accordance with their Obligations

There are situations where the market does not provide enough incentive for compliance with the applicable professional obligations of arbitrators. It should be noted that: i) the international arbitration market is considerably imperfect, being particularly rife with information asymmetries and agency problems; ii) arbitrators are not necessarily long-term players in the market; iii) the short-term gains of deviating can be larger than the long-term benefits of respecting the dominant values and rules in certain circumstances; and iv) both parties can collude with an 'arbitrator' to achieve an illicit goal. Therefore, market pressures

[44] See, on this point, Alan Scott Rau, 'On Integrity in Private Judging' (1998) 14 *Arbitration International* 115, 118.

[45] See Gary Born, *International Commercial Arbitration*, 2nd edn (Alphen aan den Rijn, Wolters Kluwer Law & Business, 2014) 1234. ('[a]n arbitrator's reputation, with both parties and appointing authorities, is materially damaged by overreaching on jurisdictional issues, particularly if it results in an award being annulled or denied recognition in public proceedings.')

[46] See Fernando Dias Simões, *Commercial Arbitration Between China and the Portuguese-Speaking World* (Alphen aan den Rijn, Wolters Kluwer Law & Business, 2014) 74. See also McIlwrath and Savage (n 35) 254.

alone do not always prescribe enough incentives for compliance. These four issues will be explored in turn.

i. Market Imperfections in International Arbitration: Lack of Information and Principal-agent Problems

Establishing that it is in the arbitrators' best interest to uphold their professional and ethical obligations relies on the assumption that the different actors selecting arbitrators not only prefer arbitrators who uphold these obligations but are also able to identify and select the arbitrators who respect them. However, as often identified in the economic literature, almost no market possesses the characteristics that allow perfect market outcomes.[47] Indeed, perfect competition scenarios rely on several assumptions that are not fully encountered in real-life scenarios, most notably the rationality of the agents, lack of barriers to entry, or perfect information.[48]

These general limitations in markets' functioning also occur in relation to international commercial arbitration. In particular, the lack of perfect information is a dominant feature of arbitration. Many parties and counsel lack information regarding arbitrators' true quality – ie, their actual level of independence, impartiality, and technical expertise in crafting awards.[49] This is especially exacerbated due to the confidential nature of most arbitral proceedings. Parties, therefore, usually have to depend on their counsel to overcome their lack of knowledge when trying to select the most appropriate arbitrator. However, even law firms' knowledge of arbitrators might vary significantly.

Closely linked to this idea, it should be noted that principal-agent problems may arise in the context of selecting arbitrators. A risk would be the possibility of counsel or (more rarely) board members of arbitral institutions 'capturing' the decision to further their own interests. For example, counsel may select not the arbitrator that best serves the interests of their clients but, instead, those that best conform to their own understanding of what an arbitrator should be or who might be most helpful to their own career choices. For example, counsel could attempt to 'trade' appointments – ie, attempting to increase the number of one's own appointments by expressly or implicitly appointing another member of the arbitral community with the intent that the appointee would appoint them back in the future. It should be noted that since parties often lack the level of information necessary to select the arbitrator, counsel often takes over this choice in practice.[50]

[47] See, for all, Francis M Bator, 'The Anatomy of Market Failure' (1958) 72 *The Quarterly Journal of Economics* 351.

[48] Indeed, modern economics that predict how agents act increasingly relies on the concepts of bounded rationality, norm-based rationality, and empirically determined rationality. See David Colander, 'The Death of Neoclassical Economics' (2000) 22 *Journal of the History of Economic Thought* 127, 136.

[49] Detailing the imperfections of the international arbitration market, see Catherine A Rogers, 'The Vocation of the International Arbitrator' (2004) 20 *American University International Law Review* 957, 967. Also expressing doubts on the ability of the market to provide a well-functioning and just system of arbitration, see Carrie Menkel-Meadow, 'Ethics Issues in Arbitration and Related Dispute Resolution Processes: What's Happening and What's Not Arbitration Symposium' (2001) 56 *University of Miami Law Review* 949, 950.

[50] See Bentolila (n 38) 152. It should be noted that in the White & Case and Queen Mary's survey on Choices in International Arbitration (2010), 68% of the corporate counsel surveyed said that they were not confident that they could make an informed choice of an arbitrator without the input of external counsel.

Still, imperfect information and principal-agent problems are present across markets and usually allow the creation of incentives that reward market actors who produce better services at lower prices than their competitors, albeit imperfectly. In international commercial arbitration, the increasing competition between law firms and arbitral institutions partially curtails the possibility of these decisions being 'captured' by these actors. It also must be borne in mind that the high level of sophistication of most international arbitration users allows them to better guarantee their long-term interests.

To this effect, law firms certainly are aware that losing arbitral proceedings may result in future loss of revenues from disgruntled clients who are either unhappy with their counsels' commitment to their interests or the perceived unfairness of the arbitral proceeding. Therefore, they have a strong incentive to optimise the choice of an arbitrator in a way that secures the interests of the party and its perception of arbitration as a fair method of solving disputes. Similarly, the people within arbitral institutions with the power to choose arbitrators have to take into consideration that systematic 'poor' choices may result in: i) a loss of reputation of that particular arbitral institution; and ii) a loss in the trust of commercial arbitration as a whole.

ii. The Problem of the Non-repeating 'Player' in the Regulation of International Commercial Arbitration

The idea that market incentives lead arbitrators to comply with their duties also hinges on the assumption that arbitrators intend to engage in the market repeatedly, ie, they are looking to be appointed arbitrators in different cases. The risk of 'losing' reputation by infringing norms is a concern mainly for those arbitrators who intend to continue operating in this market.[51] It should be noted, however, that not all arbitrators are, or intend to be, 'repeating' players. Indeed, without any requirements of professionalisation, someone with no incentive to consider the long-term effects of reputation may be appointed to an arbitral tribunal.[52]

Such concerns do not seem to play a considerable role in international commercial arbitration. As detailed in chapter three, the selection of arbitrators usually follows conservative trends, with parties and arbitral institutions usually selecting those deeply embedded within the arbitral community. As previously noted, obtaining a first appointment is a process that usually requires prospective arbitrators to previously commit seriously to the field.[53] There are, therefore, reasons to believe that purely 'non-repeating' players are rare.[54] Further, most arbitrators, even if not particularly concerned about how their

[51] See Susan D Franck, 'The Role of International Arbitrators' (2005) 12 *ILSA Journal of International and Comparative Law* 499, 517. See also João Ilhão Moreira, 'The Insider/Outsider Divide and the Ethics of Commercial Arbitrators' (2022) 19 *Manchester Journal of International Economic Law* 132.

[52] A variation of this problem relates to the situation where a particular party is the only realistic source of appointments to an arbitrator. As noted by Paulson: 'In the case of an arbitrator who considers that his only chance lies with the party which has already named him once, this might result in more or less dissimulated, but nevertheless systemic, favouritism.' Jan Paulsson, 'Ethics, Elitism, Eligibility' (1997) 14 *Journal of International Arbitration* 13, 14. The limitations on reappointments noted above and in the previous chapter should, however, be borne in mind.

[53] See Simões (n 46) 74.

[54] See Tay (n 32) 126.

reputation will affect the likelihood of being appointed again as an arbitrator, will have to consider how unethical acts will affect their pursuit of other professional activities, most importantly as counsel in international arbitration.[55]

iii. Large One-off payments as a Potential Incentive for Deviation

Finally, it should be noted that purely monetary incentives do not guarantee that arbitrators will not deviate from fulfilling their obligations. One simple example would be a party offering an arbitrator a one-off payment that is bigger than the expected cost to their reputation and possible civil and criminal consequences, such as the risk of liability and detection by criminal authorities. A more benign variant of the same problem is a prospective arbitrator who would be obliged to recuse himself or herself from a case but would calculate that the reputational cost would be inferior to the fees obtained from accepting it. In these cases, the 'rational' arbitrator – ie, the arbitrator concerned only about maximising their material self-interest (an unlikely category)[56] – would decide to deviate from their professional obligations.

Two notes about this topic are important, however. Arbitrators do not try only to maximise income but also have other concerns such as their social relationships, work satisfaction, feelings of achievement, and, importantly for this discussion, a sense of personal integrity and reputation.[57] These considerations often override the prospect of financial gain, leading arbitrators to comply with their professional and ethical obligations even if it would not be in their strict financial best interest to do so. This is an idea that will be picked up again at the end of this chapter.[58]

Also, it should also be noted that arbitral proceedings have mechanisms to deal with situations where one of the parties tries to subvert the arbitral proceedings by, for example, offering an illicit payment to one or more elements of the arbitral tribunal. The adversarial nature of arbitration creates a large incentive for the other party to monitor any wrongdoing. Parties will, therefore, often devote considerable resources to determining whether an arbitrator has not complied with any of the relevant rules. As it will be explored in chapter eight, the aggrieved party has several legal mechanisms by which to react in this situation, which include: i) requesting the arbitral award to be annulled; ii) requesting that the award is not recognised and enforced; and iii) requesting damages from the arbitrators that engage in such behaviours.

[55] As noted by Schultz and Kovacs: 'Most arbitrators have other sources of income, typically legal counsel work, which usually are more lucrative, both in total and for equal time and effort. For such arbitrators, which likely form the great majority of arbitrators, it makes no economic sense to engage in certain behaviour [...that...] reduces their chance of being used as counsel.' Thomas Schultz and Robert Kovacs, 'The Law Is What the Arbitrator Had for Breakfast: How Income, Reputation, Justice, and Reprimand Act as Determinants of Arbitrator Behaviour' in Julio César Betancourt (ed), *Defining issues in international arbitration: celebrating 100 years of the Chartered Institute of Arbitrators* (Oxford, Oxford University Press, 2016) 246.

[56] 'The evidence from cognitive psychology and behavioural sociology has indicated that economic factors and calculations, and a rational calculation of the economic costs and benefits, play at best a limited role in decisions made by individuals, groups and even commercial organisations.' Hodges (n 1) 109.

[57] See on this point, more generally, Richard A Posner, 'Judicial Behavior and Performance: An Economic Approach' (2004) 32 *Florida State University Law Review* 1259, 1260. See also Hodges (n 1) 60.

[58] See ch 7, section IV.

iv. *The Problem of Cooperative Strategies by Parties to Subvert the Arbitral Proceedings*

The current system, however, provides fewer safeguards regarding cooperative strategies between both parties and arbitrators to subvert arbitration. In some circumstances, parties may have an interest in using arbitral proceedings, in collusion with arbitrators, to accomplish specific illicit goals.[59] A possibility would be, for example, both parties ordering the arbitral tribunal to ignore the fact that a contract was obtained through the corruption of public officials or that the underlying contract was established to abet a money laundering scheme. While it is extremely hard to know how common these kinds of situations are, it is possible that parties rely on arbitration as a way of avoiding the prying eyes of national courts.[60]

If any such agreement and award are kept secret so as not to damage the arbitrator's reputation, and none of the parties is interested in reneging on the illegal agreement, the market will not produce incentives to avoid this kind of behaviour. Further, parties will likely avoid the usage of mainstream arbitral institutions or well-known arbitrators, using instead service providers less concerned with the long-term effect of reputation costs.[61] In these circumstances, however, such actions may rise to the level of criminal offences and may be prosecuted by criminal authorities and public enforcement agencies. The role of criminal law in controlling arbitrators' behaviour will be explored further in chapter eight.

II. Entrance into the Profession and its Effect on the Compliance with Professional Obligations

Closely linking to the question of how market incentives shape arbitrators' compliance with professional and ethical obligations, it is important to analyse how access to the profession shapes this same question. Indeed, the long informal process of qualification and networking that the vast majority of arbitrators have to undertake prior to obtaining an appointment might influence the level of compliance with professional and ethical norms. First, the difficulties of accessing the arbitral profession may help to establish an environment where most arbitrators are aware of and committed to the dominant values of international arbitration. Speculatively, one may argue that the same process may also pre-select a subset of the total population that may be less predisposed to deviating from accepted norms. These two ideas will be explored in turn.

[59] For a discussion of this and related cases, see Bernardo M Cremades and David Cairns, 'Trans-National Public Policy in International Arbitral Decision-Making: The Cases of Bribery, Money Laundering and Fraud' in Kristine Karsten and Andrew Berkeley (eds), *Arbitration : money laundering, corruption and fraud* (Paris, ICC, 2003).

[60] See Domitille Baizeau and Tessa Hayes, 'The Arbitral Tribunal's Duty and Power to Address Corruption Sua Sponte' in Andrea Menaker (ed), *International Arbitration and the Rule of Law: Contribution and Conformity*, vol 19 (Alphen aan den Rijn, Kluwer Law International, 2017) 234. It should be noted that such cases are not unheard off. The well-known ICC Case No. 1110, decided in 1963 by Judge Lundgreen, involved a case where both parties, in practice, asked the tribunal to decide their case in accordance with the terms of reference and ignore any practices of corruption. Cremades and Cairns (n 59) 79.

[61] Some parties may, however, choose a reputable arbitral institution precisely to give a veneer of legitimacy to corrupt dealings. See Baizeau and Hayes (n 60) 234.

A. The Difficult Process of Entering the Arbitral Profession and the Learning of Dominant Norms

Due to the market characteristics discussed above and in more detail in chapter three, entrance into practice as an arbitrator is a complex and challenging process that demands a significant investment of time and money into creating the networks and technical expertise that will increase the likelihood of a first appointment. Becoming and maintaining a position as an arbitrator often involves a long process of: i) acquiring practical experience in the field; ii) participating in community gatherings, such as attending conferences and joining professional associations; and iii) 'courting' and networking with other members of the community.[62]

This long process also provides an environment where future members of the community of arbitrators learn the written and unwritten norms dominant within the community. It must be noted that both in domestic and international commercial arbitration, arbitrators often do not undertake specialised professional training (although more has become available over the years and increased in popularity).[63] To be considered for most appointments, a would-be arbitrator often has to participate in this 'socialisation' process that usually lasts a considerable number of years. In this process, would-be arbitrators necessarily learn the dominant discourses and tenets of the profession.

These socialisation processes have, therefore, conceivably, a positive effect on compliance. Through the cumulation of academic learning, practical experience and participation in events, would-be arbitrators become proficient in how concepts such as impartiality, independence or confidentiality should guide arbitrators' behaviour. These same experiences expose would-be arbitrators to practical examples of situations where professional and ethical obligations are at stake. Through these processes, members of the community become familiar with the key sources of professional duties, be it legislation provisions, court decisions, or the community-driven soft law and commentary that shapes the content of these norms.

In practice, the efforts undertaken by the would-be members of the community in entering the field provide a similar function to the training and qualification through exams found in many professions. While no formal training is required, the significant amount of participation within the arbitral community before most members have a realistic possibility of entering the roster of international arbitrators provides a surrogate for the mandatory education and training demanded in other professions.

However, the way that this process takes place is markedly different for arbitrators. In most learned professions, a formal process of qualification ends with a candidate being declared, in a binary fashion, qualified or unqualified. The informal process of qualification that allows one to enter the arbitral profession instead produces an environment where

[62] See Dolores Bentolila, *Arbitrators as Lawmakers* (Alphen aan den Rijn, Kluwer Law International, 2017) 150; Fernando Dias Simões, *Commercial Arbitration Between China and the Portuguese-Speaking World* (Alphen aan den Rijn, Wolters Kluwer Law & Business, 2014) 74; Joshua DH Karton, *The Culture of International Arbitration and The Evolution of Contract Law* (Oxford, Oxford University Press, 2013) 59. See also McIlwrath and Savage (n 35) 254.

[63] Typical cases include the training courses organised by CIArb and the advance arbitrator training developed by ICC. However as noted by McIlwrath and Savage 'Our impression, at any rate, is that many or most of the world's leading arbitrators have no formal training or qualifications as arbitrators.' McIlwrath and Savage (n 35) 254.

each prospective arbitrator is bestowed with more or less legitimacy and visibility within the community. Due to the tendency of parties and other appointing authorities to select amongst exclusively elite members, the vast majority of appointments will, therefore, tend to flow to those who participated extensively in the informal process of qualification described above.

B. Entrance in the Market and the Pre-selection of a Particular 'Population'

As discussed in chapter three, the particularities of the arbitral market, namely the difficulties of accessing the profession and the inability to outcompete more experienced members through lower prices, lead to only a very small number of would-be entrants actually entering this market.[64] Indeed, only a selected few of the many active members of the arbitral community become arbitrators.[65] The difficulties of entering the market might influence the level of compliance of international commercial arbitrators due to how it pre-selects who enters this field. In particular, it arguably: i) allows the weeding-out of those not sufficiently committed to the profession and its values;[66] and ii) selects from those who might be less inclined to norm-breaking behaviour.

i. Pre-selection of 'True-believers' in the Virtues of International Arbitration and the Role of the Arbitrator

Regarding the first idea, it is important to note that the large amount of 'investment' needed to attempt to access the role of arbitrator and the incertitude and the significant time frame for the eventual recoupment of this investment might discourage those not sincerely committed to the field. Further, entering the arbitral community is not a simple process of cumulating 'markers' of technical expertise, such as writing articles and mingling with other members within conferences and associations. Instead, entrance and progress in the community both involve a long process in which each member is typically at the same time a competitor – as each member is usually vying for the same appointments and business opportunities – and a juror – since each member evaluates each other's legitimacy, technical expertise, and potential value as a contact.

This system might, therefore, allow the community to weed out members who do not conform to pre-defined notions of what an arbitrator should be. The repeated interactions between the arbitral community and the prospective arbitrator before they are allowed to enter the small 'circle' of arbitrators provide many opportunities for the members to evaluate whether they conform to what is considered acceptable behaviour and become acquainted with the written and unwritten rules of the community. If a member does not consistently commit to this area of law and its gatherings in a way which is considered appropriate by other members, it might diminish their chances of entering the roster of usual arbitrators.

[64] Karton (n 62) 59.
[65] See Paulsson (n 52) 19.
[66] See Emmanuel Gaillard, 'Sociology of International Arbitration' (2015) 31 *Arbitration International* 1, 13.

This long process might contribute to pre-selecting a population as arbitrators, which is tendentially and disproportionally composed of people who are truly committed to the values of arbitration.[67] This is important as such a population might be more inclined to forego personal financial gains in order to conform to normative understandings of how an arbitrator should act. This means that the population of those currently composing the arbitrators' roster might be more inclined to refuse to break a norm accepted within the arbitral community even when breaking such a norm would yield a net benefit for the arbitrator concerned.

ii. Possible Pre-selection of a Population that Due to its Characteristics Might be Less Inclined to Engage in Norm-breaking Behaviour

Finally, it should be noted that the population that composes international arbitrators is a highly pre-selected set of individuals who are almost always older[68] and already possess successful careers, most often within the legal or academic professions. Such a population might be less inclined to violate norms.[69] While plenty of evidence suggests that successful, well-established individuals are not immune from engaging in norm-breaking activity, such members of society will often be more risk-averse. They will often prize more dearly adherence to norms and social respectability within their professional circles. Arbitrators, who often are individuals at either the peak or the twilight of their professional careers, might be a population that, on average, will not display a preference for risky activity.

There is also an indication that the market also pre-selects those members who are perceived as being of good character and displaying integrity – ie, those who appear more committed to upholding virtuous behaviours. For the reasons discussed in chapter three, members displaying such characteristics will be more palatable choices as arbitrators. It is plausible that the perception of such characteristics correlates to non-norm-breaking behaviour to some extent. While outliers will naturally be present, it is conceivable that the characteristics favoured by the market in an arbitrator tend to form a population of members less interested in norm-breaking activity.

III. Social Rewards, Social Sanctions and Transmission of Information within Arbitration

The next step in understanding what leads arbitrators to fulfil their professional and ethical obligations involves exploring in more detail the relationship between the arbitrator

[67] Although cynics may perceive the support of members of the arbitral community for the expansion of international arbitration to be self-interested, many members of the community do support international arbitration as a matter of principle. See Stacy I Strong, 'Clash of Cultures: Epistemic Communities, Negotiation Theory, and International Lawmaking' (2016) 50 *Akron Law Review* 495, 520.

[68] See Mirèze Philippe, 'How Has Female Participation at ICC Evolved? ICC Arbitrators, Court Members and Court's Secretariat' (2017) 3 *ICC Dispute Resolution Bulletin* 37, 42.

[69] In regard to the idea that an older population is less likely to engage in crime, it has been a truism of criminology that age negatively correlates with criminal behaviour. For a discussion, see, among many others, Travis Hirschi and Michael Gottfredson, 'Age and the Explanation of Crime' (1983) 89 *American Journal of Sociology* 552.

and the 'arbitral community' – ie, the growing number of arbitrators, practitioners, and academics which have engaged in the arbitral trade and over time have established durable professional and sometimes personal relations between themselves. As discussed above and in chapter three, the market mechanics of international commercial arbitration incentivise strong links among all participants in this market. In turn, the interplay between the arbitral community and its constituent members is a crucial factor in understanding why the prevalent attitude amongst international arbitrators has been complying with dominant values.

Two key ideas are particularly relevant in understanding how the arbitral community contributes to an environment where arbitrators comply with their professional obligations. First, the arbitral community offers social rewards and visibility to members who comply with desirable behaviour and, conversely, penalises those who do not. Second, the arbitral community provides a network where information regarding compliance and arbitrators' professional and ethical 'credentials' is transmitted. These ideas will be explored in turn.

A. The Role of the Arbitral Community in Rewarding and Sanctioning Members

The role of the arbitral community in guaranteeing that professional and ethical rules are followed does not stop at the moment of entrance by only 'admitting' well-connected members who are well-versed in the canons and discourses of international arbitration. It is instead a continuous process by which members who comply with professional obligations are rewarded, and members who comply poorly with professional obligations and demonstrate questionable ethical behaviour face community-driven sanctions. These processes are, however, not necessarily straightforward due to the imperfect and asymmetric level of information the different players in the market have.

i. The Arbitral Community's Role in Rewarding Members

Cultivating relationships and involvement with the community is essential to increase the likelihood of being appointed as an arbitrator. As discussed in more detail in chapter three, the arbitral community has a significant influence over which prospective arbitrators ultimately enter the market. Decisions regarding who gets appointed are often taken by community members acting as heads of arbitral institutions, counsel, or co-arbitrators; therefore, a good relationship with all these actors is essential for an arbitrator. Consequently, establishing and maintaining relationships with the arbitral community is a permanent game that arbitrators know they cannot abandon and where they often invest considerable amounts of time and money.

This influence gives the community as a whole leverage over the individual arbitrators and incentivises arbitrators to comply with the norms dominant in the community. Members who are deemed 'worthy' by the community – ie, are knowledgeable, well-liked,[70]

[70] As noted by Moore: 'The standing of a professional with his nominal peers is, not surprisingly, a mixture of various overt and informal criteria, not infrequently mixed with personal judgments verging on the professional.' Wilbert Ellis Moore, *The Professions: Roles and Rules* (New York, Russell Sage Foundation, 1970) 150.

and ethically sound – are, in theory, rewarded by the community with appointments to arbitral tribunals, speaking engagements, and elected and non-elected positions in arbitral institutions and professional organisations.[71] The arbitral community and its members have a clear interest in enforcing standards of behaviour that promote the legitimacy and usage of international arbitration. Therefore, they will have an interest in reappointing and rewarding members who contribute to the success of the field.

It is, however, difficult to determine how much progression and maintenance within the roster of active arbitrators is a result of perfect compliance with their professional obligations. Arbitrators' success is partially a function of previous success. Very well-connected and well-known arbitrators might continue finding work even if peers do not strongly rate their performance. Some have noted that after an arbitrator assumes a certain level of importance and notoriety within the community, it is very difficult to displace them from their position in the market. Still, the fact that most successful arbitrators are very frequently credited for the quality of their work and ethical attitude may indicate that complying arbitrators are recognised and rewarded by the community.[72]

ii. The Role of the Arbitral Community in Punishing Members

The community further provides social sanctions for members who deviate from desirable behaviour.[73] In the context of a reasonably small community where there is a significant incentive to know the other players and the latest evolutions in the field, members will have their actions scrutinised and may face criticism if they infringe on the professional norms of the profession. In theory, expressions of disapproval may take different forms, from criticism in more formal venues, such as academic and non-academic articles or speeches given in arbitral conferences, to more informal ways, such as the transmission of disapproval face-to-face.

It is important to note that in the world of international arbitration, clearly directed open criticism of a particular arbitrator in a public forum is beyond rare.[74] The collegiate nature of the arbitration, where all members look to improve their social standings, likely

[71] Moore's description of how prestige among professionals is messaged is very much applicable in the world of arbitration. The author notes that it can range from very subtle and informal deference, such as developed consensus among professionals concerning unusual skill or judgement to ceremonial behaviour, such as election to honorific offices in professional associations, by citations and awards, testimonial dinners, and the like. ibid 154.

[72] See, eg, Chamber and Partners list of most in-demand international arbitrators available at chambers.com/guide/, last accessed 12 April 2020, where 'preparedness' is one of most often pointed characteristics of top arbitrators, usually in conjunction with mentions of 'experience' and 'knowledge'.

[73] The existence of a system of social sanctions is by no means a particularity of the arbitral community. Indeed, all groups utilise, to different extents, ostracism and gossip, as well as other informal sanctions, as a punishment to those who violate in-group norms. See Chandra Sekhar Sripada and Stephen Stich, 'A Framework for the Psychology of Norms' in Stephen Stich (ed), *Collected Papers, Volume 2: Knowledge, Rationality, and Morality, 1978–2010* (Oxford, Oxford University Press, 2012) 293.

[74] Jan Paulson's criticism of Judge Abner Mikva for his actions as an arbitrator within the Loewen Arbitration, an arbitral NAFTA dispute that opposed the Loewen corporation to the US, represents one of such rare instances. See Jan Paulsson, 'Moral Hazard in International Dispute Resolution' (2010) 25 *ICSID Review* 339, 345. See also V Veeder, 'The Historical Keystone to International Arbitration: The Party-Appointed Arbitrator – From Miami to Geneva' in David Caron and others (eds), *Practising Virtue: Inside International Arbitration* (Oxford, Oxford University Press, 2015) 129.

discourages a confrontational approach.[75] Criticism of peer behaviour in open forums is often undertaken through other methods such as 'war stories' where a member will recount an anecdotal story from his professional experience, often presenting him/herself as a principled character facing objectionable behaviour from an unnamed antagonist.[76] In the same vein, arbitral institutions do not adopt a 'name and shame' attitude. While some voices have requested arbitral institutions to be more forthcoming regarding past experience with particular arbitrators, arbitral institutions usually do not make any information regarding particular arbitrators' performance or behaviour public.[77]

The fact that, within the arbitral community, public criticism of a particular arbitrator is rare does not mean that the community does not provide negative reviews of bad performance or poor ethical behaviour. This, however, takes place through personal contacts, through which members of the community express displeasure to other members of the community about arbitrators they have worked with. This takes place most often before a party appoints an arbitrator to an arbitral proceeding. Typically, before making an appointment, counsel to the parties looks to gather information among peers about the characteristics of a potential appointee. In these contacts, information about the previous performance of that particular arbitrator is often shared and considered when deciding the appointment.

B. The Role of the Community in Transmitting Information

Closely related to the idea discussed above, it is important to note that the arbitral community works as a network where information about potential arbitrators is transmitted. In the professional regulation literature, the idea of 'asymmetric information' – in this particular context, the idea that 'consumers' are usually unable to fully determine the 'quality' and true expertise of a professional working in a specialised field – is often used as a justification for the need to intervene in these markets. These arguments have, however, not spurred significant interventions in the international arbitration market. Instead, inter-community linkages are used by those within the community to overcome these issues.

In the context of international commercial arbitration, where most arbitral awards and almost all arbitral tribunals and arbitral institutions' decisions are not available to third parties, the consumers – ie, the parties who use arbitral services – may have, at least in theory, some difficulty in making an informed decision when selecting an arbitrator.[78] Due to the difficulties of evaluating available information, parties often rely on the advice

[75] The reluctance to criticise the judgement or skill of a fellow professional is not, however, a particularity of arbitrators and can be found in other professions as a manifestation of collegiality. See Moore (n 70) 110.

[76] Noting the relevance of 'war stories' as an informal method of social control in the legal profession, see Wendel (n 23) 1984.

[77] See David Hacking, 'Arbitration Is Only as Good as Its Arbitrators' in Loukas Mistelis and Stefan Kröll (eds), *International Arbitration and International Commercial Law: Synergy, Convergence, and Evolution : Liber Amicorum Eric Bergsten* (Alphen aan den Rijn, Kluwer Law International, 2011) 227. See also, Catherine A Rogers, 'The Arbitrator and the Arbitration Procedure, Transparency in Arbitrator Selection' in Christian Klausegger and others (eds), *Austrian Yearbook on International Arbitration 2016* (Wien, Manz'sche Verlags-und Universitätsbuchhandlung, 2016) 80.

[78] It should be noted that some information regarding the 'quality' of arbitrators can be obtained from the profiles that some arbitrators provide or are organised by specialised publications. Further, information can be inferred from the academic and non-academic publications many arbitrators produce, allowing to gather some information

of, and sometimes fully delegate their choice to, their in-house and external legal counsel. These, in turn, often rely on their professional networks within and outside the law firms to obtain further information regarding suitable candidates.

Figure 7.1 Data on 'Where do you find your information about arbitrators?' adapted from QMUL's '*2018 International Arbitration Survey: The Evolution of International Arbitration*

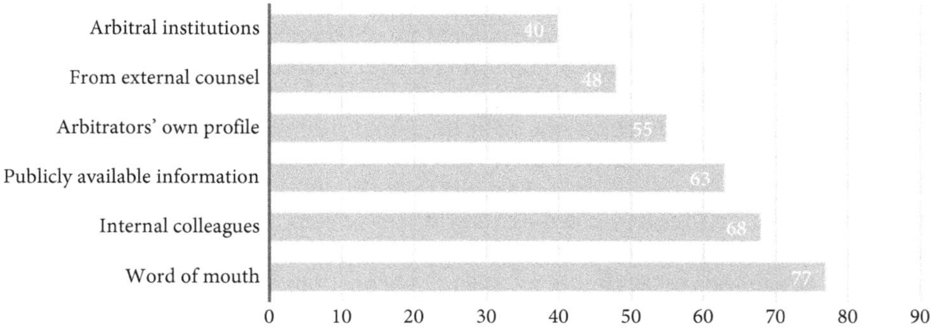

In this regard, the arbitral community functions as a network through which information about arbitrators can be communicated. Informal contacts among members of the community allow for determining the professional expertise and ethical credentials of a prospective appointee.[79] The proximity among the members of this community and the repeated interactions among them facilitate these contacts and give members the confidence to approach other members regarding such issues.[80] As each member is incentivised to network within the community, they end up functioning as another point through which information is distributed.

If the members of the arbitral community were not so proactive in establishing networks with other members, information about the quality of each individual member would be more difficult to access. In this respect, the closed nature of the community spontaneously creates not only a system of 'rewards' and 'punishments' – mostly in the form of appointments and importance within the community or lack thereof – but also the mechanisms through which information regarding compliance is transmitted through the community.

IV. The International Commercial Arbitration Market and Community as Catalysts for the 'Internalisation' of Norms

Much of the discussion undertaken in this chapter regarding why international arbitrators comply with norms has been based on an analysis of how the market and the arbitral

regarding the technical knowledge of the arbitrator regarding certain areas of law or their understandings of how arbitral proceedings should be conducted.

[79] McIlwrath and Savage (n 35) 253. Some have noted the imperfect nature of such mechanisms. See, eg, Michael Mcilwrath, 'Grading the Arbitrator' (2007) 73 *The Journal of the Chartered Institute of Arbitrators* 224, 224.

[80] As noted by Bermann: 'There may not be any other field of legal practice in which practitioners from around the world so regularly interact at conferences, symposia, training sessions and other events'. George A Bermann, 'American Exceptionalism in International Arbitration' in Arthur W Rovine (ed), *Contemporary Issues*

community often intertwine to reward international arbitrators with long-term monetary and non-monetary gains by complying with norms. This assumes that norm compliance is driven by self-interest, at least defined in a broad sense. While it was also argued that the particular way the market is set tends to accumulate those truly committed to the values of arbitration, the thrust of the argument relied on the idea that lack of price competition and the reasonably closed nature of the arbitral community leads arbitrators to comply with norms as this is, in most circumstances, in their best interest.

It is important to note that decisions to comply are often not a reflection of an 'amoral calculator', who calculates personal economic and non-economic benefits and costs from complying. Certain norms are followed because the subjects of the norm have simply internalised that certain behaviour is 'the right thing to do' or 'the way things are done'.[81] This process by which an agent accepts a set of norms and values and acts in accordance with them is what can be called internalisation. Internalisation has a powerful effect in regulating behaviour and is often noted as a key driver of compliance.[82] Sometimes, this process becomes so ingrained that compliance with norms becomes driven not by rationalised options but appears as an almost automatic, subconscious behaviour. As noted by a commentator:

> When I'd had my coffee this morning and went upstairs to get dressed for work, I never considered being a nudist for the day.[83]

What does this mean in regard to international arbitrators? First, it reminds us that arbitrators will respond to situations not only by callously calculating future gains and losses of money, social position, or their moral views regarding a certain issue or ideological preferences. Their compliance will also reflect how much arbitrators have internalised their role and their functions. Conceivably, an arbitrator does not fully consider the advantages and costs of, for example, complying with the norm that determines its obligation of allowing a party to present a document – they simply comply with a norm they have internalised. It should be noted that in the world of arbitration, where many choices are made in a high-stakes environment by elite actors, decisions are expected to be heavily rationalised. Still, many other choices are undertaken routinely or as reflections of internalised roles.

Second, it raises the question of whether there are reasons to believe that the level of internalisation of norms by arbitrators will be significantly different from that of other professionals. In this respect, some of the particularities of the international arbitration market and community that have already been discussed should be recalled. These allow speculation that within the arbitral community, there might be a higher level of

in International Arbitration and Mediation: The Fordham Papers (2011) (Leiden, Martinus Nijhoff Publishers, 2012) 3.

[81] As noted by Kagan, Gunningham and Thornton: 'Sociological explanations of law-abidingness in individuals (among taxpayers, for example) suggest three basic motivations. One is fear of detection and punishment by government enforcement agents. The second is fear of humiliation or disgrace in the eyes of family members or social peers. The third is an internalized sense of duty, that is the desire to conform to internalized norms and beliefs about the right thing to do.' Robert Kagan, Neil Gunningham and D Thornton, 'Fear, Duty, and Regulatory Compliance: Lessons from Three Research Projects' in Christine Parker and Vibeke Nielsen (eds), *Explaining Compliance: Business Responses to Regulation* (Cheltenham, Edward Elgar Publishing, 2011).

[82] See Dennis H Wrong, 'The Oversocialized Conception of Man in Modern Sociology' (1961) 26 *American Sociological Review* 183.

[83] See Joshua M Epstein, 'Learning to Be Thoughtless: Social Norms and Individual Computation' (2001) 18 *Computational Economics* 9.

internalisation to the role and rules specific to the profession compared with other professions and their respective roles and rules. In particular, it is worth noting that: i) compliance is often a result of observing compliance in others; ii) internalisation is often the result of learned experiences; and iii) compliance with norms is more prevalent when there is a belief that these are the result of a fair process.

With regard to the first idea, it should be noted that, as discussed above, in the market conditions of international arbitration, due to the existence of reputational competition between arbitrators, it is expected that in most circumstances, arbitrators will find it in their best interest to adhere to the norms, and therefore non-compliance will be low. In turn, compliance appears to also be a result of personally observing others complying or, more generally, the belief that others are complying.[84] Therefore, compliance by international arbitrators may conceivably be exacerbated as a result of compliance being the dominant observed behaviour in the field.

Another relevant point discussed above is important to recall: entrance to the community demands a long process of committing to arbitration practice. This is expressed in practical terms by acquiring work and academic experience, joining community gatherings, and networking. It was argued that this long process forces would-be arbitrators, in most cases, to get familiar with the tenets of the field and may help exclude those uncommitted to the values of the field. It is also conceivable that this aids the process of internalisation and reinforcement of values.[85] It is important to note that education can provide people with information that shapes their attitudes and values, inducing compliant behaviour.[86]

Finally, the process for which norms are created and imposed on the subjects seems to considerably influence the amount of internalisation and compliance.[87] When the subjects of norms perceive these to be produced by a legitimate authority, there is a greater tendency to comply.[88] Also, norms produced within a fair process, especially those where subjects consider having some degree of control over the process, tend to produce more compliance.[89] Regarding international arbitrators, and as discussed in chapter five, most norms result from an interactive process between the members of the community where norms slowly enter a commonly held set of values, principles, and rules.[90] Since the norms applicable to international commercial arbitrators are rarely imposed in a top-down fashion but rather are a collective creation by the community, it is conceivable that arbitrators more easily internalise them.

[84] See, eg, the oft-noted fact in tax compliance literature that people are more willing to pay taxes if they believe that their friends and other citizens pay taxes. Eric A Posner, 'Law and Social Norms: The Case of Tax Compliance' (2000) 86 *Virginia Law Review* 1781, 1784.

[85] The same basic notion can be expressed in a different way, by emphasising a common 'culture of arbitration' which in turn drives compliant behaviour. See, eg, Ginsburg noting 'Actors engaged in repeated interaction over time produce culture. [The] common training and expertise, combined with interactive practices, produces a common set of expectations. These expectations, in turn, shape behaviour, though they are also subject to change as new norms arise'. Tom Ginsburg, 'The Culture of Arbitration' (2003) 36 *The Vanderbilt Journal of Transnational Law* 1335, 1337.

[86] See Jon G Sutinen and K Kuperan, 'A Socio-economic Theory of Regulatory Compliance' (1999) 26 *International Journal of Social Economics* 174, 184.

[87] See ibid 182.

[88] For a discussion see, Tom R Tyler, *Why People Obey the Law* (New Haven, Yale University Press, 1990) 7.

[89] See also ibid.

[90] As noted by Bermann: 'The international arbitration community is in itself a densely integrated one, with widely shared assumptions and expectations concerning the ground rules for conduct in arbitration'. Bermann (n 80) 3.

8

Enforcement of Arbitrators' Professional and Ethical Rules

Chapter seven explored how a set of incentives and the particular structure of the arbitral community tends to create an environment where arbitrators typically comply with their professional and ethical obligations. The underlying argument rested on the idea that the particular mechanisms of the arbitration market created long-term economic incentives for arbitrators to comply with their professional and ethical obligations. It further argued that the particular structure of the arbitral market leads to an environment where those highly committed to the field and its dominant values are more likely to be selected for arbitral appointments. Finally, it posited that the arbitral market contributed to a highly cohesive community where members cultivate close relations, allowing for an environment where, within the community, information regarding the professional and ethical qualities of the members is transmitted.

This chapter completes the analysis of the grid of incentives leading arbitrators to comply with their professional and ethical duties by examining how other institutions and mechanisms play a role in enforcing these obligations.[1] To further explore these mechanisms and institutions, this chapter will focus on the role played by: i) arbitral institutions; ii) professional associations; and iii) national courts in imposing these obligations. It will further analyse the role played by civil and criminal liability in enforcing these obligations. Throughout this chapter, a particular concern will be understanding not only how these institutions and mechanisms enforce these obligations but also their limitations and how these mechanisms feed into the reputation and economic mechanisms that dominate this market.

I. The Role of Arbitral Institutions in Enforcing Professional and Ethical Rules

Arbitral institutions play a vital role in the development of arbitral proceedings and the arbitrators' services market.[2] As discussed in chapter two, arbitral institutions have long been

[1] It is worth noting that there have been voices requesting a more proactive attitude of arbitral institutions in enforcing arbitrators' ethical standards. See Katia Fach Goméz, *Key Duties of International Investment Arbitrators: A Transnational Study of Legal and Ethical Dilemmas* (Springer Berlin Heidelberg, 2018) 14. Also, arguing for arbitral institutions to play a role in relation to arbitrators, akin to what the bar plays in relation to lawyers, see Catherine A Rogers, 'The Vocation of the International Arbitrator' (2004) 20 *American University International Law Review* 957, 1011.

[2] See Katherine L Lynch, *The Forces of Economic Globalization: Challenges to the Regime of International Commercial Arbitration* (Alphen aan den Rijn, Kluwer Law International, 2003) 110.

fundamental to the development and adoption of international arbitration and are crucial meeting points of the arbitration community. Their role is, therefore unsurprisingly, key in guaranteeing that arbitrators comply with their professional obligations.[3] In analysing how arbitral institutions influence compliance and enforcement of arbitrators' professional obligations, the following sections will focus in particular on their role in: i) overseeing arbitrators' behaviour within arbitral proceedings under their institutional rules; and ii) influencing behaviour through their selections of arbitrators.

A. The Role of the Arbitral Institutions in Overseeing Arbitrators' Behaviour within Arbitral Proceedings

Arbitral institutions, in their role as organisers of proceedings, usually have considerable powers within their rules to oversee arbitrators' behaviour.[4] While there is considerable variance in the involvement of these institutions, with some taking a more interventionist role and others a more hands-off approach,[5] arbitral institutions often work as a safety net which guarantees users an institutional system of remedies against abuses of the process.[6] Arbitral institution involvement may include, amongst others: i) playing a role in selecting or confirming arbitrators; ii) providing a forum for arbitrators to be challenged; and iii) taking measures to guarantee that arbitrators act efficiently. These two last roles will be addressed in this section, and the first will be picked up again when discussing arbitral institutions' interventions in the arbitral market.[7]

i. Arbitral Institutions' Powers to Decide Challenges and Revoke the Appointment of Arbitrators

Arbitral institutions' function as a forum for parties to challenge arbitrators is one of the key roles usually associated with them. While the exact language of the institutional rules varies significantly, it often allows arbitral institutions considerable latitude to remove arbitrators that deviate from acceptable behaviour.[8] Namely, it allows parties to have a remedy against arbitrators who: i) failed to comply with their requirements to be independent or impartial by, for example, failing to disclose a connection with one of the parties or act in a partisan way during the proceedings; or ii) fail to advance an arbitration with reasonable diligence

[3] See Rogers (n 1) 983.

[4] Still, it is important to note that arbitral institutions do not undertake the roles typically associated with professional regulators. Namely, they do not establish training requirements, undertake licensing or accreditation or demand formal continuing professional development requirements.

[5] For an overview, see Rémy Gerbay, *The Functions of Arbitral Institutions* (Alphen aan den Rijn, Kluwer Law International, 2016) 54.

[6] See Janice Lee, 'The Evolving Role of Institutional Arbitration in Preserving Parties' Due Process Rights' (2017) 10 *Contemporary Asia Arbitration Journal* 235.

[7] See ch 8, section I.B.

[8] Eg, Art 14, ICC Rules 2021 establishes that 'A challenge of an arbitrator, whether for an alleged lack of impartiality or independence, or otherwise, shall be made by the submission to the Secretariat of a written statement [...]'. Other arbitral institution rules establish a closed list of grounds that allow an arbitrator to be challenged. However, even those are often constructed broadly. See, eg, Art 10, LCIA Rules 2020.

and dispatch.[9] Often, arbitral institutions also have the power to remove an arbitrator on their own motion if they consider that a serious breach has been committed.[10]

In practice, arbitral institutions' ability to decide a challenge and remove an arbitrator works as a way of these institutions 'sanctioning' arbitrators who deviate from their obligations.[11] Being removed from their position represents to arbitrators: i) a 'direct cost' since they may lose their ability to, totally or partially, claim fees in relation to that case; and ii) an 'indirect cost' since it may diminish their reputation within the arbitral community and arbitral institutions in particular.[12] The concern with these costs strongly incentivises arbitrators to comply with accepted behaviour and, in particular, with the applicable rules of the institution. It is important to note, however, that a decision by an arbitral institution to remove an arbitrator is not a common occurrence.

Figure 8.1 Breakdown of arbitral institutions' arbitral cases[13]

Institution	Number of new cases	Number of challenges	Challenges upheld	% Successful challenges
ICC (2020)	946	92	5	5.4%
LCIA (2020)	407	6	1	16.6%
SCC (2020)	213	19	2	10.5%
HKIAC (2020)	318	1	1	100%
SIAC (2020)	1080	4	1	25%

As can be seen from the figures above, both challenges and arbitral institutions' decisions to remove an arbitrator are relatively rare occurrences.[14] This is the case even when taking into consideration the situations where an arbitrator voluntarily steps down following a challenge.[15] Since the decision to remove an arbitrator can often disrupt the smooth continuation of the arbitral proceedings, arbitral institutions are wary of taking this option, having to weigh the gravity of the infringement against the practicalities of continuing the

[9] For a discussion in the ICC Rules context, see Eric A Schwartz and Yves Derains, *Guide to the ICC Rules of Arbitration*, 2nd edn (Alphen aan den Rijn, Kluwer Law International, 2005) 184.

[10] The ICC Rules uses language that allows the institution broad discretion to remove an arbitrator. Namely, the ICC Court may remove an arbitrator when it 'decides that the arbitrator is prevented de jure or de facto from fulfilling the arbitrator's functions, or that the arbitrator is not fulfilling those functions in accordance with the Rules or within the prescribed time limits'. See ICC 2021 Arbitration Rules, Art 15(2) Also using broad language allowing a removal of an arbitrator by the institution, see LCIA 2020, Arbitration Rules 10(1).

[11] See Dolores Bentolila, *Arbitrators as Lawmakers* (Alphen aan den Rijn, Kluwer Law International, 2017) 249.

[12] It is important to note that traditionally decisions on arbitrators' challenges were not publicised by arbitral institutions. See, Alec Stone Sweet and Florian Grisel, *The Evolution of International Arbitration: Judicialization, Governance, Legitimacy* (Oxford, Oxford University Press, 2017) 227. This is a practice that has somewhat evolved. In this sense, the LCIA has since 2011 made publicly available a database with decisions on arbitral challenges. Starting from 2015, the ICC has also changed its policy to start communicating to parties the reasons underlying their decisions on challenges to arbitrators. It is important to note that even in the case of LCIA, while some of the decisions are public, the name of the arbitrator is generally redacted.

[13] Data from the websites of the different arbitral institutions.

[14] See also Gary Born, *International Commercial Arbitration*, 2nd edn (Alphen aan den Rijn, Wolters Kluwer Law & Business 2014) 1914, noting, however, that challenges have become more common in recent years.

[15] See ibid 1920.

arbitration.[16] Still, the possibility of parties reacting through arbitral institutions against violations of arbitrators' obligations is an important safeguard to ensure that a readily accessible and quick deciding forum is available to the parties.

ii. Discretionary Determination of Fees to Encourage Arbitrators to Conduct Proceedings Efficiently

A more recent instrument that some arbitral institutions started to use in order to incentivise arbitrators to comply with professional goals is to adapt arbitrators' fees.[17] In particular, some arbitral institutions, most notably the ICC, reward arbitrators by increasing their fees when conducting proceedings efficiently and reducing them when arbitrators are inefficient.[18] In this context, efficiency primarily means rapidness and diligence in finalising the proceedings. The advantage of this instrument is that it allows arbitral institutions to shape arbitrators' behaviour without having to undertake more disruptive measures, such as removing an arbitrator.[19] Still, this is far from a universal approach, with most arbitral institutions preferring not to discretionarily change arbitrators' fees as such discretion makes costs and earnings less predictable for both parties and arbitrators.

B. Arbitral Institutions' Power to Shape the Market for Arbitrators and their Effect on Compliance with Professional Obligations

In addition to their powers to oversee arbitral proceedings, arbitral institutions also are essential players in the market for arbitrators. Through their appointment decisions and, to a lesser extent, through their selections to arbitrators' lists, arbitral institutions have, in practice, a great influence over which arbitrators become successful in the market and which do not. Their selections, therefore, have the potential to influence compliance and be used to enforce professional norms. With the aim of better understanding how these selections influence compliance, the following sections will focus on: i) how competition

[16] 'A successful challenge, in particular, can severely disrupt the arbitration if it occurs at an advanced stage of the proceedings.' Schwartz and Derains (n 9) 184. See also Lucy Gordon-Vrbo and Dominik Vock, 'Commentary on the Swiss Rules, Article 12 [Removal of an Arbitrator]' in Manuel Arroyo (ed), *Arbitration in Switzerland: The Practitioner's Guide*, 2nd edn (Alphen aan den Rijn, Kluwer Law International, 2018) 587.

[17] See Barbara Alicja Warwas, *The Liability of Arbitral Institutions: Legitimacy Challenges and Functional Responses* (The Hague, TMC Asser Press, 2017) 68. See also, SIAC Code of Ethics 1.3.: 'The prospective arbitrator confirms that he understands that the Registrar of SIAC will take into account any failure by the prospective arbitrator to discharge his duties to ensure the fair, expeditious, economical and final determination of the dispute when fixing the quantum of fees payable to the arbitrator.'

[18] See ICC Arbitration Rules, Appx III, Art 2. See also Vienna International Arbitral Centre 2018 Rules, Art 44(7) and SCC Rules, Art 49(3): 'In finally determining the Costs of the Arbitration, the Board shall have regard to the extent to which the Arbitral Tribunal has acted in an efficient and expeditious manner.'

[19] A similar measure would be to publicise the names of tardy or unethical arbitrators. See Stephan Wilske, 'The Duty of Arbitral Institutions to Preserve the Integrity of Arbitral Proceedings' (2017) 10 *Contemporary Asia Arbitration Journal* 201, 215. See also Chinese Arbitration Association, Taipei Rules Art 41 which establishes 'if the arbitral tribunal fails to render its final award within the time limit prescribed in or agreed pursuant to Article 21 of the Arbitration Law, CAA may make the names of the arbitrators public in its journals without giving prior notice'. It is worth noting that, as discussed in ch 7, section III.A.ii, public shaming of arbitrators is, however, an option almost never used by arbitral institutions.

between arbitral institutions provides incentives for these to guarantee compliance by arbitrators; and ii) how arbitral institutions play a role in determining who successfully enters the market, tending to invite in those committed to the field.

i. Competitive Pressures Leading Arbitral Institutions to Intervene in the Arbitrators' Market to Guarantee Compliance with Professional Norms

In chapter three, when discussing the market for arbitral institutions, it was noted that, despite charging fees for their services, arbitral institutions do not act in a way fully akin to commercial entities.[20] However, it was also noted that arbitral institutions are increasingly competing in a global market.[21] As arbitral institutions gradually expand their operations more globally, a new era where arbitral institutions increasingly face off in the same markets has emerged. Guaranteeing that the arbitral proceedings established under the banner of the institution are perceived as 'efficient' and 'high-quality' is a key aspect of maintaining their competitive edge in the market.[22] This competition, in turn, creates pressure in the downstream market for arbitrators for the latter to comply with these goals.

Figure 8.2 Representation of the relationship between the market for arbitral institutions and arbitrators

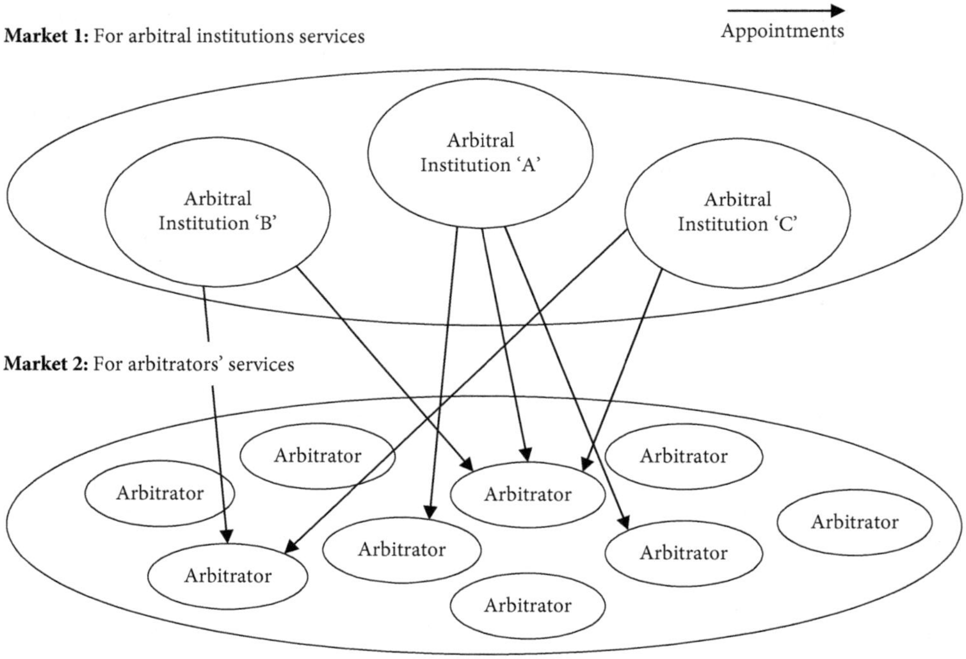

[20] See ch 3, section I.A.

[21] See Fernando Dias Simões, 'A Dispute Resolution Center for the Brics?' in Rostam J Neuwirth, Alexandr Svetlicinii and Denis De Castro Halis (eds), *The BRICS-Lawyers' Guide to Global Cooperation* (Cambridge, Cambridge University Press, 2017) 303.

[22] See Warwas (n 17) 38.

Arbitral institutions benefit from selecting arbitrators who help them ensure the reputation of the arbitral institution and, more widely, arbitration as a system of resolving disputes.[23] The higher the level of competitive pressure on the arbitral institutions market ('Market 1'), the higher the pressure they will conceivably put on arbitrators ('Market 2') for these to act in a way that will reflect positively on the institution. Conceivably, the inner dynamics of arbitral institutions may help exacerbate this tendency as the professional future of those working within arbitral institutions is often linked to the institution's success. Indeed, holding a position or working within an arbitral institution is often used successfully as a stepping stone to increase the likelihood of being appointed in arbitration cases.

In any case, arbitrators are well aware of the importance of being on arbitral institutions' radars and maintaining a relationship with them.[24] Therefore, they will likely adapt their behaviour in order to comply with arbitral institutions' preferences and conceivably increase the likelihood of being appointed. Bad previous experiences, such as lack of responsiveness or efficiency by an arbitrator, are certainly taken into consideration by the arbitral institution when undertaking future appointments.[25] Conversely, arbitrators perceived to excel by an institution may see the likelihood of being appointed again increase. Consequently, the need to satisfy arbitral institutions provides a strong incentive for arbitrators to avoid acting in ways that are considered improper within arbitral circles.

To this extent, arbitral institutions have the potential to play the role of powerbrokers in determining which arbitrators become successful and to discipline what the 'arbitral community' perceives as unwanted behaviour by arbitrators. While arbitral institutions do not have by legal statute the power to stop arbitrators from continuing to operate in the market, they have de facto the capability to severely curtail the ability of an arbitrator who has performed unethically to find future appointments. It should be noted that arbitral institutions usually do not make formal decisions to stop appointing an arbitrator in future proceedings. Still, more informally, those within an institution may decide not to consider an arbitrator in future instances.[26]

ii. The Role of Arbitral Institutions in Selecting who Successfully Enters the Profession and its Influence on Compliance

Another way arbitral institutions influence compliance relates to their key role in selecting who enters the 'profession.' As discussed in chapter three, arbitral institutions are often the source of the first appointment in an arbitrator's career and are usually important in the

[23] See Stephen R Bond, 'The International Arbitrator: From the Perspective of the ICC International Court of Arbitration' (1991) 12 *Northwestern Journal of International Law & Business* 1, 8.

[24] Noting the link between 'super arbitrators' and arbitral institutions, see Florian Grisel, 'Competition and Cooperation in International Commercial Arbitration: The Birth of a Transnational Legal Profession: Grisel' (2017) 51 *Law & Society Review* 790, 818.

[25] The power of arbitral institutions to create pressure on arbitrators through the implicit threat of (informal) 'blacklisting' has been noted. See Ksenia Polonskaya, 'Arbitral Institutions' Response to Perceived Legitimacy Deficits: Promoting Diversity, Transparency and Expedition in Investor-State Arbitration' in Freya Baetens (ed), *Legitimacy of Unseen Actors in International Adjudication*, 1st edn (Cambridge, Cambridge University Press, 2019) 371.

[26] See Wilske (n 19) 215.

early career of many arbitrators.[27] Being less pressured than parties to appoint highly influential and experienced arbitrators, arbitral institutions sometimes take the opportunity to appoint more junior members of the community, especially in the context of smaller-scale, single-arbitrator proceedings.[28] Since previous experience serving as an arbitrator is one of the key considerations to be appointed,[29] arbitral institutions' role in 'recruiting' members into the community is, therefore, central.

The role of arbitral institutions in selecting who enters the market extends beyond simply providing first appointments. Another important example of how an arbitral institution may play a role in helping a prospective arbitrator's career is by adding their name to the institution's roster of arbitrators. These are lists of arbitrators that, depending on the rules of the institution, may be relied upon by the institution in future appointments. Another example is inviting a potential member to participate as a speaker in one of the arbitral institutions' events. These decisions by arbitral institutions, while not guaranteeing appointments, signal quality and trust in that individual, helping the market identify those who are appropriate to be selected as arbitrators.

Since, as explored above, arbitral institutions rely on a reputation as a fair and independent institution as a key tool for competing in the market, they will benefit from scouting prospective arbitrators who will help them improve this reputation.[30] Arbitral institutions, therefore, have an incentive to maintain the close-knit nature of international arbitration, only adding new members they have vetted and considered committed to the arbitral enterprise.[31] Since arbitral institutions develop relationships with many community members and can observe previous work undertaken by prospective arbitrators who have acted as counsel, these institutions are arguably in a particularly good position to undertake this function.

II. The Role of Professional Associations in Enforcing Arbitrators' Professional Norms

Beyond arbitral institutions, other organisations play a role in enforcing arbitrators' obligations. In this regard, it is important to analyse both the role played by: i) arbitral professional associations, ie, the voluntary associations that encompass professionals linked to arbitration; and ii) the role played by other professional associations that, albeit not directed to arbitration, might have members that also work as arbitrators. In particular, because many arbitrators are also practising lawyers, local bar associations could play a

[27] See Tony Cole and others, 'Arbitration in the Americas: Report on a Survey of Arbitration Practitioners' (Leicester, University of Leicester, 2018) 29, 45, available at ciarglobal.com, last accessed 12 November 2023.

[28] See Rémy Gerbay, "How Does a New Arbitrator Get Their First Appointment?', A Q&A Session with Remy Gerbay (Interview Given to Lexis PSL Arbitration)' (Social Science Research Network, 2014) SSRN Scholarly Paper ID 2519505 2.

[29] See Lucy Greenwood and Mark Baker, 'Getting a Better Balance on International Arbitration Tribunals' (2012) 28 *Arbitration International* 653, 658.

[30] See Franz T Schwarz and Christian W Konrad, *The Vienna Rules: A Commentary on International Arbitration in Austria* (Alphen aan den Rijn, Kluwer Law International BV, 2009) 121: 'of course, the VIAC, like any arbitral institution, strives to appoint arbitrators of quality, as a poor selection and offended parties will reflect badly on the institution's reputation'.

[31] See Rogers (n 1) 975.

part in regulating arbitration. As it will be seen, both kinds of associations play, however, a limited role. This will be seen in turn.

A. The Role of Arbitral Professional Associations

Chapters four and five argued that arbitral professional associations were considerably different from professional associations in other fields. One of the key aspects of this difference is that arbitral professional associations, despite actively developing professional norms, rarely intervene in enforcing those same standards.[32] In the same vein, they also do not filter entrance, as membership is not a prerequisite to act in the market. Also, these associations are typically open to anyone wishing to join.[33] In this sense, their direct role in enforcing professional norms may be qualified as minimal.[34] They mostly play an indirect role by reinforcing the close-knit nature of the arbitral community. This allows information about compliance to flow through the community in the fashion described in chapter seven, allowing reputation sanctions to work better in this market.

A notable exception to this is the Chartered Institute of Arbitrators (CIArb). Founded as The Institute of Arbitrators in 1915, the Chartered Institute of Arbitrators comes closer in both aims and functioning to a professional association in the English tradition. It filters entrance by determining different grades of membership that can only be achieved by undertaking training organised by the Institute and demonstrating achievement in arbitration.[35] Pursuant to its by-laws, CIArb also has the power to investigate and sanction misconduct allegations by its members, a unique characteristic amongst the professional associations in the arbitration field.[36]

Two notes regarding the disciplining powers of CIArb are important. First, actual usage of these powers by CIArb seems rare,[37] with information only having been made

[32] See Cameron L Sabin, 'The Adjudicatory Boat without a Keel: Private Arbitration and the Need for Public Oversight of Arbitrators' (2001) 87 *Iowa Law Review* 1337, 1354.

[33] This is the case of international arbitration associations such as the International Council for International Arbitration (ICCA) that invites membership both from individuals and corporations, not determining specific prerequisites for those wishing to join. In the same vein, national arbitral associations are usually open to any wishing to join. As an example the Club Español de Arbitraje (CEA) determines in Art 6 of its by-laws that membership should be composed of those that have 'ample experience in arbitration'. In practice, it does not, however, establish a filter of experience for membership. In the same vein, the Comité Français de l'Arbitrage (CFA) establishes in Art 6 of its by-laws that membership is open to all jurists or representatives of the business world interested in arbitration.

[34] It should be noted that some national arbitral associations have in their statutes provisions that allow disciplining their members. To this effect, using broad language, the CEA by-laws, in its Art 11, has powers to, inter alia, expel its members that display behaviour that seriously affects the 'interests of the association'. See also CFA by-laws allowing expulsion of members which incur in a 'serious breach'. From communications with members of the respective arbitral communities, it is apparent that these provisions have, however, not been used to discipline members who have breached ethical duties within arbitral proceedings.

[35] The CIArb establishes three membership categories: 'Associate', 'Member' and 'Fellow'. Associate, the lowest of the aforementioned categories, demands successfully completing one of CIArb's introductory courses or a minimum of six months' experience in dispute avoidance or dispute management.

[36] See, CIArb's Royal Charter Bye-Laws and Schedule to the Bye-Laws, Art 5(6).

[37] Sceptics have noted that industry self-regulation is often marked by weak enforcement and secretive and mild sanctioning. See Neil Gunningham and Joseph Rees, 'Industry Self-Regulation: An Institutional Perspective' (1997) 19 *Law & Policy* 363, 370.

available in very few instances.[38] Second, despite CIArb's popularity in and outside England, participation in this association is by no means universal. Many of the most active arbitrators are not affiliated with CIArb. Due to the voluntary nature of an association like CIArb, it is plausible that very strong enforcement could deter some participants from joining the association. This would be the case, particularly, in those environments where joining a particular association is not understood as key to being successful as an arbitrator. As discussed, in the arbitration market, despite arbitrators often joining multiple associations, membership in any particular one is not considered essential to operate in the market.

Still, the fact that CIArb cumulates the ability to discipline its members with one of the highest memberships amongst arbitral associations seems to indicate that resistance by the association's members is not the main factor explaining why these rarely enforce ethical obligations. Rather, it appears to be outside of arbitral associations' scope to assume these functions. Indeed, no significant voices inside the arbitral community push arbitral associations to be more proactive in this regard. Again, it is important to note that, as explored in chapter three, since arbitrators largely depend on their integration in the community to continue operating in the market, formal decisions to 'expel' or 'suspend' a member are usually unnecessary. Instead, informal shunning of a member has largely the same effect.

B. The Role of Other Professional Associations

The potential role of other professional associations should also be noted. As most arbitrators cumulate this role with membership in another profession, their actions as arbitrators can sometimes fall under the scope of the disciplinary powers of other professional associations. Since arbitrators most often cumulate work as legal counsel, local legal bars, in particular, could theoretically exercise some level of discipline over arbitrators.[39] Arguably, some violations of professional norms by arbitrators could be construed, depending on the exact wording of the relevant statutory and ethical rules, as a violation of their local bar's ethical rules and open, in this way, an avenue for disciplinary action by the bar.[40]

Still, it should be noted that lawyers' local bars have usually not taken a proactive attitude in enforcing and disciplining lawyers in relation to their role as arbitrators. Exceptionally, some jurisdictions have enacted specific rules of conduct for domestic and international arbitrators.[41] However, in most circumstances, it is generally understood that professional rules designed to regulate an attorney-client relationship do not specifically apply when a

[38] It is important to note that CIArb does not make available comprehensive statistics on its disciplinary proceedings. See Report from The Club des Juristes, Report: The Arbitrators' Liability, June 2017, available at: staging.leclubdesjuristes.com/wp-content/uploads/2017/06/CDJ_Rapports_Responsabilit%C3%A9-de-l%C2%B9arbitre_Juin-2017_UK_web.pdf, last accessed 1 April 2019.

[39] See Born (n 14) 2892.

[40] See Shari Maynard, 'The Current State of Arbitrator Ethics and Party Recourse Against Grievances' (2016) 8 *Yearbook on Arbitration and Mediation* 204, 217.

[41] See, eg, Code of Conduct for Italian Lawyers approved by the National Bar Council during the session of 31 January 2014, Art 61.

lawyer acts as an arbitrator.[42] In a broader sense, local bars' disinterest in regulating international arbitration might derive from the notion that the field is only participated by a small, often elite, subsection of the legal profession that could be put at a disadvantage if a stringent understanding of local norms would apply.[43]

III. The Role of Courts in Enforcing Arbitrators' Professional and Ethical Obligations

Following an analysis of the role of arbitral institutions and professional associations in enforcing arbitrators' professional norms, it is important to analyse the role played by national courts in this regard. While national courts have mostly limited powers to intervene in arbitral proceedings under the current arbitration legislative frameworks, they still hold powers that allow them to review the actions undertaken by arbitrators. As will be seen, this allows courts to enforce arbitrators' professional obligations indirectly. Two important types of power in this regard are usually afforded to courts: i) deciding the removal of an arbitrator following a challenge by one of the parties; and ii) at the seat or the place of enforcement annulling or refusing to enforce an arbitral award. These will be analysed in turn.

A. National Courts' Power to Remove an Arbitrator from Arbitral Proceedings

The first important power of national courts to regulate arbitrators relates to the possibility of removing an arbitrator from an arbitral proceeding. During arbitral proceedings, parties are usually entitled to recourse to national courts at the seat of arbitration if one or more of the arbitrators fail to comply with essential obligations.[44] While the exact wording of the applicable provisions changes between jurisdictions, parties are usually entitled to challenge an arbitrator if: i) there are justifiable doubts as to the arbitrator's impartiality or independence; or ii) the arbitrator fails to perform his duties within a reasonable time frame.[45] Typically, courts only intervene after a first decision is taken by the arbitral tribunal itself or the arbitral institution responsible for organising the proceedings.[46]

[42] See Born (n 14) 1970.

[43] For the same reasons, local bar associations are usually uninterested in regulating the conduct of their lawyers operating as counsel in international arbitrations, especially those taking place abroad. See Catherine A Rogers, 'Fit and Function in Legal Ethics: Developing a Code of Conduct for International Arbitration' (2001) 23 *Michigan Journal of International Law* 341, 341.

[44] It is important to note that a few jurisdictions do not allow interlocutory challenges of arbitrators. This is the case of the US, where the FAA does not envision interlocutory judicial challenges of arbitrators. See Born (n 14) 1928. Other jurisdictions only allow national courts to hear challenges in the case of ad hoc arbitrations. See ibid 1926.

[45] See UNCITRAL Model Law, Arts 12 and 14.

[46] To this effect, the UNCITRAL Model Law allows parties to challenge an arbitrator in case the arbitrator does not voluntarily withdraw from their position. The first decision will be made by the arbitral tribunal who will

In this sense, the possibility of parties requesting courts to revoke an arbitrator's mandate plays a regulatory role, as it modifies the grid of incentives an arbitrator faces. It plays an effect similar to the removal by an arbitral institution: by removing an arbitrator, a court imposes a direct cost on an arbitrator since they may be unable to recover fees from the case.[47] Further, a high-profile removal from a case by a court might affect the arbitrator's reputation[48] and, in this sense, affect an arbitrator's ability to find further appointments in this field.[49] However, not all court decisions to remove an arbitrator will necessarily affect reputation in the same way. As will be discussed below, the arbitral community plays an important role in mediating these effects.

B. The Regulatory Effect of Annulling or Refusing Enforcement of an Arbitral Award

Under the current system, both national courts at the seat of arbitration and the courts of the jurisdiction where enforcement is sought may, in theory, scrutinise the award.[50] At the seat of arbitration, national courts may, under some circumstances, review requests to set aside the award in accordance with the grounds prescribed in the law of the seat. This usually includes serious violations of due process guarantees, such as the arbitral tribunal not allowing the possibility of a party presenting their case or formal requirements, such as the tribunal not being constituted in accordance with the agreement of the parties.[51] Importantly, it further allows the court to annul awards that violate public policy, such as an award that would run against the dominant moral considerations in that jurisdiction.[52]

Further, in the jurisdiction where enforcement of an award is sought, national courts may refuse to recognise and enforce the award against the limited grounds prescribed in the New York Convention or where, in the rare cases that the Convention would not be applicable, the grounds defined by the law of the state where the enforcement takes place. These most often overlap with the grounds provided for setting aside an award.[53] Article V of the New York Convention, the key provision in this aspect, provides seven grounds that allow the court to not recognise and enforce the award, including the invalidity of the arbitration agreement, lack of proper notice of the arbitration proceedings,

decide whether there are reasons to remove the arbitrator. If the tribunal refuses the challenge, the party will usually have the possibility of requesting the competent national court to review this decision. Rules from arbitral institutions, however, may allow it to first review the challenge in lieu of the arbitral tribunal. See, eg, ICC 2021 Arbitration Rules, Art 14.

[47] See English Arbitration Act 1996, Art 24(4).

[48] Conceivably, also the reputation of the arbitral institution responsible for the appointment may be affected. See Karel Daele, *Challenge and Disqualification of Arbitrators in International Arbitration* (Alphen aan den Rijn, Kluwer Law International, 2012) 218.

[49] Conversely, a strong pre-existing reputation can conceivably help, to an extent, shield arbitrators from challenges. Noting that in the well-known *AT&T Corporation and Another v Saudi Cable Company* case, the strong reputation and experience of the chairman of the arbitration were (amongst several other factors) considered in dismissing a challenge, see ibid 284.

[50] See also ch 2, section I.C.

[51] See UNCITRAL Model Law, Art 34.

[52] For a discussion on the concept of international public policy, see ch 6, section IV.A.

[53] See UNCITRAL Model Law, Arts 34 and 36.

the award dealing with differences beyond the scope of the arbitration, and the award being against the public policy of the state.[54]

Together with the possibility of setting aside an award, the possibility of an arbitral award being refused enforcement operates as an incentive for arbitrators to comply with their professional and ethical obligations. Courts provide a public forum that will review arbitrators' actions. Having an award set aside or refused enforcement may affect the position of an arbitrator within the community, as a negative review of the actions taken during the proceedings may conceivably affect an arbitrator's reputation. However, it is important to note that the effects of these national courts' interventions are more limited than could be otherwise anticipated as the arbitral community mediates its influence on the market. The arbitral community often expects courts to have a hands-off approach regarding arbitration.[55] These ideas will be explored in more detail next.

i. Setting Aside an Arbitral Award and Refusing Enforcement as Incentives for Compliance

When a losing party in an arbitral proceeding applies to have the arbitral award set aside or applies to have the enforcement of the award refused, these often involve arguments related to the acts and decisions taken by the arbitrators in the panel. Losing parties often argue that the arbitrators have violated due process principles or that the arbitral award violated the public policy of the concerned jurisdiction. By petitioning a court to set aside or stop enforcement of an arbitral award, the parties allow an arbitral tribunal to review the behaviour of arbitrators. While these are sometimes used merely as a dilatory tactic to avoid prompt enforcement, they also have the ability to affect arbitrators' incentives.

Arbitrators and the broader arbitral community pay considerable attention to the decisions of courts that scrutinise awards, especially those that decide to set aside or refuse enforcement. In a context where many arbitral awards are confidential, the information provided by courts – whose decisions are almost always publicly available – is a relevant source of information regarding the general 'quality' of arbitral proceedings in a particular jurisdiction but also, in some circumstances, allow information to be obtained regarding specific arbitrators.[56] Even when the arbitrator's name is not mentioned in the court decision, sometimes arbitration insiders can identify the relevant arbitrator, and such information might circulate within the community.

It is, therefore, conceivable that arbitrators incorporate the risk of their award being annulled or not enforced when deciding how to act in this market. Having a decision annulled or enforcement refused conceivably invites unwanted scrutiny of the actions of the arbitrators involved. As these events are relatively rare and the community closely monitors

[54] For an analysis of these grounds, see Emmanuel Gaillard and George A Bermann, *Guide on the Convention on the Recognition and Enforcement of Foreign Arbitral Awards: New York, 1958* (Leiden, Brill, 2017) 129.

[55] See Juslian DM Lew, 'Does National Court Involvement Undermine the International Arbitration Process' (2008) 24 *American University International Law Review* 489, 537.

[56] Enforcement proceedings have been noted to provide one of the rare opportunities to glimpse inside the arbitral system. Catherine A Rogers, 'Transparency in International Commercial Arbitration' (2006) 54 *Kansas Law Review* 1301, 1313.

judicial decisions related to arbitration, these cases are often widely discussed. Given that arbitration largely operates as a reputation market, arbitrators are, therefore, incentivised to avoid having their award set aside or refused enforcement since any allegation of misconduct made in a court of law against an arbitrator can easily become public and possibly diminish the arbitrator's position within the community.[57]

Moreover, other factors may also explain why arbitrators take steps to avoid being challenged, see their awards set aside or refused enforcement. In the context where most arbitrators are deeply committed to the field, they may feel severely uncomfortable regarding challenges made by the parties or having their award set aside or refused enforcement by a court. For arbitrators, misconduct allegations likely carry a personal element beyond simply a damaged reputation in the market.[58] Indeed, in more general terms, a strong aversion to being overturned by judicial decision-makers, be it arbitrators or national judges, is often identified.[59]

Overall, and independently of the reason that leads arbitrators to want to avoid court decisions not confirming their awards, it is clear that courts, both at the seat and the place of enforcement, do provide a mechanism for enforcing regulatory norms of behaviour in the market. By creating strings of decisions that punish certain behaviours, courts also act as enforcers of the dominant values regarding arbitration. As is to be expected, the competent national courts at the jurisdictions where arbitrations are most commonly seated – places like London, Geneva, Paris or Singapore – play an enhanced enforcing role in this aspect.

ii. The Practical Limits to the Courts Acting as 'Regulators' of the Behaviour of Commercial Arbitrators

The power of courts to regulate the behaviour of international commercial arbitrators is, however, more limited than otherwise would be expected. First, a decision by the court to annul and not enforce an award does not often impose a direct cost on arbitrators. Even if the award is annulled or determined not to be enforceable, arbitrators will usually retain their fees (notwithstanding the liability risks discussed below). In this aspect, the effect of courts' decisions takes place mostly through affecting arbitrators' reputations. However, it is important to note that having decisions confirmed or annulled is only one of the many aspects that comprise an arbitrator's reputation. Having a decision annulled may not significantly affect an arbitrator's career, especially a well-established one, as long as the facts that transpire are not perceived to be particularly scandalous.

It should further be noted that it is far from automatic that any court's decision would affect an arbitrator's reputation. Indeed, the arbitral community often bands together to

[57] As Karton notes: 'Rendering an award that is the subject of a successful challenge implies (in arbitrators' perception, if not always in fact) a failure on the part of the tribunal. It is a black mark on an arbitrator's résumé and may even affect his or her ability to garner future appointments.' Joshua DH Karton, *The Culture of International Arbitration and The Evolution of Contract Law* (Oxford, Oxford University Press, 2013) 48. See also, Sam Luttrell, *Bias Challenges in International Commercial Arbitration: The Need for a 'real Danger' Test* (Alphen aan den Rijn, Kluwer Law International, 2009) 254.

[58] Luttrell (n 57) 254.

[59] See Susan D Franck, 'The Role of International Arbitrators' (2005) 12 *ILSA Journal of International and Comparative Law* 499, 512.

criticise particular judicial decisions that it sees as not in line with best arbitral practices or are otherwise unfair, siding with the arbitrators' behaviour.[60] In this sense, the arbitral community mediates the influence courts have on the arbitral market. While the arbitral community offers a closely-knit network through which information regarding arbitrators can pass, it also comments on and contextualises those decisions. Through the many informal contacts taken in professional settings, community gatherings, and sometimes academic discussions, the arbitral community ascertains if a deviation actually occurred and how serious it was.

Another important limitation to courts' intervention in the arbitration market is the restricted role courts are expected to play.[61] As discussed in chapter two, most legislators have constructed a framework with limited grounds to allow court intervention. Also, the dominant narrative establishes that courts should respect the autonomy of arbitral tribunals and avoid full reviews of the merits of the case.[62] As discussed in chapter four, some level of regulatory competition also takes place with jurisdictions that over-intervene in arbitral proceedings being shunned and running the risk of parties delocalising their proceedings to other jurisdictions. To the extent judges follow the dominant 'pro-arbitration' understandings and feel motivated by the enterprise of attracting arbitral proceedings to the jurisdiction, their intervention will be typically limited.[63]

Altogether, it is not surprising that the setting aside or refusals of enforcement of international arbitration awards are relatively rare in most jurisdictions.[64] Typically, courts only annul or refuse enforcement if arbitrators seriously infringe on their obligations. In the cases where national courts overextend their review, an arbitrator's position in the market will often not be affected as the community will understand it as an unwarranted decision. Still, courts play a role that can be defined 'as the north point on a compass that keeps arbitral proceedings on course'.[65] They provide a safety mechanism that helps guarantee that parties have a recourse mechanism in case deviations happen and a forum whose power to review actions remains an important deterrent against complacent arbitrators.[66]

[60] Observing that '[s]ome less-developed' jurisdictions have taken decisions refusing to enforce awards that were 'manifestly wrong', see Born (n 14) 3716.

[61] In this sense, national courts have been argued as having to 'strike an exceedingly fine balance between party autonomy and a minimum competence for national judicial review' as 'too much judicial review will transfer real decision power from the arbitral tribunal (…) to a national court whose party neutrality may be considerably less'. William Michael Reisman, *Systems of Control in International Adjudication and Arbitration: Breakdown and Repair* (Durham, Duke University Press, 1992) 112.

[62] Defining the idea that courts will not review the substance of arbitrators' decisions contained in foreign or nondomestic arbitral awards as a 'sacrosanct principle of international arbitration', see Born (n 14) 3706.

[63] Noting the 'pro-arbitration' attitude of Hong Kong's Courts as a key to the success to Hong Kong as an arbitration hub, see Chiann Bao, 'Hong Kong Courts: International Arbitration Law in the Making' [2019] *Belgian Review of Arbitration* 615, 628.

[64] Catherine A Rogers, *Ethics in International Arbitration* (Oxford, Oxford University Press, 2014) 239. See also Jean-François Poudret and Sébastien Besson, *Comparative Law of International Arbitration* (London, Sweet & Maxwell, 2007) 845. Indicating that the statistical likelihood for a challenge of an award to be successful before the Swedish Courts of Appeal to be only around 5%, see Robin Oldenstam, 'Due Process Paranoia or Prudence?' in Patrik Schöldström and Alex Calissendorff (eds), *Stockholm Arbitration Yearbook 2019* (Alphen aan den Rijn, Kluwer Law International, 2019) 126.

[65] Rogers (n 64) 239.

[66] The power of national courts to influence the grid of incentives of arbitrators has inclusively led some to argue for a more stringent approach in reviewing arbitral awards. Most notably, Eric Posner has argued for national courts to take a 'probabilistic' merit review of arbitral awards as to incentivise arbitrators to respect mandatory rules. Eric A Posner, 'Arbitration and the Harmonization of International Commercial Law: A Defense of

IV. Civil Liability as a Mechanism to Enforce Arbitrators' Professional Obligations

Closely linked to the court's power to intervene in arbitral proceedings is the possibility of parties commencing proceedings to hold arbitrators liable for violating their legal and contractual obligations. How this can be used to help enforce arbitrators' professional obligations is reasonably straightforward. In theory, liability suits may comprise an important risk for arbitrators who do not comply with their professional and ethical obligations, potentially imposing a monetary cost on deviation.[67] However, it is important to note that many jurisdictions and arbitral institutions limit arbitrators' liability, albeit to different extents.[68] These limitations and a few examples of how the liability of arbitrators operates will be seen next.

A. Limitations of Arbitrators' Liability Through Legal Acts and Arbitral Institutions Rules

For understandable reasons, many jurisdictions limit the possibility of parties procuring damages from arbitrators, albeit to different degrees. While virtually no jurisdiction offers arbitrators full immunity from suit, in most states, some level of protection is afforded, either by expressly limiting liability in legislative frameworks or by the effect of courts' decisions. Underlying this protection are policy considerations that, albeit not uniformly accepted, have held sway inside and outside arbitration circles. The thrust of the argument relies on the idea that if arbitrators did not have at least some immunity from suit, they could face unwarranted pressure from disgruntled parties, which could advance spurious lawsuits to harass arbitrators or as a tactic to derail arbitral proceedings.[69]

The idea of establishing specific legal rules guaranteeing arbitrators' immunity has traditionally been the option of common law jurisdictions, where legislative acts and courts often curtail the extent to which an arbitrator may be held liable.[70] For example, in England and Wales, the Arbitration Act 1996 provides that 'an arbitrator is not liable for anything done or omitted to do in the discharge or purported discharge of his functions as arbitrator unless the act or omission is shown to have been in bad faith'.[71] In the US, courts have generally established an even more shielding framework for arbitrators, broadly equating arbitral immunity with judicial immunity and, therefore, guaranteeing a very protective regime.[72]

Mitsubishi' (1999) 39 *Virginia Journal of International Law* 647. This is an approach, however, not preferred by the arbitral community. See, eg, Born (n 14) 3706.

[67] See Andrew F Popper, 'In Defense of Deterrence' (2011) 75 *Albany Law Review* 181.

[68] For an overview, see Susan D Franck, 'The Liability of International Arbitrators: A Comparative Analysis and Proposal for Qualified Immunity' (2000) 20 *New York Law School Journal of International and Comparative Law* 1.

[69] See Julian DM Lew, Loukas A Mistelis and Stefan Kröll, *Comparative International Commercial Arbitration* (Alphen aan den Rijn, Kluwer Law International, 2003) 288.

[70] See Philippe Fouchard and others, *Fouchard Gaillard Goldman on International Commercial Arbitration* (Alphen aan den Rijn, Kluwer Law International, 1999) 591. See also Franck (n 68) 18.

[71] English Arbitration Act 1996, s 29(1).

[72] See Lew, Mistelis and Kröll (n 69) 292; Nadia Smahi, 'The Arbitrator's Liability and Immunity Under Swiss Law – Part I' (2016) 34 *ASA Bulletin* 876, 890.

In civil law countries, despite the fact that arbitrators' immunity has traditionally been less of a concern to courts and legislators, deference to the idea that arbitrators must be protected from liability also holds sway. For example, French courts have established a high threshold demanding arbitrators to incur 'a personal breach equivalent to wilful misrepresentation or constitutive of fraud, gross negligence, or a denial of justice', often equating the protection given to arbitrators to that given to judges.[73] Also, in Germany, the Federal Supreme Court has held that the parties implicitly agreed that the liability of an arbitrator should not go further than that of a judge, even despite the German legal provisions not expressly addressing arbitrators' immunity.[74]

Finally, it should also be taken into consideration that arbitral institutions' rules often limit the liability of arbitrators and the arbitral institutions themselves.[75] For example, the ICC establishes that: 'The arbitrators, any person appointed by the arbitral tribunal, the emergency arbitrator, the Court and its members, the ICC and its employees, and the ICC National Committees and Groups and their employees and representatives shall not be liable to any person for any act or omission in connection with the arbitration, except to the extent such limitation of liability is prohibited by applicable law.'[76] Similar provisions are also established in the LCIA, HKIAC and the SIAC rules.[77]

B. The Rare Number of Instances Arbitrators are Held Liable for Damages

Despite the restrictive legal regime, courts still sporadically hold arbitrators liable. Such instances seem, however, to come very few and far between. The oft-quoted *Raoul Duval v V* provides an example of how civil liability can provide negative consequences to arbitrators who deviate from the rules regarding independence and impartiality. In this case, the chairperson of the arbitral tribunal started to work for one of the parties the day after the arbitral tribunal issued its award, a fact he failed to disclose.[78] After successfully vacating the arbitral award, Duval sued the arbitrator for the damages caused. The Tribunal de Grand Instance, Paris, agreed that the arbitrator was contractually liable to pay the suing party the fees paid to the arbitrators, the arbitral institution and the costs of defence.

The Finnish Supreme Court case *Urho, Sirkka and Juuka Ruola v X* provides another of the few examples where an arbitrator was held liable after seriously breaching their

[73] See Cour de Cassation – Première chambre civile, Arrêt n° 2 du 15 janvier 2014 (11–17.196). See also Lew, Mistelis and Kröll (n 69) 292; Fouchard and others (n 70) 588.

[74] See Lew, Mistelis and Kröll (n 69) 292. See also Christian Hausmaninger, 'Civil Liability of Arbitrators-Comparative Analysis and Proposals for Reform' (1990) 7 *Journal of International Arbitration* 7, 36.

[75] It should be noted that even without express rules determining exclusion of liability, arbitral immunity may extend to arbitral institutions. See Hausmaninger (n 74) 39.

[76] See Art 41, ICC 2021 Arbitration Rules.

[77] See Art 31, 2020 LCIA Arbitration Rules, Art 46, 2018 HKIAC Administered Arbitration Rules and Art 38, 2016 SIAC Arbitration Rules.

[78] For a background on the facts of the case, see Michael Hwang, Katie Chung and Fong Cheng, 'Claims Against Arbitrators for Breach of Ethical Duties' in Arthur W Rovine (ed), *Contemporary Issues in International Arbitration and Mediation: The Fordham Papers 2007* (Leiden, Brill, 2008) 238.

professional obligation.[79] In this case, following a successful annulment of an arbitral award determined in an ad hoc setting, the plaintiff started proceedings against the arbitrator for the costs and expenses of the arbitration. The Finnish Supreme Court held that the arbitrator's failure to disclose that he had previously provided several legal opinions to the respondent company constituted a breach of contract. It, therefore, awarded the plaintiff the costs and expenses of the arbitration.

All in all, liability may be a consideration for arbitrators, especially considering that being sued, even if ultimately the defendant prevails, might still impose considerable costs on the sued party. Still, the risk of liability seems to play, at most, a peripheral role in enforcing arbitrators' professional obligations.[80] First, the number of cases in which an arbitrator was successfully sued seems to be too small to be a critical factor in explaining arbitrators' compliance. Further, there does not seem to be a link between jurisdictions offering less protection to an arbitrator and higher levels of compliance. Indeed, the liability of arbitrators has not been a central point of discussion in arbitral circles,[81] overall signalling that this is not, at least so far, a key concern for arbitrators.

V. Criminal Liability as a Mechanism to Enforce Arbitrators' Professional Obligations

One last point worth considering is the possibility of arbitrators being held criminally liable for actions undertaken in connection to their role as arbitrators. Criminal sanctions, most notably imprisonment, can obviously be a serious deterrent to illicit behaviour.[82] Further, criminal sanctions have the power to affect the agent by diminishing their reputation and social position.[83] In a reputation-driven market, as arbitration notably is, it is easy to understand that arbitrators would find any involvement in criminal proceedings something to be avoided at all costs.[84] Still, the option to use criminal sanctions as a way of controlling arbitrators' behaviour is a controversial issue. Criminalisation opens an avenue for states to control the actions of arbitrators,[85] either as a way to honestly try to further

[79] See Martin Maisner, *Czech and Central European Yearbook of Arbitration – 2012: Party Autonomy versus Autonomy of Arbitrators* (Alexander J Bělohlávek and Naděžda Rozehnalova eds, New York, Juris Publishing Inc, 2012) 157.

[80] See Born (n 14) 2012.

[81] Noting that the discussions on civil liability of arbitrators have often been neglected, see Hausmaninger (n 74) 8.

[82] Summarising the research on the deterrence power of criminal sanctions, see Daniel S Nagin, 'Criminal Deterrence Research at the Outset of the Twenty-First Century' (1998) 23 *Crime and Justice* 1. It is important to note that research has shown that more important than the harshness of the sentence, key factors to deterrence are the swiftness of sentencing and the likelihood of detection. See also Peter J Henning, 'Is Deterrence Relevant in Sentencing White-Collar Criminals' (2015) 61 *Wayne Law Review* 27, 47.

[83] Research has demonstrated that, eg, in the field of tax compliance, criminal proceedings, due to their strong effect on reputation and community stance, are a much more powerful deterrent than civil liability proceedings. See Steven Klepper and Daniel Nagin, 'Tax Compliance and Perceptions of the Risks of Detection and Criminal Prosecution' (1989) 23 *Law and Society Review* 209.

[84] See Lin Yifei, *Judicial Review of Arbitration: Law and Practice in China* (Alphen aan den Rijn, Kluwer Law International, 2018) 163.

[85] See Mohamed Sweify, 'Criminal Sanctions Targeting Arbitrators: An Egyptian Perspective' (2019) 11 *International Journal of Arab Arbitration* 69, 106.

guarantee the fairness of arbitral proceedings or, more cynically, as a way to influence arbitrators not to rule against the interests of the state or some of its key figures.

As a general rule, most jurisdictions have not opted to establish criminal norms specifically targeting arbitrators. Still, naturally, some serious deviations by arbitrators of their professional obligations can be construed as a violation of more general criminal provisions, such as bribery, extortion or money laundering. While this does not exclude the possibility that the threat of criminal prosecution is playing a role in dissuading arbitrators from undertaking serious criminal offences, it is important to note, as will be seen below, that criminal proceedings against arbitrators seem to be very rare.[86] This offers some support to the generally held notion that severe deviations by arbitrators from their professional norms are unusual. These ideas will be further discussed next.

A. Examples of the Criminal Norms Applicable to International Arbitrators

Usually, criminal codes do not refer particularly to arbitration. Still, they generally contain provisions that are broad enough to allow, for example, prosecution of arbitrators who accept bribes or other similarly serious acts. For example, many definitions of bribery, such as the one contained in the UK Bribery Act 2010, which defines being bribed as requesting, accepting or agreeing to accept a financial or other advantage in exchange for improperly performing a relevant function or activity,[87] can, in theory, allow criminal prosecution in situations where an arbitrator accepts an illicit payment from a party.[88] In the same vein, other criminal offences, such as fraud or forgery, may play a role in controlling arbitrators' behaviour.

Sometimes, criminal codes do have provisions that expressly mention arbitrators. This is, for example, the case of the German Criminal Code, which deals specifically with arbitrators in several different provisions. It provides, amongst other provisions, that:

> '**Section 332 (b)** – A judge or an arbitrator, who demands, allows himself to be promised or accepts a benefit for himself or for a third person in return for the fact that he performed or will in the future perform a judicial act and thereby violated or will violate his judicial duties shall be liable to imprisonment from one to ten years. In less serious cases the penalty shall be imprisonment from six months to five years. [...]
>
> **Section 339** – A judge, another public official or an arbitrator who in conducting or deciding a legal matter perverts the course of justice for the benefit or to the detriment of a party shall be liable to imprisonment from one to five years.'

Other similar provisions exist in the Swiss Criminal Code, the Austrian Criminal Code, and the Norwegian Criminal Code.[89] However, these are not exclusively aimed at arbitrators

[86] See Ramon Mullerat and Juliet Blanch, 'The Liability of Arbitrators: A Survey of Current Practice' (2007) 1 *Dispute Resolution International* 105. See also Born (n 14) 2018.

[87] See Paula Hodges and Joanne Greenaway, 'Duties of Arbitrators' in JDM Lew and others (eds), *Arbitration in England: With Chapters on Scotland and Ireland* (Alphen aan den Rijn, Kluwer Law International, 2013) 306.

[88] See UK Bribery Act 2010, s 2(4).

[89] See Swiss Criminal Code, Art 322, Austrian Criminal Code, Art 304 and Norwegian Criminal Code, Art 114.

but rather mention arbitrators alongside other agents playing similar roles, such as judges and public officials. While, in the context of arbitration, such provisions could, in theory, allow an avenue to prosecute arbitrators, they seem not to be significantly used in these jurisdictions. In this sense, they are relatively uncontroversial norms that do not seem to be a central concern of the arbitral community, with these norms receiving relatively little attention in arbitration-related literature.[90]

This is, however, not always the case. Sometimes, the passage of criminal provisions elicits strong concerns in the arbitral community, particularly if there is a concern that these provisions will not remain merely in the books and have the potential to be abused by authorities. Two examples, one resulting from one amendment to the Chinese criminal laws and another to the laws of the United Arab Emirates, deserve to be noted as they show how potential 'criminalisation' of arbitrators can lead to a strong reaction from the arbitral community at both the domestic and international level.

The first of these examples relates to an amendment to the Chinese Criminal Code providing imprisonment for those 'who intentionally run counter to facts and laws and twists the law when making a ruling in arbitration'.[91] These changes became controversial within the Chinese arbitral community, igniting a debate between those against and for the provision.[92] The debate around such provisions cannot be separated from the fact that in China, several accusations and arrests of arbitrators were made.[93] It is important to note that despite the vast size of the Chinese domestic arbitration market, most of it is largely insulated from the international arbitration practice, having many idiosyncratic legal rules and practices.[94] Therefore, such provisions have not been the subject of much attention in international arbitration circles, which often perceive Chinese domestic arbitration as an outlier in international practice.

A more highly publicised case in international circles was the reaction to the passage of a criminal provision in the United Arab Emirates in 2016, which shows an example of the international arbitration community successfully opposing a legislative transformation. In what was perceived as a too-broad construction, the United Arab Emirates Federal Penal Code provided that:

> Anyone who issues a decision, expresses an opinion, submits a report, presents a case or proves an incident in favour of or against a person, in contravention of the requirements of the duty of neutrality and integrity, while acting in his capacity as an arbitrator, expert, translator or fact-finder appointed by an administrative or judicial authority or selected by the parties, shall be punished by temporary imprisonment.[95]

Across arbitration circles, this provision was seen as opening up the possibility of dangerously prosecuting international arbitrators.[96] Distrust in the local criminal system

[90] See Born (n 14) 2017.

[91] See Chinese Criminal Code, Art 399A.

[92] See Xiaosong Duan, 'Criminal Liability of Arbitrators in China: Analysis and Proposals for Reform' (2014) 23 *Pacific Rim Law & Policy Journal* 343, 352.

[93] The most high-profile of these cases was the arrest of Wang Shengchang. For an overview of the case, see Wu Ming, 'The Strange Case of Wang Shengchang' (2007) 24 *Journal of International Arbitration* 63.

[94] See Fan Kun, *Arbitration in China: A Legal and Cultural Analysis* (Oxford, Hart Publishing, 2013) 1.

[95] See United Arab Emirates Penal Code, Art 257 (repealed).

[96] See Sweify (n 85) 70.

certainly played a role in the response against the provision. Also, it is important to note that contrary to the largely insulated Chinese domestic arbitration market, the Middle East has generally been an important source of work for international arbitrators and firms.[97] The reaction within the arbitral community was strong, with very high-profile members warning that such a measure could jeopardise arbitration in the Emirates. Further anecdotal instances of arbitrators refusing to participate in proceedings in the jurisdiction were reported.[98] Given the intense backlash against this change, the provision was changed in 2018 to explicitly carve out arbitrators from the law's scope, a decision welcomed in arbitration circles.[99]

Independently of how different countries deal with the question of criminalising serious arbitral misconducts, actual imprisonments, or even attempts to prosecute arbitrators criminally seem to be extremely rare.[100] This does not necessarily mean that arbitrators do not commonly undertake criminal behaviour.[101] The lack of criminal cases could stem instead from a lack of ability or willingness from authorities to detect and prosecute criminal behaviour. Although it is always challenging to determine the prevalence of criminal activity, from the discussions this author undertook with those within the arbitral community, the general impression seems to be that the kind of serious deviations that would amount to criminal behaviour was something they had not experienced or had knowledge of happening.

B. Examples of Criminal Proceedings Brought against Arbitrators

Despite the extremely low number of criminal cases involving arbitrators, some cases have come to light where arbitrators have been investigated or jailed following their actions in arbitral proceedings. Three reported cases of criminal investigations into arbitrators' actions offer insight into the kind of behaviour that can result in criminal prosecution. Their analysis also allows seeing how different behaviours, circumstances and perceptions of the judicial system where the prosecution took place might elicit different reactions from the arbitral community, ranging from a perception that the behaviours were unacceptable to expressions of support to the arbitrators involved.[102] As it will be seen, these perceptions may also depend on how trusted and well-known an arbitrator is within the community, with well-established figures being conceivably more likely to be supported by the community.

[97] See Yves Dezalay and Bryant G Garth, *Dealing in Virtue: International Commercial Arbitration and the Construction of a Transnational Legal Order* (Chicago, University of Chicago Press, 1996) 43.

[98] See Sweify (n 85) 71.

[99] See Sami Tannous and Matei Purice, 'The New UAE Federal Arbitration Law: Was It Worth the Wait?' (2018) 36 *ASA Bulletin* 866, 877; Alain Farhad, 'The United Arab Emirates' New Arbitration Legislation: A Giant Leap Forward?' (2019) 36 *Journal of International Arbitration* 523, 531.

[100] See Mullerat and Blanch (n 86) 105. See also Born (n 14) 2018.

[101] Noting the difficulties of quantifying 'white-collar' crime in general, see Professor Hazel Croall, *Understanding White Collar Crime* (Buckingham, McGraw-Hill Education (UK), 2001) 21.

[102] Manifestations of solidarity and even 'codes of silence' between those who share the same occupation or profession are not uncommon. See Geoffrey P Alpert, Jeffrey J Noble and Jeff Rojek, 'Solidarity and the Code of Silence' in Roger G Dunham and Geoffrey P Alpert (eds), *Critical Issues in Policing: Contemporary Readings*, 7th edn (Illinois, Waveland Press, 2015) 106.

i. The Tapie Affaire: A Case where Politics Met Arbitration Drawing Significant Media Attention

The most high-profile case of alleged arbitral misconduct within commercial arbitration is arguably the so-called *Tapie Affaire*. This case, whose full description surpasses this text's scope, was extensively reported in French and international media outlets.[103] This attention was partly due to the many well-known political actors that became entangled in the proceedings, most notably Christine Lagarde, former French Finance Minister and head of the IMF. At the core of the case were serious allegations of improper conduct and lack of impartiality of a well-established French arbitrator and former judge named Pierre Estoup, leading to complex subsequent litigation where the validity of the award was discussed and the criminal prosecution of Mr Estoup.

The case relates to a legal dispute between well-known French business tycoon, former politician and football club owner Bernard Tapie and the Crédit Lyonnais, a French state-owned bank that would eventually discharge its liabilities to another French state company called Consortium de Réalisation (CDR). Mr Tapie alleged that the bank had fraudulently profited from his stake in the Adidas sports company. After years of litigation between Mr Tapie and CDR at the state courts without reaching a conclusion, the parties agreed to refer the dispute to binding arbitration. Christine Lagarde, at the time French Finance Minister, signed off the deal, allowing the case to proceed to arbitration.[104]

The three-member arbitral tribunal, composed of Pierre Estoup, Jean-Denis Bredin, and Pierre Mazeaud, all well-known figures in French legal circles, ruled in favour of Mr Tapie in 2008, awarding him circa €400 million.[105] The French government chose not to pursue an appeal or annulment of the award in the French courts. It would, however, emerge from criminal investigations by the French authorities that Mr Estoup had extensive and undisclosed ties to Mr Tapie and his lawyer in the case. These included Mr Estoup allegedly: i) concealing previous consultancy work provided to Mr Tapie's lawyer in connection to this and other related disputes; ii) receiving information about the case after it had started from Tapie's advisors; and iii) maintaining a personal relation to Mr Tapie.

After this information came to light, the CDR group filed for revision of the award (*recours en révision*). The Paris Court of Appeal decided in February 2015 that the request was admissible and retracted the award. The Court criticised the behaviour of Mr Estoup, who, according to the Court, had 'deliberately and systematically directed the reflection of the tribunal in favour of the interests of the party that he intended to promote by collusion with the latter and his counsel'.[106] Both Mr Estoup, Mr Tapie, and his main lawyer, Mr Lantourne, were then charged with *escroquerie en bande organisée*, being, however,

[103] For a detailed summary of the facts of the case and subsequent litigation, see Clément Fouchard, "L'affaire Tapie', a Review from an Arbitration Perspective' (2017) XIV *Revista Brasileira de Arbitragem* 94.

[104] Ms Lagarde was herself brought to trial in connection with this case, being accused of 'culpable negligence' for having allowed the case to be decided by arbitration and having failed to challenge the arbitral award. The French courts ultimately decided that criminal punishment in connection with these actions was not appropriate. See Alan Redfern, 'The Importance of Being Independent: Laws of Arbitration, Rules, Guidelines – and a Disastrous Award' (2017) 6 *Indian Journal of Arbitration Law* 9, 22.

[105] Including an amount of €45 million for moral damages, a value considered abnormally high for French judicial standards. See Marc Henry, 'Arbitrage Tapie: Les Affres d'un Prejudice Moral Immoral' (2016) 34 *ASA Bulletin* 207.

[106] See HSF Notes, *Paris Court of Appeal orders the retraction of an award made where one arbitrator lacked independence: the ongoing Tapie saga*, 4 March 2015, available at: hsfnotes.com, last accessed 3 April 2020.

eventually acquitted, with the Criminal Court of Paris reportedly finding 'nothing in the case that confirmed' the allegation that the arbitration pay-out was tainted by 'fraud'.[107]

While Mr Estoup's advanced age at the time of the facts supra discussed does not provide a window on how involvement in a scandal of this nature impacts a career, the fallout of the case provides an example of how the arbitration community reacts to this sort of attention to the field. In this case, while the proceedings drew considerable concern within the French arbitral community, it was not perceived as symptomatic of deeper problems with arbitration. Rather, the whole arbitration case was perceived as atypical and 'unrepresentative' of Parisian arbitration.[108] While it was lamented that part of the general public was introduced to arbitration due to the scandalous nature of this particular case, Paris courts were praised for their handling of the proceedings, with the annulment being presented as a demonstration of the system working.[109]

ii. The Conviction of Arbitrator Yusof Holmes Abdullah as an Example of Criminal Proceedings Punishing Serious Deviations

A second reasonably high-profile case relates to the sentencing of the arbitrator Yusof Holmes Abdullah due to his misconduct in proceedings that took place in the Kuala Lumpur Regional Centre for Arbitration (KLRCA).[110] Mr Holmes, a British chartered arbitrator with a degree from the Imperial College and a permanent resident in Malaysia for over 25 years, was a well-known arbitrator in Malaysia with connections to local arbitration bodies, most notably being one of the founders of the CIArb's Malaysian branch. While not a household name in international circles, Mr Holmes had, prior to the allegations, reportedly acted as arbitrator in Malaysia, the Philippines, Thailand, Pakistan, Indonesia, Hong Kong, Singapore, Spain, and the UK.

In 2010, Mr Holmes, 66 at the time, was accused of soliciting a US£2 million bribe from a Malaysian company director in an arbitration between a Malaysian construction company and a Chinese state-owned company, in proceedings where US$8 million were at stake. Mr Holmes was the sole arbitrator in these proceedings. While this first bribery allegation was not criminally pursued, a second allegation of Mr Holmes having falsified a statement of independence presented to the KLRCA in connection with the case was brought to trial. He was eventually sentenced to six months in prison in January 2017, with the court accepting payment of a fine in lieu of carrying out the sentence.

The case of Mr Holmes is notable as one of the few reported cases where an arbitrator actually faced a conviction for an action undertaken within arbitral proceedings. It illustrates how criminal investigations can have the potential to work as a strong deterrent against the more serious deviations an arbitrator can undertake. They also demonstrate how suspicion of criminal activity by an arbitrator may lead to their 'market value' plummeting.

[107] See France 24, *French tycoon Bernard Tapie acquitted of fraud*, 9 July 2019, available at www.france24.com, last accessed 3 April 2020.

[108] Fouchard (n 103) 111.

[109] ibid. See also Jehan-Damien Le Brusq, *The Tapie saga: Paris successfully passed the test*, Kluwer Arbitration Blog, 1 September 2016, available at /arbitrationblog.kluwerarbitration.com/, last accessed 3 April 2020.

[110] See Andrea Menaker and Harpreet Dhillon, 'Article 52(1)(C)' in Julien Fouret, Rémy Gerbay and Gloria M Alvarez (eds), *The ICSID Convention, Regulations and Rules: A Practical Commentary* (Cheltenham, Edward Elgar Publishing, 2019) 612.

In the case of Mr Holmes, the moment suspicions arose, he apparently resigned from his work as an arbitrator and had, according to his lawyer, in light of the case, seen his career destroyed and left unable to work as an arbitrator again.[111]

iii. The Allegations against Peruvian Arbitrators Following the Odebrecht Scandal: Solidarity Amongst the Arbitral Community

The final example to be discussed relates to the investigations undertaken on the conduct of 16 Peruvian arbitrators who were accused of receiving bribes from the Brazilian construction company Odebrecht.[112] The case itself relates to wider corruption practices by Odebrecht, which, following numerous criminal investigations and the cooperation of several whistle-blowers, found itself at the centre of an impressive web of corruption scandals linking politicians and construction companies throughout Latin America and beyond.[113] In the particular case of Peru, Odebrecht's key executives confessed to the company bribing different governmental authorities to secure auctions for construction projects in Peru and further undertaking contractual surcharges.

While at the time of writing, not all details were fully clear, the investigations revealed a well-established and politically connected lawyer and arbitrator who had allegedly been bribed by Odebrecht and issued awards to benefit the company in exchange of generous money offers. The alleged bribe-taker had purportedly also used the money received to bribe other arbitrators on behalf of Odebrecht and illegally arrange the result of arbitral proceedings. Following the investigations, the alleged bribe-taker apparently entered into an agreement with the public prosecution office, naming 16 arbitrators as allegedly involved in the bribing schemes to award Odebrecht fraudulent arbitral awards.

It is important to note that some of the 16 arbitrators were very well-established names within the Peruvian legal market. These were the cases of Fernando Cantuarias, Franz Kundmuller, and Mario Castillo – three well-renowned arbitrators and scholars in Peru. Mr Cantuarias, in particular, was well-known even outside Peru, having strong links with international arbitral institutions and arbitral professional associations abroad.[114] Still, 14 of the 16 arbitrators, including the three arbitrators named above, were ordered to an 18-month pre-trial detention in November 2019.[115]

[111] Mr Holmes' lawyer reportedly stated: 'With this conviction, my client's career is destroyed as he won't be able to work as an arbitrator again.' The Star, '*Ex-chartered arbitrator gets jail*', 6 January 2017, available at www.thestar.com.my/, last accessed 3 April 2020.

[112] See Carlos Rios Pizarro, *Mixing Righteous and Sinners: Summary of the Odebrecht Corruption Scandal and the Peruvian Jailed Arbitrators*, Kluwer Arbitration Blog, 10 December 2019, available at arbitrationblog.kluwerarbitration.com/, last accessed 3 April 2020.

[113] For an overview of the Odebrecht corruption scandals, see Diego Zysman-Quirós, 'White-Collar Crime in South and Central America: Corporate-State Crime, Governance, and the High Impact of the Odebrecht Corruption Case' in Melissa L Rorie (ed), *The Handbook of White-Collar Crime* (Chichester, Wiley, 2019). See also, Riccardo Vecellio Segate, 'The Dis-Embedded Arbitrator: Releasing Arbitration from Corruption-Shaped Environments in the Wake of the Odebrecht Arbitral Ordeal in Peru' (2023) 12 *Social Sciences* 232.

[114] Mr Cantuarias was reportedly a member of, amongst other organisations, the Board of Reporters of Institute of Transnational Arbitration (ITA), the Latin American Group of the International Chamber of Commerce (ICC) and the Association for International Arbitration (AIA).

[115] See Radio Programas del Perú (RPP), *Juez dicta 18 meses de prisión preventiva contra Humberto Abanto y otros 13 árbitros por caso Odebrecht*, 4 November 2019, available at rpp.pe/, last accessed on 3 April 2020.

The detention of these arbitrators, particularly Mr Cantuarias, gave rise to strong manifestations of solidarity from the arbitral community. Many members of the arbitral community, inside and outside Peru, took to the media and online to express their views and show support. Further, key arbitral institutions wrote letters to the Public Prosecutor's office and the Peruvian government showing their support for and trust in Mr Cantuarias.[116] In these letters and texts, members of the arbitral community often detailed how practices, such as pre-trial conferencing between parties and arbitrator and arbitrators self-establishing fees, were not a sign of 'corruption', as alleged by the prosecution, but instead internationally accepted practices within international arbitration. It is important to note that this showing of support was not for all the accused but very much focused on the three well-established arbitrators and Mr Cantuarias in particular.

While investigations were still ongoing at the time of writing,[117] this case shows many revealing features about how criminal investigations interrelate with the arbitral community, the arbitral market and its potential regulatory effect. First, it might indicate a willingness by the arbitral community to establish distinctions between situations where they believe there was foul play and situations where there was not, walking away from the members in the first situation and showing support in the latter. Second, as discussed in chapter four, it might indicate that a large scandal may spur regulatory transformations.

Indeed, just two months after the arrests, the government of Peru published an urgent decree modifying several provisions of Peru's arbitration law.[118] These changes, poorly received by the local and regional arbitral community, were all directed at giving more protection to the Peruvian state when it acts as a party in arbitration proceedings. As per the Decree's explanatory note, the amendment resulted from the Peruvian government's belief that arbitration, albeit suitable for private disputes, is not an adequate dispute resolution for situations where the Peruvian state intervenes as a party. Namely, according to the explanatory note, it did not ensure the transparency of the proceedings or allow avoiding acts of corruption.

More broadly, this case provides an overview of how an arbitral community may react to situations it perceives as diminishing the legitimacy of the field. Following the Odebrecht investigation, as a response to the concerns that arbitration in Peru may lack transparency, the National and International Arbitration Center of the Lima Chamber of Commerce started a digital platform named '*Faro de Transparencia*' ('Transparency Lighthouse').[119] This platform provides information regarding appointed arbitrators, awards, annulment decisions and, more uniquely, decisions to sanction arbitrators.[120]

[116] Most notably Alexis Mourre (President of the ICC Court of Arbitration). See Alexis Mourre letter dated 14 November 2019, available at www.caeperu.com/noticias/pdf/alexis-mourre-presidente-de-la-corte-de-arbitraje-de-la-ICC.pdf, last accessed 3 April 2020.

[117] In December 2019, Mr Cantuarias, Mr Kundmuller, Mr Castillo and six other arbitrators were released, remaining, however, subject to significant restrictions on their freedom pending the corruption investigations.

[118] See Peruvian Urgent Decree N° 020-2020, 24 January 2020, modifying Decree-Law n° 1071.

[119] See Marianella Ventura and Irene Zegarra-Ballón, *A 'Transparency Lighthouse' for Arbitration in Peru*, Kluwer Arbitration Blog, 15 August 2020, available at arbitrationblog.kluwerarbitration.com/2020/08/15/a-transparency-lighthouse-for-arbitration-in-peru//, last accessed 4 September 2023.

[120] See Asistente Faro de Transparencia CCL, available at www.arbitrajeccl.com.pe/asistente-faro-de-transparencia-ccl, last accessed 4 September 2023. The National and International Arbitration Center of the Lima Chamber of Commerce, unlike most arbitral institutions, provides for the possibility of sanctioning arbitrators. See Art 12, Estatuto, Centro Nacional e Internacional de Arbitraje (el 'Centro') de la Cámara de Comercio de Lima.

VI. The Peripheral and Incidental Nature of 'Legal' Recourse as a Way of 'Regulating' Arbitrators

In conclusion, it should be said that the mechanisms discussed in this chapter present an effect on arbitrators' compliance that is mostly incidental. In this sense, they have not been designed to primarily affect an arbitrator's grid of incentives but rather provide a safeguard for parties. For example, parties' right to challenge arbitrators and awards appears to have been chiefly intended to protect parties' rights to due process rather than as a system primarily designed to deter unwanted arbitrator behaviour. This can be seen by the way that discussions around these mechanisms mainly focus on their 'normative' dimension rather than their 'regulatory' effect – ie, smaller consideration is paid to how these decisions systemically affect the behaviour of arbitrators compared to assuring fairness and due process in that particular instance.[121]

This is not to say that such mechanisms do not play an important effect in fostering compliance. As discussed, they can not only provide a direct cost for an arbitrator but, perhaps, more importantly, inflict an indirect cost by affecting their reputation. Also, the simple fact that these mechanisms exist might have a potential deterrent effect even if they are rarely applied in practice. Still, it is worth noting that the parties and not the arbitrator often bear the most direct cost of an arbitrator's misconduct.[122] This is typically the case of an arbitral award being refused enforcement, which, in the context of arbitrators' limited liability, typically will not directly lead to a cost to the arbitrator. This decision, however, might represent significant losses for the 'winning' party that will be unable to enforce its award and may have to repeat the proceedings to exercise its rights.

This analysis also holds for other mechanisms discussed in this chapter. As seen above, civil liability and criminal liability have not, in most circumstances, been explicitly tailored to deter arbitrators' misconduct. Instead, general legal provisions have sporadically been used as a basis to start proceedings against arbitrators. While further statutory detail on how these norms are to be interpreted in the arbitral context could bring clarity, there are sound policy reasons not to allow a pervasive usage of these mechanisms. As discussed above, they might allow unscrupulous parties to disrupt arbitral proceedings. Therefore, this means that the reputation and community-control mechanisms discussed in chapter seven will likely have to continue to play a role if the current light-touch oversight system is to continue operating. The next chapter will discuss how this will play out against the background of a changing arbitral landscape.

[121] The fact that the question of whether arbitrators may retain their fees following a challenge or an annulment of an award has not been the focus of attention can be seen as an indication that modifying arbitrators' incentives for compliance is not a primary concern of these mechanisms.

[122] See William Park, 'Arbitration in Autumn' (2011) 2 *Journal of International Dispute Settlement* 287, 292; Hodges and Greenaway (n 87) 316.

9

Reframing the Growing Pains of Commercial Arbitration: Regulatory Challenges and Achievements

I. The Arbitral Market as a Catalyst for the Dominance of the Arbitral Community Over its Regulation

This book has explored one key idea: that the unique characteristics of the international commercial arbitration market has allowed the arbitral community to develop a unique regulatory framework.[1] Two main reasons justify why the field has not developed centrally defined state-backed regulation. First, arbitration operates against the background of a continuing regulatory competition between jurisdictions and arbitral institutions to attract arbitral proceedings. This competition has led arbitration to be modelled in a way that is primarily directed to benefit dispute parties, ie, a system built on party autonomy and designed in a commercially minded and service-oriented fashion.

Second, given that many within the arbitration community benefit from the current state of affairs and are reasonably insulated from competition, the community has, for the most part, worked to keep arbitration free from the regulatory arrangements found in most other professional areas. This, of course, is not the result of any particular innate attachment of arbitrators to free-market ideals or a special kind-heartedness of the members of the arbitral community to outsiders. Instead, it is better explained as an adaptation to the characteristics of the arbitration market, where those already within it, as a general rule, benefit from more people joining the arbitral community.

Arbitrators present, therefore, a curious case of self-regulation. Although arbitrators are often perceived as occupying an elite role, the arbitral community in general and arbitrators in particular have not engaged in advancing a 'closure of the market' agenda. This book posited that this was largely derived from the fact that, in this market, incumbent arbitrators are already well protected from potential competition. It argued that arbitrators would be generally worse off if the traditional set of protections other professions enjoy – such as a monopoly over the right to offer particular services or licensing requirements – were established.[2]

[1] The power of the arbitral community to influence the design and, itself, create norms has led some to borrow the concept of 'epistemic community' to describe it. See, eg, Katherine L Lynch, *The Forces of Economic Globalization: Challenges to the Regime of International Commercial Arbitration* (Alphen aan den Rijn, Kluwer Law International, 2003) 94.

[2] See ch 4, section III.B.

Instead, current members benefit from incorporating new members as they serve as further 'nodes', helping expand the international market.[3]

In a sense, the market can be described as imperfect, fraught with barriers to entry, and lacking transparency.[4] First, the way fees are set and the strong preference for established arbitral institutions make this a market subject to low-price competition. Further, the prevalent appointment system, dominated in practice by arbitration insiders, arbitrators, and arbitral institutions, leads to a conservative approach to appointments. Parties, partly driven by strategic considerations and partly due to the difficulties in evaluating quality, tend to strongly prefer practitioners already in the market. Altogether, this gives arbitration its oft-noted 'closed club' nature.[5]

The interesting regulatory conundrum of arbitration is that these same market characteristics allow norms to be created and enforced. To explain how these norms are created and enforced, this book focused on the relationship that develops between each arbitrator and the arbitral community as a whole. Understanding how the arbitral community self-regulates demands considering not only how the arbitral community benefits from 'regulating' the behaviour of its members but also why its members participate in constructing the regulatory framework and adhere to it. Indeed, the way each member of the arbitral community adapts to the peculiar mechanics of the international arbitration market is the main driver that keeps this framework functioning.

The de facto dominance of the arbitral community over who gets to be successful in the market and the centrality of 'reputation' mechanisms lead to a unique interplay between each member and the community.[6] Within the arbitration market, each member is incentivised to advance the arbitral agenda by participating in regulatory initiatives, spreading the values of arbitration and complying with the expected behaviours of the field. Participation in this process is compensated with connections, appointments, and prestige. Non-participation and non-compliance lead the member to be forgotten by the community. In turn, the community as a whole benefits from the existence and enforcement of norms that guarantee a fair and efficient solving of disputes by arbitrators.

It is, therefore, the unique characteristics of the arbitration market that allowed the unique style of self-regulation that prevails in arbitration to emerge. This is an important notion. Arbitration is not, as some would describe it, unregulated. It is, in fact, as those within the field rapidly recognise, a field with numerous rules. While many institutions, including state legislators and courts, participate in this rule-making process, the arbitral community has a paramount role. Not only does the arbitral community produce a significant number of texts, but it also has a decisive influence over the actions of other actors.

[3] See Tom Ginsburg, 'The Culture of Arbitration' (2003) 36 *The Vanderbilt Journal of Transnational Law* 1335, 1342.

[4] Catherine Rogers' description of the arbitral market as deeply imperfect has been highly influential, becoming a common observation in many subsequent texts about arbitration. See Catherine A Rogers, 'The Vocation of the International Arbitrator' (2004) 20 *American University International Law Review* 957.

[5] See Yves Dezalay and Bryant G Garth, *Dealing in Virtue: International Commercial Arbitration and the Construction of a Transnational Legal Order* (Chicago, University of Chicago Press, 1996) 10; Rogers (n 4) 967.

[6] The idea that the arbitral community as whole benefits from the increased reputation of arbitration as a legal institution and trust in its ability in solving disputes is well summarised in the 'aphorism': 'a rising tide of arbitral business lifts all boats'. See Joshua DH Karton, *The Culture of International Arbitration and The Evolution of Contract Law* (Oxford, Oxford University Press, 2013) 57.

Furthermore, the arbitral community plays a decisive role in guaranteeing that the members of the community comply with the dominant rules. As discussed, despite lacking the formal instruments to control entrance or punish behaviour, the way that the community and market are structured ensures compliance.

II. Reframing the Strengths and Weaknesses of Arbitration as a Reflection of the Regulatory Forces at Play

Importantly, the framework described can also explain the strengths and weaknesses usually associated with arbitration. The way that the arbitration market is set does not encourage aggressive price competition between arbitrators. Instead, prices are mostly set by arbitral institutions through fee schedules, which, while subject to some level of competition, are not primed to adapt prices to market conditions. The usage of fee schedules through arbitration, while being a logical option in the context of remunerating arbitrators, makes cost arrangements less flexible. They also help explain the general perception that the market is not open. Given the difficulties of competing through lower prices, it is unsurprising that prospective arbitrators find this market difficult to enter.

It should be equally noted that these same market characteristics help explain the general perception that arbitrators comply with their ethical obligations and why arbitration has, for the most part, not been marred by scandals. The way that the market is set underpins the often-noted idea that arbitrators are wholly dependent on their reputation as ethical and efficient and, therefore, carefully guard it by considering how their actions will be perceived within the community. This is a central aspect of the environment that underpins the general tendency of arbitrators to comply with existing norms.

However, this book has argued that incentives for reputation are only part of the puzzle explaining how the regulation of arbitration works. The argument presented in this book relies on the idea that the arbitral market's specificities lead to the formation of a professional community that is unique in many aspects. The need found by arbitration service providers to develop connections and network with other members leads to a more integrated community than that found in other professions or sub-fields of law. This level of integration allows information about norms and compliance to be transmitted across members, permitting to overcome the lack of transparency the arbitral market otherwise suffers.[7] It further creates an environment where each member evaluates and is evaluated by other members.

Over time, the arbitral community and the arbitral market filter the entrance to allow only a selected few to join the small roster of those who are routinely selected to be arbitrators.[8] This pre-selection may further contribute to an environment where those acting as arbitrators are perhaps more intrinsically motivated to participate in the process of creating and enforcing norms.[9] This is important, as strictly defined self-interest does not

[7] See ch 7, section III.B.

[8] See, Magdalene D'Silva, 'Dealing in Power: Gatekeepers in Arbitrator Appointment in International Commercial Arbitration' (2014) 5 *Journal of International Dispute Settlement* 605, 633.

[9] See ch 7, section IV.

fully explain norm creation and compliance within the arbitral community.[10] In an environment where well-known arbitrators often enjoy a protected position, and deviation is sometimes difficult to identify, there are situations where it could be in the best monetary self-interest of an arbitrator to deviate.[11] The general perception that serious deviations are extremely rare brings to the forefront the notion that compliance with obligations and regulatory goals is dependent on multiple factors, such as the characteristics of who composes the arbitral community and to what extent the members of the community internalise the norms of the field.[12]

Also, and perhaps more surprisingly, this same structure and set of incentives have had the power to address more structural regulatory issues, at least to an extent. A case in point has been the many efforts by the arbitral community to increase diversity. Lack of gender diversity, in particular, has long been an issue drawing criticism from inside and outside the community.[13] While there are no direct market incentives for individuals to be concerned about diversity, indirectly, the need to protect the legitimacy of arbitration has prompted many within the community to take initiatives to correct this imbalance.[14] This has, in turn, become a collective goal of the community to which many have adhered, and although the demographics of the profession remain unbalanced, some advancement has been made.[15]

Altogether, this shows that the debates on the regulation of arbitrators have been incomplete. When discussing its own regulation, the arbitral community has simply concluded that arbitrators, in deciding to act 'ethically' or 'unethically', follow their best interest.[16] While self-interest is naturally paramount, broader considerations should be taken into account. Behavioural psychology and criminology may offer a window to understand how the particular process of 'socialisation' and the characteristics of those within the community might play an important role in understanding why arbitrators comply and deviate from their obligations.[17] It also may open new avenues to understand how arbitrators and parties can be led to produce more fair and efficient dispute resolution.[18]

[10] In more general terms, showing the complex interrelation between moral principles and self-interest, and ultimately suggesting that our understanding of moral questions is influenced, but not fully explained, by self-interest, see Peter DeScioli and others, 'Equity or Equality? Moral Judgments Follow the Money' (2014) 281 *Proceedings of the Royal Society B: Biological Sciences* 20142112.

[11] See ch 7, section I.C.

[12] See also, more generally, Christopher Hodges, 'Resetting Incentives, Remuneration and Trust' [2020] Oxford Legal Studies Research Paper No. 14/2020 21.

[13] See, eg, Michael McIlwrath and John Savage, *International Arbitration and Mediation: A Practical Guide* (Alphen aan den Rijn, Kluwer Law International, 2010) 255.

[14] Most notably the 'Arbitration Pledge' organised by the Equal Representation in Arbitration (ERA), an initiative started in 2015 that invites members of the arbitral community to pledge to take steps to address the lack of gender diversity in arbitral tribunals.

[15] See Fahira Brodlija, 'Innovative Solutions for an Age-Old Issue: How Transparency and Data Analytic Tools Can Improve Diversity in International Arbitration' (2021) 5 *Journal of Strategic Contracting and Negotiation* 24, 25.

[16] Also, some regulatory interventions, such as arbitral institutions decisions to change arbitrators' fees to reward speedy dispute resolution, seem to work with the same logic.

[17] More generally, investigating the effect of 'irrational' systematic biases in arbitrators, see Susan D Franck and others, 'Inside the Arbitrator's Mind' (2017) 66 *Emory Law Journal* 1115.

[18] For example, there have been empirical observations showing that the way financial incentives shape behaviour is less straightforward than commonly assumed. Namely, large financial rewards have been shown to crowd out intrinsic motivation and have sometimes detrimental effects on performance. See, Hodges (n 12) 24. These observations offer an interesting starting point for discussions regarding the design of counsel, arbitral institutions and arbitral tribunals' fees.

By way of conclusion, this chapter will tie in the analysis of the regulatory framework that governs arbitrators with the discussions currently taking place within the arbitration community. It will first evaluate whether the regulatory framework analysed in this book can continue to lead arbitrators to create and comply with norms in a context where the arbitral community is increasing in size and becoming more heterogeneous. As will be examined, there have been considerable transformations in the arbitration market and the arbitral community. Just a few decades ago, a small clique of insiders dominated the field, but the success of arbitration meant that relationships are no longer contained in a group where all members know each other. This has created doubts amongst some within the arbitral community about whether the sense of community has broken down and whether the pressures to comply with professional norms may be waning.

These questions will establish the groundwork to determine whether there is a case for increased 'professionalism' – ie, a case for advancing a more traditional regulation of arbitrators as a full-time profession and, in particular, a separation between the role of arbitrator and counsel in commercial arbitration. With this goal in mind, the next section will discuss why such a transformation would be unlikely. Specifically, it focuses on why state legislatures, the arbitral community, and arbitral institutions will likely not pursue such development. Despite the unlikelihood of this scenario, the last section will discuss whether professionalisation would be a positive step. As it will be seen, this is an intriguing question that entails reimagining a very distinct regulatory system.

III. How does the Regulation of Behaviour in International Commercial Arbitration Take Place in a Changing Landscape?

One of the most often noted recent changes in the characteristics of the arbitral community is its increase in size and diversity.[19] In many ways, as aforementioned, these changes have been celebrated. Given the common aspersion that arbitration was dominated by a 'white, male and stale' elite, the (limited) increase in diversity, in terms of gender, race and nationality of elite commercial arbitrators, has been welcomed by those within the community.[20] To a smaller extent, the increased number of participants has also been used to negate ideas that arbitration is dominated by a small old-boys network, notions that, until recently, were often emphasised even inside arbitration circles.

These transformations have also, however, led to some level of discomfort. As the community became increasingly heterogeneous, the idea that arbitration was entering a period where commitment to professional values was waning seemed to have taken hold around some circles. There seems to be an underlying idea that as arbitration becomes more popular and the initially small community grows exponentially, new entrants might be less

[19] See Lucy Greenwood, 'Tipping the Balance–Diversity and Inclusion in International Arbitration' (2017) 33 *Arbitration International* 99.

[20] As noted by Greenwood: 'the arbitration community has shown through its enthusiastic reception of the Pledge, that it is committed to addressing the representation of women on arbitration tribunals'. See ibid 108.

committed to the norms of the field.[21] These fears were expressed eloquently in a speech by Sundaresh Menon. In words that drew attention across the community, the Singapore Chief Justice argued:

> [i]mplied understandings or shared values no longer provide any meaningful means of shaping or influencing conduct in this context. Arbitrators can no longer consider themselves bound by peer standards, because there are no peers in the true sense, amidst all this diversity. [...][t]he absence of common or defined ethical standards to guide such a great diversity of practitioners obviously poses serious difficulties and has the potential to create an uneven battleground that can ultimately affect fairness and integrity in international arbitration.[22]

It is fair to note that the views expressed by Chief Justice Menon, albeit not a sole voice within the community, are perhaps more pessimistic than the majority view within arbitration circles.[23] Still, these views raise challenging questions. Namely, it brings to the forefront the possibility that an increased number of arbitrators and arbitral practitioners will not let the unique regulatory framework explored in this book continue providing incentives for norms to be created and enforced. The increasing number of members in the group could, in theory, jeopardise the mechanisms for divulging information about these norms and the 'quality' of each member.[24] If each member of the community, amid an increasing multitude of members, is unable to identify the quality of each peer, the reputation and peer pressure mechanisms that help guarantee compliance with ethical norms may break down.

It is certainly too early to fully anticipate how these transformations will affect the ability of the international commercial arbitration community to continue self-regulating. After all, the last two decades have been marked by continuous expansion, and while growth seems to be flattening out, the size and characteristics of the arbitration community have not yet stabilised.[25] Still, recent transformations in the field show that an increased number of arbitrators and practitioners does not necessarily mean an end to the set of incentives described in this book. The international commercial arbitration market has so far shown flexibility to accommodate these transformations and to continue to provide networks for information regarding each agent to flow.

Three developments should be noted in particular in this regard. First, as discussed in chapter five, the arbitration community is going through a process of developing and crystallising the dominant understandings of applicable norms into written codes and texts. Due to the decentralised nature of the production of these texts and the relative recency of

[21] See Catherine A Rogers, 'Regulating International Arbitrators: A Functional Approach to Developing Standards of Conduct' (2005) 41 *Stanford Journal of International Law* 53, 62.

[22] Sundaresh Menon, 'Some Cautionary Notes for an Age of Opportunity' (Chartered Institute of Arbitrators International Arbitration Conference, Penang, 22 August 2013), available at www.singaporelaw.sg/.

[23] In some arbitral circles it has become common to mention that a 'golden-age' of arbitration has passed. See, eg, David W Rivkin, 'Keynote Address: A New Contract Between Arbitrators and Parties' (2016) 18 *Asian Dispute Review* 4; William Park, 'Arbitration in Autumn' (2011) 2 *Journal of International Dispute Settlement* 287, 288.

[24] Menkel-Meadow also points out how an increasing number of actors and standards may allow the 'technocratic' arguments of lawyers and arbitrators to justify almost any practice. Carrie Menkel-Meadow, 'Ethics Issues in Arbitration and Related Dispute Resolution Processes: What's Happening and What's Not Arbitration Symposium' (2001) 56 *University of Miami Law Review* 949, 975.

[25] See Global Arbitration News, International Arbitration Statistics 2018 – Another busy year for Arbitral Institutions, 2 July 2019, available at globalarbitrationnews.com.

these efforts, it is uncertain to what extent these texts will be able to fully establish themselves as common ground. In many areas, the process of 'codifying' is still taking place. Still, how some of these texts, particularly the IBA Guidelines on Conflicts of Interest and the IBA Guidelines on Taking of Evidence, have been widely adopted allows us to anticipate that, over time, the community organically tends to gravitate to a specific set of codified norms that are communicated widely across the community.

Second, technological developments have helped information to continue flowing through a more extensive community, allowing reputation mechanisms to continue operating. The internet has become a cornerstone of dispersing information in this environment.[26] Publications with a strong online presence report on recent legal developments, the most important cases, and all the news relevant to the community.[27] Blogs, mailing lists, and social networks also allow members of the community to comment on cases and developments in the market. These information networks provide the community with a forum to discuss which behaviours are acceptable and to criticise behaviours that do not conform to the values held by the members of the community.

The increased value of information regarding arbitrators has inclusively spurred the emergence of third parties, such as Arbitrator Intelligence and Jus Mundi, that compile and analyse information on arbitrators. While, in broad terms, these companies can be seen as part of an emergent legal tech sector, these initiatives can also be seen as a logical development of the well-established practice of those within the community attempting to obtain as much information on a prospective arbitrator prior to an appointment. More importantly, they exemplify how the arbitration market is able to, at least to an extent, self-correct some of its own imperfections. As information becomes more complex and difficult to obtain, and therefore more valuable, incentives appear for agents to organise and provide, against a price, this information.

Finally, the increasing size of the community also meant that the structure of the community itself has transformed in ways that allow information to continue flowing. As international commercial arbitration expanded, some international arbitrators have looked to differentiate themselves by specialising in market niches, be it in terms of jurisdiction or areas of practice. Further, new geographical centres have assumed increasing importance.[28] Around these centres, new, smaller communities have formed. While arbitration has grown well beyond the point where even the most gregarious member of the arbitral community can know all the other members of the community, the way the community has splintered conceivably allows members to know other participants in the niche of the market they are familiar with.

This specialising also gave rise to more separate roles within the community. As noted in chapter two, some elite senior arbitrators have been changing how they organise their

[26] Arbitrators have increasingly relied on social media strategies as 'reputation' promotional tools, leading to a new level of transparency in the market. See, Niuscha Bassari, 'Arbitrators and Their Online Identity' in Maud Piers and Christian Aschauer (eds), *Arbitration in the Digital Age: The Brave New World of Arbitration* (Cambridge, Cambridge University Press, 2018) 246.

[27] Examples of such publications and forums include the Global Arbitration Review (GAR), the Kluwer Arbitration Blog and the OGEMID mailing list, amongst many others.

[28] Most notably Singapore and Hong Kong. See, eg, Neil Kaplan, 'The History and Development of Arbitration in Hong Kong Symposium: Financial Law in Hong Kong and South-East Asia' (1996) 1 *Yearbook of International Financial and Economic Law* 203.

practices, with some abandoning large, well-established law firms and establishing small legal boutiques dedicated to arbitration.[29] The increasing demands of independence and impartiality and the inner dynamics of large law firms have made it more difficult to combine being a partner at a top law firm and routinely accepting arbitral appointments. This raises important questions. Namely, it leads to the question of whether arbitrators should operate as a fully separated profession – ie whether the current practice of multiple-hatting, where arbitrators also act, in other proceedings, as counsel or experts, should be maintained or arbitrators should instead operate full-time in this role. First, however, it should be considered if such radical evolution would be even possible against the background of the transformations taking place in the dispute resolution market.

IV. The Current Transformations in the Dispute Resolution Market and the Possibility of Changes in the Regulation of Arbitrators

While some have increasingly seen arbitrators as a separate socio-professional category,[30] there does not seem to exist, at least in what commercial arbitration is concerned, a strong impetus to reform the way international arbitrators are organised. As discussed in chapter four, neither state legislatures nor parties and the arbitral community itself have found sufficient incentives to procure a transformation of the regulatory landscape. Still, a number of significant transformations in the approaches of these actors to the current market should be noted. Namely, i) some states have shown an increasing interest in creating alternatives to international arbitration; ii) parties' preferences in regard to arbitrators and dispute resolution are in continuous flux; and iii) arbitral institutions are increasingly assuming a central role in the field of arbitration.

A. Recent States' Intervention in the Dispute Resolution Market: The Creation of Alternatives to Arbitration

For the reasons noted in chapter four, state legislatures are not prime candidates to develop a stricter regulation of arbitrators.[31] As discussed in that chapter, regulatory competition, driven by the ability of parties to select where their proceedings will take place, has led states to not intensively regulate arbitrators. Still, it is worth noting that some states have shown an increasing interest in international dispute resolution. Beyond a trend of legislative acts aimed at facilitating the usage of arbitration, some states have also looked to create alternatives. Two types of initiatives should be noted: the passage of international treaties, fostering the usage of court litigation and mediation in the international sphere and the development of international commercial courts.

[29] See ch 2, section II.D.

[30] See Emmanuel Gaillard, 'Sociology of International Arbitration' (2015) 31 *Arbitration International* 1, 4.

[31] See ch 4, section III.

In relation to international treaties, three recent international conventions should be noted: the Hague Choice of Court Convention, signed in 2005; the Hague Judgments Convention, signed in 2019; and the Singapore Mediation Convention, also signed in 2019. Further, many states have created commercial courts with the specific purpose of attracting international business disputes. China, the Netherlands, France, Germany, Singapore, and Dubai, amongst others, have experimented with establishing their own models of courts dedicated to international commercial disputes.[32] In common, and typically finding inspiration in arbitration and the London Commercial Court, these courts use English, specialised judges, and fast-track procedures to broaden the appeal of the judiciary to solve international commercial disputes.[33]

So far, however, these initiatives have not significantly transformed the international dispute resolution market, making it unclear to what extent court litigation and mediation can truly become alternatives to international commercial arbitration. Also, the international commercial courts currently in operation have not seen a large caseload.[34] Despite some states seeing the potential in these venues as ways of propping up their local legal markets and helping transform their jurisdictions into international hubs of dispute resolution,[35] these courts have so far not been able to establish themselves as alternatives to international arbitration on a large scale.[36]

It is also important to note that these initiatives do not present themselves as being motivated by weaknesses perceived in arbitration but rather intended to create complementary mechanisms to arbitration.[37] In fact, they have often used arbitration-like solutions as an inspiration for their frameworks. Still, the combination of these initiatives may have

[32] See Gary F Bell, 'The New International Commercial Courts – Competing with Arbitration – The Example of the Singapore International Commercial Court' (2018) 11 *Contemporary Asia Arbitration Journal* 193, 193.

[33] See Andrew Godwin, Ian Ramsay and Miranda Webster, 'International Commercial Courts: The Singapore Experience' (2017) 18 *Melbourne Journal of International Law* 219, 221; Marta Requejo Isidro, 'International Commercial Courts in the Litigation Market' (2019) 9 *International Journal of Procedural Law* 4; Georgia Antonopoulou, 'The 'Arbitralization' of Courts: The Role of International Commercial Arbitration in the Establishment and the Procedural Design of International Commercial Courts' (2023) 14 *Journal of International Dispute Settlement* 328.

[34] An exception to this has been the London Commercial Court, which has been a significant player in the international dispute resolution market. Albeit created much earlier (1895) than the current generation of international commercial courts, it has been often presented as a blueprint for the current crop of international commercial courts. For a typology of the different generations of international commercial courts, see Weixia Gu and Jacky Tam, 'The Global Rise of International Commercial Courts: Typology and Power Dynamics' (2021) 22 *Chicago Journal of International Law* 443.

[35] See Stephan Wilske, 'International Commercial Courts and Arbitration – Alternatives, Substitutes or Trojan Horse' (2018) 11 *Contemporary Asia Arbitration Journal* 153, 156.

[36] The Singapore International Commercial Court (SICC) has been perhaps the most successful of the recent wave of international commercial courts. As of the end of 2021, the SICC had a docket of 83 first instance matters. Of these, 73 were transfers from the Singapore High Court and 10 were fresh filings. See SICC, 'The year 2021 in review' (February 2022) www.sicc.gov.sg/docs/default-source/modules-document/media-resources/sicc-news-no-27-(feb-2021)_bc09f7f5-2053-4508-8ff1-5fca6031d46e.pdf, last accessed 14 November 2023. It is important to note that many of the SICC's cases are cases filed in the Singapore High Court and that the High Court may determine that a specific case should come within the jurisdiction of the SICC, even if a jurisdiction agreement does not exist. See Bell (n 32) 212.

[37] See Godwin, Ramsay and Webster (n 33) 223; Requejo Isidro (n 33) 34. Despite often affirming a complementary role to arbitration, perceived weaknesses of arbitration have been seen as playing a role in the development of these courts. See Dalma R Demeter and Kayleigh M Smith, 'The Implications of International Commercial Courts on Arbitration' (2016) 33 *Journal of International Arbitration* 441, 442.

the potential to create a competitive framework for arbitration.[38] In this way, it also allows states to indirectly regulate arbitration. By upping the competitiveness of the alternatives to arbitration, states conceivably create pressure on arbitration providers to improve their quality/price ratio and address issues that would lead users to prefer other dispute resolution mechanisms.[39]

B. Parties Changing Preferences as a Catalyst for 'Regulatory' Changes

Even if states are not interested or capable of transforming the regulation of arbitration, other actors may operate these changes. As an example, parties can 'force' arbitrators to become more professionalised by displaying a systematic preference for arbitrators operating full-time and appointing only those integrated within professional organisations that train, examine and supervise arbitrators. In the same vein, parties can have the same effect by selecting arbitral institutions that would be more akin to professional associations – ie, selecting arbitral institutions that would take a more hands-on approach in training, vetting and regulating arbitrators' behaviour.[40]

Over time, these changes can happen. As discussed in chapter two, preferences changed in the 1980s and 1990s, showing an increased appointment of those who had a more robust specialised knowledge in arbitration instead of those with a background outside law or even in law but outside arbitration.[41] Some indications seem to point to the idea that the market is showing an increasing preference for those supported by teams, allowing them to deal with the progressively escalating technical and factual complexity of arbitral proceedings.[42] Still, currently, no trend of a systemic preference for 'professional' arbitrators by parties can be identified.

While futurology regarding market preferences is a notoriously challenging endeavour, one can characterise the likelihood of parties starting to systematically prefer 'professionalised' arbitrators as unlikely. It is true that, as markets mature, specialisation typically takes place as it allows competitive advantages for those who specialise. However, in arbitration, it seems that, for most operating in the market, the increased business opportunities of offering more than one type of service trump the benefits of specialisation. Furthermore, there is a strong overlap between the skills and knowledge needed to be an effective counsel and an arbitrator, leading to a lower benefit in specialising exclusively in one of these roles.

Decisions to appoint arbitrators are often complex strategic decisions, where the parties are not necessarily always trying to appoint the 'best' arbitrator, in the sense of the most

[38] See M Hwang, 'Commercial Courts and International Arbitration – Competitors or Partners?' (2015) 31 *Arbitration International* 193, 194.

[39] See Demeter and Smith (n 37) 469.

[40] Albeit most arbitral institutions have not taken serious steps to regulate arbitrators in a way akin to a professional association, there have been voices requesting a more proactive role, most notably Rogers. See Rogers (n 21) 110.

[41] See ch 2, section II.

[42] See Thomas Schultz and Robert Kovacs, 'The Rise of a Third Generation of Arbitrators? Fifteen Years After Dezalay and Garth' (2012) 28 *Arbitration International* 161, 171.

well-prepared or the one most able to conclude the proceedings in an 'efficient' way. Often, these decisions involve many other calculations, such as which prospective arbitrator would prove more advantageous for the party or more knowledgeable about the substantive issues at play.[43] This means that while general trends might continue to move, it is likely that arbitrators with different profiles will continue to be selected, ranging between those who are more 'professionalised' and others who are undertaking appointments in a more limited way.

C. The Power of the Arbitral Community and Arbitral Institutions to Determine 'Regulatory' Changes

If the market is not likely to organically lead to fully 'professionalised' arbitrators, other candidates could still perform this change. For example, the arbitral community could spontaneously self-regulate by determining the unacceptability of awards issued by 'part-time' arbitrators or those without 'accepted' qualifications. In a sense, any such radical transformation taking place is also an unlikely proposition. A proposal, for example, to outright eliminate the possibility of cumulating accepting appointments as arbitrator and counsel or the introduction of mandatory licensing would certainly receive opposition from most within the community,[44] be it due to authentic disagreement with the merits of any such proposal or more cynically due to the fact that any such transformation would negatively affect their income prospects.[45]

However, more measured steps are far from outside of the realm of possibility.[46] The arbitral community has sometimes adopted understandings that do not necessarily conform to the best short-term interests of its elite members or even the majority of its members. Arguably, this was the case with the IBA Guidelines on Conflicts of Interest, discussed in chapter six, which opted for solutions that limited the ability of well-positioned arbitrators, namely those within large law firms, to be appointed more frequently.[47] In theory, the arbitral community could further expand the definition of conflicts of interest, independence and impartiality, leading to a higher number of arbitrators opting to take arbitral appointments as their full-time professional endeavour.

Given their increasing importance derived from their growing caseload, arbitral institutions are an even more likely candidate to operate these changes. They could do so by selecting to primarily appoint 'full-time' arbitrators and, in this way, create further incentives

[43] See Grant Hanessian and Lawrence W Newman, *International Arbitration Checklists*, 2nd edn (New York, Juris Publishing Inc, 2009) 45.

[44] See, eg, Gary Born, *International Commercial Arbitration*, 2nd edn (Alphen aan den Rijn, Wolters Kluwer Law & Business, 2014) 2048.

[45] Noting resistance by the international arbitration community to proposals for express ethical regulation or even self-regulation to be 'inevitable', see Catherine A Rogers, *Ethics in International Arbitration* (Oxford, Oxford University Press, 2014) 225.

[46] Franck, eg, comments: 'As the international arbitration constituency continues to expand arbitrators should give into their impulse to professionalize the services they render. By seeking out opportunities to enhance their independence and impartiality, this will benefit the integrity of international arbitration by confirming the neutrality and fairness of the underlying process.' Susan D Franck, 'The Role of International Arbitrators' (2005) 12 *ILSA Journal of International and Comparative Law* 499, 520.

[47] See David A Lawson, 'Impartiality and Independence of International Arbitrators' (2005) 23 *ASA Bull.* 22, 37.

for arbitrators to professionalise. Alternatively, in an even more radical departure from current practices, arbitral institutions could assume a role more akin to those of traditional professional associations in other fields. They could start determining mandatory qualifications for arbitrators,[48] providing mandatory training for those wanting to be appointed, or creating and enforcing ethical codes in a similar way to how professional bodies self-regulate other professionals.[49]

In a way, this is also an unlikely outcome. Arbitral institutions are generally headed by either arbitrators or those with close ties to the field. To an extent, they depend on the arbitral community to attract parties to the institution. Therefore, arbitral institutions will typically not look to alienate the arbitral community. That said, these institutions have the ability to take steps that are not in line with the strict, short-term interests of current arbitrators. Due to their market power, arbitral institutions can, in practice, impose policy solutions that may not be the preference of arbitrators or parties. Some of the steps undertaken to increase transparency,[50] diversity of arbitration rosters[51] or efficiency of proceedings[52] may be used as examples of arbitral institutions deviating from the short-term interest of members of the community to promote the long-term legitimacy of arbitration.

V. Should a Separation between the Function of Arbitrator and Counsel be Encouraged?

Altogether, while the market for dispute resolution is in flux, a radical transformation in the way arbitrators provide their services is an unlikely outcome. While arbitral institutions and the arbitral community more generally could, if they so wished, force the 'professionalisation' of arbitrators by pushing for further separation of the function of arbitrators from other professional functions and regulating the entrance into the market, there seems to be no pressure to undertake any such radical transformations. Still, it is worth discussing

[48] In the context of other fields of arbitration, arbitral institutions do sometimes take a more hands-on approach in establishing explicit requirements for arbitrators. This is the case of sports arbitration where the Court of Arbitration for Sport maintains a closed list of arbitrators that must have 'appropriate legal training, recognized competence with regard to sports law and/or international arbitration, a good knowledge of sport in general and a good command of at least one CAS working language'. Philippe Cavalieros and Janet Kim, 'Can the Arbitral Community Learn from Sports Arbitration?' (2015) 32 *Journal of International Arbitration* 237, 247.

[49] There are a few examples of arbitral institutions taking a more proactive role in the enforcement of arbitral obligations. Most notably the AAA and the Milan Chamber of Arbitration (CAM) have indicated that they may withdraw an arbitrator from their lists that fails to disclose a conflict of interest in a proceeding. See Katia Fach Gomėz, *Key Duties of International Investment Arbitrators: A Transnational Study of Legal and Ethical Dilemmas* (Berlin, Springer Berlin Heidelberg, 2018) 69.

[50] Eg, the decision of the ICC to publish limited information relating to arbitrators sitting in ICC cases, allowing parties to know how many ICC cases arbitrators have seated on, can in theory be a drawback to elite arbitrators as it might allow them to be challenged in future proceedings or allow criticism for accepting too many appointments. The very limited information disclosed limits, however, any significant drawback for arbitrators.

[51] Efforts of some arbitral institutions to increase the diversity of the arbitrators appointed, namely trying to achieve more gender parity, rather than directed at benefiting the current roster of elite arbitrators (which is overwhelmingly composed by men) seem to be an attempt to counteract ideas that arbitration lacks diversity, which, as aforementioned, became a common criticism of arbitration.

[52] See, eg, the examples of arbitral institutions reducing arbitrators' fees in case of delayed awards. Ch 8, section I.B.

whether such regulatory changes would be positive in the sense of producing a fairer and more efficient dispute resolution system, especially given that through small steps, such as an increasingly stricter understanding of independence and impartiality, separation of the profession can, de facto, be reached.

Within arbitral circles, discussions around this topic are usually framed with reference to the concept of 'double-hatting' – ie, the practice of simultaneously combining the roles of arbitrator and counsel in different cases.[53] It is important to note that while to an extent contentious in the context of investment arbitration, the practice of double-hatting, perhaps surprising for those outside the field, is largely uncontroversial within commercial arbitration circles.[54] However, forbidding 'double-hatting' and 'professionalisation' are not precisely coinciding concepts. The latter would refer to a broader process of acquiring the characteristics typical of the profession, including a monopoly of the 'professionals' over the possibility of offering services in the area and the existence of state-backed enforcement of formalised codes of ethics.

Arguments can be made in favour of further separating the role of 'arbitrator' and 'counsel', either by forcing a professionalisation of arbitrators or limiting double-hatting. If, as argued in chapter seven, part of the incentives leading arbitrators to comply with professional and ethical norms derive from reputation mechanisms, limiting the possibility of those not operating in the market long-term accepting appointments would arguably help these reputation mechanisms to operate better.[55] Also, limiting the possibility of cumulating appointments as arbitrator and counsel would, to an extent, limit the possibility of 'trading' appointments – ie, a practice of appointing a particular member as an arbitrator with the implicit or even explicit agreement of being appointed by the same member as an arbitrator in another proceeding.[56]

Such changes would probably not find any traction within the arbitral community. Tradition, given that being an arbitrator has not been historically a full-time pursuit,[57] and perhaps self-interest, as few in the community would be interested in changing the current status quo, helps explain this resistance. Those within the community have used several arguments to justify opposition to a prohibition of double-hatting.[58] Some have a more practical bent by pointing out that forbidding counsel to act as arbitrators would significantly weaken the pool of talent available to act as an arbitrator.[59] Others focus on a more normative dimension, arguing that limiting double hatting would restrict parties' rights to

[53] See Malcolm Langford, Daniel Behn and Runar Hilleren Lie, 'The Revolving Door in International Investment Arbitration' (2017) 20 *Journal of International Economic Law* 301, 321.

[54] See Malcolm Langford, Daniel Behn and Runar Hilleren Lie, 'The Ethics and Empirics of Double Hatting' (2017) 6 *ESIL Reflection* 6.

[55] In the context of international investment arbitration, it has been hypothesised that 'repeat-arbitrators', by opposition to 'one-short arbitrators', work as 'guardians of the regime'. Malcolm Langford and Daniel Behn, 'Managing Backlash: The Evolving Investment Treaty Arbitrator?' (2018) 29 *European Journal of International Law* 551, 565.

[56] See Thomas Buergenthal, 'The Proliferation of Disputes, Dispute Settlement Procedures and Respect for the Rule of Law' (2006) 22 *Arbitration International* 495, 498.

[57] See Gaillard (n 30) 4.

[58] See Dennis H Hranitzky and Eduardo Silva Romero, 'The 'Double Hat' Debate in International Arbitration' *New York Law Journal* (14 June 2010) available at www.law.com/newyorklawjournal/, last accessed on 9 April 2020.

[59] See, in the context of investment arbitration, Langford, Behn and Lie (n 53) 322.

freely select their arbitrator and, in this sense, infringe their autonomy – one of the cornerstones of arbitration.[60]

A further note is warranted. Establishing arbitrators as a fully separate profession would probably significantly change the underlying mechanisms shaping the regulation of the field. This would not necessarily mean that arbitrators would be similar to other professions. Arbitration would still be transnational in nature and likely would not be regulated across national lines.[61] Even in a model where arbitrators would be a separate profession, it would still be a market marked by low levels of price competition, and that would tend to be a space difficult to enter for those not heavily invested in the field. Still, it would be possible that if arbitrators were a separate profession, they would push for measures to further entrench their position, such as the usage of 'closed lists' of arbitrators by arbitral institutions.[62]

A separate arbitral profession would mean the emergence of a more 'polarised' community where each member would be less inclined to interact with others as peers.[63] In the current field, there are high incentives for engagement with the community, where those who participate in community initiatives and gatherings see the likelihood of being appointed as an arbitrator increase. This creates incentives for wide participation in self-regulatory initiatives. In a polarised field where those operating as counsel cannot be directly 'rewarded' with the potential of appointments as arbitrators, it would be likely that their engagement with the rest of the community would wane.[64] Interactions would, therefore, move to relations between two poles: those specialising in acting as counsel who would operate in practice as 'service-acquirers' and those specialising as arbitrators who would act as 'service providers'.

How the arbitral community would adapt to such an environment is not fully knowable, but certainly, a significantly different way of creating and enforcing norms would emerge. Any changes in this regard should, therefore, be carefully considered. A fully professionalised and regulated arbitral profession could perhaps bring a semblance of legitimacy to the field and could address the issues of 'one-shot' arbitrators not concerned with reputation.[65] It could, however, also bring unpredictable changes to arbitration. The current design of commercial arbitration was largely the work of the arbitral community itself. These self-regulatory efforts are not fully altruistic but rather the by-product of a complex 'game'

[60] See Born (n 44) 2048.

[61] The increasingly transnational nature of professions, such as elite lawyers and accountants, has been a topic progressively explored in the sociology of professions. Still strategies of closure in these elite subsects of their professional communities is significantly distinct of the situation found in arbitration. For an overview of closure professional strategies in a transnational setting, see James R Faulconbridge and Daniel Muzio, 'Professions in a Globalizing World: Towards a Transnational Sociology of the Professions' (2012) 27 *International Sociology* 136.

[62] Latvia is noteworthy for determining a mandatory system of closed-lists for arbitral institutions. This is a heavily criticised departure from international practice. See Toms Kruminš, 'Arbitration in Latvia: A Cautionary Tale?' (2017) 34 *Journal of International Arbitration* 303, 324.

[63] See Gaillard (n 30) 14.

[64] This would not, however, necessarily mean a breakdown of the ability of arbitration to continue producing its own regulatory framework. To an extent, arbitrators would likely be incentivised to interact with each other and with counsel and participate in the initiatives regarding their own status and applicable norms. Even counsel would, to an extent. be interested in participating in the community as they would likely still be invested in the state of arbitration as a whole.

[65] See Franck (n 46) 517. See also João Ilhão Moreira, 'The Insider/Outsider Divide and the Ethics of Commercial Arbitrators.' (2022) 19 *Manchester Journal of International Economic Law* 132.

through which elite members offer valuable work time legitimising arbitration and, in exchange, receive networking opportunities and community prestige that ultimately translate into appointments and success.

If the benefits of networking and community prestige would drop for a significant number of participants, the members of the arbitral community could conceivably quit participating in the creation (and, to an extent, in the enforcement) of the professional norms existing in the field. This would give rise to a vacuum that other players would certainly fill. Arbitral institutions would possibly be sufficiently incentivised to take a more proactive role in regulating arbitrators and creating and enforcing norms to maintain the legitimacy of arbitration.[66] Likely, a smaller cadre of professionalised arbitrators would continue regulating efforts. It would, however, run the danger to advance a closure agenda that arbitration has so far avoided.

[66] In this context, it is worth noting that the 'legitimacy' of international arbitration has been increasingly presented as having to satisfy not only parties ('party legitimacy') or the arbitral community ('community legitimacy'), but also needs to take into account the interests of national societies ('national legitimacy') and global society as a whole ('global legitimacy'). See Stephan Schill, 'Developing a Framework for the Legitimacy of International Arbitration' in Albert Jan van den Berg (ed), *Legitimacy: Myths, Realities, Challenges* (Alphen aan den Rijn, Wolters Kluwer Law & Business, 2015) 827.

BIBLIOGRAPHY

Abbott A, 'The Order of Professionalization: An Empirical Analysis' (1991) 18 *Work and Occupations* 355

——, *The System of Professions: An Essay on the Division of Expert Labor* (Chicago, University of Chicago Press, 2014)

Abel RL, 'Comparative Sociology of Legal Professions: An Exploratory Essay' (1985) 10 *American Bar Foundation Research Journal* 5

——, *American Lawyers* (Oxford, Oxford University Press, 1989)

——, *The Making of the English Legal Profession* (Washington, Beard Books, 1998)

Aksen G, 'Taming the Twin Dragons of International Arbitration: Cost and Delay' in Patricia Shaughnessy and Sherlin Tung (eds), *The Powers and Duties of an Arbitrator: Liber Amicorum Pierre A. Karrer* (Alphen aan den Rijn, Kluwer Law International, 2017)

Alessi D, 'Enforcing Arbitrator's Obligations: Rethinking International Commercial Arbitrators' Liability' (2014) 31 *Journal of International Arbitration* 735

Allen N and Mallett D, 'Arbitrator Disclosure – No Room For The Colour Blind' (2011) 7 *Asian International Arbitration Journal* 118

Alpert GP, Noble JJ and Rojek J, 'Solidarity and the Code of Silence' in Roger G Dunham and Geoffrey P Alpert (eds), *Critical Issues in Policing: Contemporary Readings*, 7th edn (Illinois, Waveland Press, 2015)

Antonopoulou G, 'The "Arbitralization" of Courts: The Role of International Commercial Arbitration in the Establishment and the Procedural Design of International Commercial Courts' (2023) 14 *Journal of International Dispute Settlement* 328

Ashbaugh H, 'Ethical Issues Related to the Provision of Audit and Non-Audit Services: Evidence from Academic Research' (2004) 52 *Journal of Business Ethics* 143

Badelt C, 'Entrepreneurship in Nonprofit Organizations: Its Role in Theory and in the Real World Nonprofit Sector' in Helmut K Anheier and Avner Ben-Ner (eds), *The Study of Nonprofit Enterprise: Theories and Approaches* (New York, Springer Science & Business Media, 2003)

Baizeau D and Hayes T, 'The Arbitral Tribunal's Duty and Power to Address Corruption Sua Sponte' in Andrea Menaker (ed), *International Arbitration and the Rule of Law: Contribution and Conformity*, vol 19 (Alphen aan den Rijn, Kluwer Law International, 2017)

Baldwin R, Cave M and Lodge M, *Understanding Regulation: Theory, Strategy, and Practice*, 2nd edn (Oxford, Oxford University Press, 2012)

Baldwin R, Scott CD and Hood C, *A Reader on Regulation* (Oxford, Oxford University Press, 1998)

Bantekas I, *An Introduction to International Arbitration* (Cambridge, Cambridge University Press, 2015)

Bao C, 'Hong Kong Courts: International Arbitration Law in the Making' [2019] *Belgian Review of Arbitration* 615

Bassari N, 'Arbitrators and Their Online Identity' in Maud Piers and Christian Aschauer (eds), *Arbitration in the Digital Age: The Brave New World of Arbitration* (Cambridge, Cambridge University Press, 2018)

Bator FM, 'The Anatomy of Market Failure' (1958) 72 *The Quarterly Journal of Economics* 351

Becker HS, *Sociological Work: Method and Substance* (London, Routledge, 1976)

Bell GF, 'The New International Commercial Courts – Competing with Arbitration – The Example of the Singapore International Commercial Court' (2018) 11 *Contemporary Asia Arbitration Journal* 193

Benson BL, 'An Exploration of the Impact of Modern Arbitration Statutes on the Development of Arbitration in the United States' (1995) 11 *Journal of Law, Economics, & Organization* 479

Bentolila D, *Arbitrators as Lawmakers* (Alphen aan den Rijn, Kluwer Law International, 2017)

Berger KP, 'Common Law vs. Civil Law in International Arbitration: The Beginning or the End?' (2019) 36 *Journal of International Arbitration* 295

Berger KP and Jensen JO, 'Due Process Paranoia and the Procedural Judgment Rule: A Safe Harbour for Procedural Management Decisions by International Arbitrators' (2016) 32 *Arbitration International* 415

Bermann GA, 'American Exceptionalism in International Arbitration' in Arthur W Rovine (ed), *Contemporary Issues in International Arbitration and Mediation: The Fordham Papers (2011)* (Leiden, Martinus Nijhoff Publishers, 2012)

Bettencourt JC and Marks T, 'The Chartered Institute of Arbitrators' in JDM Lew and others (eds), *Arbitration in England: With Chapters on Scotland and Ireland* (Alphen aan den Rijn, Kluwer Law International. 2013)

Bevilacqua T and Ugarte R, 'Ensuring Party Equality in the Process of Designating Arbitrators in Multiparty Arbitration: An Update on the Governing Provisions' (2010) 27 *Journal of International Arbitration* 9

Bietz H, 'On the State and Efficiency of International Arbitration – Could the German `Relevance Method` Be Useful or Not?' (2014) 12 *SchiedsVZ* 121

Bishop D and Reed L, 'Practical Guidelines for Interviewing, Selecting and Challenging Party-Appointed Arbitrators in International Commercial Arbitration' (1998) 14 *Arbitration International* 395

Black J, 'Constitutionalising Self-Regulation' (1996) 59 *The Modern Law Review* 24

Blackaby N, 'Public Interest and Investment Treaty Arbitration' in Albert Jan van den Berg (ed), *International Commercial Arbitration: Important Contemporary Questions* (Alphen aan den Rijn, Kluwer Law International, 2003)

Blendon RJ, Benson JM and Hero JO, 'Public Trust in Physicians – U.S. Medicine in International Perspective' (2014) 371 *New England Journal of Medicine* 1570

Böckstiegel K-H, 'Arbitrator's Case Management: Experiences and Suggestions' in Gerald Aksen and others (eds), *Global reflections on international law, commerce and dispute resolution : liber amicorum in honour of Robert Briner* (Paris, ICC Publishing, 2005)

——, 'Do Institutions Really Add Value to the Arbitral Process?' in Bernard Hanotiau and Alexis Mourre (eds), *Dossier IX Players' Interaction in International Arbitration* (Paris, ICC Publishing, 2012)

Bolton SC and Muzio D, 'Can't Live with 'Em; Can't Live without 'Em: Gendered Segmentation in the Legal Profession' (2007) 41 *Sociology* 47

Bond SR, 'The International Arbitrator: From the Perspective of the ICC International Court of Arbitration' (1991) 12 *Northwestern Journal of International Law & Business* 1

Boon A, 'Professionalism under the Legal Services Act 2007' (2010) 17 *International Journal of the Legal Profession* 195

Borbély A, 'Agency in Conflict Resolution as a Manager–Lawyer Issue: Theory and Implications for Research' (2011) 4 *Negotiation and Conflict Management Research* 129

Born G, *International Commercial Arbitration: Commentary and Materials* (Alphen aan den Rijn, Kluwer Law International, 2001)

——, *International Arbitration: Law and Practice* (Alphen aan den Rijn, Kluwer Law International, 2012)

——, *International Commercial Arbitration*, 2nd edn, (Alphen aan den Rijn, Wolters Kluwer Law & Business, 2014)

Bouzarjomehri S and Amini E, 'Public Policy as Ground for Refusal of International Arbitral Awards – A Comparison Between Different Judicial Practices' (2016) 9 *Journal of Politics and Law* 81

Brazolo LR di, 'International Arbitration and Domestic Law' in Giuditta Cordero-Moss (ed), *International Commercial Arbitration: Different Forms and Their Features* (Cambridge, Cambridge University Press, 2013)

Brekoulakis SL, 'Introduction: The Evolution and Future of International Arbitration' in Stavros L Brekoulakis, Julian DM Lew and Loukas A Mistelis (eds), *The Evolution and Future of International Arbitration* (Alphen aan den Rijn, Kluwer Law International, 2016)

Brodlija F, 'Innovative Solutions for an Age-Old Issue: How Transparency and Data Analytic Tools Can Improve Diversity in International Arbitration' (2021) 5 *Journal of Strategic Contracting and Negotiation* 24

Brower CN, 'W(h)Ither International Commercial Arbitration? The Goff Lecture 2007' (2008) 24 *Arbitration International* 181

Brower CN and Rosenberg CB, 'The Death of the Two-Headed Nightingale: Why the Paulsson – van Den Berg Presumption That Party-Appointed Arbitrators Are Untrustworthy Is Wrongheaded' (2013) 29 *Arbitration International* 7

Brutger R and Strezhnev A, 'International Investment Disputes, Media Coverage, and Backlash Against International Law' (2022) 66 *Journal of Conflict Resolution* 983

Buchanan MA, 'Public Policy and International Commercial Arbitration' (1988) 26 *American Business Law Journal* 511

Buchner-Jeziorska A and Evetts J, 'Regulating Professionals: The Polish Example' (1997) 12 *International Sociology* 61

Buergenthal T, 'The Proliferation of Disputes, Dispute Settlement Procedures and Respect for the Rule of Law' (2006) 22 *Arbitration International* 495

Bühring-Uhle C, Kirchhoff L and Scherer G, *Arbitration and Mediation in International Business* (Alphen aan den Rijn, Kluwer Law International BV, 2006)

Bulter H, 'Unlocking the Law: Building on the Work of Professor Larry E. Ribstein' (2013) 38 *International Review of Law and Economics* 2

Burrage M, *Revolution and the Making of the Contemporary Legal Profession: England, France, and the United States* (Oxford, Oxford University Press, 2006)

Cabrillo F and Fitzpatrick S, *The Economics of Courts and Litigation* (Cheltenham, Edward Elgar Publishing, 2008)

Cairns D, 'The Spanish Application of the UNCITRAL Model Law on International Commercial Arbitration' (2006) 22 *Arbitration International* 573

Caplow T, *The Sociology of Work* (Minnesota, University of Minnesota Press, 1954)

Carbonneau TE, 'The Exercise of Contract Freedom in the Making of Arbitration Agreements' (2003) 36 *Vanderbilt Journal of Transnational Law* 1189

—— *Law and Practice of Arbitration*, 5th edn (New York, Juris Publishing Inc, 2014)

——, 'The Elaboration of a French Court Doctrine on International Commercial Arbitration: A Study in Liberal Civilian Judicial Creativity' (1980) 55 *Tulane Law Review* 1

Carducci G, 'The Arbitration Reform in France: Domestic and International Arbitration Law' (2012) 28 *Arbitration International* 125

Caron DD, 'Light and Dark in International Arbitration: The Virtues, Risks and Limits of Transparency' in Hong Kong International Arbitration (ed), *International Arbitration: Issues, Perspectives and Practice: Liber Amicorum Neil Kaplan* (Alphen aan den Rijn, Kluwer Law International, 2019)

Carter JH, 'The Culture of Arbitration and the Defense of Arbitral Legitimacy' in David D Caron and others (eds), *Practising Virtue: Inside International Arbitration* (Oxford, Oxford University Press, 2015)

Carter JH and Fellas J, *International Commercial Arbitration in New York* (Oxford, Oxford University Press, 2010)

Casella A, 'On Market Integration and the Development of Institutions: The Case of International Commercial Arbitration' (1996) 40 *European Economic Review* 155

Catenaccio P, 'Cultural Variation in Arbitration Journals: The International Court of Arbitration Bulletin and the Arbitration Journal Compared' in Vijay Kumar Bhatia, Christopher Candlin and Maurizio Gotti (eds), *Discourse and Practice in International Commercial Arbitration: Issues, Challenges and Prospects* (London, Ashgate Publishing Ltd, 2012)

Cavalieros P and Kim J, 'Can the Arbitral Community Learn from Sports Arbitration?' (2015) 32 *Journal of International Arbitration* 237

Chaserant C and Harnay S, 'Self-Regulation of the Legal Profession and Quality in the Market for Legal Services: An Economic Analysis of Lawyers' Reputation' (2015) 39 *European Journal of Law and Economics* 431

Choi SJ, 'The Problem with Arbitration Agreements' (2003) 36 *Vanderbilt Journal of Transnational Law* 1233

Chua W-F and Clegg S, 'Professional Closure: The Case of British Nursing' (1990) 19 *Theory and Society* 135

Chung Y and Ha H-Y, 'Arbitrator Acceptability in International Commercial Arbitration: The Trading Firm Perspective' (2016) 27 *International Journal of Conflict Management* 379

Clay T, 'Qui Sont Les Arbitres Internationaux?: Approche Sociologique' in Rosell (ed), *Les arbitres internationaux* (Paris, Société de Législation Comparée, 2005)

——, 'El Mercado Del Arbitraje' (2014) 7 *Arbitraje: revista de arbitraje comercial y de inversiones* 15

Colander D, 'The Death of Neoclassical Economics' (2000) 22 *Journal of the History of Economic Thought* 127

Cordero-Moss G, *International Commercial Arbitration: Different Forms and Their Features* (Cambridge, Cambridge University Press, 2013)

Coulson R, 'Will the Growth of Alternative Dispute Resolution (ADR) in American Be Replicated in Europe' (1992) 9 *Journal of International Arbitration* 39

Cremades BM and Cairns D, 'Trans-National Public Policy in International Arbitral Decisionmaking: The Cases of Bribery, Money Laundering and Fraud' in Kristine Karsten and Andrew Berkeley (eds), *Arbitration: money laundering, corruption and fraud* (Paris, ICC, 2003)

Cremades BM and Cortes R, 'The Principle of Confidentiality in Arbitration: A Necessary Crisis' (2013) 23 *Journal of Arbitration Studies* 25

Croall PH, *Understanding White Collar Crime* (Buckingham, McGraw-Hill Education (UK), 2001)

Crompton R, 'Professions in the Current Context' (1990) 4 *Work, Employment and Society* 147

Daele K, *Challenge and Disqualification of Arbitrators in International Arbitration* (Alphen aan den Rijn, Kluwer Law International, 2012)

Dasser F and Igbokwe EO, 'The Award and the Courts, Efficient Drafting of the Arbitral Award: Traditional Ways Revisited – Lesson Learned from the Past?' in Christian Klausegger and others (eds), *Austrian Yearbook on International Arbitration 2019* (Wien, Manz'sche Verlags-und Universitätsbuchhandlung, 2019)

de Witt Wijnen O, Voser N and Rao N, 'Background Information on the IBA Guidelines on Conflicts of Interest in International Arbitration' (2004) 5 *Business Law International* 433

Delvolvé J-L, 'Multipartism: The Dutco Decision of the French Cour de Cassation' (1993) 9 *Arbitration International* 197

Demeter DR and Smith KM, 'The Implications of International Commercial Courts on Arbitration' (2016) 33 *Journal of International Arbitration* 441

Denzin NK and Mettlin CJ, 'Incomplete Professionalization: The Case of Pharmacy' (1968) 46 *Social Forces* 375

Derains Y, 'Le Professionnalisme Des Arbitres Internationaux' [2019] *Revue de l'Arbitrage* 659

DeScioli P and others, 'Equity or Equality? Moral Judgments Follow the Money' (2014) 281 *Proceedings of the Royal Society B: Biological Sciences* 20142112

Dezalay Y and Garth BG, 'Merchants of Law as Moral Entrepreneurs: Constructing International Justice from the Competition for Transnational Business Disputes' (1995) 29 *Law & Society Review* 27

——, *Dealing in Virtue: International Commercial Arbitration and the Construction of a Transnational Legal Order* (Chicago, University of Chicago Press, 1996)

Donaldson T, 'Are Business Managers "Professionals"?' (2000) 10 *Business Ethics Quarterly* 83

Draetta U, 'The Dynamics of Deliberation Meetings in Arbitration: Some Personal Considerations' [2011] *International Business Law Journal* 219

——, 'The Transnational Procedural Rules for Arbitration and the Risks of Overregulation and Bureaucratization' (2015) 33 *ASA Bulletin* 327

——, 'Cooperation among Arbitrators in International Arbitration' (2016) 5 *Indian Journal of Arbitration Law* 107

Drahozal CR, 'Commercial Norms, Commercial Codes, and International Commercial Arbitration' (2000) 33 *Vanderbilt Journal of Transnational Law* 79

——, 'In Defense of Southland: Reexamining the Legislative History of the Federal Arbitration Act' (2002) 78 *Notre Dame Law Review* 101

——, 'Arbitrator Selection and Regulatory Competition in International Arbitration Law' in Christopher R Drahozal and Richard W Naimark (eds), *Towards a Science of International Arbitration: Collected Empirical Research* (Alphen aan den Rijn, Kluwer Law International, 2004)

——, 'Regulatory Competition and the Location of International Arbitration Proceedings' (2004) 24 *International Review of Law and Economics* 371

——, 'Arbitration by the Numbers: The State of Empirical Research on International Commercial Arbitration' (2006) 22 *Arbitration International* 291

Drahozal CR and Naimark RW, *Towards a Science of International Arbitration: Collected Empirical Research* (Alphen aan den Rijn, Kluwer Law International BV, 2005)

D'Silva M, 'Dealing in Power: Gatekeepers in Arbitrator Appointment in International Commercial Arbitration' (2014) 5 *Journal of International Dispute Settlement* 605

Duan X, 'Criminal Liability of Arbitrators in China: Analysis and Proposals for Reform' (2014) 23 *Pacific Rim Law & Policy Journal* 343

Durant LV, 'Gender Bias and Legal Profession: A Discussion of Why There Are Still So Few Women on the Bench' (2004) 4 *University of Maryland Law Journal of Race, Religion, Gender & Class* 181

Eidenmüller H, 'The Transnational Law Market, Regulatory Competition, and Transnational Corporations' (2011) 18 *Indiana Journal of Global Legal Studies* 707

Eisenberg T and Macey JR, 'Was Arthur Andersen Different? An Empirical Examination of Major Accounting Firm Audits of Large Clients' (2004) 1 *Journal of Empirical Legal Studies* 263

Ellenbogen G, 'English Arbitration Practice' (1952) 17 *Law and Contemporary Problems* 656

Epstein JM, 'Learning to Be Thoughtless: Social Norms and Individual Computation' (2001) 18 *Computational Economics* 9

Fach Goméz K, *Key Duties of International Investment Arbitrators: A Transnational Study of Legal and Ethical Dilemmas* (Cham, Springer Berlin Heidelberg, 2018)

Fan K, *Arbitration in China: A Legal and Cultural Analysis* (Oxford, Hart Publishing, 2013)

Farhad A, 'The United Arab Emirates' New Arbitration Legislation: A Giant Leap Forward?' (2019) 36 *Journal of International Arbitration* 523

Faulconbridge JR and Muzio D, 'Legal Education, Globalization, and Cultures of Professional Practice Symposium: Empirical Research on the Legal Profession: Insights from Theory and Practice' (2009) 22 *Georgetown Journal of Legal Ethics* 1335

——, 'Professions in a Globalizing World: Towards a Transnational Sociology of the Professions' (2012) 27 *International Sociology* 136

Fernández Arroyo DP, 'Soft Law and Arbitral Procedure: A Conditioned But Inescapable Couple' (2018) 7 *European International Arbitration Review* 71

Fernández Rozas JC, 'Clearer Ethics Guidelines and Comparative Standards for Arbitrators' in Bernardo María Cremades, Miguel Angel Fernández-Ballesteros and David Arias Lozano (eds), *Liber amicorum Bernardo Cremades* (Madrid, La Ley, 2010)

Fernandez-Armesto J, 'Salient Issues of International Arbitration' (2012) 27 *American University International Law Review* 721

Flood J and Caiger A, 'Lawyers and Arbitration: The Juridification of Construction Disputes' (1993) 56 *The Modern Law Review* 412

Fortese F and Hemmi L, 'Procedural Fairness and Efficiency in International Arbitration' (2015) 3 *Groningen Journal of International Law* 110

Fouchard C, '"L'affaire Tapie", a Review from an Arbitration Perspective' (2017) XIV *Revista Brasileira de Arbitragem* 94

Fouchard P, 'Conclusion' [1990] *Revue de l'Arbitrage* 483

Fouchard P and others, *Fouchard Gaillard Goldman on International Commercial Arbitration* (Alphen aan den Rijn, Kluwer Law International, 1999)

Franck SD, 'The Liability of International Arbitrators: A Comparative Analysis and Proposal for Qualified Immunity' (2000) 20 *New York Law School Journal of International and Comparative Law* 1

——, 'The Role of International Arbitrators' (2005) 12 *ILSA Journal of International and Comparative Law* 499

——, 'Empirically Evaluating Claims About Investment Treaty Arbitration' (2007) 86 *North Caroline Law Review* 1

——, 'The Diversity Challenge: Exploring the Invisible College of International Arbitration' (2014) 53 *Columbia Journal of Transnational Law* 429

——, 'Inside the Arbitrator's Mind' (2017) 66 *Emory Law Journal* 1115

Frankel MS, 'Professional Codes: Why, How, and with What Impact?' (1989) 8 *Journal of Business Ethics* 109

Freidson E, 'The Changing Nature of Professional Control' (1984) 10 *Annual Review of Sociology* 1

——, *Profession of Medicine: A Study of the Sociology of Applied Knowledge* (Chicago, University of Chicago Press, 1988)

——, 'The Theory of Professions: State of the Art' in Robert Dingwall and Philip Lewis (eds), *The Sociology of the Professions: Lawyers, Doctors and Others* (Paris, Quid Pro, LLC, 2014)

Gaillard E, *The Review of International Arbitral Awards* (New York, Juris Publishing Inc, 2010)

——, 'International Arbitration as a Transnational System of Justice' in Albert Jan Van Den Berg (ed), *Arbitration – The Next Fifty Years* (Alphen aan den Rijn, Kluwer Law International, 2012)

——, 'Sociology of International Arbitration' (2015) 31 *Arbitration International* 1

Gaillard E and Bermann GA, *Guide on the Convention on the Recognition and Enforcement of Foreign Arbitral Awards: New York, 1958* (Leiden, Brill, 2017)

Galindo Gil P, 'Ley de Arbitraje, Artículo 1 [Ámbito de Aplicación]' in Carlos González-Bueno (ed), *Comentarios a la Ley de Arbitraje* (Madrid, Consejo General del Notariado, 2014)

George E, 'A Historical Reflection on Arbitration and the Corporation as an Object of Economic Governance' (2017) 39 *Western New England* 557

Gerbay R, 'Is the End Nigh Again? An Empirical Assessment of the "Judicialization" of International Arbitration' (2014) 25 *American Journal of International Arbitration* 223

——, '"How Does a New Arbitrator Get Their First Appointment?", A Q&A Session with Remy Gerbay (Interview Given to Lexis PSL Arbitration)' (Social Science Research Network 2014) SSRN Scholarly Paper ID 2519505

——, *The Functions of Arbitral Institutions* (Alphen aan den Rijn, Kluwer Law International, 2016)

Ginsburg T, 'The Culture of Arbitration' (2003) 36 *The Vanderbilt Journal of Transnational Law* 1335

Glaeser EL (ed), *The Governance of Not-for-Profit Organizations* (Chicago, University of Chicago Press, 2006)

Glossner O, 'Sociological Aspects of International Commercial Arbitration' (1982) 10 *International Business Lawyer* 311

Godwin A, Ramsay I and Webster M, 'International Commercial Courts: The Singapore Experience' (2017) 18 *Melbourne Journal of International Law* 219

Goldstein MJ, 'A Career in International Commercial Arbitration' in Salli Swartz (ed), *Careers in International Law* (American Bar Association, 2008)

Gomez-Acebo, *Party-Appointed Arbitrators in International Commercial Arbitration* (Alphen aan den Rijn, Kluwer Law International, 2016)

Goode WJ, 'Community Within a Community: The Professions' (1957) 22 *American Sociological Review* 194

——, 'The Librarian: From Occupation to Profession?' (1961) 31 *The Library Quarterly: Information, Community, Policy* 306

Gordon-Vrbo L and Vock D, 'Commentary on the Swiss Rules, Article 12 [Removal of an Arbitrator]' in Manuel Arroyo (ed), *Arbitration in Switzerland: The Practitioner's Guide*, 2nd edn (Alphen aan den Rijn, Kluwer Law International, 2018)

Gotshal S, 'Arbitration and the Lawyer's Place in the Business Community' (1956) 11 *The Business Lawyer* 52

Graving RJ, 'The International Commercial Arbitration Institutions: How Good A Job Are They Doing?' (1989) 4 *American University International Law Review* 319

Greenberg S, Kee C and Weeramantry JR, *International Commercial Arbitration: An Asia-Pacific Perspective* (Cambridge, Cambridge University Press, 2011)

Greenwood L, 'The Rise, Fall and Rise of International Arbitration: A View from 2030' (2011) 77 *Arbitration International* 435

——, 'Tipping the Balance–Diversity and Inclusion in International Arbitration' (2017) 33 *Arbitration International* 99

Greenwood L and Baker M, 'Getting a Better Balance on International Arbitration Tribunals' (2012) 28 *Arbitration International* 653

——, 'Are Challenges Overused in International Arbitration?' (2013) 30 *Journal of International Arbitration* 101

Grisel F, 'Treaty-Making between Public Authority and Private Interests: The Genealogy of the Convention on the Recognition and Enforcement of Foreign Arbitral Awards' (2017) 28 *European Journal of International Law* 73

——, 'Competition and Cooperation in International Commercial Arbitration: The Birth of a Transnational Legal Profession: Grisel' (2017) 51 *Law & Society Review* 790

Gu W and Tam J, 'The Global Rise of International Commercial Courts: Typology and Power Dynamics' (2021) 22 *Chicago Journal of International Law* 443

Gunningham N and Rees J, 'Industry Self-Regulation: An Institutional Perspective' (1997) 19 *Law & Policy* 363

Gunz HP and Gunz SP, 'Hired Professional to Hired Gun: An Identity Theory Approach to Understanding the Ethical Behaviour of Professionals in Non-Professional Organizations' (2007) 60 *Human Relations* 851

——, 'Client Capture and the Professional Service Firm' (2008) 45 *American Business Law Journal* 685

Gunz HP, Gunz SP and Dinovitzer R, 'Professional Ethics: Origins, Applications, and Developments' in Laura Empson and others (eds), *The Oxford Handbook of Professional Service Firms* (Oxford, Oxford University Press, 2015)

Habegger P, 'The Arbitrator's Duty of Efficiency: A Call for Increased Utilization of Arbitral Powers' in Patricia Shaughnessy and Sherlin Tung (eds), *The Powers and Duties of an Arbitrator: Liber Amicorum Pierre A. Karrer* (Alphen aan den Rijn, Kluwer Law International, 2017)

——, 'Saving Time and Costs in Arbitration' in Manuel Arroyo (ed), *Arbitration in Switzerland: The Practitioner's Guide*, 2nd edn (Alphen aan den Rijn, Kluwer Law International, 2018)

Hacking D, 'Arbitration Is Only as Good as Its Arbitrators' in Loukas Mistelis and Stefan Kröll (eds), *International Arbitration and International Commercial Law: Synergy, Convergence, and Evolution : Liber Amicorum Eric Bergsten* (Alphen aan den Rijn, Kluwer Law International, 2011)

Hale T, *Between Interests and Law: The Politics of Transnational Commercial Disputes* (Cambridge, Cambridge University Press, 2015)

Hanessian G and Newman LW, *International Arbitration Checklists*, 2nd edn (New York, Juris Publishing Inc, 2009)

Hanotiau B and Block G, 'The Law of 19 May 1998 Amending Belgian Arbitration Legislation' (1999) 15 *Arbitration International* 97

Harten G van, 'Perceived Bias in Investment Arbitration' in Michael Waibel and others (eds), *The Backlash Against Investment Arbitration: Perceptions and Reality* (Alphen aan den Rijn, Kluwer Law International, 2010)

Hascher D, 'Independence and Impartiality of Arbitrators: 3 Issues' (2012) 27 *American University of International Law Review* 789

Hausmaninger C, 'Civil Liability of Arbitrators-Comparative Analysis and Proposals for Reform' (1990) 7 *Journal of International Arbitration* 7

Heitzmann P, 'Arbitration and Criminal Liability for Competition Law Violations in Europe' in Gordon Blanke and Phillip Landolt (eds), *EU and US Antitrust Arbitration: a Handbook for Practitioners*, vol 1 (Alphen aan den Rijn, Kluwer Law International, 2011)

Helmer EV, 'International Commercial Arbitration: Americanized, Civilized, or Harmonized' (2003) 19 *Ohio State Journal on Dispute Resolution* 35

Henning PJ, 'Is Deterrence Relevant in Sentencing White-Collar Criminals' (2015) 61 *Wayne Law Review* 27

Henry M, 'Arbitrage Tapie: Les Affres d'un Prejudice Moral Immoral' (2016) 34 *ASA Bulletin* 207

Heremans T, *Professional Services in the EU Internal Market : Quality Regulation and Self-Regulation* (Oxford, Hart Publishing, 2012)

Herrmann G, 'UNCITRAL's Work Towards a Model Law on International Commercial Arbitration' (1984) 4 *Pace Law Review* 537

Hirschi T and Gottfredson M, 'Age and the Explanation of Crime' (1983) 89 *American Journal of Sociology* 552

Hobér K, 'Arbitration Reform in Sweden' (2001) 17 *Arbitration International* 351

Hodges C, *Law and Corporate Behaviour : Integrating Theories of Regulation, Enforcement, Compliance and Ethics* (Oxford, Hart Publishing, 2015)

——, 'Resetting Incentives, Remuneration and Trust' [2020] Oxford Legal Studies Research Paper No. 14/2020

Hodges P, 'The Arbitrator and the Arbitration Procedure, The Proliferation of "Soft Laws" in International Arbitration: Time to Draw the Line?' in Christian Klausegger and others (eds), *Austrian Yearbook on International Arbitration 2015* (Wien, Manz'sche Verlags, 2015)

——, 'Equality of Arms in International Arbitration: Who Is the Best Arbiter of Fairness in the Conduct of Proceedings?' in Andrea Menaker (ed), *International arbitration and the rule of law: contribution and conformity* (Alphen aan den Rijn, Kluwer Law International, 2017)

Hodges P and Greenaway J, 'Duties of Arbitrators' in JDM Lew and others (eds), *Arbitration in England: With Chapters on Scotland and Ireland* (Alphen aan den Rijn, Kluwer Law International, 2013)

Horvath G, 'Guerrilla Tactics in Arbitration, an Ethical Battle: Is There Need for a Universal Code of Ethics?' in Christian Klausegger and others (eds), *Austrian Yearbook on International Arbitration 2011* (Wien, Manz'sche Verlags-und Universitätsbuchhandlung, 2011)

Horvath GJ and Wilske S, *Guerrilla Tactics in International Arbitration* (Alphen aan den Rijn, Kluwer Law International, 2013)

Hranitzky DH and Romero ES, 'The "Double Hat" Debate in International Arbitration' (2010) 14 *New York Law Journal*

Huber SK, 'State Regulation of Arbitration Proceedings: Judicial Review of Arbitration Awards by State Courts' (2009) 10 *Cardozo Journal of Dispute Resolution* 509

Hunter M, 'Ethics of the International Arbitrator' (1987) 53 *Arbitration International* 219

Hwang M, 'Commercial Courts and International Arbitration – Competitors or Partners?' (2015) 31 *Arbitration International* 193

Hwang M, Chung K and Cheng F, 'Claims Against Arbitrators for Breach of Ethical Duties' in Arthur W Rovine (ed), *Contemporary Issues in International Arbitration and Mediation: The Fordham Papers 2007* (Leiden, Brill, 2008)

Hwang M and Lim K, 'Corruption in Arbitration: Law and Reality' (2012) 8 *Asian International Arbitration Journal* 1

Jamin C, 'Services juridiques : la fin des professions?' (2012) 1 *Pouvoirs* 33

Jarrosson C, 'Les Frontières de l'arbitrage' [2001] *Revue de l'arbitrage* 5

Jemielniak J, *Legal Interpretation in International Commercial Arbitration* (London, Ashgate Publishing Ltd, 2014)

Jensen JO, 'Setting Aside Arbitral Awards in Model Law Jurisdictions: The Singapore Approach from a German Perspective' (2015) 4 *European International Arbitration Review* 55

Kachwaha S, 'The Arbitration Law of India: A Critical Analysis' (2005) 1 *Asian International Arbitration Journal* 105

Kagan R, Gunningham N and Thornton D, 'Fear, Duty, and Regulatory Compliance: Lessons from Three Research Projects' in Christine Parker and Vibeke Nielsen (eds), *Explaining Compliance: Business Responses to Regulation* (Cheltenham, Edward Elgar Publishing, 2011)

Kalicki JE and Raouf MA (eds), 'Personal Reflections from Leading Arbitrators: Transcript of Luncheon Panelists' Remarks', *Evolution and Adaptation: The Future of International Arbitration* (Alphen aan den Rijn, Kluwer Law International, 2019)

Kaplan N, 'The History and Development of Arbitration in Hong Kong Symposium: Financial Law in Hong Kong and South-East Asia' (1996) 1 *Yearbook of International Financial and Economic Law* 203

——, 'The Role of the State in Protecting the System of Arbitration' (2015) 81 *Arbitration: The International Journal of Arbitration, Mediation and Dispute Management* 452

Karsten K, 'Money Laundering: How It Works and Why You Should Be Concerned' in Kristine Karsten and Andrew Berkeley (eds), *Arbitration: money laundering, corruption and fraud* (Paris, ICC Publishing, 2003)

Karton JDH, *The Culture of International Arbitration and The Evolution of Contract Law* (Oxford, Oxford University Press, 2013)

Kaufmann-Kohler G, 'Soft Law in International Arbitration: Codification and Normativity' (2010) 1 *Journal of International Dispute Settlement* 283

Kaufmann-Kohler G and Rigozzi A, *International Arbitration: Law and Practice in Switzerland* (Oxford, Oxford University Press, 2015)

Kaufmann-Kohler G and Stucki B, *International Arbitration in Switzerland: A Handbook for Practitioners* (Alphen aan den Rijn, Kluwer Law International, 2004)

Kellor F, *American Arbitration: Its History, Functions and Achievements* (Washington, Beard Books, 1948)

Kerr M, *As Far as I Remember* (Oxford, Hart Publishing, 2002)

Kim HH, 'Market Uncertainty and Socially Embedded Reputation' (2009) 68 *American Journal of Economics and Sociology* 679

Klepper S and Nagin D, 'Tax Compliance and Perceptions of the Risks of Detection and Criminal Prosecution' (1989) 23 *Law and Society Review* 209

Koepp J and Ason A, 'An Anti-Enforcement Bias? The Application of the Substantive Public Policy Exception in Polish Annulment Proceedings' (2018) 35 *Journal of International Arbitration* 157

Koh WSW, 'Think Quality Not Quantity: Repeat Appointments and Arbitrator Challenges' (2017) 34 *Journal of International Arbitration* 711

Kronke H, 'The Role of Private International Law: UNIDROIT and the Geneva Conventions on Arbitration' in Michel Erpelding, Burkhard Hess and Hélène Ruiz Fabri (eds), *Peace Through Law* (Baden-Baden, Nomos Verlagsgesellschaft mbH & Co KG, 2019)

Kronke H, Nacimiento P and Otto D, *Recognition and Enforcement of Foreign Arbitral Awards: A Global Commentary on the New York Convention* (Alphen aan den Rijn, Kluwer Law International, BV 2010)

Krumiņš T, 'Arbitration in Latvia: A Cautionary Tale?' (2017) 34 *Journal of International Arbitration* 303

Kühner D, 'The Revised IBA Rules on the Taking of Evidence in International Arbitration' (2010) 27 *Journal of International Arbitration* 667

Lalive P, 'Transnational (or Truly International) Public Policy and International Arbitration' in Pieter Sanders (ed), *Comparative Arbitration Practice and Public Policy in Arbitration* (Alphen aan den Rijn, Kluwer Law and Taxation Publishers, 1987)

Lamm CB, Pham HT and Moloo R, 'Fraud and Corruption in International Arbitration' in Miguel Angel Fernandez-Ballester; and David Arias Lozano (eds), *Liber amicorum Bernardo Cremades* (Madrid, Wolters Kluwer España, 2010)

Landau T and Weeramantry R, 'A Pause for Thought' in AJ van den Berg (ed), *International arbitration: the coming of a new age?* (Alphen aan den Rijn, Kluwer Law International, 2013)

Landes WM and Posner RA, 'The Private Enforcement of Law' (1975) 4 *The Journal of Legal Studies* 1

Langford M and Behn D, 'Managing Backlash: The Evolving Investment Treaty Arbitrator?' (2018) 29 *European Journal of International Law* 551

Langford M, Behn D and Lie RH, 'The Ethics and Empirics of Double Hatting' (2017) 6 *ESIL Reflection* 1

——, 'The Revolving Door in International Investment Arbitration' (2017) 20 Journal of International Economic Law 301

Larson MS, *The Rise of Professionalism: A Sociological Analysis* (Berkeley,University of California Press, 1977)

Lawson DA, 'Impartiality and Independence of International Arbitrators' (2005) 23 *ASA Bulletin* 22

Leaua C, 'Factors Taken into Consideration by the Parties When Appointing an Arbitrator' (2012) 33 *Procedia – Social and Behavioral Sciences* 925

Lee J, 'The Evolving Role of Institutional Arbitration in Preserving Parties' Due Process Rights' (2017) 10 *Contemporary Asia Arbitration Journal* 235

Lein E and others, 'Factors Influencing International Litigants' Decisions to Bring Commercial Claims to the London Based Courts' (Gov.UK, 2015)

Lew JDM, 'Does National Court Involvement Undermine the International Arbitration Process' (2008) 24 *American University International Law Review* 489

Lew JDM and Holm M, 'Development of the Arbitral System in England' in Julian DM Lew and others (eds), *Arbitration in England: With Chapters on Scotland and Ireland* (Alphen aan den Rijn, Kluwer Law International, 2013)

Lew JDM, Mistelis LA and Kröll S, *Comparative International Commercial Arbitration* (Alphen aan den Rijn, Kluwer Law International, 2003)

Lin Y, *Judicial Review of Arbitration: Law and Practice in China* (Alphen aan den Rijn, Kluwer Law International, 2018)

Lo CW-H and Snape E, 'Lawyers in the People's Republic of China: A Study of Commitment and Professionalization' (2005) 53 *The American Journal of Comparative Law* 433

López CAM, 'Practical Criteria for Selecting International Arbitrators' (2014) 31 *Journal of International Arbitration* 795

Lovett SL, 'The Employee-Lawyer: A Candid Reflection on the True Roles and Responsibilities of In-House Counsel' (2015) 34 *Journal of Law and Commerce* 113

Lüth F and Wagner PK, 'Soft Law in International Arbitration – Some Thoughts on Legitimacy' [2012] *StudZR* 14

Luttrell S, *Bias Challenges in International Commercial Arbitration: The Need for a 'real Danger' Test* (Alphen aan den Rijn, Kluwer Law International, 2009)

Ly FD, 'The Place of Arbitration in the Conflict of Laws of International Commercial Arbitration: An Exercise in Arbitration Planning' (1991) 12 *Northwestern Journal of International Law & Business* 48

Lynch KL, *The Forces of Economic Globalization: Challenges to the Regime of International Commercial Arbitration* (Alphen aan den Rijn, Kluwer Law International, 2003)

MacArthur E, 'Regulatory Competition and the Growth of International Arbitration in Singapore' (2018) 23 *Appeal: Review of Current Law and Law Reform* 165

Macassey L, 'International Commercial Arbitration – Its Origin, Development and Importance' (1938) 24 *American Bar Association Journal* 518

Macdonald KM, *The Sociology of the Professions* (London, SAGE Publications, 2013)

Macey JR and Sale HA, 'Observations on the Role of Commodification, Independence and Governance in the Accounting Industry' (2003) 48 *Villanova Law Review* 1167

Maisner M, *Czech and Central European Yearbook of Arbitration – 2012: Party Autonomy versus Autonomy of Arbitrators* (Alexander J Bělohlávek and Naděžda Rozehnalova eds, New York, Juris Publishing Inc, 2012)

Martin AR, Sussman E and Scherer M, 'Success in International Arbitration: No Shortcuts' (2014) 21 *Dispute Resolution Magazine* 27

Martin J and Hunter H, 'Arbitration Procedure in England: Past, Present and Future' (1985) 1 *Arbitration International* 82

——, 'Judicial Assistance for the Arbitrator' in Julian DM Lew (ed), *Contemporary Problems in International Arbitration* (Dordrecht, Springer Netherlands, 1987)

Mayer P, 'Effect of International Public Policy in International Arbitration?' in Loukas A Mistelis (ed), *Pervasive Problems in International Arbitration* (Alphen aan den Rijn, Kluwer Law International, 2006)

Maynard S, 'The Current State of Arbitrator Ethics and Party Recourse Against Grievances' (2016) 8 *Yearbook on Arbitration and Mediation* 204

McDougall A de L, 'International Arbitration and Money Laundering' (2004) 20 *American University International Law Review* 1021

Mcilwrath M, 'Grading the Arbitrator' (2007) 73 *The Journal of the Chartered Institute of Arbitrators* 224

McIlwrath M and Savage J, *International Arbitration and Mediation: A Practical Guide* (Alphen aan den Rijn, Kluwer Law International, 2010)

McIlwrath M and Schroeder R, 'Transparency In International Arbitration: What Are Arbitrators And Institutions Afraid Of?' in Arthur W Rovine (ed), *Contemporary Issues in International Arbitration and Mediation: The Fordham Papers (2010)* (Leiden, Brill | Nijhoff, 2011)

Mclaren DE, 'Party-Appointed vs List-Appointed Arbitrators: A Comparison' (2003) 20 *Journal of International Arbitration* 233

Melis W, 'The Role of Individuals in International Arbitration' in Patricia Shaughnessy and Sherlin Tung (eds), *The Powers and Duties of an Arbitrator: Liber Amicorum Pierre A. Karrer* (Alphen aan den Rijn, Kluwer Law International, 2017)

Menaker A and Dhillon H, 'Article 52(1)(C)' in Julien Fouret, Rémy Gerbay and Gloria M Alvarez (eds), *The ICSID Convention, Regulations and Rules: A Practical Commentary* (Cheltenham, Edward Elgar Publishing, 2019)

Menkel-Meadow C, 'Ethics Issues in Arbitration and Related Dispute Resolution Processes: What's Happening and What's Not Arbitration Symposium' (2001) 56 *University of Miami Law Review* 949

Michaels R, 'Dreaming Law without a State: Scholarship on Autonomous International Arbitration as Utopian Literature' (2013) 1 *London Review of International Law* 35

——, 'Roles and Roles Perceptions of International Arbitrators' in Walter Mattli and Thomas Dietz (eds), *International Arbitration and Global Governance: Contending Theories and Evidence* (Oxford, Oxford University Press, 2014)

Mistelis L, 'International Arbitration – Corporate Attitudes and Practices – 12 Perceptions Tested: Myths, Data and Analysis' (2004) 15 *American Review of International Arbitration* 525

Mohtashami R and Tannous S, 'Arbitration at the Dubai International Financial Centre: A Common Law Jurisdiction in the Middle East' (2009) 25 *Arbitration International* 173

Moore WE, *The Professions: Roles and Rules* (New York, Russell Sage Foundation, 1970)

Moreira JI, 'The Limits to Voluntary Arbitration in Establishing a Fair, Independent and Accessible Dispute Resolution Mechanism Outside Large Contractual Disputes' in Leonardo de Oliveira and Sara Hourani (eds), *Access to Justice in Arbitration: Concept, Context and Practice* (Alphen aan den Rijn, Kluwer Law International, 2020)

——, 'Arbitration Vis-à-Vis Other Professions: A Sociology of Professions Account of International Commercial Arbitrators' (2022) 49 *Journal of Law and Society* 48

——, 'The Insider/Outsider Divide and the Ethics of Commercial Arbitrators' (2022) 19 *Manchester Journal of International Economic Law* 132

Moreira JI and Vecellio Segate R, 'The "It" Arbitrator: Why Do Corporations Not Act as Arbitrators?' (2021) 12 *Journal of International Dispute Settlement* 525

Moses ML, *The Principles and Practice of International Commercial Arbitration* (Cambridge, Cambridge University Press, 2012)

Mourre A, 'Arbitration and Criminal Law: Reflections on the Duties of the Arbitrator' (2006) 22 *Arbitration International* 95

Mullerat R and Blanch J, 'The Liability of Arbitrators: A Survey of Current Practice' (2007) 1 *Dispute Resolution International* 99

Muniz JT de P and Basílio ATP, *Arbitration Law of Brazil: Practice and Procedure* (New York, Juris Publishing Inc, 2006)

Mustill MJ, 'Arbitration: History and Background' (1989) 6 *Journal of International Arbitration* 43

Nagin DS, 'Criminal Deterrence Research at the Outset of the Twenty-First Century' (1998) 23 *Crime and Justice* 1

Naimark RW, 'Building a Fact-Based Global Database-The Countdown' (2003) 20 *Journal of International Arbitration* 105

Naimark RW and Keer SE, 'Post-Award Experience in International Commercial Arbitration' in Christopher R Drahozal and Richard W Naimark (eds), *Towards a Science of International Arbitration: Collected Empirical Research* (Alphen aan den Rijn, Kluwer Law International BV, 2005)

Neal M and Morgan J, 'The Professionalization of Everyone?: A Comparative Study of the Development of the Professions in the United Kingdom and Germany' (2000) 16 *European Sociological Review* 9

Ng J, 'When the Arbitrator Creates the Conflict: Understanding Arbitrator Ethics through the IBA Guidelines on Conflict of Interest and Published Challenges' (2015) 2 *McGill Journal of Dispute Resolution* 23

O'Connor EO and Rutledge PB, 'Arbitration, the Law Market, and the Law of Lawyering' (2014) 38 *International Review of Law and Economics* 87

Ogus A, 'Rethinking Self-Regulation' (1995) 15 *Oxford Journal of Legal Studies* 97

Oldenstam R, 'Due Process Paranoia or Prudence?' in Patrik Schöldström and Alex Calissendorff (eds), *Stockholm Arbitration Yearbook 2019* (Alphen aan den Rijn, Kluwer Law International, 2019)

Olson M, *The Logic of Collective Action: Public Goods and the Theory of Groups* (Cambridge, MA, Harvard Univ Press 1971)

O'Malley ND, *Rules of Evidence in International Arbitration: An Annotated Guide* (Abingdon, Taylor & Francis, 2013)

Onyema E, 'Drafting an Effective Arbitration Agreement in International Commercial Contracts' (2003) 7 *Vindobona Journal of International Commercial Law & Arbitration* 277

——, *International Commercial Arbitration and the Arbitrator's Contract* (London, Routledge, 2010)

Park W, 'The Procedural Soft Law of International Arbitration: Non-Governmental Instruments' in Loukas A Mistelis (ed), *Pervasive Problems in International Arbitration* (Alphen aan den Rijn, Kluwer Law International, 2006)

——, 'Arbitrator Integrity' in Michael Waibel and others (eds), *The Backlash Against Investment Arbitration: Perceptions and Reality* (Alphen aan den Rijn, Kluwer Law International, 2010)

——, 'Arbitration in Autumn' (2011) 2 *Journal of International Dispute Settlement* 287

——, 'Rectitude in International Arbitration' (2011) 27 *Arbitration International* 473

——, 'Procedural Tension in International Arbitration: Arbitration in Autumn' in John Norton Moore (ed), *International Arbitration: Contemporary Issues and Innovations* (Leiden, Martinus Nijhoff Publishers, 2013)

Parkin F, *Marxism and Class Theory: A Bourgeois Critique* (New York, Columbia University Press, 1983)

Partasides C, 'The Fourth Arbitrator? The Role of Secretaries to Tribunals in International Arbitration' (2002) 18 *Arbitration International* 147

Paulsson J, 'Ethics, Elitism, Eligibility' (1997) 14 *Journal of International Arbitration* 13

——, 'Moral Hazard in International Dispute Resolution' (2010) 25 *ICSID Review* 339

——, *The Idea of Arbitration* (Oxford, Oxford University Press, 2013)

Paulsson J, Rawding N and Reed L, *The Freshfields Guide to Arbitration Clauses in International Contracts* (Alphen aan den Rijn, Kluwer Law International BV, 2011)

Pavic V, 'Bribery and International Commercial Arbitration – The Role of Mandatory Rules and Public Policy' (2012) 43 *Victoria University of Wellington Law Review* 661

Philippe M, 'How Has Female Participation at ICC Evolved? ICC Arbitrators, Court Members and Court's Secretariat' (2017) 3 *ICC Dispute Resolution Bulletin* 37

Philipsen N, 'Recent Developments in the Regulation of Auditors: An Economic Perspective' in Niels Philipsen and Guangdong Xu (eds), *The Role of Law and Regulation in Sustaining Financial Markets* (London, Routledge, 2014)

Phillips PG, 'A Lawyer's Approach to Commercial Arbitration' (1934) 44 *The Yale Law Journal* 31

Pierce JVH, Carter JR and Cinotti DN, 'Challenging and Enforcing International Arbitral Awards in New York' in James H Carter and John Fellas (eds), *International Commercial Arbitration in New York*, 2nd edn (Oxford, Oxford University Press, 2016)

Pilawa D, 'Sifting through the Arbitrators for the Woman, the Minority, the Newcomer Notes' (2019) 51 *Case Western Reserve Journal of International Law* 395

Plotkin J, Yazar O and Krasula M, 'YCAP and CJCA Interview of Marek Krasula Features' (2021) 2 *Canadian Journal of Commercial Arbitration* 92

Polkinghorne M and Gill BA, 'Due Process Paranoia: Need We Be Cruel to Be Kind?' 34 *Journal of International Arbitration* 935

Polonskaya K, 'Arbitral Institutions' Response to Perceived Legitimacy Deficits: Promoting Diversity, Transparency and Expedition in Investor-State Arbitration' in Freya Baetens (ed), *Legitimacy of Unseen Actors in International Adjudication* (Cambridge, Cambridge University Press, 2019)

Popper AF, 'In Defense of Deterrence' (2011) 75 *Albany Law Review* 181

Posner EA, 'Arbitration and the Harmonization of International Commercial Law: A Defense of Mitsubishi' (1999) 39 *Virginia Journal of International Law* 647

——, 'Law and Social Norms: The Case of Tax Compliance' (2000) 86 *Virginia Law Review* 1781

Posner RA, 'Theories of Economic Regulation' (1974) 5 *Bell Journal of Economics and Management Science* 335

——, 'Judicial Behavior and Performance: An Economic Approach' (2004) 32 *Florida State University Law Review* 1259

Posthuma RA, Dworkin JB and Swift MS, 'Arbitrator Acceptability: Does Justice Matter? Arbitrator Acceptability' (2000) 39 *Industrial Relations: A Journal of Economy and Society* 313

Poudret J-F and Besson S, *Comparative Law of International Arbitration* (London, Sweet & Maxwell, 2007)

Puig S, 'Social Capital in the Arbitration Market' (2014) 25 *European Journal of International Law* 387

Quiroga MG, 'Reflexiones y Propuestas Prácticas a La Luz Del Arbitraje Internacional En La Ley 60/2003' (2006) 3 *Revista Brasileira de Arbitragem* 71

Raouf MA, 'Emergence of New Arbitral Centres in Asia and Africa: Competition, Cooperation and Contribution to the Rule of Law' in Stavros L Brekoulakis, Julian DM Lew and Loukas A Mistelis (eds), *The Evolution and Future of International Arbitration* (Alphen aan den Rijn, Kluwer Law International, 2016)

Rau AS, 'On Integrity in Private Judging' (1998) 14 *Arbitration International* 115

Redbird B, 'The New Closed Shop? The Economic and Structural Effects of Occupational Licensure' (2017) 82 *American Sociological Review* 600

Redfern A, 'The Importance of Being Independent: Laws of Arbitration, Rules, Guidelines – and a Disastrous Award' (2017) 6 *Indian Journal of Arbitration Law* 9

Redfern A and Hunter M, *Law and Practice of International Commercial Arbitration* (London, Sweet & Maxwell, 2004)

Reisman WM, *Systems of Control in International Adjudication and Arbitration: Breakdown and Repair* (Durham, Duke University Press, 1992)

Requejo Isidro M, 'International Commercial Courts in the Litigation Market' (2019) 9 *International Journal of Procedural Law* 4

Reuben RC, 'Constitutional Gravity: A Unitary Theory of Alternative Dispute Resolution and Public Civil Justice' (1999) 47 *UCLA Law Review* 949

Reymond C, 'L'Arbitration Act, 1996 – Convergence et Originalité' [1997] *Revue de l'Arbitrage* 45

Rivkin DW, 'The Revised IBA Rules on the Taking of Evidence' in Arthur W Rovine (ed), *Contemporary Issues in International Arbitration and Mediation* (Leiden, Brill Academic Publishers 2012)

——, 'Keynote Address: A New Contract Between Arbitrators and Parties' (2016) 18 *Asian Dispute Review* 4

Roebuck D, *Early English Arbitration* (Oxford, The Arbitration Press, 2008)

——, *Mediation and Arbitration in the Middle Ages: England 1154 to 1558* (Oxford, Holo Books, The Arbitration Press 2013)

——, *The Golden Age of Arbitration: Dispute Resolution Under Elizabeth I* (Oxford, Holo Books, The Arbitration Press 2015)

——, *Arbitration and Mediation in Seventeenth-Century England* (Oxford, Holo Books The Arbitration Press, 2017)

Roebuck D, Boorman FC and Markless R, *English Arbitration and Mediation in the Long Eighteenth Century* (Oxford, Holo Books The Arbitration Press, 2019)

Roebuck D and Fumichon BD, *Roman Arbitration* (Oxford, The Arbitration Press, 2004)

Rogers CA, 'Fit and Function in Legal Ethics: Developing a Code of Conduct for International Arbitration' (2001) 23 *Michigan Journal of International Law* 341

——, 'The Vocation of the International Arbitrator' (2004) 20 *American University International Law Review* 957

——, 'Regulating International Arbitrators: A Functional Approach to Developing Standards of Conduct' (2005) 41 *Stanford Journal of International Law* 53

——, 'Transparency in International Commercial Arbitration' (2006) 54 *Kansas Law Review* 1301

——, 'The Arrival of the "Have-Nots" in International Arbitration' (2007) 8 *Nevada Law Journal* 341

——, *Ethics in International Arbitration* (Oxford, Oxford University Press, 2014)

——, 'The Arbitrator and the Arbitration Procedure, Transparency in Arbitrator Selection' in Christian Klausegger and others (eds), *Austrian Yearbook on International Arbitration 2016* (Wein, Manz'sche Verlags-und Universitätsbuchhandlung, 2016)

Romero ES, Jolivet E and Grisel F, 'Aux origines de l'arbitrage commercial contemporain : l'émergence de l'arbitrage CCI (1920–1958)' [2016] *Revue de l'arbitrage* 403

Rosenthal MS, 'Arbitration in the Settlement of International Trade Disputes' (1946) 11 *Law and Contemporary Problems* 808

Rubino-Sammartano M, *International Arbitration Law and Practice*, 3rd edn (New York, Juris Publishing Inc, 2014)

Rutledge PB, 'Toward a Contractual Approach for Arbitral Immunity' (2004) 39 *Georgia Law Review* 151

Sabin CL, 'The Adjudicatory Boat without a Keel: Private Arbitration and the Need for Public Oversight of Arbitrators' (2001) 87 *Iowa Law Review* 1337

Sackville R, 'Why Do Judges Make Law: Some Aspects of Judicial Law Making' (2001) 5 *University of Western Sydney Law Review* 59

Salim M and Belinda M, 'Survey: Arbitral Institutions Can Do More to Foster Legitimacy. True or False? in Albert Jan van den Bert (ed)', *Legitimacy: Myths, Realities, Challenges* (Alphen aan den Rijn, Wolters Kluwer Law & Business, 2015)

Saks M, 'Defining a Profession: The Role of Knowledge and Expertise' (2012) 2 *Professions and Professionalism* 1

Sanders P, 'The Making of the Convention', *Enforcing arbitration awards under the New York Convention: experience and prospects* (UN, 1999)
Scherer M, 'Limits of the IBA Rules on the Taking of Evidence: Document Production Based on Contractual or Statutory Rights' (2010) 13 *International Arbitration Law Review* 195
Scheu J, *Creation and Implementation of a Multilateral Investment Court* (Baden-Baden, Nomos, 2022)
Schill S, 'Developing a Framework for the Legitimacy of International Arbitration' in Albert Jan van den Berg (ed), *Legitimacy: Myths, Realities, Challenges* (Alphen aan den Rijn, Wolters Kluwer Law & Business, 2015)
——, 'Conceptions of Legitimacy of International Arbitration' in David Caron and others (eds), *Practising Virtue: Inside International Arbitration* (Oxford, Oxford University Press, 2015)
Schinazi M, *The Three Ages of International Commercial Arbitration* (Cambridge, Cambridge University Press, 2021)
Schlaepfer AV and Girod C, 'Institutional vs. Ad Hoc Arbitration' in Gabrielle Kaufmann-Kohler and Blaise Stucki (eds), *International Arbitration in Switzerland: A Handbook for Practitioners* (Alphen aan den Rijn, Kluwer Law International, 2004)
Schmitz AJ, 'Ending a Mud Bowl: Defining Arbitration's Finality through Functional Analysis' (2002) 37 *Georgia Law Review* 123
Schultz T and Kovacs R, 'The Rise of a Third Generation of Arbitrators?' (2012) 28 *Arbitration International* 161
——, 'The Law Is What the Arbitrator Had for Breakfast: How Income, Reputation, Justice, and Reprimand Act as Determinants of Arbitrator Behaviour' in Julio César Betancourt (ed), *Defining issues in international arbitration: celebrating 100 years of the Chartered Institute of Arbitrators* (Oxford, Oxford University Press, 2016)
Schulz J, 'Arbitrating Arbitrability: How the U.S. Supreme Court Empowered the Arbitrator at the Expense of the Judge and the Average Joe Comment' (2010) 44 *Loyola of Los Angeles Law Review* 1269
Schwartz EA, 'The ICC Arbitration Rules and the UNCITRAL Model Law' (1993) 9 *Arbitration International* 231
Schwartz EA and Derains Y, *Guide to the ICC Rules of Arbitration*, 2nd edn (Alphen aan den Rijn, Kluwer Law International, 2005)
Schwarz FT and Konrad CW, *The Vienna Rules: A Commentary on International Arbitration in Austria* (Alphen aan den Rijn, Kluwer Law International BV, 2009)
Sciulli D, 'Continental Sociology of Professions Today: Conceptual Contributions' (2005) 53 *Current Sociology* 915
Seppälä, CR, 'Why Finland Should Adopt the UNCITRAL Model Law on International Commercial Arbitration' (2017) 34 *Journal of International Arbitration* 585
Sgard J, 'A Tale of Three Cities: The Construction of International Commercial Arbitration' in Gregoire Mallard and Jerome Sgard (eds), *Contractual Knowledge* (Cambridge, Cambridge University Press, 2016)
Silberman L, 'The New York Convention After Fifty Years: Some Reflections on the Role of National Law' (2009) 38 *Georgia Journal of International & Comparative Law* 25
Simões FD, *Commercial Arbitration Between China and the Portuguese-Speaking World* (Alphen aan den Rijn, Kluwer Law & Business, 2014)
——, 'A Dispute Resolution Center for the Brics?' in Rostam J Neuwirth, Alexandr Svetlicinii and Denis De Castro Halis (eds), *The BRICS-Lawyers' Guide to Global Cooperation* (Cambridge, Cambridge University Press, 2017)
Slate WKI, 'Cost and Time Effectiveness of Arbitration' (2010) 3 *Contemporary Asia Arbitration Journal* 182
Smahi N, 'The Arbitrator's Liability and Immunity Under Swiss Law – Part I' (2016) 34 *ASA Bulletin* 876
Sripada CS and Stich S, 'A Framework for the Psychology of Norms' in Stephen Stich (ed), *Collected Papers, Volume 2: Knowledge, Rationality, and Morality, 1978–2010* (Oxford, Oxford University Press, 2012)
Stein SJ and Wotman DR, 'International Commercial Arbitration in the 1980s: A Comparison of the Major Arbitral Systems and Rules' (1983) 38 *The Business Lawyer* 1685
Steingruber AM, *Consent in International Arbitration* (Oxford, Oxford University Press, 2012)
Stigler G, 'The Theory of Economic Regulation' (1971) 2 *Bell Journal of Economics* 3
Stone Sweet A and Grisel F, *The Evolution of International Arbitration: Judicialization, Governance, Legitimacy* (Oxford, Oxford University Press, 2017)
Strong SI, 'Clash of Cultures: Epistemic Communities, Negotiation Theory, and International Lawmaking' (2016) 50 *Akron Law Review* 495
Sutinen JG and Kuperan K, 'A Socio-economic Theory of Regulatory Compliance' (1999) 26 *International Journal of Social Economics* 174
Sweify M, 'Criminal Sanctions Targeting Arbitrators: An Egyptian Perspective' (2019) 11 *International Journal of Arab Arbitration* 69
Szalai IS, 'Modern Arbitration Values and the First World War' (2007) 49 *The American Journal of Legal History* 355
Tannous S and Purice M, 'The New UAE Federal Arbitration Law: Was It Worth the Wait?' (2018) 36 *ASA Bulletin* 866

Tao J, 'Arbitration Law of the PRC' in Loukas A. Mistelis (ed), *Concise International Arbitration*, 2nd edn (Alphen aan den Rijn, Kluwer Law International, 2015)

Tay YJ, 'Reflections on the Selection of Arbitrators in International Arbitration' in AJ van den Berg (ed), *International Arbitration: The Coming of a New Age?* (Alphen aan den Rijn, Kluwer Law International, 2013)

Teichmann F, Boticiu SR and Sergi BS, 'Compliance Issues in Arbitration Proceedings – Bribery, Money Laundering and Other Abuses' [2023] *Journal of Financial Crime*

Torgbor E, 'Overview of the Disposition of Courts Towards Arbitration in Africa' in Emilia Onyema (ed), *Rethinking the role of African national courts in arbitration* (Alphen aan den Rijn, Kluwer Law International, 2018)

Twining W and others, 'The Role of Academics in the Legal System' in Mark Tushnet and Peter Cane (eds), *The Oxford Handbook of Legal Studies* (Oxford, Oxford University Press, 2005)

Tyler TR, *Why People Obey the Law* (New Haven, Yale University Press, 1990)

van den Berg AJ, 'Dissenting Opinions by Party-Appointed Arbitrators in Investment Arbitration' in Mahnoush H Arsanjani, J Katz Cogan, RD Sloane and S Wiessner (eds), *Looking to the future: essays on international law in honor of W. Michael Reisman* (Leiden, Martinus Nijhoff Publishers, 2011)

Vecellio Segate R, 'The Dis-Embedded Arbitrator: Releasing Arbitration from Corruption-Shaped Environments in the Wake of the Odebrecht Arbitral Ordeal in Peru' (2023) 12 *Social Sciences* 232

Veeder V, 'La Nouvelle Loi Anglaise Sur l'arbitrage de 1996: La Naissance d'un Magnifique Éléphant' [1997] *Revue de l'Arbitrage* 3

——, 'Gala Dinner Address: Memories from ICCA's First Fifty Years' in AJ van den Berg (ed), *Arbitration: The Next Fifty Years* (Alphen aan den Rijn, Kluwer Law International, 2012)

——, 'The Historical Keystone to International Arbitration: The Party-Appointed Arbitrator – From Miami to Geneva' in David Caron and others (eds), *Practising Virtue: Inside International Arbitration* (Oxford, Oxford University Press, 2015)

——, 'Who Are the Arbitrators?' in Albert Jan van den Berg (ed), *Legitimacy: Myths, Realities, Challenges, ICCA Congress Series, Volume 18* (Alphen aan den Rijn, Kluwer Law International, 2015)

Veeder V and Dye B, 'Lord Bramwell's Arbitration Code 1884–1889' (1992) 8 *Arbitration International* 329

Verbist H and Schäfer E, *ICC Arbitration in Practice*, 2nd edn (Alphen aan den Rijn, Kluwer Law International, 2015)

Von Mehren RB, 'The Eco-Swiss Case and International Arbitration' (2003) 19 *Arbitration International* 465

Wagner G, 'Dispute Resolution as a Product: Competition between Civil Justice Systems' in Horst Eidenmüller (ed), *Regulatory Competition in Contract Law and Dispute Resolution* (London, Bloomsbury Publishing, 2013)

Waibel M and others (eds), *The Backlash Against Investment Arbitration: Perceptions and Reality* (Alphen aan den Rijn, Kluwer Law International, 2010)

Warwas BA, *The Liability of Arbitral Institutions: Legitimacy Challenges and Functional Responses* (The Hague, TMC Asser Press, 2017)

Webster TH and Buhler DM, *Handbook of ICC Arbitration: Commentary, Precedents, Materials* (London, Sweet & Maxwell, 2014)

Wendel WB, 'Nonlegal Regulation of the Legal Profession: Social Norms in Professional Communities' (2001) 54 *Vanderbilt Law Review* 1953

Werner J, 'Competition within the Arbitration Industry' (1985) 2 *Journal of International Arbitration* 5

——, 'International Commercial Arbitrators: From Merchant to Academic to Skilled Professional Focus on International ADR' (1997) 4 *Dispute Resolution Magazine* 22

Whelan CJ and Ziv N, 'Privatizing Professionalism: Client Control of Lawyers' Ethics Colloquium: Globalization and the Legal Profession' (2011) 80 *Fordham Law Review* 2577

White LC, *International Non-Governmental Organizations: Their Purposes, Methods, and Accomplishments* (New Brunswick, Rutgers University Press, 1951)

Wilensky HL, 'The Professionalization of Everyone?' (1964) 70 *American Journal of Sociology* 137

Wilske S, 'The Duty of Arbitral Institutions to Preserve the Integrity of Arbitral Proceedings' (2017) 10 *Contemporary Asia Arbitration Journal* 201

——, 'International Commercial Courts and Arbitration – Alternatives, Substitutes or Trojan Horse' (2018) 11 *Contemporary Asia Arbitration Journal* 153

——, 'International Arbitration and Its Dark Sides, in Particular Corruption: What Arbitral Institutions Could and Should Do to Tackle Such Unwelcome Issues' (2019) 12 *Contemporary Asia Arbitration Journal* 147

Wolff R, *New York Convention on the Recognition and Enforcement of Foreign Arbitral Awards: A Commentary* (Munchin, CH Beck, 2019)

Wrong DH, 'The Oversocialized Conception of Man in Modern Sociology' (1961) 26 *American Sociological Review* 183

Wu M, 'The Strange Case of Wang Shengchang' (2007) 24 *Journal of International Arbitration* 63

Zysman-Quirós D, 'White-Collar Crime in South and Central America: Corporate-State Crime, Governance, and the High Impact of the Odebrecht Corruption Case' in Melissa L Rorie (ed), *The Handbook of White-Collar Crime* (Chichester, Wiley, 2019)

INDEX

References to figures are indicated by *f* followed by page number.

Printed in the USA
CPSIA information can be obtained
at www.ICGtesting.com
LVHW050515050824
787367LV00005B/103